Aid and Arms to the Third World

An Analysis of the Distribution and Impact of US Official Transfers

R. D. McKinlay
and
A. Mughan

Frances Pinter (Publishers), London

First published in Great Britain in 1984 by
Frances Pinter (Publishers) Limited
5 Dryden Street, London WC2E 9NW

British Library Cataloguing in Publication Data

McKinlay, R. D.
    Aid and arms to the Third World.
    1. Underdeveloped areas—Munitions
    2. Underdeveloped areas—Foreign relations
    I. Title   II. Mughan, A.

    ISBN 0-903804-87-5

Typeset by Joshua Associates, Oxford
Printed by SRP Ltd., Exeter

Aid and Arms to the Third World

Contents

List of Abbreviations

United Nations Statistical Yearbook	UNSY
United Nations Yearbook of National Account Statistics	UNYNAS
United Nations Yearbook of International Trade Statistics	UNYITS
International Monetary Fund International Financial Statistics	IMFIFS
International Monetary Fund Balance of Payments Yearbook	IMFBPY
Europa Yearbook	EY
Statesman's Yearbook	SY
Keesing's Contemporary Archives	KCA
Political Handbook and Atlas of the World	PHAW
US Overseas Loans and Grants	USOLG
Stockholm International Peace Research Institute World Armaments and Disarmament Yearbook	SIPRI
Stockholm International Peace Research Institute worksheets	SIPRI-ws

Acknowledgements

The research for this book was funded by a grant (HR5343) from the Social Science Research Council (UK). A number of other institutions also contributed to its completion. The Stockholm International Peace Research Institute, and in particular Signe Landgren-Backstrom, kindly allowed us access to data not available from its publications. Our home universities, Lancaster and Cardiff respectively, provided us with general institutional support, as did the Australian National, Northwestern and Odense universities at various times over the course of the project. While too many to name individually, a large number of people also contributed to the project through assistance in the collection and coding of the data or through comments on various drafts of the manuscript. In this second category, we would like to single out Misty Gerner, Des King, Bruce Moon and Phil Schrodt. Indeed, Bruce Moon went far above and beyond the call of duty in the time and attention he devoted to informed and insightful comment and discussion. Finally, our thanks go to Joe Whittaker for devising one of the statistical test procedures.

1 A Conceptualisation and Research Design

Official transfers

Definition

The principal concern of this book lies in the analysis of resource transfers between national governments, i.e. 'official' transfers. While it is true that a large number of resources are transferred between governments, in terms of dollar value, volume and political significance, the major transfers in the world at the present time are economic aid, military assistance and arms sales and it is on these that we focus our analysis. But before proceeding to this analysis, we need to elaborate the similarities and differences between them. This is not a problematic exercise since there exists broad agreement not only on how each is defined, but also on how each is differentiated from the others. The criteria of differentiation that are commonly used are the degree of concessionality involved in the transfer and the immediate object funded by it. As a preface to our analysis, therefore, we shall now define each of the three transfers and evaluate them against these two criteria. Our general argument will be that the differentiation afforded by these criteria is one of degree, and not of kind. In other words, the criteria do not afford a categorical distinction between economic aid, military assistance and arms sales.

Economic aid is generally defined in terms of intergovernmental financial transfers that are allocated for the promotion of economic development in the recipient country. There are two main sources for this transfer: individual governments and intergovernmental organisations, like the United Nations, the European Community, the International Monetary Fund and the World Bank. The former are bilateral transfers and the latter multilateral. Governments and intergovernmental agencies do not monopolise the transfer of aid, however. Non-governmental agencies, especially international ones like OXFAM and the Red Cross, also transfer concessional funds to the Third World. But such transfers are excluded from our analysis, partly for conceptual reasons (the standard definition of aid relates only to official transfers) and partly because their volume is very small in relation to official transfers.

Economic aid can vary along a number of other dimensions in addition to source. It can, for example, assume a variety of different forms ranging from a direct cash transfer to the transfer of goods or services. Equally, it can be allocated for use only in specified projects, such as, for example, the construction of a dam or steel mill or it can be allocated to general programmes so that the recipient has some discretion in spending it within the general framework of, say, a planned or already operational welfare or development programme.[1]

Military assistance is the military analogue of economic aid and, as such, is defined as intergovernmental concessionary transfers allocated for military, as opposed to economic, development purposes. Unlike economic aid, however, military assistance comes entirely from individual governments; there are no multilateral military assistance programmes and, at least officially, non-governmental groups do not provide military assistance. But, albeit relatively rarely, governments may provide such assistance to non-governmental national groups. Almost invariably, this situation arises in the context of domestic conflict and, since such transfers are generally seen as a contravention of international norms, they are usually 'hidden'. Thus, unofficial reports have it that the United States of America currently supplies military assistance to Egypt, which then supplies arms to the guerrilla forces rebelling against the Soviet-backed regime in Afghanistan. Precisely because it is unofficial, however, such assistance is excluded from our analysis. Furthermore, it is likely to be very small in volume relative to official transfers of military assistance.

Like economic aid, military assistance can take a variety of different forms. It may, for example, be direct cash support for the recipient's military budget. Alternatively, it may be the provision of services, perhaps in the form of advisers or training or the provision of goods—in the form of weapons systems, for example.[2]

Arms sales are commercial arms transfers between governments. As in the case of military assistance, intergovernmental organisations do not engage in this transfer, although some transfers may be intergovernmental in the narrow sense that two or more suppliers co-operate in the design and production of particular weapons systems. Like military assistance, however, arms sales do not always take place on a purely bilateral, government-to-government basis. Private individuals and companies do legally and publicly buy and sell arms, but their activities are always monitored and controlled by governments, usually through a system of obligatory export licences. Private arms sales are excluded from our analysis partly because they are not fully intergovernmental—indeed, except for the provision of the export licence, they are likely not to involve governments at all—and partly because in relation to official transfers they are small in both value and volume. Excluded for the same reasons are 'black market' arms sales.[3]

Most often arms sales take the form of the transfer of weapons systems. To the extent that these systems are sold and their complexity entails ongoing running costs, perhaps in the form of software and back-up systems requiring the employment of nationals of the supplier country, arms sales, unlike economic aid and military assistance, normally make no direct cash contribution to the recipient's budget.

Thus, the three official transfers have in common that they can come from a variety of different sources, although bilateral transfers between governments are by far the most important in terms of both value and volume. Each may also assume a variety of forms. Where they differ, however, at least in principle, is in their degree of concessionality and the object of funding. If only because they entail a grant element, economic aid and military assistance are concessionary in nature, whereas arms sales, being commercial by definition, are not. The three transfers can, in principle, be equally clearly differentiated with regard to their object of funding. Economic aid is intended to promote economic development in the recipient countries and military assistance and arms sales to promote military development. But while these differentiations do undoubtedly tell us something about the form and purpose of the individual transfers, to hold to them too rigidly obscures a more complex and less orderly reality.

In the first place, economic aid and military assistance are not entirely concessionary in the sense of being without commercial features. Equally, arms sales are not fully commercial in the sense of being without concessionary elements. Economic aid and military assistance comprise both grants and loans. The concessionary elements in such loans are that they may entail a substantial grace period during which repayment is suspended or they may have an extended amortisation period attached to them or, most commonly, the rate of interest on them may be lower than the commercial market rate. Economic aid and military assistance can also deviate often from full concessionality in that they may be 'tied' as to both the form and source of expenditure. Real economic costs, for example, could be visited on an aid recipient that found itself tied to a type or volume of expenditure that it had neither anticipated nor desired. The recipient could also find itself in the same disadvantageous position if the expenditure of its aid receipt were tied to the purchase of products from the supplier country that were priced above the lowest available market rate. Arms sales show a similar blend of the concessionary and commercial. Such sales usually involve both cash and credit arrangements and a significant concessionary element can creep into them when the loans, or credit, involve a grace period, an extended amortisation period or interest rates below the market level. The system of weapons procurement and production can also dilute the purely commercial character of arms sales. Since this system is not subject to open market forces, there can be no such thing as a free market price for most weapons and it is possible for them to be transferred for political reasons at a price that does not reflect their 'true' production cost. Finally, arms sales can be overtly or covertly located in a larger economic aid or military assistance package so that, even though the supplier government may hold that the arms are being sold at the commercial rate, there may be offsetting concessionary elements in the larger package.

Thus, while the balance may vary from one to the other, all three transfers contain both commercial and concessionary elements and cannot be rigidly classified on the basis of one or other of them. A second barrier to their categorical

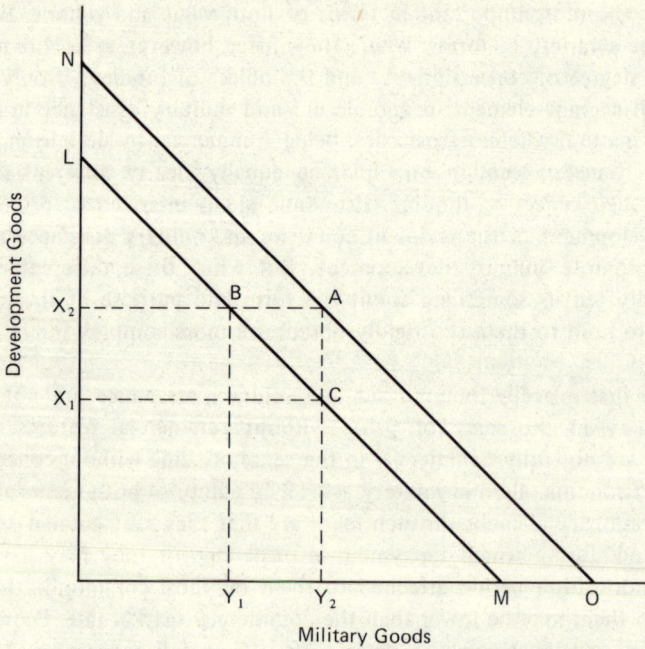

Figure 1.1 Production possibility curve for choice between development and
military goods

separation and classification lies in their *de facto* substitutability. That is,
economic aid can be used to secure military goods, while military assistance
and arms purchases can underwrite development goods. This argument is illustrated most easily through the device of the production-possibility curve de-
picted in Figure 1.1 and on which we have placed developments goods on one
axis and military goods on the other.[4] Imagine that a country has a choice
between development and military goods, it could either spend all its available
income on one of them or on some combination, which would be determined
by its placement on the line LM in Figure 1.1. The receipt of economic aid
or military assistance from an outside supplier will push the LM income line
out to a new position, NO, leaving the country with the same choice but enabling
it to buy more of either set of goods. The precise expenditure pattern of a
hypothetical country might be set at point A, indicating the purchase of X_2
amount of development goods and Y_2 of military ones. If, prior to receiving
the supplement to this income, this hypothetical country planned the expenditure pattern indicated by point C on the curve (X_1 amount of development
and Y_2 of military goods), then the receipt has led to an increase in development goods to the amount of $X_2 - X_1$. In other words, whether the receipt had
taken the form of economic aid or military assistance, it would have led to

the procurement of more development goods. Similarly, had B (Y_1 amount of military and X_2 of development goods) been the previously envisaged expenditure pattern, the receipt of either economic aid or military assistance would have led to an increase of $Y_2 - Y_1$ in the procurement of military goods.[5]

Much the same argument holds if we consider the relationship between economic aid and arms sales. At its simplest, the receipt of economic aid could free resources that were then used to purchase imported arms. Alternatively, the purchase of what are perceived as necessary armaments could push out the line LM either because the purchase itself contained a concessional element or because it provided a positive import effect (i.e. foreign arms can be purchased at a lower cost than producing them domestically). But whatever the precise formula, economic aid and arms sales can act as substitutes for each other, even if less readily than economic aid and military assistance can.

Two conclusions follow from this discussion of the interrelationship of the three major official transfers in the contemporary world: economic aid, military assistance and arms sales. The first is that, while hardly the same phenomenon, the three are not as categorically separable as their formal titles suggest. The second conclusion follows directly from this recognition of their complexity and is that the uses to which each is put by suppliers and the impact of each on the military, economic, social and political development of recipients is a matter for investigation rather than assertion. It is precisely such an investigation that lies at the heart of this book.

Conceptualisation

Having provided clear and uncontroversial definitions of the central phenomena in our study, i.e. the three major official transfers of economic aid, military assistance and arms sales, we shall now proceed to the important task of presenting a more general conceptualisation of them. In contrast to clear definitions, such conceptualisations are not a prerequisite of empirical research, but it is generally accepted that higher level concept formation, which is essentially what we mean by the phrase 'more general conceptualisation', does constitute a prerequisite for the type of research that, like ours, is orientated to the generation of empirical theories having explanatory and nomothetic content. The principal advantage of this kind of conceptualisation is its ability to direct specific pieces of research to more general considerations and to facilitate the integration of disparate sets of findings into a single body of knowledge. In this particular case, the conceptualisation that we have developed increases our ability to understand and evaluate the role of official transfers in the structure and workings of the larger international system.[6]

The starting point of this conceptualisation is that official transfers take place without coercion. Recipients do not coerce suppliers into providing them with resources, nor do suppliers coerce recipients into accepting the resources that they choose to transfer. There is, in short, a supply of, and demand for, official transfers. Given their scale and scope, a myriad of factors could be invoked to explain the prevailing pattern of demand and supply. We suggest, however, that this myriad can be ordered and simplified through the concepts of first-order and second-order demand and supply utilities.

On the demand side, the primary first-order utility of official transfers is the perception that they can enhance the power capabilities of recipients. Even if one disagreed with the practice of measuring power purely in terms of capabilities, preferring perhaps to see it more in relational terms, it cannot be denied that capabilities are an extraordinarily important component of any power relation. Equally, it cannot be denied that official transfers can serve to increase general military capabilities, as well as any number of economic capabilities, e.g. budget revenues, international liquidity and investment.

This first-order demand utility leads to a second-order one. For any recipient to seek to increase or supplement its power capabilities is rarely an end in its own right; it is more usually a means to a further end, or to a second-order utility. Increased capabilities may be necessary to the realisation of a large variety of political, economic or social ends that can be either domestic or international in nature. These ends can include, for example, the improvement of the recipient's international status, the achievement of supremacy in a local power struggle, the promotion of the sectional interests of its ruling elite, the stimulation of infrastructural development, the expansion of social welfare programmes, and so on.

On the supply side, the attraction of official transfers for the supplier is that they enable it potentially to achieve two main first-order utilities: leverage and commitment. There are a number of ways in which official transfers can provide the supplier with leverage over recipients' behaviour. At the very minimum, the attachment of conditions to transfers inevitably entails some degree of intervention, benign or otherwise, in the internal affairs of recipients. More importantly, precisely because official transfers are commonly perceived as attractive to recipients (they possess, in other words, demand utilities), the supplier can manipulate its own transfers to reward or reinforce certain types of behaviour. Positive reinforcement occurs when the promise of transfers is used as an inducement or bribe to influence the behaviour of recipients, whereas negative reinforcement entails using the threat of reducing or witholding transfers as a coercive means of achieving the same end. Supplier leverage can also grow out of a situation where transfers involve goods or services that require continuing support in the form, say, of spare parts, maintenance or advice. Finally, leverage can develop when the transfers themselves involve some element of repayment and the recipient runs into debt-servicing problems. In this situation, the ability minimally to reschedule the debt once again provides the supplier with a potential source of influence, perhaps even control, over certain aspects of recipient behaviour.

The second first-order utility of official transfers for the supplier is that their preferential allocation allows it to demonstrate its commitment to recipients and this demonstration can itself spur co-operative behaviour on the latters' part. The commitment potential of official transfers is largely a function of some of their own key characteristics. In the first place, they are explicitly intergovernmental so that, unlike, say, with trade or investment, supplier governments are in full control of the flow of official transfers to recipient countries. In the second place, official transfers are very visible, which is a prerequisite for the signalling of commitment to other domestic and international political actors. Stated differently, supplier governments not only control official transfers, but are also seen to be in control of them. Finally, since official transfers involve the distribution of, what are from the perspective of the recipient, scarce and desirable commodities, namely power capabilities, they cannot but represent an important, as well as visible, means for a supplier government to signal its commitment to, or register its support for, another government.

As with recipients, however, it seems to us that suppliers do not pursue the first-order utilities of leverage and commitment as ends in themselves. Instead they are intended to provide the means of realising a set of suppliers' second-order utilities which is very varied and variable in content. This variation reflects the fact that the identity of these second-order utilities is conditioned by the supplier's foreign policy interests within the recipient population and these interests themselves can vary from one supplier to another and/or for the same supplier across time. In general, however, suppliers' interests in the Third World cover such areas as trade, investment, security, regional power balances and the form of domestic political arrangement. Leverage and commitment provide suppliers with the means to promote or protect what each perceives to be its interests.

But just as benefits can incur costs, the pursuit of their first-order and second-order demand and supply utilities can lead to both recipient and supplier of official transfers incurring disutilities. On the demand side, the recipient can experience two major first-order disutilities, which are themselves directly created by the supplier's main first-order utilities. In the first place, the recipient can find itself caught in a relationship of dependence on the supplier. This situation occurs when the recipient, subjected to a high degree of leverage from the supplier, is persuaded or coerced to undertake a series of actions or policies that it would not otherwise have undertaken. In the second place, supplier commitment may lead a recipient into the position where it is, perhaps mistakenly and counterproductively from the point of view of its own foreign policy interests, aligned in the public eye not only with that supplier, but also with all its general policies.

Even though these two disutilities are, in a sense, the obverse of supplier utilities, there is not necessarily a zero-sum relationship between the interests of supplier and recipient. For example, if a supplier uses its leverage to bring about policies that the recipient would have pursued anyway or could pursue without incurring any perceived cost, then neither recipient nor supplier experiences any disutilities. Equally, in the specific context of commitment, a recipient may positively court identification with a particular supplier since an indication of that supplier's commitment could be transformed into a power capability in its relations with other recipient countries.

But a recipient can also experience a second-order disutility to the extent that the supplement to its power capabilities afforded by its receipt of official transfers, i.e. the first-order demand utility, may not actually assist it to achieve the desired second-order utilities. If, for example, arms are purchased to redress a regional imbalance in, say, military preparedness, but the recipient finds that its neighbours are receiving proportionately similar transfers from another supplier, then a second-order utility has become a disutility in that the recipient has at the very least incurred economic costs without coming anywhere nearer to the original objective of redressing the regional imbalance. Furthermore, to the extent that official transfers, albeit inadvertently, encourage corruption or displace local production, the recipient might find its ability to pursue its own second-order utilities undermined or impaired in the long term.

Equally, the supplier can experience disutilities, of which there are four principal first-order varieties. Firstly, counter-leverage can develop when the recipient finds itself in a position to be able to dictate the terms or conditions of official transfers. This situation arises most generally when the recipient possesses, or has the right to, something to which it attaches lesser value than a supplier or competing suppliers to whom the object in question has an important second-order utility. It might be the case, for example, that a supplier is anxious to ensure its international security by establishing a military base in some strategically important foreign country. Provided that this country has no objection in principle to such a base, its relative diffidence places it in a stronger bargaining position than the anxious supplier promising, probably among other things, official transfers in return for permission to build the base. The recipient's bargaining position is even stronger if a number of suppliers are vying for the same permission. Indeed, generally speaking, if supplier X is in competition with supplier Y and both are interested in potential recipient Z, then as long as Z is willing to accept transfers from either supplier, its ability to play one off against the other inevitably increases its bargaining power.

A second, and most serious, first-order supplier disutility is escalating commitment. This relationship arises when a supplier finds itself continually increasing the volume of its transfers to a recipient while at best coming no nearer to achieving its original second-order utility(ies) *vis-à-vis* that recipient. Thus, for example, the supplier may wish, among other things, to uphold the government of a particular recipient in face of domestic insurgency. If, however, the domestic insurgency persists or increases despite the supplier's transfers then, short of abandoning its original goal, the supplier will be obliged to escalate or intensify its commitment to that recipient.

A third first-order disutility is likely to develop when a supplier's leverage and commitment potential is reduced as the direct consequence of transfers from competing suppliers. Stated succinctly, a supplier can 'call the tune' only when it monopolises the flow of transfers to a recipient. Once the recipient finds itself able to diversify the sources of the transfers that it receives then, other things being equal, it will reduce its first-order demand disutilities and simultaneously increase first-order supplier disutilities. Under these circumstances, if the original supplier wishes to maintain its utilities, then it would have to respond to the emergence of competition minimally by increasing its transfers. Were the other suppliers to respond in a like manner, then a situation of escalating transfers with little utility gain for any supplier would once again transpire.

A fourth first-order disutility for the supplier relates to the costs of official transfers. Broadly speaking, these costs can be either economic or political. Other things being equal, both economic and military aid, to the extent that they involve concessionality and/or constitute deficits on its balance of payments, entail a real economic cost for the supplier. Suppliers are, of course, well aware of such costs and this awareness helps to explain why aid often takes the form of loans or is tied to the recipient meeting certain conditions favourable to the supplier. Indeed, one of the great attractions to suppliers of the sale of arms is that this is a means of reducing their economic cost. That is, to the extent that the production of arms for export offsets their research and development costs or can bring economies of scale to their domestic production, then suppliers can achieve a very real economic gain through their sale abroad. On the other hand, it may be that the production of arms for an export market can require their modification to suit the local circumstances of the recipient and this can reduce the economic benefits that the supplier draws from their sale. Furthermore, to the extent that arms production is essentially independent of market forces, it can entail economic inefficiencies so that expanding their production for an export market can simply intensify these inefficiencies and consume investment capital that might have been employed to greater comparative advantage in other areas of domestic production.

As well as such economic costs, official transfers can involve potentially more serious and damaging political costs and these can be either domestic or international in nature. Domestic political costs accrue to any supplier government if criticism of its transfer programme leads it to lose popular or legislative support. Such criticism may be founded on either the opportunity cost argument (i.e. critics would prefer the money to be spent at home) or on allegations of the transfers failing to achieve their objectives. In so far as international political costs follow exactly the same pattern, a supplier's transfer programme leads to a decline in its general level of Third World support. Such a decline can result, for example, from recipients' charges of insufficient volume of transfers or of excessive supplier leverage in exchange for transfers.

Finally, a supplier can experience second-order disutilities, essentially as a direct result of the transfers failing to realise the supplier's second-order utilities. If, for example, a supplier is concerned to manipulate the leverage and commitment potential of its official transfers to promote its trading interests with a recipient, the failure to do so results in the supplier experiencing a second-order disutility. What is more, this disutility could be compounded by first-order disutilities relating, for example, to economic and political costs.

Both recipient and supplier, then, can experience a series of first-order and second-order utilities and disutilities. On some occasions, the utilities of one partner to the relationship may be synonymous with the disutilities of the other, i.e. the relationship is zero-sum. On other occasions, however, an increase in, say, a utility for one need not entail a disutility for the other. It would, in other words, be misleading to conceive of the relationship between one partner's utilities and the other's disutilities as being necessarily and inevitably zero-sum. Instead, the relationship is better viewed in terms of a net utility, i.e. the balance of utilities and disutilities, for either or both supplier and recipient. Each one's net utilities then become able to increase or decrease with the other's or to vary independently of it.

Having elaborated our general conceptualisation of official transfers, we can now point to its two substantial advantages. Firstly, its very generality enables us to integrate into it much of the extant research on official transfers. The 'tying' of aid, for example, can now be interpreted as one of the means by which the supplier of a transfer can seek to reduce one of its disutilities, i.e. economic cost. But at the same time, 'tying' is likely to reduce the transfer's first-order demand utility to the recipient, which, in turn, can mitigate the first-order utility that the transfer affords the supplier. In other words, the mechanics of the interrelationship between recipient and supplier can produce a situation in which, especially from the perspective of the supplier, 'tying' is a self-defeating strategy.

In other research, various writers have suggested that aid programmes should be terminated. The reasons that they give for termination, however, are often mutually contradictory and this is because they tend to focus their attention on some utilities and/or disutilities to the neglect of others. One school of thought claims, for example, that aid programmes should be terminated, or at least massively restructured, because they do not promote development. Aid is therefore assumed to be solely a means of achieving the same specific second-order utility, i.e. development, for both recipient and supplier. But this assumption could well be misplaced since there are plenty of other utilities to which either partner to the transfer relationship may attach higher priority. Another school of thought recommends the termination of aid on the grounds that it is an essentially ineffective form of blackmail. Focusing at least initially on first-order supplier disutilities, the effectiveness of this argument hinges on demonstrating the supplier's failure to achieve its desired second-order utilities.

Rarely, however, is this failure systematically addressed, never mind demonstrated. More importantly still, and relatedly, the issue in this argument is not solely the realisation of a specific second-order utility or set of them, but whether aid effectively produces an acceptable change to the advantage of the supplier in the balance of utilities and disutilities afforded by its aid programme, i.e. in its net utilities. Again, this issue is not comprehensively addressed by this school of thought. Finally, we come to the school of thought that holds that economic aid should be terminated because it is too successful in structuring recipients' pattern of development to their own long-term disadvantage. Thus, because its emphasis is on demand disutilities rather than utilities, the members of this school hold that aid should be terminated because it achieves too effectively what the previous school thought it did not achieve well enough.[7]

The second advantage of the evaluation of this conceptualisation is that it lends itself to a more general picture of the role and importance of official transfers in the international system. In short, it makes it apparent that they do not exist in isolation, but are embedded in a larger matrix of utility calculations on the part of both supplier and recipient. Whether at the level of first-order or second-order utilities, therefore, the explanation of the pattern of official transfers in the international system is to be found in these calculations.

Research design

Research objectives

Broadly speaking, our research focus is an analysis of US official transfers to the Third World over the period 1950-79. It is an analysis that has two specific objectives: the first being to identify the factors that structure the distributions of these transfers and the second to assess the impact of these same transfers.

The first of these objectives constitutes our distribution analysis and its focus is the explanation of the substantial variation in the volume of US official transfers received by Third World countries in any one year. Put another way, our objective is simply to explain why some Third World countries receive larger volumes of a transfer than others.[8] The analysis itself is carried out on a bi-annual basis over the period 1950-79.[9]

In the normal course of events, any transfer, provided that it is not trivial in volume, will entail consequences, or impacts, for supplier and recipient alike. While, as will be explained shortly, we make no claim to provide a comprehensive analysis of these impacts, our second, and necessarily more limited research objective is to make at least some contribution to an assessment of the impact of official transfers.

The first objective, then, relates to the identification of the factors that structure, and thus explain, the distribution of official transfers. The conceptualisation that we have elaborated has already set us on the path to achieving this objective. There can be no distribution without an existing demand and the existence of this demand can be explained by the first-order and second-order utilities that official transfers promise to recipients. But this promise need not always be realised, and anticipated utilities may even become disutilities. The upshot of this situation is not only that there is nothing immutable about the demand for official transfers in general, but also that the demand curve for one or all countries can easily change over time. As long as certain conditions prevail, however, the demand for official transfers, even though they entail some degree of risk for the recipient, is unlikely to disappear altogether. These conditions are a substantial discrepancy in capabilities between supplier and recipient, the pursuit on the part of the recipient of goals, or second-order utilities, for which it deems an expansion of its domestic capabilities to be necessary and, finally, a continuing perception on the part of the recipient that official transfers confer on it a positive net utility. While the negation of any one or more of these conditions could well remove the demand for, and consequently the supply of, official transfers, it is the case that over the three decades from 1950 to 1979, there has persisted in the Third World a generally high level of demand for them. To be sure, there have been some changes in this demand pattern; some Organisation of Petroleum Exporting Countries (OPEC) and other newly industrialising countries no longer solicit economic aid, for example. None the less, the demand for official transfers is, generally speaking, still strong.

While the existence of a demand for transfers may precede the supply of them, the demand itself explains neither the existence of the aggregate supply nor the variation in its distribution among the population of potential recipients. Our conceptualisation does, however, provide the basis for a satisfactory explanation of both these aspects of the supply side of official transfers. What is more, this explanation guides the empirical analysis in subsequent chapters of this book. It has already been argued that official transfers enable the supplier to establish commitment and leverage relations with recipients. But because, as was the case with recipients, suppliers' first-order utilities can become first-order disutilities, there is nothing immutable about the supply of transfers and, at any given point in time, the volume of transfers to any single recipient or to all of them is in part a function balance between the two. Still more importantly, though, their volume is a function of the second-order utilities that the supplier wishes to realise and for which the first-order utilities are no more than the means. It follows, therefore, that the volume of official transfers allocated to a recipient is a function of that country's standing in relation to the supplier's foreign policy interests, i.e. second-order utilities. Put another way, the variation in the supplier's annual distribution of official transfers reflects the relative priority it attaches to the population of potential recipients and this variation in priority in turn reflects how intensely the recipient enshrines the foreign policy interests of the supplier. The guiding hypothesis of our distribution analysis is that the volume of official transfers, precisely because these are a means by which the supplier promotes and protects its foreign policy interests, will vary as a function of the importance of Third World countries to the foreign policy interests of the United States.

Our second research objective relates essentially to net second-order utilities. In focusing on the impact of transfers, we are in effect examining how well both supplier and recipient achieve their respective second-order utilities. In contrast to our 'distribution' objective, therefore, it is more of a descriptive task. But this is not to say that it is a trivial one for the net utility of transfers for both supplier and recipient has a critical influence on the aggregate demand for, and supply of, them. Thus, while perhaps not of the same theoretical interest as that of their distribution, the question of the impact of transfers none the less has a substantial theoretical, to say nothing of practical, importance.

Execution of research objectives

We turn now to the question of how we are to go about the execution of our 'distribution' and 'impact' research objectives. Up to this point, our conceptualisation of official transfers has posited that they constitute a means through which suppliers can pursue their foreign policy interests, but it has done little to specify precisely what these interests are. This is because it is our view that the identification of the foreign policy interests structuring a supplier's distribution of its official transfers is the proper domain of empirical inquiry, particularly since these interests are likely to vary from one supplier to another and for the same supplier from one time point to another.

In point of fact, our selection of foreign policy interests to be tested in relation to US official transfers has been guided, if not constrained, by the general literature on that country's foreign policy. These interests have been grouped into four clusters, with each cluster forming the basis of a separate analysis and chapter in the book. In order of their presentation, these clusters profile: (1) power politics; (2) competition with communism; (3) economic interests; and (4) socio-political interests. A comprehensive list of the variables making up each cluster, together with their sources, is presented in Appendix A.

Broadly speaking, our strategy of analysis is to search for relationships between these four clusters of foreign policy interests and the volume of US official transfers to Third World recipients. To make the analysis manageable and comprehensible, the four clusters are always treated separately, although we realise that there is some inter-relationship between them. The search for relationships within clusters is built around two complementary statistical techniques, one-way analysis of variance (ANOVA) and multiple regression analysis. With ANOVA, we allocate recipients annually to one of the zero, small, medium or large categories depending on the volume of the transfer that they receive for that year. This process is carried out separately for each of the three official transfers. The actual mechanics of defining the four recipient categories is uniform across both transfers and time and is fully described in Appendix B. The existence of a systematic bivariate relationship between the level of transfer receipt and any of the foreign policy interest variables enables us to impute a structuring effect to that variable.

The second step in our analysis is the regression of each official transfer on all four clusters of foreign policy interests separately. We use multiple regression because it is an analytical technique that has a number of advantages over the one-way ANOVA design. Its multivariate character permits the estimation of the relative importance of a number of explanatory variables through the comparison of their beta weight values; it potentially reduces the number of statistically (and, hence, theoretically) significant explanatory variables; and, finally, it can identify explanatory variables which, in bivariate terms, may show no relationship with the dependant variables, but which may do so once the confounding effects of other explanatory variables are controlled. Its major shortcoming, on the other hand, is multicollinearity. We have sought to circumvent this problem through the use of high tolerance levels in the regression equations, but this strategy runs the risk of being over-stringent in the identification of significant explanatory variables.[10] Since this is not a problem with one-way ANOVA, our complementary use of the two techniques maximises the advantages and minimises the limitations of each of them individually.

Our use of multiple regression does generate a difficulty, however, and this stems from the fact that there are a large number of cases that do not receive one or other transfer during the period of the analysis. Such is the case in all years for military assistance and arms sales and from 1968 onwards for economic aid. These non-recipients are excluded from our regression analyses since they are sufficiently numerous to distort their outcome. They cannot, however, simply be assumed to be the mirror-image of recipients with regard to their relationship to the clusters of foreign policy interests, so discriminant analysis is used to differentiate them from recipients on the basis of these clusters. Only then is regression analysis used to determine why recipients vary in the volume of transfers that they are allocated by the United States. In other words, the military assistance, arms sales and post-1968 economic aid programmes are treated as involving two stages of decision-making. The first is the selection stage where, juxtaposing recipients and non-recipients of the individual transfer, we employ, when possible, discriminant analysis to determine whether the variables comprising each cluster can significantly differentiate the two groups one from the other. If they do, we can conclude that these variables identify the criteria on the basis of which selection for inclusion in the recipient population is made. Allocation is the second stage and it is characterised by the use of multiple regression analysis to identify the criteria determining which recipients get what amount of the transfer in question.

Generally speaking, the distribution analysis runs from 1950 to 1979 and the foreign policy, or independent, variables are lagged against the transfers by one year in all the statistical analyses. In other words, the 1951 transfers are related to observations on the foreign policy variables for 1950 and this practice is repeated for each subsequent alternate year up to 1979. Alternate years only are analysed simply to make our findings more manageable and easily presentable. Nothing is lost through this selectivity since the magnitude of each transfer's correlation with itself from one year to the next is invariably very high (see Chapter 2).

With regard to the impact side of our analysis, we find ourselves without much established theoretical guidance as to which variables can be expected to have been affected by US official transfers. Only the various *dependencia* models appear to have any relevance here, but we have chosen not to let them dictate our impact study, partly because they have a number of conceptual and empirical limitations and partly because too close an adherence to their strictures would proscribe the examination of other potentially interesting and important variables.

An alternative approach would be simply to assess the impact of transfers on variables measuring the second-order utilities of supplier and recipient. But this approach presents two major problems. Firstly, it assumes that we can identify these utilities. To be sure, we have already made this assumption with regard to the United States and its clusters of foreign policy interests, but this is a single case and a great deal is known about its foreign policy goals. By contrast, we know very little about the second-order utilities of the scores of US transfer recipients. In other words, while there is no logical reason why the second-order utilities of transfer recipients should not be identified, there is every practical reason why they should not be. If only for this reason, we make no claim to having a systematic and theoretically interesting set of recipient second-order utilities upon which the impact of US official transfers can be assessed. Secondly, impact can be both intended and unintended. Suppose, for example, that the United States wished to promote its trading interests solely through its official transfers. If our attention were monopolised by this one foreign policy goal, the analysis could well overlook an unintended, but none the less theoretically important say, investment effect, which, in turn, may or may not rank in the recipient's set of second-order utilities. In short, no impact study should blind itself to the possibility of unintended, as well as intended, effects.

Given these difficulties, our solution, which is only partial, is to focus on the performance of recipients. Admittedly, the concept of performance is both very open-ended in empirical terms and at a low level of abstraction in conceptual terms, but it is, none the less, useful in the specific context of this study. Our measure of performance is rate of change on the individual variables comprising the four clusters used in the distribution analysis and it is a concept that can be examined from the perspective of either the supplier or the recipient. The former perspective asks the question whether the supplier's realisation of a previously defined second-order utility varies systematically across the different categories of transfer receipt level. For example, if recipients' trade with communist countries was found in the distribution analysis to be a second-order supply utility and was also found in the impact analysis to have increased least quickly in the high recipient category and most quickly in the zero category, then we could conclude that the United States has realised one of its foreign policy goals.

The recipients' performance perspective is less neatly defined and more *ad hoc* simply because we are not aware a priori of the identity of recipients' second-order utilities. All that we can do is to trawl the widest range of variables possible and hope to come across systematic patterns of change on what can reasonably be construed as recipients' second-order utilities and disutilities. Thus, if it were found, for example, that the diversification of recipients' exports had proceeded most quickly in the zero recipient category and least quickly in the high one, then to the extent that export diversification can be assumed to be a second-order recipient utility, the transfer in question could reasonably be interpreted as having promoted a second-order disutility for its recipients.

The mechanics of the impact analysis involve initially categorising our population of Third World countries into zero, small, medium and large recipients, the basis of the categorisation being the volume of the transfer in question that each has received over an aggregated four-year period (see Appendix C for further details). Performance is then measured by the mean annual change within each category over the four-year period stretching from the first year of the aggregated transfer receipt to the year immediately following this same aggregated receipt. Thus, if recipients are categorised on the basis of the period 1950-3, their performance is estimated over the period 1950-4.[11] The extra year is added so that the prerequisite of temporal asymmetry is present in those instances in which we choose to draw causal inference from observed covariation. The impact or otherwise of official transfers is assessed by comparing the mean annual change in each of the four recipient categories in a simple analysis of variance design. It should be noted that the selection of four-year periods over which to assess impact is somewhat arbitrary; we ended up choosing this time span in preference to others because it is long enough to give an impact effect the opportunity to mature and manifest itself and it is short enough not to be insensitive to change in this same effect over a longer time period. Indeed, its sensitivity to such change is deliberately enhanced through the use of a form of moving average, i.e. of periods over which performance is examined that are not mutually exclusive of each other. The periods are in fact 1950-4, 1952-6, 1954-8, and so on all the way through to 1974-8.

In conceptual terms, the impact analysis itself is conducted on two related levels. On the first of them, we look for covariation between the volume of transfer receipt and the rate of growth on the individual performance variables. The presence of such covariation enables us to conclude simply that the United States is allied through the particular transfer with Third World countries displaying certain performance rates. We may, for example, find significant covariation between aid transfers and rates of growth of, say, military expenditure. But it is important to note that all that we observe is covariation; no dependence one on the other is implied to exist between the two variables. The discovery of covariation is still an interesting finding, however, since its presence has, at least potentially, substantial implications for an understanding of how transfers have an impact on performance. If we find, for example, that in distributing its aid, the United States rewards countries with higher levels of military expenditure, then it becomes important, in the context of the achievement of its second-order utilities, to draw attention to the fact that it also secures an association with Third World countries displaying higher growth rates on this same variable.

The second level involves the evaluation of impact in terms of the narrower and more specific phenomenon of causation. Covariation is a necessary, but not sufficient, condition of causation and, as such, causation can perhaps be best seen as a second, less inclusive stage in the analysis of covariation. If causality is to be established, a number of conditions in addition to covariation need to be present. In particular, there has to be a temporal asymmetry between the variables in the relationship, a sound argument as to why the transfer could effect systematic variation in the performance indicator and, finally, good reason to believe that what we are seeing is not, in fact, a spurious relationship, i.e. to believe that the observed covariation is due to the impact of the transfer itself and not to some uncontrolled variable standing outside the relationship.

When impact is considered at the level of causation, the transfer receipts are seen as acting as independent variables in contrast to the dependent variables that they were in the earlier distribution analysis. Equally, the role of the foreign policy variables on which impact is assessed is reversed; they have become the dependent variables in the causal analysis. In short, the covariation and causation impact analyses differ with regard to the relationships of independence and dependence between the constituent variables. The covariation analysis assumes no such relationships, whereas the causation analysis explicitly tests for its existence. In the context of our study, however, neither impact analysis is in any sense superior to the other since a particular performance pattern may be caused by the receipt of US transfers, but even if it is not so caused, the simple fact of covariation between performance and transfer receipts may none the less have substantial importance for the realisation of US foreign policy objectives. In short, it may be that the United States is content to allow its transfers simply to reinforce performance patterns caused by other factors rather than seek to cause the patterns itself. Whatever the 'cause', the end result is the same from the perspective of the United States' realisation of its second-order impact utilities.

The study as a whole covers the years 1950–79 and its population of potential recipients is essentially all non-OECD countries that are not members of the communist bloc. Communist countries are excluded on the atheoretical grounds of problems of data availability. Each member of the population is included from 1950 onwards unless it became independent in a later year. If this is the case, its date of inclusion is its year of independence provided that its actual declaration of independence preceded 1 July and the following year if it succeeded this mid-year date. Missing data problems have meant that some countries have been included in the analysis only after they had been independent for a number of years. A full list of our population, together with their year of independence (if post-1950) and year of inclusion, is given in Appendix D.

Finally, in both the distribution and impact studies, we analyse official transfers in per capita, as well as gross, terms. This represents an effort on our behalf to distinguish between United States absolute and relative preferences in its dealings with Third World countries. That is, since these countries vary so substantially in population size, we include in the analysis a measure of relative, or per capita, preference, as well as one of absolute, or gross, preference. This distinction is important for the light it throws on the calculus underlying the distribution of US official transfers. If country A has half the population of country B and both receive the same gross transfer, then the two countries are accorded the same absolute preference, but A has twice the relative preference.

Design problems

Any research project will find itself confronted with two types of difficulty. The first relates to problems of conceptualisation and design and the second to technical difficulties like multicollinearity and outliers. This section is concerned with the first type since these constitute the more fundamental issues that ultimately determine the worth or otherwise of our project. Difficulties of the technical type will be addressed as they crop up in the course of the analysis. Here we shall consider in turn conceptual problems inherent in the design of the distribution study, in the distinction between distribution and impact and, finally, in the design of the impact study.

The most important problem in the distributional analysis relates to the question of the validity of the volume of an official transfer as an operational measure of supplier commitment and leverage. To appreciate this problem and our resolution of it, it is helpful to review briefly the logic underlying the distributional part of the larger study. We in fact take the dollar value allocations of official transfers to reflect the United States' priority ranking of Third World states, a priority that can be either absolute or relative in form depending on whether the transfer is measured in gross or per capita terms. Our assumption then is that the priority ranking accorded to recipients is a function of their at least potential contribution to the realisation of US foreign policy goals, i.e. the greater their actual or potential contribution the larger the volume of one or other transfer they receive. Since the principal objective of the distributional analysis is to identify these goals, this assumption is not problematic; if it is invalid, the analysis will identify no such interests, i.e. the assumption will have been put to the empirical test. We also assume that, while the distribution of official transfers itself reflects a hierarchy of foreign policy goals, they do so precisely because they afford the supplier with a means of promoting and protecting these goals through the commitment and leverage potential that is inherent in the transfers. In other words, if official transfers did not afford the supplier these utilities, then it would not deploy them in the first place.

Where we do encounter a validity problem is in the assumption that the volume of official transfers is an equally valid measure of both commitment and leverage. Other things being equal, it stands to reason that greater volume does indicate greater utility potential for the supplier, but it could be argued that this equation is more valid for commitment than it is for leverage. The grounds for such an argument are that supplier leverage is in part a function of recipient need so that if a country is in dire need of a transfer because of, say, a capital shortage or the outbreak of external conflict, then a relatively small volume of the appropriate transfer would likely create disproportionate leverage. To take empirical account of this type of need would be an extraordinarily difficult task since it would basically require the profiling and measurement of the needs of all our recipient countries. Still worse, we would, in fact, have to profile and measure recipients' perceptions of their needs as it is well known that it is the perception of need rather than 'objective' need that determines behaviour.

Paradoxically, however, it is the complication created by the importance of perceived need that provides us with the first of several ways out of this validity problem. That is, perceived need will in all likelihood be assessed by recipients in relative terms. For example, Third World countries vary in their per capita income and all probably seek to achieve positive growth rates, but it is unlikely that the wealthier among them seek lower growth rates than the poorer as long as there are still wealthier countries to act as a comparison group. In this respect, perceived need is likely to show less variation than absolute need. Thus, while it may be that, from the perspective of need, we could only assume that supplier leverage will increase with transfer volume when need is constant across all recipients, it seems entirely likely that recipients' perception of need, which is itself a relative phenomenon, would show little variation across recipients so that supplier leverage can, once again, be reasonably assumed to increase with transfer volume.

A second reason why the problem of need is not overly burdensome in the context of this analysis is that, following the logic of the relationship of perceived need to leverage, it would still be essential to take account of the volume of the transfer. In other words, holding volume constant, while it would be accurate to argue that an increase in recipient need will produce greater leverage for the supplier of the transfer, it is equally tenable that, holding need constant, an increase in volume will also produce greater leverage. Of course, this relationship will hold only up to the point at which recipient demand is fully satisfied, but we know that the demand for transfers continues to outstrip their supply since Third World countries constantly demand more of them.[12] Thus, since aggregate demand exceeds aggregate supply, the marginal utility returns on increasing levels of transfers, although diminishing, would not approach zero. In this respect, volume can be taken as a valid indicator of leverage.

Finally, it should be reiterated that leverage is not solely a function of need, whether it be perceived or absolute. As was argued earlier, it is also in large part a direct function of the absolute size of the transfer.

In sum, then, while the measurement of leverage undeniably presents more problems than the measurement of commitment, there seems to be no overwhelming reason why, other things being equal, the volume of a transfer cannot be accepted as an equally valid measure of both first-order supplier utilities.

A related observation is that official transfers are not the only means for a supplier to establish commitment and leverage relations. Governments can also signal commitment through, for example, treaties and other diplomatic ties, but these generally either correlate highly with official transfers or are not especially important *vis-à-vis* the Third World. Governments can also use alternative forms of leverage, such as the threat of force. However, except for extreme circumstances, official transfers are a much more acceptable and efficient way of exercising leverage, not least because they are in demand.

Another potentially serious validity problem concerns the commitment and leverage relations that may be developed by non-governmental agencies or actors, primarily through their trade and investment links with Third World countries. At least in principle, such links could give rise to a situation where a supplier government has a substantial foreign policy interest in a recipient, but allocates it only a relatively small volume of official transfers on the grounds that non-governmental actors sharing broadly the same values and goals have already developed strong commitment and leverage relations, thereby attenuating the need for the government in question to do so. The problem that this situation creates for us is that our analysis would not uncover the expected relationship between official transfers and US foreign policy interests. There are three reasons, however, why this situation is, in fact, unlikely to arise.

First of all, except in extreme circumstances like boycotts or embargoes, Western governments find it very difficult to control trade or investment flows so that they would be unlikely to seek to pursue their first-order utilities of commitment and leverage through agencies that they do not control. Secondly, a substantial commitment to a Third World country by, say, a transnational corporation might well lead a supplier government to distrust this commitment since it is a potential source of counter-leverage for the recipient. Once again, therefore, no government is likely to entrust the pursuit of its foreign policy interests to an actor that it does not fully control. Finally, while commitment and leverage relations can indeed be developed by non-governmental actors, it seems to us that similar relations between governments are qualitatively different precisely because they are intergovernmental. What is more, these doubts notwithstanding, even if a low volume of transfers were made to a Third World country that contributed markedly to, say, US foreign policy interests, either our analysis would detect it or, at worst, it would weaken our results if undetected. In the first of these instances, our one-way ANOVA analysis could identify such a situation by yielding a profile of high interest value in the zero recipient category, a relatively low value in the small category and larger ones in the medium and high categories. In the second instance, all that we can say is that we think it in fact preferable to err on the side of conservatism in the sense of producing weaker results rather than artificially inflated ones.

The second set of conceptualisation and design problems concerns the distinction between distribution and impact. While obviously sound at the level of common sense, it is a difficult distinction to maintain at a more rigorous level of analysis. For a start, the probable existence of a feedback loop from impact to distribution means that the two are always likely to be compounded, perhaps so much so as to be to all intents and purposes inseparable either conceptually or empirically. In addition, decision-makers may not only evaluate impact effects differently, but may also differ in the way in, or extent to, which they build them into subsequent distribution decisions. In effect, therefore, it is, strictly speaking, impossible to draw a categorical distinction between the distribution and impact of official transfers. At any one time, a distributional pattern may be no more than the sum total of previous impact evaluations on the part of the supplier. Rather than invalidating the analytical distinction between distribution and impact, however, this difficulty simply alerts us to the need to be prepared to look for the explanation of changing distributional patterns in earlier impacts. What is more, since this is an empirical problem it is one to which we can easily address ourselves because of the length of the time period covered by our analysis.

The third set of conceptualisation and design problems concerns the impact analysis side of the study. This analysis raises several problems, the first of which relates to the level of our approach. Impact studies can be either micro or macro in their level of analysis. Micro-level studies are most often carried out in the context of a single country and they usually examine the immediate consequences of the receipt of a transfer. A study of the external funding of a new irrigation system, for example, would investigate the effects of this system on the political, economic and social organisation of the locality. Micro effects do not inform our impact analysis, however. Rather, we adopt a macro-level approach that is concerned to look for the generalised effects of a number of transfers on principal aggregates, such as per capita income, across a large number of countries. This analytical focus is not intended to imply the superiority of the macro approach; the two approaches yield different types of information and have different payoffs. In this sense, they are better viewed as being complementary rather than as being rivals.[13]

A second problem with our impact study is its general lack of a theoretical or conceptual base. This problem simply reflects the fact that we do not have, or know of, a theory (i.e. a set of interrelated explanatory hypotheses) of impact to test. To state this limitation in its extreme form, we have no a priori theoretical reason to search for impacts in particular areas so that the impact analysis that we do undertake is essentially an *ad hoc* empiricist one. While we cannot deny this characteristic of the analysis, its extent should be qualified on three counts. In the first place, it is unavoidable precisely because there exists no theory to test. Even though *dependencia* models do cover the impact of official transfers, their assertions are simply not in a testable form. Secondly, any study of impacts must always confront the issue of intended and unintended effects. In other words, even if a theory existed that predicted certain outcomes, it could well be that many interesting and important outcomes would fall outside its predictions so that to the extent that an impact analysis was fully guided by the theory, it would risk overlooking important unintended outcomes. This is an important reason why impact studies in general are often deliberately *ad hoc* in character. Thirdly, it should be remembered that we are not completely reduced to *ad hoc* empiricism in this particular study. Generally speaking, supplier and recipient second-order utilities guide our search for impacts. This guidance is undoubtedly stronger on the supplier side of the analysis since we already know much about US foreign policy interests and goals and therefore are provided with a 'natural' focus in our examination of impacts. Indeed, the question of whether the United States actually achieves the interests that it promotes through its transfer programmes acts as a perfect bridge between the distribution and impact parts of the study. But since we have no rationale to enable us to identify recipient second-order utilities, we are undeniably on weaker ground in the recipient side of the impact analysis. On this matter, while readily admitting that it is basically an empiricist 'defence', we can only say that our impact analysis does cover a wide array of potential recipient interests.

The third problem in our impact analysis derives from the lack of controls in it. As noted previously, impact is examined in terms of either covariation or causation, but both are bivariate, at least in the context of this study. Examining impact in terms of covariation produces no insurmountable difficulties in this regard. Thus, if it turns out, for example, that Third World countries' rate of growth of trade with the communist bloc increases inversely with the receipt of US transfers, we can unproblematically conclude that the two variables covary, a conclusion that may well have some interest in its own right. If, however, we wish to go beyond this simple statement and interpret the co-variation to mean that US official transfers deter communist bloc trade, we are then making a causal impact statement that is massively more problematic than its simple covariation predecessor.

Perhaps the best way of conveying the problems associated with causal impact statements is to describe the type of research design that would be necessary for the unambiguous identification of this type of impact. Most appropriate would be the classical experimental design that would subject recipients to periods of transfers and no transfers under identical conditions. But this design cannot be used simply because we are in no position to manipulate supplier-recipient relations in a laboratory setting or in a quasi-laboratory field setting. There are, however, two possible alternative designs. The first would involve ideally the randomised selection of recipients and non-recipients, but, again, this design cannot be realised perfectly when the researcher has no control over the flow of transfers. Occasionally, we do in this study approximate this design by accident. Thus, for example, we may find that recipients and non-recipients of a transfer do not differ in their levels of per capita income, but transfer recipients enjoy significantly higher rates of growth on this variable. Under these circumstances, the initial similarity in levels of per capita income allows us to conclude that the variable itself does not explain the differences in its own rate of growth across the two transfer recipient groups. In other words, albeit by accident, we have effectively controlled for one possible explanation of the differential growth rates in per capita income. As it turns out, we make extensive use of this 'partial control' design in our individual impact analyses. A final possible research design involves using multiple regression analysis to explain the variation in a particular performance variable by means of a series of independent variables. We could then introduce volume of official transfers into the equation to determine whether it added significantly to the equation's explanatory power. If it did and if we also had good reason to believe that it should, we could then legitimately draw a causal inference about the impact of an official transfer on some particular dimension of recipient performance.

While feasible in theory, each of these designs raises immense practical difficulties of implementation. The classical experimental design is impossible to execute because we simply cannot manipulate both countries and transfers to form experimental and control groups. The multiple regression design is impracticable because we could not conceivably attempt to produce an explanation for each of a huge array of performance variables. The randomised design is sometimes partially practicable by accident and we end up being able to use it on a large number of occasions. The net result of these practical difficulties is that we are most often forced back onto our bivariate analyses despite their substantial problems of control. In short, we have no choice but to run the risk of either finding results that are, in fact, artefacts since their presence is a function of one or more confounded variables or of missing 'real' causal relationships whose absence is a function of one or more intervening variables not figuring in the analysis.

On the other hand, it should be noted that we are not entirely helpless in the face of these difficulties since, paradoxically, we can put the interface between distribution and impact to our immediate advantage. That is, the very fact that our distribution analyses tell which variables structure, i.e. are important to, supplier transfer decisions, gives us some indication of the identity of those variables whose rate of growth the supplier is likely to wish to influence. Furthermore, in those instances in which we wish to go beyond noting simple covariation and impute causality, we can carefully evaluate the grounds for wishing to draw the causal inference in the first place and at the same time articulate any relevant caveats that we may wish to make about it.

In summary, then, it cannot but be concluded that the distribution design in our study is substantially more robust than is the impact design. In the latter case, we do not indulge altogether in *ad hoc* empiricism, but equally we are far from generating empirical theory. In the case of the distribution analysis, by contrast, we do have the basis for an empirical theory since our general working hypothesis is that the distribution of official transfers is a function of the importance of potential recipients to the foreign policy interests of the supplier and that this interest is promoted and protected through the commitment and leverage potential inherent in official transfers for which there is a greater demand than supply. With regard to this particular study, having identified and justified the four main clusters of foreign policy interests that we should expect the United States to wish to promote, these interests, if corroborated, will constitute our empirical theory explaining the distribution of US official transfers.

Format of presentation

From Chapter 2 onwards, this book can be divided into three parts, the first part consisting of Chapters 2 and 3, the second of Chapters 4, 5, 6 and 7 and the third of Chapter 8.

Essentially, Chapters 2 and 3 provide the descriptive background to our subsequent analysis of the US official transfer programme. Chapter 2 starts with an elaboration of the rationale for the individual economic aid, military assistance and arms sales programmes, especially over the period stretching from the end of the Second World War to 1979. This elaboration is followed by an examination of the institutional setting in which the individual programmes have evolved and by a quantitative profile of the evolution of these programmes over the three decades since 1950. The primary purpose of this chapter is descriptive, but it also highlights a number of interesting and important interrelationships between the three transfer programmes.

Since the United States has often pursued its foreign policy goals through alliances with other, sympathetic states, Chapter 3 describes the evolution of its relations in a Third World context with its major allies, the Federal Republic of Germany (FRG), France, Japan and the United Kingdom (UK), since 1950. Changes in the alliance are graphed by means of a longitudinal examination of the interaction between US official transfer programmes and the equivalent programmes of its individual allies. In a second section of the chapter, this exercise is repeated for the economic aid programmes of the United States on the one hand and a number of multilateral agencies on the other, namely, the World Bank, the European Community (EC) and the United Nations Organisation (UN). The basic purpose of both sets of analyses is to determine the extent, if any, to which US hegemony in the international official transfers market has been eroded over the period stretching from 1950 to 1979.

The most substantively important part of the book is Chapters 4 to 7 inclusive since it is in these chapters that we investigate the relationship between US foreign policy interests and official transfers within the framework of our distribution and impact research design. Differing only in their substantive focus (i.e. the cluster of foreign policy interests that they investigate), these four chapters follow the same organisational format. But although treated separately, the clusters of interests should not be viewed as being rigidly independent of each other. Rather, their separation is best viewed as a necessary simplifying device and the conceptual overlap between them is explicitly recognised in our analysis by several variables appearing in more than one chapter. Equally, however, the degree of overlap should not be overstated; the clusters do enjoy an unambiguous internal coherence and do reflect analytically separable aspects of the United States' overall foreign policy since the onset of the Cold War.

The first section that is common to all four chapters is the introductory one and it is divided into two parts, the first of which we call the theoretical rationale. This rationale elaborates in some detail why we should expect a relationship to exist between the particular cluster of US foreign policy interests and official transfers.[14] The second part of this opening section outlines our operationalisation of these foreign policy interests. Taken over the four chapters, we cover a wide array of such interests and this is so for two reasons. Firstly, it is necessary because we have no a priori way of knowing which specific foreign policy interests, if any, are salient. Indeed, precisely because transfers are deployed to promote these interests in general, it seems to us that the identification of which interests are served by which transfers is best made empirically. Secondly, to use a wide array satisfies a more methodological point, which is that since it is not difficult to find relationships in the social sciences, a sustained effort must be made to reject relationships so that comparative evaluation becomes possible. In other words, this strategy enables us to evaluate rival explanations more systematically.

This introductory section is followed in each of Chapters 4 to 7 by the substantively important body of the chapter, namely the presentation and discussion of our findings. This is a complex and potentially confusing task that we have sought to simplify by creating a division of labour between the presentation of the findings and the interpretation of them. Thus, we have two parts in each chapter, Findings and Interpretation, each of which is further subdivided into distribution and impact analyses. The second section of each of the four chapters then becomes the presentation of our distribution and impact findings sequentially. What is more, each of these subdivisions treats the transfers of economic aid, military assistance and arms sales separately and sequentially. This format is then repeated in the third section of each of the four chapters, namely, the Interpretation section.

It is worth recapitulating at this point that our analysis of each transfer's distribution proceeds on two levels, bivariate and multivariate. The bivariate analysis involves simple ANOVAs in which the individual foreign policy interest variables are arrayed across the zero, small, medium and high recipient categories for each transfer. The multivariate analysis, on the other hand, comprises one or two stages, depending on the number of zero recipients of the transfer in question. The first stage is selection and it comes into play where the number of non-recipients is large, i.e. for military assistance and arms sales in every year and for economic aid from 1968 onwards. Where their number is small, as in the case of economic aid prior to 1968, this stage is omitted altogether. Selection is executed through discriminant analysis, a technique that determines whether the particular set of foreign policy interest variables distinguishes recipients and non-recipients of the transfer. The second multivariate stage is allocation and, with the sole exception of economic aid before 1968, it is executed only on those Third World countries actually receiving one or other transfer. The purpose of the allocation stage is to identify the variables actually determining which recipients get what amount of the transfers. When it comes to the impact findings, they are purely bivariate and their presentation consists of arraying the performance indicators' mean annual rate of growth over a four-year period across the aggregated zero, small, medium and large transfer recipient categories.

The third section common to Chapters 4 to 7 is the one involving the interpretation of the previously presented findings. While the distinction between findings and interpretation is difficult to maintain rigorously, the two components can none the less be analytically distinguished on the basis of their relative amounts of descriptive and evaluative content. Our general strategy is to maintain the distinction to the extent possible by outlining our findings in a rote, descriptive manner and then interpreting them against the theoretical rationale outlined at the outset of each chapter. We decided against fusing the two endeavours in a single treatment so as to maximise both clarity and simplicity of presentation and the opportunity for readers perhaps to develop alternative interpretations of the findings that we present. On the other hand, given that the Findings sections are replete with detailed quantitative results, some readers might prefer to skip over them and proceed directly to the Interpretation section of each chapter where our overall view, or Interpretation, of the previously enumerated findings is presented.

Matching its Findings counterpart, the Interpretation section is made up of separate distribution and impact subsections. In the former, our essential aim is to determine whether or not each chapter's cluster of foreign policy interests can be concluded to have significantly influenced the distribution of one or other official transfer, whereas the impact subsection is concerned to evaluate its findings against imputed supplier second-order utilities and recipient first-order and second-order utilities.

The final part of the book is made up of the concluding chapter and there the conclusions about the distribution and impact of US official transfers are integrated into a more general discussion of the changing role of the United States in the international political system.

Notes

1. For a good survey of the large number of issues associated with economic aid, see C. R. Frank, *et al., Assisting Developing Countries* (New York: Praeger, 1972); E. K. Hawkins, *The Principles of Development Aid* (London: Penguin, 1970); R. F. Mikesell, *Economics of Foreign Aid* (London: Weidenfeld and Nicholson, 1968); D. Wall, *The Charity of Nations* (New York: Basic Books, 1973); and J. White, *The Politics of Foreign Aid* (London: Bodley Head, 1974).

2. Military assistance and arms sales are most often treated as a single official transfer. Again, for a good survey of a large number of issues associated with this transfer, see A. H. Cahn, *et al., Controlling Future Arms Trade* (New York: McGraw-Hill, 1977); P. J. Farley, *et al., Arms Across the Sea* (Washington D.C.: The Brookings Institution, 1978); R. E. Harkavy, *The Arms Trade and International Systems* (Cambridge, Mass.: Ballinger, 1975); S. G. Neuman and R. E. Harkavy, eds, *Arms Transfers in the Modern World* (New York: Praeger, 1980); U. Ra'anan *et al.,* eds, *Arms Transfers to the Third World* (Boulder: Westview, 1978); A. J. Pierre, ed., *Arms Transfers and American Foreign Policy* (New York: New York University Press, 1979); A. J. Pierre, *The Global Politics of Arms Sales* (Princeton, N.J.: Princeton Universtiy Press, 1981); J. Stanley and M. Pearton, *The International Trade in Arms* (London: Chatto and Windus, 1972); and Stockholm International Peace Research Institute, *The Arms Trade with the Third World* (London: Paul Elek, 1971).

3. Insight into the black market in arms can be entertainingly gained from A. Sampson, *The Arms Bazaar* (New York: The Viking Press, 1977).

4. In actual fact, production-possibility curves are concave to make allowances for economies of scale. This refinement need not concern us, however, since it does not affect the basis of the general argument.

5. In practice, the inter-substitutability of transfers is not perfect. For example, military assistance may entail transfers that the recipient could not purchase, but this small proviso does not undermine the main thrust of the argument.

6. For a more general methodological discussion of the role of concept formation model construction and empirical research, see P. Abel, *Model Building in Sociology* (London: Weidenfeld and Nicholson, 1971); C. G. Hempel, *Fundamentals of Concept Formation in Empirical Science* (Chicago: University of Chiago Press, 1969); A. Przeworski and H. Teune, *The Logic of Comparative Social Inquiry* (New York: Wiley, 1970); and G. Sartori, 'Concept Misformation in Comparative Politics', *American Political Science Review*, 64 (December 1970), pp. 1033–53. For a more extended discussion of the general epistemological assumptions underlying our particular piece of research, a discussion that is illustrated by examples from the area of international relations, see D. A. Zinnes, *Contemporary Research in International Relations* (New York: Free Press, 1976).

7. For examples of these three positions on the usefulness of aid, see respectively, P. T. Bauer, *Dissent on Development* (London: Weidenfeld and Nicholson, 1971); H. J. Morgenthau, 'Preface to a Political Theory of Foreign Aid' in R. A. Goldwin, ed, *Why Foreign Aid?* (Chicago: Rand McNally, 1962); and T. Hayter, *Aid as Imperialism* (London: Penguin, 1970).

8. An alternative focus for a distribution analysis is the explanation of variation in total transfers allocations not over recipients, but over time. In other words, the question asked would be why the volume of, say, economic aid increases over some time periods and declines over others. Since we consider this focus theoretically less important and interesting than that on variation across recipients over time, we make no systematic analysis of it in this study. None the less, we do touch on it when it becomes relevant to our larger concerns. See especially the quantitative profiles of the individual transfers in Chapter 2.

9. Ideally, the time period chosen for any study would represent an interval of time that has some general 'theoretical' importance. 1950, our starting year, does have this importance in the sense that it marks the post-war commencement of official transfer programmes to the Third World. Our final year, 1979, has no such importance and was chosen simply because it was the latest year for which relevant data were available. It can only be defended, therefore, on the grounds that we wished to make our findings as up-to-date as possible, as well as to cover the maximum time period possible.

10. The tolerance level we actually use does not allow any independent variable to enter the regression equation if 50 per cent or more of its variance can be explained by the other independent variables.

11. The individual transfers are aggregated over a four-year period, e.g. 1950–3. Change in performance on each variable is assessed, however, over the period 1950–4, a time span that actually covers five years. None the less, since performance is defined as the mean annual change from 1950–4 and since the mean is calculated over four change intervals (1950–1, 1951–2, 1952–3 and 1953–4), we refer to the aggregated units in the impact analysis as four-year periods.

12. For the most recent evidence of persistent Third World demands for more

transfers, we only have to look at these countries' demands for a New International Economic Order (NIEO), a dimension of which is increased aid transfers. See, for example, H. O. Bergesen, *et al.*, eds, *The Recalcitrant Rich* (London: Frances Pinter, 1982). Third World countries have been less vocal on the question of arms sales, although it is altogether clear that they are generally opposed to any restraints on these transfers. This opposition can be clearly seen in the chapters dealing with the control of arms sales in any of the books cited in the second footnote for this chapter.

13. The distinction between micro and macro studies is, of course, a fluid one. One of the most widely studied areas in the context of general aid and technology transfers to the Third World is the so-called 'green revolution'. These studies are for the most part good illustrations of impact analyses that, although primarily micro in orientation, none the less have macro connotations. One highly sophisticated such study is: United Nations Research Institute for Social Development, *The Social and Economic Implications of the Large-scale Introduction of New Varieties of Food* (United Nations: Geneva, 1974).

14. This strategy conforms to the realist position in the philosophy of science to the effect that, before formulating a hypothesis, the researcher should have a clear reason or set of reasons as to why the relationship contained in the hypothesis should be expected to exist. For statements of this position, see R. Harre, *The Principles of Scientific Thinking* (London: Macmillan, 1970); and R. Keat and J. Urry, *Social Science as Science* (London: Routledge and Kegan Paul, 1975).

2 A Descriptive Profile of US Official Transfers

The development of US transfers before 1950

While the US programme of official transfers is usually dated from Roosevelt's World War II Lend–Lease Programme, there had, in fact, been an important precursor to this venture some twenty-five years earlier. Prior to 1914 the United States had been a debtor nation but World War I, in liquidating many European holdings in the United States, served not only to transform Western Europe into a debtor area, but also to transform the United States into a creditor nation. Indeed, it loaned approximately $7 billion to its European allies from the time of the outbreak of war in 1914 to the signing of the Armistice some four years later. It also sold arms to these same allies and these twin novel developments gave rise to the Wilsonian concept of the United States as the 'arsenal of democracy'.

The inter-war period saw the continuation of the flow of US arms and loans to Europe, although it did drop to levels substantially below those of the war period. Arms sales, however, became a matter of controversy. There was a generally widespread feeling that the unrestricted international trade in arms had contributed substantially to the outbreak of World War I and, as a result, a number of efforts to restrict their flow were instigated. The first such effort was the St. Germain Convention of 1919, but it was not implemented because the United States failed to ratify it. The more ambitious Geneva Convention of 1925 sought to establish both prohibited zones and the government licensing of arms sales, but it also failed to come into effect.

Widespread concern over arms transfers persisted, however and, in the United States, it culminated in the establishment of the Senate Munitions Committee in 1934. Popularly known as the Nye Committee, this body was particularly concerned about private, commercial weapons sales, believing them to be antithetical to world peace. Under the influence of its chairman, Senator Nye, it reasoned that as long as weapons could be sold for profit, some groups would have a distinct interest in ensuring the persistence of the highest possible level of demand for them. Therefore, it eventually came to recommend, among other things, the close governmental regulation of private arms manufacture, the establishment of a Munitions Control Board and the development of arms control legislation by the League of Nations. Overtaken by events, however, these recommendations were ignored in the short term, but one of them, namely the governmental regulation of all arms sales has become an institutional feature of the post-World War II arms market. All arms sales, be they intergovernmental or private, now require government export licences.

But while the US transfer of arms and loans may date back to at least World War I, it was only with the country's retreat from isolationism during and after World War II that such transfers were consciously and consistently integrated into the overall foreign policy design of the United States. The watershed of this development was the 1939 revision of the country's neutrality legislation so that arms could henceforth be transferred to belligerents. In consequence, Roosevelt was authorised, in the early days of the war, to send fifty destroyers to Britain without charge. While perhaps trivial in isolation, this transfer was extraordinarily important in the long term because it set the pattern of using US assistance to achieve foreign policy goals. What is more, this practice has spread to other donor states and has become ever more elaborate and explicit with the passage of time.

The full implications of the United States' change of policy towards belligerents are perhaps best brought out by examining the transfer of the destroyers from the standpoint of our model of official transfers. In having its demand for assistance granted, the recipient gained a first-order utility, i.e. an increase in its power capabilities. This increase then enabled it to pursue more effectively a second-order utility, the conflict with Germany. The United States as supplier was equally able to achieve the first-order utilities of demonstrating commitment to Britain and obtaining leverage over it, both of which led to the United States' subsequent receipt of base rights on British territory. These rights were the quid pro quo of the original transfer and constituted the supplier's second-order utility. Necessarily, though, the grant of these rights represented a first-order disutility for Britain, just as had the cost of the destroyers for the United States. Both countries, however, deemed their respective utilities to outweigh the costs of their disutilities. In short, the episode is an excellent illustration of positive net utilities for both supplier and recipient.

This initial transfer was followed in March 1941 by the adoption of the Lend–Lease Programme, which permitted the US President 'to authorise the manufacture of defense articles . . . for any foreign government whose defense he deemed vital to the defense of the United States'. The Japanese attack on Pearl Harbor in December 1941 brought a rapid acceleration in Lend–Lease so that by the end of the war, the United States had transferred some $48 billion worth of such articles to its allies. But the onset of the Cold War meant that, with the cessation of hostilities, the flow of US transfers did not decline sharply, as it had done after World War I. Whatever the reasons for the outbreak of the Cold War, its impact on subsequent US foreign policy cannot be understated. It is important, therefore, to establish at the outset its significance for the continued development of US official transfers.[1]

In 1946, the Truman administration received and immediately endorsed an 8,000-word telegram from the chargé d'affaires in its Moscow embassy, George F. Kennan. This telegram was in response to a State Department request for an explanation of Soviet behaviour. Its basic theme was that the USSR, being 'impervious to [the] logic of reason', but 'highly sensitive to [the] logic of force', would expand beyond its own borders unless it met with 'strong resistance'.[2] In Kennan's opinion, the appropriate US response to the threat of Soviet expansionism was 'long-term vigilant containment' and, although he never specified its means, the philosophy of containment became the leitmotif of a Truman administration whose originality lay in developing the means by which this overriding foreign policy goal could be realised. Figuring prominently among these means were official transfers.

The utility of these transfers for the United States was defended at length when, in response to Britain's 1947 announcement that it could no longer supply economic and military aid to a Greece and Turkey beset by communist insurgents, President Truman appeared before the US Congress to request a $400 million aid package. It was on this occasion that the Truman Doctrine was first articulated. It held essentially that there existed in the world two ways of life, one based on freedom and the other on coercion and that it was in the direct interest of world peace and US security that free people be defended against communist aggression. Since the newly-created United Nations Organisation was inadequate and ill-suited to this task, the responsibility for containing communism fell to the United States. One of the principal ways in which this country could 'assist free peoples to work out their own destinies' was through the use of official transfers. Thus, President Truman declared 'I believe that our help should be primarily through economic and financial aid, which is essential to economic stability and orderly political processes'.[3]

Later that same year, the European Economic Recovery Programme, popularly known as the Marshall Plan, was passed by Congress. Involving $17 billion in aid, this project was the most ambitious transfer programme to date. Essentially, it represented an enormous transfer of economic assistance that would enable Western Europe to rebuild its war-ravaged economy and the various first-order and second-order utilities to both supplier and recipients of this transfer were staggering. Marshall himself appears to have viewed the whole plan in narrow economic or humanitarian terms, declaring in June 1947, for example: 'Our policy is directed not against any country or doctrine but against hunger, poverty, desperation and chaos.'[4] But there were others both inside the Truman administration and in Western Europe who clearly viewed it in terms of second-order utilities of a more political or security nature.

This security emphasis was reflected in subsequent developments in both Europe and the United States. In March 1948 Belgium, Britain, France, Luxembourg and the Netherlands signed a mutual assistance pact in Brussels that was clearly directed at the Soviet Union. This event took place in the midst of a debate within the Truman administration, between people like Marshall and Forrestal, on the relative merits of economic and military assistance. In June of the same year, Senator Vandenberg, following the Forrestal 'military' line, gained congressional approval for the initiation of US negotiations with the Brussels Pact countries. These negotiations culminated in the establishment of a formal, peacetime military alliance, the North Atlantic Treaty Organisation (NATO), between the United States and Western Europe. Significantly, on the very same day that Congress ratified the NATO Treaty (25 July 1949), Truman sent a message to Congress requesting it to pass legislation that would authorise 'military aid to free nations to enable them to protect themselves against the threat of aggression'. This request was granted and the Mutual Defense Assistance Act was enacted in October 1949.

This increasing, if not greater, emphasis on the military, as well as economic, capabilities of America's allies was given further impetus by the publication in early 1950 of a National Security Council report entitled 'United States Objectives and Programs for National Security'. This report echoed the bipolarity theme first stated in the Truman Doctrine, but interpreted it less in terms of different ways of life and more in terms of a clash between fundamentally antithetical objectives and ideals in a world whose international division of power had been radically and irrevocably altered. This intepretation led it to call for 'world leadership' from the United States and to emphasise the need for a 'rapid build-up of political, economic and military strength in the free world'. In short, the principal authors of this report, Acheson and Nitze, disagreed with Marshall's view that the primary threat to world peace was social and economic chaos in Europe and that this could be averted through US economic assistance. In their eyes, the threat was nothing less than domination by Soviet ideology and military power. What is more, it was a threat that was seen as being world-wide, not just European, in scope.

This projection of US concerns beyond Western Europe was not new. President Truman had already anticipated it in his inaugural address of 1949. This was his famous 'Point Four' speech and in it he drew Americans' attention to the problems of the world's underdeveloped areas. Echoing many of the sentiments earlier directed at Western Europe, Truman called for US assistance to those 'peace-loving' and 'free' people in under-developed areas so that they, through 'a program of development based on concepts of democratic fair dealing', could learn to help themselves to 'achieve the decent, satisfying life that is the right of all people'. With Acheson's increasing influence on American foreign policy after 1949, this 'world leadership' theme gathered momentum and any doubt as to US sincerity and determination on the matter was dispelled when the North Koreans crossed the 38th parallel in June 1950.

This brief outline highlights several points that are particularly important to an understanding of the development of US official transfers in the post-World War II period. In the first place, this period saw the unambiguous institutionalisation of official transfers as a feature of US foreign policy. In the second place, the advent of the Cold War combined with the collapse of the Euro-centric state system served to ensure that the United States would not, indeed could not, return to the 'Fortress America' mentality that it had adopted between the two world wars. Thirdly, it was clear by 1950 that containment was to be the principal US response to what it perceived to be a global ideological and military threat posed by communism in general and the Soviet Union in particular. What is more, official transfers were to be the principal, although not exclusive, means by which the containment strategy was to be implemented. Finally, congressional reservations notwithstanding, the commitment of US troops in Korea emphasised that containment was not to be limited to Western Europe. In short, official transfers emerged as an institutionalised and integral part of overall US foreign policy and, at least in principle, these transfers were to be made available to those countries that were to become known as the Third World.

The development of US official transfers after 1950

The institutional setting

Five major pieces of legislation constitute the formal setting of the United States overall official transfer programme. The first, which has already been mentioned, was the Mutual Defense Assistance Act of 1949. This was replaced in 1951 by the Mutual Security Act, which represented not a change of direction in foreign policy, but an attempt to rationalise the administrative procedures provided for by its direct predecessor. Under the 1949 Act, the various aid programmes that had been undertaken by the Government were administered with relatively little co-ordination and the objective of the Mutual Security Act was to remedy this situation by establishing the position of Director of Mutual Security within the Executive Office of the President. The incumbent of this office charged the Department of Defense, the Mutual Security Agency and the Technical Cooperation Administration to deal with the distribution of military assistance, economic aid and technical assistance respectively. This basic structure was further reorganised in 1953 when the Mutual Security Agency and Technical Cooperation Administration gave way to the Foreign Operations Administration. Then, in 1955 the fledgeling Foreign Operations Administration was abolished and, emphasising the key foreign policy role of official transfers, overall responsibility for all assistance programmes passed into the hands of the Department of State, although the Defense Department maintained a key role in the administration, if not allocation, of military assistance. This broad division of responsibility has persisted to the present time.

The inauguration of President Kennedy in 1960 promised 'new directions' to meet 'new challenges' and, true to form, the third important piece of official transfer legislation, the Foreign Assistance Act, came to see the light of day shortly afterwards in 1961. This Act separated economic and military assistance more clearly than its predecessors had done and also represented yet another attempt to rationalise the formal decision-making structure with regard to official transfers. Its major innovation was to create the Agency for International

Development (AID) within the Department of State, while leaving unaltered the general division of responsibility between the Departments of Defense and State. Also unchanged was the debate within the US Government about the purpose of official transfers. Thus, on the one hand, we see President Kennedy asserting:

There exists, in the 1960s, a historic opportunity for a major economic assistance effort by the free industrialised nations to move more than half the people of the less developed nations into self-sustained economic growth . . . To achieve these new goals we will need to renew the spirit of common effort which lay behind our past efforts . . . to meet the new problems which confront us . . . [5]

But, on the other hand, the Foreign Assistance Act that was passed by Congress was decidedly less innovative and forward-looking. Indeed, it seemed to speak hardly at all to this 'historic opportunity'. It boldly asserts:

The Congress recognizes that the peace of the world and the security of the United States are endangered so long as international communism and the countries it controls continue by threat of military action, by use of economic pressure, by international subversion, or other means to attempt to bring under their domination peoples now free and independent and continue to deny the rights of freedom and self-government to peoples and countries once free but now subject to such domination . . . In enacting this legislation it is therefore the intention of Congress to promote the peace of the world and the foreign policy, security and general welfare of the United States . . . by improving the ability of friendly countries and international organisations to deter, or if necessary, defeat Communist or Communist-supported aggression . . . [6]

Despite this apparent confusion of purpose, what did become clearer under this new Act was the distinction between grants of military assistance and cash or credit arms sales. Sales as such were not novel. The 1949 Mutual Defense Act had made provision for them, terming them 'reimbursable aid'. Numerous amendments to its successor, the Mutual Security Act, had also authorised the sale of excess stock, the use of military assistance funds for credit sales, the capitalisation of a Foreign Military Sales Revolving Fund (permitting the re-use of loan repayments) and a Department of Defense guaranty reserve system. But starting in 1962, such cash and credit sales came to be known as the Foreign Military Sales Program (FMS) and to be distinguished from grant transactions within the Military Assistance Programme (MAP).

The birth of this distinction was due, in part at least, to the increasing attraction of the FMS programme for US policy-makers. Speaking in 1963, the President explained this attraction thus: 'it is essential that we make every effort to prosecute the program of selling US equipment to our allies. Not only will this decrease the net outflow of gold from this country, but it also ties in our military aid to foreign policy.'[7] This theme was reiterated in 1966 when President Johnson emphasised: 'We will shift our military aid programs from grant aid to sales whenever possible'.[8] This increased emphasis on sales led in 1968 to the fourth major piece of legislation on official transfers, the Foreign Military

Sales Act. Never intended to replace the 1961 Foreign Assistance Act, this 1968 Act simply created a clear division of labour between economic and military assistance and cash or credit sales. The former were to be covered by the old Act and the latter by the new one. But sales were not to be so indiscriminate as to undermine military transfers as instruments of US foreign policy. The 1968 Act stated:

It authorises sales by the United States Government to friendly countries having sufficient wealth to maintain and equip their own military forces at adequate strength, or assume progressively larger shares of the cost thereof, without undue burden to their economies, in accordance with the restraints and control measures specified herein and in furtherance of the security objectives of the United States . . .[9]

It further provided that:

all such sales be approved only when they are consistent with the foreign policy interests of the United States, the purposes of the foreign assistance program of the United States as embodied in the Foreign Assistance Act of 1961, as amended, the extent and character of the military requirement and the economic and financial capability of the recipient country, with particular regard being given, where appropriate, to proper balance among such sales, grant military assistance, and economic assistance as well as to the impact of the sales on programs of social and economic development and on existing incipient arms races.[10]

Despite these changes of emphasis after 1950, however, the President continued to control US official transfers. To be sure, the various congressional acts had outlined the broad parameters within which he had to operate, but these were of such a vague and wide-ranging nature that they could hardly be interpreted as a real constraint on presidential discretion. Furthermore, the complex of administrative agencies charged with planning, programming, funding and implementing the transfer programmes were directly responsible to the President. Congress's only real sanction, potential or otherwise, over the President was its authorisation of the annual appropriations that were submitted to it as part of the overall presidential budget, but even this sanction could be exercised only with regard to the economic and military assistance programmes since the sale of arms did not require any direct financial authorisation. This situation lasted until 1973 when, as part of the general congressional reaction against the 'imperial presidency', the Senate Foreign Relations Committee, under Fulbright's chairmanship, prepared legislation that was designed to effect a radical change in the official transfer programmes. The military assistance programme was to be phased out over four years, while 'the State and Defense Departments [were to get] out of the arms sales business and get these transactions back to a free enterprise, commercial basis, where they belong'.[11]

This proposed legislation never came into being, however, although it did trigger a series of repercussions. In December 1974, a law was enacted which provided that Congress could block any government-to-government sale of over $25 million. Meanwhile, the President also signed a bill phasing out MAP by 30 September 1977. Finally, the Senate Foreign Relations Committee set up a Foreign Assistance Sub-committee under Humphrey in 1975. The Humphrey Committee rejected the Fulbright plan to return arms sales to the private sector on the grounds that it would further weaken congressional control over them. After considering a number of ways whereby Congress could, in fact, increase its control over arms sales, the committee sponsored a series of recommendations that was signed into law in 1976 under the form of the International Security Assistance and Arms Export Control Act, the fifth important piece of official transfers legislation.

This Act was essentially a supplement to the 1968 Foreign Military Sales Act and its major provisions were that all arms sales of more than $25 million in value must be submitted to Congress, which then has thirty days in which to implement a concurrent veto should it so choose, that all non-NATO sales over $25 million must be on a government-to-government basis, and, finally, that the President had to submit to Congress a country-by-country justification for sales. Although intended to limit the President's discretion, this legislation basically left his authority intact in so far as Congress still only enters the discussion of any arms transfer at a very late stage and its latitude for action remains constrained by both substantial lobbying pressure from domestic arms manufacturers and the presidential reprimand that its blocking of a proposed transfer would seriously harm the United States' relations with the recipient country concerned.[12]

A quantitative profile

Having described the general institutional setting of official transfers, we now present a quantitative profile of them. But before elaborating this profile, two important issues need to be addressed. The first of them concerns whether we treat economic aid, military assistance and arms sales jointly or separately and the second the sources from which we derive our quantitative data. We shall now deal with each of them in turn.

With regard to the first of these issues, the three transfers will be analysed separately, a strategy that may seem paradoxical in view of the fact that we earlier argued for their inter-substitutability. The point of this argument, however, is not that the transfers are identical, but that economic and military aid in particular can often be interchanged in the uses to which they are put by recipients. In other words, its purpose is only to caution against viewing them as being categorically different from each other. Certainly, they are not generally held to be identical by either donor or recipient governments and this is perhaps the single best reason for treating them separately. After all, if governments are guided in their decisions by this perception, to aggregate the transfers would in all likelihood entail the loss of a substantial amount of valuable information. It is certainly clear in the case of the United States, for example, that the perception of the transfers' distinctiveness reigns. Not only is each transfer covered by its own legislation, but also successive presidential administrations have attached different priorities to the individual transfers at different points in time and have consequently employed different mixes of them to pursue their foreign policy goals. Finally, the transfers are best treated separately if only for the empirical reason that there is substantial variation in their individual total dollar value and distribution among Third World countries and this variation needs to be explained.

The second problem to be resolved concerns our data sources. They are of two types, national and international, and we have taken the view that, generally speaking, the latter are preferable since the intergovernmental organisations collecting them introduce a standardisation that improves the international comparability of their data. Despite this general preference, however, we do use US government figures to measure that country's economic aid flows to Third World countries instead of those produced by the Development Assistance Committee (DAC) of the Organization for Economic Cooperation and Development (OECD). We make this choice simply because, while the DAC figures may be comparable across all OECD suppliers of aid, they are published only from 1960 onwards, whereas the official US figures are available from 1950. What is more, we lose nothing by this choice. Table 2.1 shows that the US and DAC figures are, in fact, very similar in terms of both their dollar value and, more importantly, their intercorrelation across recipients is very high, averaging out over the nineteen years at 0.95 with a range of no more than 0.85 to 0.99. In other words, the two operational definitions of economic aid are all but the same.[13]

We are on less certain ground, however, with regard to official US statistics on military assistance and arms transfers. Our problem here is basically that it is difficult to validate these statistics since no intergovernmental organisation disseminates similar data. This situation contrasts markedly with the one prevailing in the inter-war period when the League of Nations published figures on arms transfers. And, indeed, there have been proposals that its successor, the UN, does likewise. In 1965, for example, Malta proposed the establishment of a system of UN publicity about arms transfers only to find itself defeated by its fellow members in a vote on the issue. Similarly, when Demark, Iceland Malta and Norway collectively proposed in 1968 that the UN Secretary General should look into publishing statistics on arms transfers, opposition, particularly from the Third World, proved to be so strong that the proposal was not even put to the vote. In view of this situation, the only non-governmental source of arms data is the Stockholm International Peace Research Institute (SIPRI), which uses its own, individual accounting system to collect annual data on the transfer of major weapons systems between states. We make extensive use of

Table 2.1 Volume of (in current $m.) and correlations between US economic aid by US Government and OECD sources

	Volume		Correlation		Volume		Correlation
	Govt.	OECD			Govt.	OECD	
1960	2,637	2,476	0.98	1970	2,528	2,524	0.99
1961	2,870	3,203	0.87	1971	2,583	2,677	0.95
1962	3,740	3,208	0.97	1972	2,698	2,426	0.91
1963	3,660	3,426	0.97	1973	2,496	2,188	0.97
1964	3,335	3,418	0.95	1974	2,221	2,194	0.99
1965	3,169	3,535	0.97	1975	2,803	2,526	0.87
1966	3,788	3,536	0.98	1976	4,059	2,679	0.85
1967	3,082	3,518	0.94	1977	3,322	2,715	0.92
1968	3,214	3,488	0.96	1978	3,766	3,219	0.97
1969	2,466	2,612	0.97	1979	3,821	NA	–

this data in our analysis.[14] Indeed, we really have no choice but to do so since, with the notable exception of the United States; national governments do not release details of their arms transfers broken down by recipient. Thus, the SIPRI data have two inestimable advantages: their availability from 1950 onwards and their comparability both across countries and across time. But, equally, they have the disadvantage of being rather limited in what they define as arms, i.e. major weapons systems.[15] For this reason, as well as for our analytical focus being principally on US transfers, we use official US military assistance and arms sales data to measure the transfers.[16]

Table 2.2 details the relationship between the SIPRI figures and the official US figures for military assistance and arms sales. Given the relatively restricted SIPRI definition of what constitutes arms, it is not surprising that its transfer estimates differ from the United States'. That this difference is not overly important, however, is indicated by the fact that the correlations between the estimates from the two sources are generally substantial.

To recapitulate briefly, then, official US figures constitute the dependent variables in our analyses of the distribution and impact of individual official transfers. Thus, all three of the transfers at the heart of this study are operationally defined by the US Government. This is not a problem, however, since its conceptual definition of each transfer conforms closely to that given in Chapter 1. Moreover, its operational definition of economic aid at least is very similar in volume to, and correlates almost perfectly with, the standardised US aid figures disseminated by the OECD. It is regrettable that the US military assistance and arms sales figures cannot be similarly validated, but there is simply no point of comparison for them that is equivalent to the OECD. Their unofficial character notwithstanding, the SIPRI arms sales figures are a source of confidence on this matter. While they can only be expected to differ in magnitude because of definitional dissimilarities, they none the less correlate highly with official US estimates.

Table 2.2 Volume of US transfers (in constant $m.) under Foreign Military Sales Program (FMS) and Military Assistance Program (MAP) from US Government sources and of US transfers of major weapons systems from SIPRI sources (SIPRI) together with correlations between each of FMS and MAP with SIPRI for alternate years, 1951–79

	Volume*			Correlations	
	FMS†	MAP†	SIPRI	FMS–SIPRI	MAP–SIPRI
1951	–	239	73	–	0.41
1953	–	861	184	–	0.62
1955	–	999	315	–	0.93
1957	–	1,409	319	–	0.46
1959	–	1,358	277	–	0.90
1961	–	1,106	241	–	0.28
1963	–	1,444	342	–	0.65
1965	–	1,425	435	–	0.53
1967	166	1,588	343	0.60	0.51
1969	349	2,396	837	0.55	0.58
1971	581	3,111	689	0.65	0.48
1973	739	4,236	621	0.59	0.13
1975	1,719	527	1,356	0.94	0.04
1977	3,627	–	2,793	0.72	–
1979	2,885	–	NA	NA	–

*SIPRI figures are put into constant prices based on a three-nation basket of deflators. To facilitate comparisons we have put FMS and MAP figures into 1970 prices deflated by the US general price index.

†FMS figures are not given for 1951–65 due to their small size, while MAP figures are not given for 1977–9 for the same reason.

Having addressed these issues, we now turn to the two major concerns of this section of the chapter. The first of them is to present a descriptive profile of the respective distributions of aid, military assistance and arms sales over the period 1950–79. These profiles comprise the same informational segments, namely the dollar volume of the transfer, the correlation of this volume in one year with that in the next (1950-1, 1951-2, etc.), the size of the recipient population, the correlation between gross and per capita receipts and, where relevant, the relations between the principal components of the transfers. The second concern is to examine, again on a purely descriptive level, the nature of the relations between the three transfer programmes.

To take the economic aid programme first, Figure 2.1 shows that, when expressed in constant dollar terms, its volume has varied substantially over time. Generally rising from 1950 to the early 1960s, its dollar value contracts more or less continuously between 1966 and 1974. It then stabilises more or less at its mid-1950s level, which is itself only half of the value it reaches at its high point in the mid-1960s.

Table 2.3 presents our next segment of information on the aid programme,

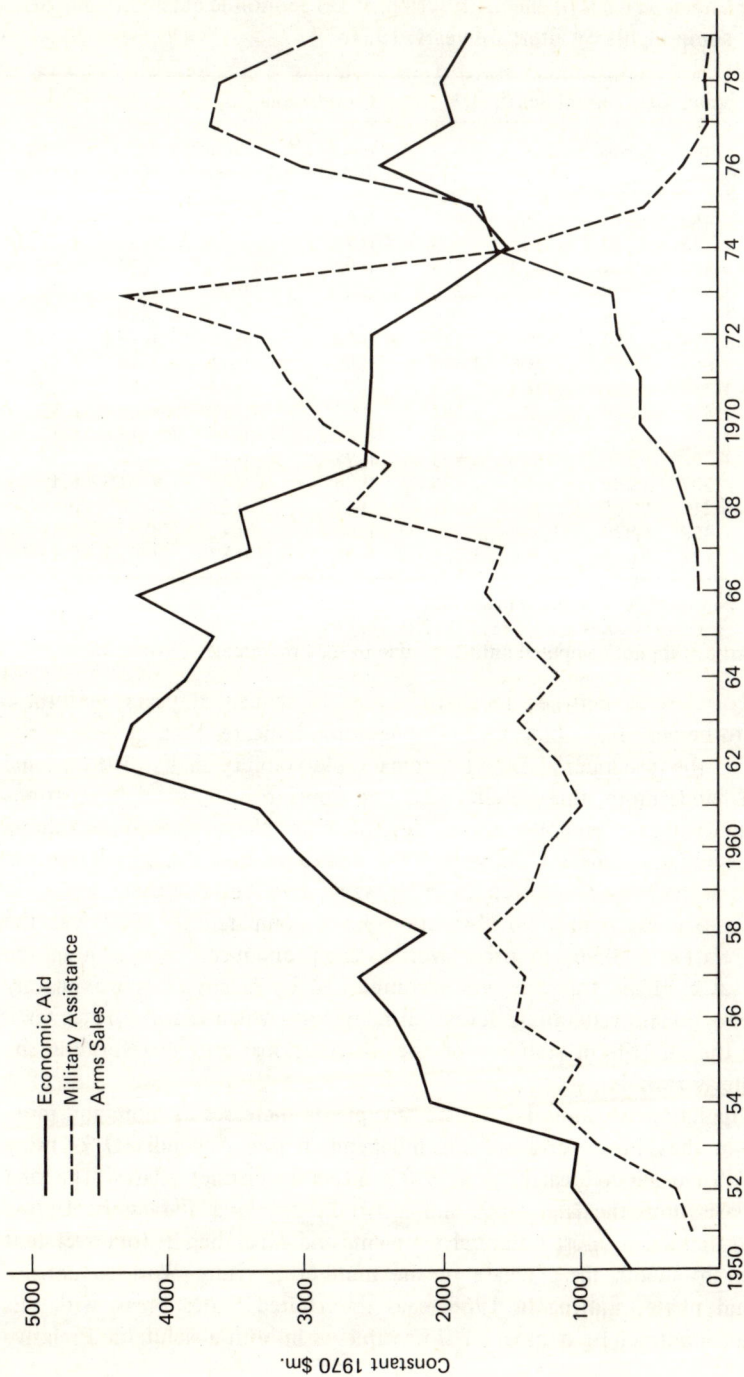

Figure 2.1 Flow of annual transfers of US economic aid, military assistance and arms sales to the Third World in constant 1970 $m., 1950–79.

Table 2.3 Characteristics of the distribution of US economic aid and its major components by alternate years, 1951–79

	Volume (in current $m.)*				Correlations			
	Grants	Loans	SSA	Total	Aid at t/† Aid at $t + 1$	Grants/‡ Loans	SSA/ 'Other'	Gross per cap.
1951	452	245	359	697	0.65	–	0.00	0.68
1953	768	40	534	808	0.77	–	0.23	0.47
1955	1,521	244	1,413	1,765	0.92	–	0.26	0.55
1957	1,508	708	1,287	2,218	0.83	0.20	0.26	0.29
1959	1,405	955	1,006	2,360	0.89	0.30	0.20	0.17
1961	1,716	1,154	982	2,870	0.93	0.52	0.18	0.20
1963	1,666	1,994	606	3,660	0.96	0.41	0.10	0.12
1965	1,258	1,911	465	3,169	0.97	0.23	0.05	0.20
1967	1,398	1,684	746	3,082	0.97	0.18	0.08	0.36
1969	1,187	1,279	416	2,466	0.89	0.21	0.18	0.37
1971	1,324	1,259	538	2,583	0.97	0.14	0.29	0.55
1973	1,207	1,289	601	2,496	0.96	0.47	0.41	0.40
1975	1,218	1,585	841	2,803	0.57	0.23	0.16	0.52
1977	1,402	1,920	1,642	3,322	0.97	0.47	0.37	0.67
1979	2,174	1,647	1,906	3,821	0.99	0.87	0.03	0.65

*Total economic aid = grants + loans = SSA + 'other'.
†The $t/t + 1$ correlations are for 1950/1, 1952/3, etc.
‡Correlations are not computed until 1957 due to the low volume of loans.

i.e. the correlations between its distributions in sequential years, and these turn out to be very high. Indeed, their magnitude indicates that, at least in the short term, the programme enjoys a remarkable stability in its distributional criteria. What is more, this stability seems to hold, irrespective of fluctuations in absolute volume. In dollar terms, for example, the programme's volume remains essentially constant between 1971 and 1972 and the correlation between the transfer's distribution in these same two years is 0.86. 1973, by contrast, sees a sharp drop in absolute volume compared to 1972, yet the same correlation is 0.96. In other words, the pronounced reduction in the absolute value of aid transfers was accomplished by means of approximately equal proportionate reductions across all recipients, which is still further testimony to the short-term stability of the distributional criteria informing the programme as a whole.

The population of potential transfer recipients increases as more and more countries in the Third World become independent (see Appendix D for more details). US aid allocations themselves fall into two distinct phases. The first of them lasts until the late 1960s and, generally speaking, it sees the United States granting aid to most potential recipients and expanding its total recipient population to match the increase in the number of Third World countries. The second phase, starting in 1968, sees the United States break with this pattern and contract its number of aid recipients in both absolute and relative (i.e. the number of recipients as a percentage of all potential recipients) terms. Thus, up to and including 1967, an average 13 per cent of Third World countries receive no US aid. Between 1968 and 1979, this figure more than doubles, to reach 27 per cent.[17]

Gross and per capita aid are respectively measures of absolute and relative preference and their correlation is always positive and generally significant. There is, however, some considerable variation in its actual value with the correlation coefficients ranging in magnitude from 0.12 to 0.68 (see Table 2.3).[18] Thus, while the gross and per capita aid distribution clearly overlap, they are far from being the same phenomenon and merit separate analysis.

Up to this point, we have described the principal characteristics of economic aid as an undifferentiated whole, but it is a transfer that can also be interestingly and pertinently examined in terms of its two component parts, grants and loans. While parsimony and manageability oblige us to analyse only total aid (grants + loans) in our larger study, the distinction between the two components is important in principle since those Third World countries receiving a higher ratio of grants to loans are receiving greater concessionality. As we shall see a little later, it is also the case that the two components stand in different relations to the other two US transfers. Table 2.3 shows that grants initially outweigh loans in the US economic aid programme. The gap begins to narrow, however, in the late 1950s until loans actually come to exceed grants in dollar value from the early 1960s onwards, although the margin of difference is not usually very substantial. In terms of their interrelationship, the correlation between grants and loans is always positive, but is usually not very high and varies substantially to average out at 0.37 over the 1955–79 period. It is apparent, therefore, that the expansion in total US economic aid from the late 1950s onwards is constituted primarily of increases in loans, its less concessional component. The contraction from the late 1960s, by contrast, is achieved by cutting loans and grants in relatively equal proportions. It is also apparent that concessionality, as measured by the ratio of grants to loans, varies across recipients as well as across time.

A second way of disaggregating total economic aid is to distinguish between Security Supporting Assistance (SSA) and 'Other' aid (where the latter is defined simply as total aid minus SSA). Although SSA is administered by the Agency for International Development, its definition makes it sound remarkably like military assistance.[19] Leaving this comparison aside for the moment, SSA fluctuates markedly in volume, being as low as 13 per cent of total aid allocations in 1964 and as high as 86 per cent in 1950. Generally speaking, however, its proportionate volume is highest through the 1950s, declines in the 1960s and increases again in the 1970s (see Table 2.3). Its correlation with 'Other' economic aid, although variable, is generally low and actually insignificant in most years. This pattern would seem to confirm the suspicion, aroused by the transfer's definition, that SSA is, in fact, a distinctive form of economic aid. We shall return to this point shortly.

The distribution of military assistance to the Third World follows a different pattern overall to that of aid (see Figure 2.1). Its volume increases steadily up to 1958 and then stabilises for the next ten years. The year 1958 is of additional significance because it is the first year in which military assistance transfers to the Third World exceed, at least in terms of their dollar value, those to the West. Indeed, particularly in the early 1950s, this programme is dominated by Western Europe with the consequence that military assistance flows to the Third World in such small volumes that our analysis of them can begin only in 1953. After 1958, US transfers to Western Europe decreasingly take the form of military assistance and increasingly of arms sales. Military assistance transfers to the Third World, in contrast, begin to increase sharply from 1967, overtaking economic aid in dollar value for the first time in 1970 and continuing to rise until 1973 after which time they decay exponentially down to 1977. This is the year in which the institutionalised Military Assistance Program was to be phased out with any transfers that continued being on a country-by-country basis after Congressional authorisation. Given the small sums involved after 1975, we terminate our analysis of military assistance in this year.

Averaging out at 0.93 with a range of 0.76 to 0.99, the year-by-year correlations indicate a high level of at least short-term continuity in the distribution of military assistance over the 1953–75 period. What is more, as with aid, the magnitude of these correlations does not vary systematically with increases or decreases in the total dollar value of the transfer. In other words, expansions or contractions in the total supply of military assistance are executed on a proportional basis and so do not entail substantial changes in the programme's distributional criteria.

Where the economic aid and military assistance programmes do differ, however, is in the size of their respective recipient populations. Over the three decades covered by our study, from 70 to 90 per cent of Third World countries receive economic aid in any one year, whereas a much smaller proportion receives military assistance. In fact, the absolute number of military assistance recipients increases gradually to reach a high point of 41 in 1964, but then starts to decline to 29 in 1975. The increasing size of the Third World means that there is a more marked, but still generally incremental, decay in the percentage of recipients from around 50 per cent in the mid-1950s to around 30 per cent in the mid-1970s.[20]

Ranging from 0.59 to 0.94 and averaging out at 0.84, the annual correlations between gross and per capita military assistance are generally higher than they are in the case of economic aid. In conceptual terms, therefore, there is a substantial overlap in the absolute and relative preference expressed through military assistance. But this overlap notwithstanding, the distinction between the gross and per capita forms of the transfer will be retained in our analysis.

The distribution of US arms sales is yet another story. Until 1970, arms sales to the Third World were so small that our analysis of them begins only in that year. Previously, Western European countries were by far the most important recipients of US arms sales, but the dollar value of Third World sales overtook European sales in 1975. Figure 2.1 shows 1974 to have been a particularly important year in the growth of the US arms trade with the Third World since it was the first year in which the United States transferred more arms than economic aid. Perhaps still more interestingly, this figure shows that the downgrading of the military assistance programme is matched almost perfectly by an increase in the value of arms sales. In other words, the cycle of military assistance being superseded by arms sales after itself having superseded economic aid is repeated for the Third World some twenty years after it characterised the pattern of US transfers to Western European countries. The parallel between these two sets of cycles only serves to emphasise that US official transfers are not allocated randomly. Rather, they conform to well-defined and identifiable patterns, patterns which themselves are not immutable.

As with both economic aid and military assistance, the inter-year correlations for arms sales are very high, averaging out at 0.94 for the 1970-9 period with a range of 0.80 to 0.99. Again, therefore, there would seem to be a marked degree of short-term continuity in US arms sales policy towards individual Third World countries, even during the programme's rapid expansion in the 1970s. The proportion of these countries receiving arms transfers, however, is more akin to that for military assistance than for economic aid. It increases from around 25 per cent in the early 1970s to close to 40 per cent by the close of the same decade.[21] Finally, the correlations between gross and per capita arms sales fall between those for military assistance and economic aid (averaging out at 0.77, 0.84 and 0.43 respectively). While undoubtedly substantial, the correlation between the two arms sales distributions is not sufficient to invalidate our analysing them separately, just as we do for aid and military assistance.

Having described the main distributional characteristics of the individual transfers, we turn now to examine their interrelationship. More specifically, we shall look sequentially at the relationships between aid and military assistance, aid and arms sales and military assistance and arms sales.

Table 2.4 shows economic aid and military assistance to be positively and significantly related throughout the period of our analysis except for 1975, but we attach no substantive importance to this exception since 1975 is the last year in which any substantial amount of military assistance flows to the Third World. Despite some fluctuations in the magnitude of the correlations between the two programmes, they do tend to be relatively stable over time, even during periods of expansion or contraction of one or other programme. In general, therefore, higher receipts of economic aid also entail higher levels of military assistance, although this overlap is hardly sufficiently pronounced to suggest that the two programmes are coterminous in the sense of pursuing the same goals.

Table 2.4 Correlations of US economic aid and its principal components with military assistance by alternate years, 1953–75

	Total Aid*/ Mlt. Assist.	Aid Grants/ Mlt. Assist.	Aid Loans/ Mlt. Assist.†	SSA/ Mlt. Assist.	'Other' Aid/ Mlt. Assist.
1953	0.45	0.46	–	0.73	−0.04
1955	0.34	0.30	–	0.33	0.16
1957	0.68	0.86	0.03	0.89	0.11
1959	0.44	0.62	0.06	0.62	0.13
1961	0.50	0.73	0.15	0.82	0.21
1963	0.45	0.73	0.20	0.74	0.30
1965	0.44	0.82	0.13	0.82	0.22
1967	0.63	0.87	0.08	0.85	0.19
1969	0.62	0.94	0.05	0.94	0.27
1971	0.75	0.45	0.04	0.94	0.37
1973	0.77	0.84	0.48	0.95	0.42
1975	0.17	0.11	0.14	0.09	0.16

*Total economic aid = grants + loans = SSA + 'other'.
†Correlations are not computed until 1957 due to the low volume of loans.

A different set of conclusions emerges, however, when we relate military assistance to the different components of economic aid (i.e. grants vs. loans on the one hand and SSA vs. 'Other' aid on the other). Table 2.4 shows that, with the minor exception of the years 1972–4, the correlations between loans and military assistance are generally significant, whereas those between grants and military assistance are not only positive and significant, but also very high. Indeed, after military assistance reaches its first growth peak in 1957, the transfer's correlation with aid grants is generally in excess of 0.75. Thus, military assistance recipients are both allocated more US aid and receive it in a more concessionary form. A similarly contrasting picture emerges when we examine how SSA and 'Other' aid are each related to military assistance. The correlations are low or insignificant in the case of 'Other' aid, but are positively and highly significant in that of SSA. In other words, this is yet further evidence that SSA is to most intents and purposes military assistance by another name.

In marked contrast, economic aid, no matter how conceptualised, is insignificantly related to arms sales. Thus, while it is conceivable that the US aid and arms sales programmes are indirectly complementary in the sense that they are structured to pursue essentially similar general objectives tailored to suit the different circumstances of particular recipients, it is clear that these two programmes do not enjoy the direct complementarity that the aid and military assistance programmes do. None the less, it is worth emphasising that aid and arms sales are not negatively related and, in this respect, are not directed at distinctly different recipient populations.[22]

Finally, we come to the relationship between the military assistance and arms sales programmes, a relationship that can be examined only for the first half of the 1970s. As would be expected given both these transfers' relationship to aid, no significant associations emerge in this relatively short period of time.[23] What makes this finding interesting is that it emphasises that while arms sales might replace military assistance transfers in aggregate terms, they do not substitute for them on an individual country basis. Indeed, the evidence indicates that it is, in fact, economic aid that substitutes for such military assistance transfers.

Conclusion

We can now summarise the main conclusions to be drawn from the last two sections of this chapter, i.e. those sections dealing with the United States' post-1950 official transfer programmes. With regard to their institutional setting, the most salient characteristic of the US official transfer programmes has been continuity, which has manifested itself in both general policy statements and the location of decision-making power in the Executive Office of the Presidency. Those programme changes that have taken place have tended to be administrative, relatively superficial and designed primarily to improve domestic co-ordination. Indeed, it has been argued that these administrative changes were implemented, at least in part, for public relations purposes. It is also clear that a fairly unambiguous legislative distinction has been retained between economic aid, military assistance and arms sales. Finally, the President has always enjoyed a high degree of autonomy in designing the transfer programmes. To be sure, he has been constrained by legislation, but it is legislation that has been open-ended and that has indicated when he could not make transfers rather than when he could. Under these circumstances, the onus has never really fallen on the President to justify individual transfers, or even the programmes at large, except to declare them vital to US interests. The only inroad into presidential autonomy that has been consistently available to Congress has been its ability to reduce appropriations for economic and military aid and it has regularly made use of this ability since the very first appropriation by Truman under the 1949 Mutual Defense Assistance Act. But it is not an ability that gives it any control over the more important issue of how much goes where once the appropriation has been granted. In the case of arms transfers involving cash, Congress has had little control since no funds need to be appropriated for these transfers. It has influenced credit sales only when a further capitalisation of the credit fund has been required. Even taking account of the 1976 International Security Assistance and Arms Export Control Act, then, congressional input into the whole complex of official transfers has been so slight that any control that it may claim to have in this area is more formal than real.

The quantitative profiles of the three transfers indicate the need for, and importance of, examining their distribution and impact separately. The three display different growth and/or decay paths, the transfers are made to different numbers of recipients and often they are not related one to the other. Their separateness, however, should not be overemphasised, especially outside the area of statistical analysis. After all, a 'global' perspective reminds us of their substitutability, of the similarity in the OECD and Third World countries' transfer growth and decay cycles and of the symbiosis, albeit limited, between economic and military assistance.

Notes

1. The literature on the Cold War is positively legion. For a good representation of it, see T. G. Paterson, ed., *The Origins of the Cold War* (Lexington: Heath, 1974).
2. G. F. Kennan, *Memoirs, 1925–50* (Boston: Little, Brown, 1967), p. 293.
3. H. S. Truman, 'The Truman Doctrine: Special Message to the Congress on Greece and Turkey, March 12 1947', *Public Papers of the Presidents of the United States, Harry S. Truman* (Washington, DC: US Government Printing Office, 1947).
4. G. C. Marshall, 'European Initiative Essential to Economic Recovery', *Department of State Bulletin*, **16**, 15 June 1947.
5. Excerpt from the Message of the President to Congress on foreign aid, transmitted on 22 March 1961. Quoted in J. M. Nelson, *Aid, Influence and Foreign Policy* (New York, Macmillan, 1968), p. 4.
6. Quoted in US Department of Defense, *Military Assistance Facts,* 1968.
7. Quoted in US Department of Defense, *Military Assistance and Foreign Military Sales Facts,* 1967.
8. Ibid.
9. Quoted in US Department of Defense, *Military Asistance and Foreign Military Sales Facts,* 1974.
10. Ibid. This change was compatible with the emerging Nixon Doctrine, although the burden-sharing aspect of this Doctrine had been anticipated earlier in the 1960s. See the quotations attached to notes 7 and 8.
11. Quoted in R. M. Moose and D. L. Spiegel, 'Congress and Arms Transfers', in A. J. Pierre, ed., *Arms Transfers and American Foreign Policy* (New York: New York University Press, 1979).
    It might be noted that Fulbright's desire ran counter to all the attempts at legislation in the inter-war period. Senator Nye had sought legislation that would precisely make governments assume responsibility for arms sales from the private sector since private arms merchants were seen as having a vested interest in promoting armed conflict to realise greater sales for their wares.
12. For more detailed treatments of what we term the institutional setting, see, for example P. J. Farley, *et al., Arms Across the Sea* (Washington, DC: Brookings, 1978); D. J. Louscher, 'The Rise of Military Sales as a US Foreign Assistance Instrument', *Orbis,* **20** (1977); S. Scott-Morrison, 'The Arms Export Control Act', *Stanford Journal of International Studies,* **14** (1979); and A. J. Pierre, ed., *Arms Transfers and American Foreign Policy* (New York: New York University Press, 1979).
13. Our source for the OECD aid figures is a Development Assistance Committee

publication that appears at irregular intervals and that is entitled *Geographical Distribution of Financial Flows to Less Developed Countries* (Paris: OECD). Our sources for the US figures are the following official publications: *US Foreign Assistance, 1945-61* (Washington DC: AID Statistics and Reports Division, 1962). This publication provided our 1950-7 US aid figures. Our 1958-61 aid figures came from: *US Overseas Loans and Grants, 1945-64* (Washington DC: AID Statistics and Reports Division, 1965). Although covering different periods, the subsequent publications that we use as a data source carry the same title as this last one. Our 1962-5 figures came from the publication covering the period 1945-71; our 1966-75 figures from that covering the period 1945-75; and our 1976-9 figures from the publication covering the 1945-79 period.

14. The US Department of State's Arms Control and Disarmament Agency (ACDA) also published arms transfer figures for major suppliers and recipients. We cannot make use of this data, however, since ACDA publishes breakdowns for suppliers and recipients independently so that it is impossible to ascertain how many arms any one supplier transfers to any one recipient.

15. Personal experience leaves us in no doubt that SIPRI makes painstaking and imaginative efforts to produce reliable arms transfer figures. An outline of the data collection methods used can be found in any recent edition of the SIPRI annual publication entitled *World Armaments and Disarmament Yearbook*. The data collection methods used inevitably leave some doubts as to the reliability of the estimates produced. But these doubts notwithstanding, SIPRI provides the best cross-national, longitudinal arms transfer estimates available outside classified sources. The figures that we use in this study are not available in any SIPRI publication, but were kindly made available to us directly from the Institute's files.

There are two other observations on the SIPRI figures that we would like to make. The first is that the Institute uses its own accounting system so that the actual dollar values that it generates have no meaning outside comparisons of its figures across countries and/or across time. The second is that, concerning itself only with major weapons systems, SIPRI does not distinguish between arms sales and military assistance. Thus, we do not, indeed cannot, use its figures for the United States as the dependent variable in our distribution and impact analysis. Instead, we use the SIPRI figures only for other arms suppliers or when we wish to make a direct comparison between the United States and other suppliers.

16. The US military assistance and arms sales figures up to and including 1977 are taken from: Department of Defense, DSAA, *Fiscal Year Series* (Washington, DC: Department of Defense, 1978). The figures for 1978 and 1979 are taken from the appropriate edition of the annual publication, Department of Defense, *Military Assistance and Arms Sales Facts* (Washington, DC: Department of Defense, 1978 and 1979 respectively). Earlier editions of this second publication show the figures that it gives to overlap perfectly with those found in the *Fiscal Year Series*.

All the figures reflect deliveries rather than commitments. The total military assistance deliveries are the sum of the figures to be found under the following individual headings in these two sets of publications: Military Assistance Program (MAP) Deliveries, Military Assistance Service Fund

(MASF) Deliveries, Excess MAP Deliveries, Excess MASF Deliveries, International Military Education and Training MAP Deliveries and, finally, MASF Training Deliveries.

17. It is this increase in both the relative and absolute number of aid non-recipients that leads us to use discriminant analysis in the examination of the distribution of this transfer from 1969 onwards. The actual percentage of Third World countries not receiving US aid changes as follows: 11 (1965), 12 (1967), 28 (1969), 24 (1971), 28 (1973), 22 (1975), 23 (1977) and 22 (1979).

18. It should be noted that when we report average correlations, these have been calculated over every single year and, unlike our tabular presentations, not just over alternate years.

19. The introductory section of our US aid data source, *US Overseas Loans and Grants,* defines SSA as 'grants and loans from the Supporting Assistance appropriation (excluding funds used for Population Programs) as well as obligations from appropriations for Contingency, Special Assistance, Defense Support, Direct Forces Support, Joint Control Area'. A clearer and more helpful definition is found in the US Department of State's *International Relations Dictionary* (Washington, DC: Department of State Publication 9172, 1980). Here SSA is presented as one of five components of military assistance and defined as 'SSA which promotes economic and political stability in areas where the United States has special foreign policy security interests'.

20. The absolute numbers of military assistance recipients are: 12 (1953), 22 (1955), 25 (1957), 26 (1959), 31 (1961), 41 (1963), 36 (1965), 38 (1967), 35 (1969), 37 (1971), 30 (1973) and 29 (1975). As a proportion of our population of Third World countries, these numbers are: 30 (1953), 51 (1955), 51 (1957), 50 (1959), 42 (1961), 51 (1963), 42 (1965), 42 (1967), 37 (1969), 38 (1971), 31 (1973) and 28 (1975).

21. The absolute numbers of arms sales recipients are: 25 (1971), 25 (1973), 34 (1975), 35 (1977) and 38 (1979). As a proportion of our population of Third World countries, these numbers are: 26 (1971), 25 (1973), 34 (1975), 35 (1977) and 38 (1979).

22. The simple correlations range from 0.01 to 0.21 and average out over the 1970–9 period at 0.08.

23. The mean correlation over the period 1970–5 is −0.02 and its value varies very little around this mean.

3   Other Western Suppliers

Introduction

As noted in the previous chapter, the United States' first substantial economic aid and arms transfers after World War II were channelled to Western Europe. The aid transfers were seen as a temporary measure whose immediate purpose was to facilitate the reconstruction of the region's war-ravaged economies and, generally speaking, this goal was achieved so that the transfers were brought to an end more or less on schedule. No similarly temporary status was envisaged for the arms transfers; they continued (and still do) long after the United States terminated its aid transfers. Progressively, however, the arms transfers changed from an assistance to a commercial sales basis and shrank in volume relative to similar transfers to the Third World.

The eventual economic recovery of Western Europe and, later, Japan added a substantial new dimension to the global pattern of aid and arms transfers to Third World countries since it meant that these Western countries came to switch from their initial status of recipient to that of supplier. Broadly speaking, by 1960 France, the Federal Republic of Germany (FRG) and the United Kingdom (UK) had all developed and institutionalised their own economic aid programmes.[1] Japan's aid programme was slower to get off the ground, but it was on a par with those of the other three suppliers by the late 1960s and, taken together, these four countries are now responsible for the great majority of non-US Western bilateral aid.[2]

Antedating even the institutionalisation of these national bilateral aid programmes is the emergence in the years immediately following World War II of two major multilateral aid-granting agencies, the World Bank and the United Nations (UN). These two programmes were then joined at the start of 1960 by a third multilateral agency formed by the member-states of the European Community (EC).[3]

A further source of economic aid to the Third World is the communist bloc, but it is excluded from consideration in this chapter since it is dealt with at length in Chapter 5. This exclusion notwithstanding, however, it is clear that the post-war period has seen a substantial diversification in the sources of economic aid available to Third World countries. But it should be emphasised that the bulk of this diversification followed upon the initial 'lead' of the United States.

There has also been some diversification in the sources of arms transfers, although this diversification, at least in source as opposed to volume, has been far less pronounced than in the case of economic aid.[4] Thus, in addition to the United States, France, the UK and the FRG now have very substantial arms sales programmes and, like the United States', these become non-trivial in volume only from the beginning of the 1970s.[5] Unlike with aid, there are no multilateral sources of arms transfers.

Over the period since 1945, then, the US transfer initiative has been copied with the result that there has been a substantial diversification in the Western sources of supply of both aid and arms sales that are available to the Third World. In regard to this development, this chapter has two objectives and the first of them is simply to document the growth and scale of the supplier diversification. The rationale immediately underlying this exercise is to contribute to a more general understanding, at a descriptive level, of the evolution of Western official transfer patterns and, in so doing, to complement the descriptive profile of specifically US transfers presented in the last chapter. Thus, treating economic aid and arms sales separately, the next section of this chapter documents the growth in their respective volumes over time for each major supplier. It then examines the degree and form of the overlap between the individual transfer programmes of the United States and the counterparts of the other major Western suppliers.

Occupying the subsequent section of the chapter, our second, and more substantively important, objective is to consider the implications of this supplier diversification for the effectiveness of the United States' aid and arms sales programmes. Stated somewhat differently, this section uses the previously presented descriptive information to confront the issue of the consequences of diversification for US first-order supply utilities.

The diversification of Western suppliers

Economic aid

The general developmental pattern of US bilateral economic aid has already been set out in the last chapter. It will be remembered that as of 1962, the volume of US aid started to decline in absolute terms and, as of 1969, also in terms of the proportion of Third World countries receiving this transfer. Table 3.1 highlights starkly that the US programme declined not only in absolute dollar value, but also in relation to the equivalent programmes of all the four other bilateral suppliers. Indeed, while US aid became smaller and smaller in volume from the mid-1960s, French, German, Japanese and UK aid transfers became ever larger over this same period. The US decline is even sharper in relation to the multilateral suppliers, although it is very noticeable that virtually all the change in the US position *vis-à-vis* the multilateral agencies stemmed from a massive increase in the volume of World Bank aid transfers. United Nations and EC aid transfers were, by contrast, trivial in volume and more or less stable in value over time and for these reasons will not be analysed further in this chapter.

Table 3.1 Aggregate annual flows of economic aid from the major bilateral and multilateral suppliers for alternate years, 1961-78 (in current $m)

Bilateral suppliers

	USA	France	FRG	Japan	UK
1961	3,203	338	286	36	180
1963	3,426	652	306	80	220
1965	3,535	426	615	187	383
1967	3,518	434	553	276	397
1969	2,612	498	500	374	350
1971	2,677	494	604	500	470
1973	2,188	598	872	858	406
1975	2,526	927	1,346	1,062	484
1977	2,715	819	1,187	1,019	490
1978	3,219	1,004	1,759	1,681	717

Multilateral suppliers

	World Bank			UN	EC
	IBRD	IFC	IDA		
1961	442	4	101	87	103
1963	314	21	254	154	105
1965	636	27	302	173	146
1967	530	49	350	168	158
1969	1,299	86	428	205	167
1971	1,690	94	562	254	174
1973	1,578	136	1,695	211	223
1975	3,449	211	1,763	223	241
1977	5,172	187	1,424	188	44
1978	5,193	322	2,421	430	68

In addition to aggregate volume, the US aid programme had also declined with respect to the exclusivity of the recipients of this transfer, i.e. with respect to the extent to which Third World countries received their non-communist bloc aid exclusively from the United States. The first noteworthy feature of Table 3.2 in this respect is its documentation of the extent of this decline. It clearly demonstrates that US aid recipients did not remain impervious to the attentions of other bilateral and multilateral suppliers as, indeed perhaps because, the programme was run down during the 1960s and 1970s. The simple fact of the matter is that each of France, the FRG, Japan, the United Kingdom and the World Bank expanded its pool of aid recipients even before the United States contracted its pool so that the actual number of Third World countries receiving aid exclusively from the United States could not but progressively decline. Indeed, if the other four bilateral suppliers are treated as a single group, they and, to a lesser extent, the World Bank can be seen to have all but fully penetrated the US aid population by 1978. It should be noted, however, that

Table 3.2 Proportion of countries receiving and not receiving economic aid for dyads of US–France (Fr), US–FRG, US–Japan (J), US–UK, US–All Four major bilateral suppliers (MBS), and US–World Bank (WB) for alternate years, 1961–78 (in percentages)

	US–$\overline{\text{Fr}}$	$\overline{\text{US}}$–Fr	US–$\overline{\text{FRG}}$	$\overline{\text{US}}$–FRG	US–$\overline{\text{J}}$	$\overline{\text{US}}$–J
1961	68.5	12.3	60.3	0.0	76.7	0.0
1963	66.3	3.8	45.0	1.3	81.3	0.0
1965	63.5	1.2	28.2	1.2	81.2	0.0
1967	58.9	4.4	20.0	5.6	71.1	1.1
1969	49.5	8.4	12.6	12.6	58.9	2.1
1971	44.9	9.2	15.3	13.3	53.1	2.0
1973	44.1	12.7	12.7	17.6	42.2	6.9
1975	39.6	5.0	5.0	14.9	37.6	5.0
1977	43.6	6.9	6.9	13.9	29.7	9.9
1978	37.6	8.9	4.0	13.9	23.8	8.9

	US–$\overline{\text{UK}}$	$\overline{\text{US}}$–UK	US–$\overline{\text{MBS}}$	$\overline{\text{US}}$–MBS	US–$\overline{\text{WB}}$	$\overline{\text{US}}$–WB
1961	68.5	0.0	37.0	12.3	60.3	0.0
1963	63.8	0.0	21.3	5.0	67.5	0.0
1965	57.6	3.5	10.6	5.9	55.3	1.2
1967	53.3	3.3	8.9	10.0	50.0	2.2
1969	43.2	9.5	7.4	21.1	25.3	8.4
1971	40.8	8.2	5.1	18.4	22.4	8.2
1973	28.4	9.8	3.9	20.6	20.6	12.7
1975	26.7	9.9	1.0	18.8	13.9	7.9
1977	28.7	5.0	2.0	16.8	10.9	6.9
1978	24.8	7.9	1.0	18.8	7.9	10.9

US–$\overline{\text{Fr}}$ = Percentage of countries receiving economic aid from the USA, but not from France.

$\overline{\text{US}}$–Fr = Percentage of countries receiving economic aid from France, but not from the USA.

despite the expansion of the aid-granting activities of these alternative Western suppliers, the net effect of the contraction of the US programme is to increase the proportion of Third World countries receiving no Western bilateral aid at all. Although not shown in the table, the proportion of such countries increased from a fairly stable mean of 3.6 per cent in the 1960s, to 5.1 per cent in 1971, 6.9 per cent in 1975 and 9.9 per cent in 1978.

The second noteworthy feature of Table 3.2 concerns the variation in the extent to which each of France, the FRG, Japan and the United Kingdom penetrate the US aid population. The proportion of recipients that each of them has in common with the United States was roughly the same in 1961, but evolved differently thereafter. In membership terms, the FRG's aid programme overlapped with the United States' most closely and France's the least closely. Japan and the United Kingdom ended up at much the same point of overlap in 1978, although it is noticeable that as the Japanese programme 'took off' in the 1970s, its membership distinctiveness *vis-à-vis* the US programme decayed substantially more rapidly than the United Kingdom's.

The conclusion of declining United States' exclusivity is only reinforced if we take a more sensitive measure of overlap, or penetration, than just common membership, namely the proportion of its total aid that the United States bestowed on Third World recipients that it has in common with one or more of the other Western suppliers. Table 3.3 shows that this proportion in fact increased as US exclusivity declined. Indeed, if France, the FRG, Japan and the United Kingdom are treated as a single group, by 1978 no portion of the United States' aid budget flowed to Third World countries to which it could claim exclusivity. On the other hand, a substantial portion of the allies' combined aid budget went to countries receiving no economic aid from the United States.

Table 3.3's second similarity to Table 3.2 is that it also shows considerable variation in the pattern of the US aid programme's overlap with the aid programmes of the individual allies. Again, the largest proportion of US aid flowed to those recipients that it had in common with the FRG and the smallest proportion to those it had in common with France. Japan and the United Kingdom again found themselves between these two 'extremes' with Japan generally closer to the German end of the spectrum and the United Kingdom somewhat closer to the French end of it. What is more, this same broad pattern prevails when we look at the proportion of total US aid flowing to Third World countries receiving aid from the United States, but not from the individual allies. By 1978, virtually no US aid was channelled to countries that did not also receive aid from the FRG, whereas more than half of its total flowed to countries not receiving it from France.

But the simple fact of penetration cannot itself be taken to indicate that the aid programmes of the United States and of the other bilateral and multilateral suppliers were in any sense at odds. After all, it is entirely conceivable that, as allies subordinate to US leadership, the other suppliers simply reinforced US policy by transferring aid in the same proportions and to the same Third World countries as the United States. This scenario is not borne out by the evidence, however. It is apparent from Table 3.4 that there was, in fact, a marked lack of overlap in the relationship between the US aid programme and those of France, the FRG, Japan, the United Kingdom and the World Bank individually.[6] This lack of overlap manifests itself in two ways. Firstly, there was considerable variation in the number of countries simultaneously receiving aid from the United States and one or other supplier. Secondly, there was equally pronounced variation in the joint distributions (as measured by the correlation coefficients) of the various aid programmes. Thus, there is little evidence that the individual allies or, for that matter, the World Bank docilely followed the US lead in determining the destination and dollar value of their respective economic aid allocations. What is more, this conclusion is only strengthened by a third feature

Table 3.3 Proportion of total aid allocated for dyads of US-Fr, US-FRG, US-J, US-UK, US-all four major bilateral suppliers, and US-WB for alternate years, 1961–78 (in percentages)*

	US(Fr)	(US)Fr	US-$\overline{Fr}$	$\overline{US}$-Fr	US(FRG)	(US)FRG	US-$\overline{FRG}$	$\overline{US}$-FRG
1961	12.7	40.2	87.3	59.8	55.6	100.0	44.4	0.0
1963	15.8	93.3	84.2	6.8	77.5	100.0	22.5	0.3
1965	23.4	98.1	76.5	1.9	90.1	100.0	9.9	0.2
1967	30.5	85.4	69.5	14.5	92.8	98.9	7.2	1.1
1969	56.8	82.5	43.1	17.5	96.0	87.2	4.0	12.8
1971	74.1	68.0	25.9	32.0	95.3	92.2	4.7	7.8
1973	64.8	67.7	35.2	32.3	96.4	86.7	3.6	13.3
1975	56.9	79.2	43.1	20.8	96.4	93.4	3.6	6.6
1977	43.5	79.0	56.5	21.0	98.2	92.6	1.8	7.4
1978	53.1	74.1	46.9	25.6	99.4	83.5	0.6	16.5

	US(J)	(US)J	US-$\overline{J}$	$\overline{US}$-J	US(UK)	(US)UK	US-$\overline{UK}$	$\overline{US}$-UK
1961	19.3	100.0	80.7	0.0	31.2	100.0	68.8	0.0
1963	51.3	100.0	48.7	0.0	55.4	100.0	32.7	0.0
1965	48.4	100.0	51.6	0.0	59.6	93.5	40.4	6.5
1967	63.4	100.0	36.6	0.4	68.0	94.2	32.0	5.8
1969	69.4	99.0	30.6	1.1	66.6	86.0	33.4	14.0
1971	75.3	97.8	24.7	2.2	76.4	86.2	23.6	13.8
1973	73.7	90.9	26.3	9.1	59.6	83.3	40.4	16.7
1975	65.5	94.1	34.5	5.9	71.3	97.1	28.7	2.9
1977	61.7	85.7	38.3	14.3	52.8	98.4	47.2	1.6
1978	64.5	88.9	35.5	11.1	61.0	97.6	39.0	2.4

	US(MBS)	(US)MBS	US–$\overline{\text{MBS}}$	$\overline{\text{US}}$–MBS	US(WB)	(US)WB	US–$\overline{\text{WB}}$	$\overline{\text{US}}$–WB
1961	71.8	76.0	28.2	59.8	36.5	100.0	63.5	0.0
1963	89.1	96.4	10.9	3.6	61.4	100.0	38.6	0.0
1965	95.1	97.9	4.9	2.1	64.2	99.3	35.8	0.7
1967	95.9	94.4	4.1	5.6	60.4	98.7	39.6	1.3
1969	96.6	88.1	3.4	11.8	73.2	96.7	26.8	3.3
1971	97.9	86.4	2.1	13.6	76.5	80.9	23.5	19.1
1973	97.7	83.4	2.3	16.6	66.2	81.8	33.8	18.0
1975	96.9	90.6	3.1	9.4	93.5	96.3	6.5	3.7
1977	99.1	88.2	0.9	11.8	67.0	89.3	33.0	10.7
1978	100.0	85.4	0.0	14.6	70.1	84.3	30.9	15.7

US(Fr) = Percentage of total US aid and allocated to countries receiving aid from both the USA and France.

(US)Fr = Percentage of total French aid allocated to countries receiving aid from both the USA and France.

US–$\overline{\text{Fr}}$ = Percentage of total US aid allocated to countries receiving aid from the USA, but not from France.

$\overline{\text{US}}$–Fr = Percentage of total French aid allocated to countries receiving aid from France, but not from the USA.

Table 3.4 Simple correlations between the economic aid transfers of the USA and the major bilateral and multilateral suppliers for joint recipients for alternate years, 1961–78

	US–Fr	US–FRG	US–J	US–UK	US–WB
1961	−0.26 (11)*	0.66[†] (17)	0.91[†] (5)	0.51[†] (11)	0.94[†] (17)
1963	0.0 (20)	0.88[†] (37)	0.89[†] (8)	0.83[†] (22)	0.87[†] (19)
1965	−0.11 (23)	0.79[†] (53)	0.77[†] (8)	0.72[†] (28)	0.84[†] (30)
1967	−0.20 (25)	0.66[†] (60)	0.31 (14)	0.72[†] (30)	0.92[†] (33)
1969	−0.17 (25)	0.64[†] (60)	0.28 (16)	0.61[†] (31)	0.75[†] (48)
1971	0.21 (31)	0.70[†] (60)	0.54[†] (23)	0.59[†] (35)	0.72[†] (53)
1973	−0.19 (26)	0.31[†] (58)	0.34[†] (28)	0.29[†] (42)	0.58[†] (50)
1975	−0.02 (35)	0.71[†] (70)	0.70[†] (37)	0.61[†] (48)	0.44[†] (61)
1977	−0.05 (31)	0.47[†] (69)	0.53[†] (45)	0.26[†] (46)	0.54[†] (64)
1978	−0.01 (34)	0.50[†] (68)	0.52[†] (48)	0.22 (47)	0.29[†] (64)

　* Indicates the number of countries receiving aid from both the USA and the particular supplier in question. The correlation coefficient is estimated across these countries only.
　† Indicates a significant relationship at the 0.05 level or higher.

of Table 3.4, i.e. the common tendency for these same allocations to become more weakly related to the United States', especially over the course of the 1970s.

Arms sales

The second transfer for which we have comparable, longitudinal data is arms sales. As was the case with economic aid, the developmental pattern of US arms sales over the period of this analysis has already been elaborated in Chapter 2, where official figures were seen to indicate that US arms sales 'took off' in dollar volume only in 1969.[7] The United States certainly sold arms to the Third World prior to this time, but only in very small amounts.

　Starting with 1969 figures, Table 3.5 documents the development of the US arms sales programme in relation to those of the other major Western suppliers of this transfer. Japan is excluded from the table because, with the exception of $1m worth in 1969, it transferred no arms to the Third World during

Table 3.5 Aggregate annual arms transfers of major bilateral suppliers for alternate years, 1969–78 (in constant $m)

	USA	Fr	FRG	UK
1969	837	83	26	196
1971	689	130	15	214
1973	621	287	2	183
1975	1,356	241	81	366
1977	2,793	829	57	303
1978	3,848	835	160	258

this period. The immediately striking feature of the table is just how clearly it highlights the contrasting developmental patterns of the US arms sales and economic aid programmes. At a minimum, and in sharp contrast to the aid programme, there is no evidence of a secular decline in the United States' primacy with respect to the absolute value of Western arms transfers to the Third World. Indeed, if anything, the table suggests that, except for a lapse in the first half of the 1970s, its primacy in this respect became ever more pronounced. Perhaps not the least reason for this difference between the two programmes is that two of the United States' major international economic competitors, the FRG and Japan, were hardly active in the arms sales market whereas each had become an increasingly prominent supplier of economic aid.

It is another question, however, as to whether the expansion of the US arms sales programme was associated with an increase in its pool of exclusive recipients of this transfer.[8] Taking the other three suppliers as a single group, Table 3.6 indicates that, in fact, it was not. At best, the United States was, in aggregate terms, successful only at maintaining the exclusivity that it enjoyed at the onset of the expansion. But it is also noticeable that despite an increase in the proportion of Third World countries actually purchasing Western arms, this observation generally held for the allies as well. In other words, both the United States and its allies might export more arms to more countries in the 1970s, but neither succeeded in expanding its pool of exclusive recipients because Third World countries increasingly tended to diversify their sources of supply.

Disaggregating the other suppliers in Table 3.6 is an interesting exercise because it shows the same pattern of national variation as does economic aid. Just as France was the least willing to share the United States' aid burden, it was the most willing to penetrate its potentially lucrative arms sales population. Its small volume of sales notwithstanding, the FRG was the least willing to penetrate this market and, while a little closer to the FRG position, the United Kingdom stood between these two 'extremes'. Similarly, France expanded somewhat its pool of exclusive recipients *vis-à-vis* the United States, whereas the FRG and the United Kingdom pools remained more or less stable in size throughout the 1970s.

Table 3.6 Proportion of countries receiving and not receiving arms sales for
dyads of US-Fr, US-FRG, US-UK, and US-All three major suppliers
(MS) for alternate years, 1969-78 (in percentages)*

	US-$\overline{\text{Fr}}$	$\overline{\text{US}}$-Fr	US-$\overline{\text{FRG}}$	$\overline{\text{US}}$-FRG
1969	15.8	8.4	21.1	0.0
1971	23.5	7.1	28.6	2.0
1973	16.7	8.8	20.6	0.0
1975	20.8	10.9	25.7	1.0
1977	17.8	11.9	30.7	3.0
1978	14.9	13.9	28.7	2.0

	US-$\overline{\text{UK}}$	$\overline{\text{US}}$-UK	US-$\overline{\text{MS}}$	$\overline{\text{US}}$-MS
1969	16.8	9.5	10.5	15.8
1971	20.4	10.2	16.3	16.3
1973	14.7	7.8	11.8	13.7
1975	15.8	6.9	10.9	13.9
1977	23.8	9.9	10.9	16.8
1978	24.8	8.9	10.9	21.8

*US-$\overline{\text{Fr}}$ = Percentage of countries receiving arms transfers from the USA, but not from France.
$\overline{\text{US}}$-Fr = Percentage of countries receiving arms transfers from France, but not from the USA.

Table 3.7 indicates that even if the United States was successful in maintaining an exclusive pool of arms recipients, the importance of this achievement should not be overstated since this group of countries purchased arms on no more than a very small scale. That is, the proportion of all US arms going to Third World countries also purchasing arms from one or more of the other Western suppliers almost doubled between 1969 and 1978 so that the United States' exclusive recipients accounted for only just over 4 per cent of its total arms sales by 1978. This development is not unique to the United States, however; French and UK arms sales also went in increasing proportion to common recipients.

None the less, the very fact that both the United States and its allies at least maintained their original exclusivity emphasises that, in contrast to economic aid, there was little overlap in the membership of their respective arms sales programmes. Unlike with economic aid, therefore, we cannot now proceed to examine the overlap within the three pools of recipients which received arms from both the United States and one or other of France, the FRG and the United Kingdom. The problem is that, ranging from 1 to 22 over three countries and six test periods and averaging out at less than 9, the number of countries to be found in these common recipient pools is generally too small for reliable correlational analysis. Still, bearing this caveat in mind, it is worth noting that, if executed, this analysis does tentatively confirm the impression

Table 3.7 Proportion of total arms transfers allocated for dyads of US–Fr, US–FRG, US–UK, and US–All three major suppliers (MS) for alternate years, 1969–78 (percentages)*

	US(Fr)	(US)Fr	US–F̄r	ŪS–Fr	US(FRG)	(US)FRG	US–F̄RG	ŪS–FRG
1969	31.7	78.4	68.3	21.7	14.0	100.0	86.0	0.0
1971	33.5	39.3	66.4	60.7	2.3	66.7	97.7	33.3
1973	10.6	50.2	89.4	49.8	1.1	100.0	98.9	0.0
1975	52.2	83.0	47.8	17.0	11.9	95.0	88.0	5.0
1977	51.9	75.2	48.1	24.8	4.4	73.7	95.6	26.3
1978	70.2	86.3	29.8	13.7	16.1	93.8	83.9	6.2

	US(UK)	(US)UK	US–ŪK	ŪS–UK	US(MS)	(US)MS	US–M̄S	ŪS–MS
1969	33.1	60.7	66.9	39.3	49.2	68.8	50.8	31.2
1971	57.6	46.3	42.3	53.7	61.1	44.6	38.9	55.4
1973	71.0	66.1	29.0	33.9	74.7	56.6	25.3	43.4
1975	80.5	87.7	19.5	22.3	85.5	86.9	14.5	13.1
1977	79.3	56.1	20.7	43.9	94.3	70.2	5.7	29.8
1978	41.1	79.4	58.9	20.6	95.6	85.9	4.3	14.1

*US(Fr) = Percentage of total US arms transfers allocated to countries receiving arms transfers from both the USA and France.
(US)Fr = Percentage of total French arms transfers allocated to countries receiving arms transfers from both the USA and France.
US–F̄r = Percentage of total US arms transfers allocated to countries receiving arms tranfers from the USA, but not from France.
ŪS–Fr = Percentage of total French arms transfers allocated to countries receiving arms transfers from France, but not from the USA.

of a limited overlap between the arms sales programmes of the United States and its individual allies. Less than one-third of the individual correlation co-efficients achieve statistical significance and their interrelationship varies in direction over the six years within each of the three recipient pools.[9]

The consequences of Western diversification

Economic aid

The United States' decline from hegemony in face of the rise of other Western suppliers of bilateral and multilateral aid is beyond dispute. Our objective here is to draw out the implications of this development for the aid programme's realisation of its first-order commitment and leverage utilities.

At least as manifested in its own aid programme, there has undoubtedly been a substantial decline in US commitment to the Third World and it is a decline that is apparent in both the absolute value of its aid transfers and the proportion of countries receiving them. It is tempting to proceed to equate this decline in commitment with a commensurate decline in leverage, but this temptation should be avoided for a number of reasons. At a minimum, aggregate volume does not itself determine the leverage potential of a transfer. A far more important determinant is whether or not recipients are exclusively dependent on a single supplier for their transfer allocations. But even if this is indeed the case, to the extent that few Third World countries are still solely dependent on the United States, we would still seem obliged to conclude that the leverage inherent in the US aid programme had been substantially eroded by the mid-1960s and this process continued, albeit at a slower pace, into the 1970s.

While attractive in its simplicity, however, this conclusion could well be erroneous and misleading since it is based on the assumption that the other Western suppliers competed with the United States for influence in the Third World. But it might be that their penetration of the US aid population was welcomed and encouraged by this supplier as part of an informally orchestrated strategy of 'sharing its aid burden' with other Western suppliers whose economies had begun to recover from the ravages of World War II and with whom the United States had by and large a commonality of interest in the Third World.[10] In other words, the other suppliers' penetration might equally well be interpreted to signal that co-operation under US aegis became the defining characteristic of the Western aid relationship in the Third World.

But had this scheme been adopted so as to maintain the US aid programme's leverage potential despite its contraction, the scheme itself is likely to have crystallised in one or both of two forms. Either the United States could impose a uniform percentage reduction on all its individual aid allocations and arrange for other suppliers to 'take up the slack' or it could exclude a number of former recipients from the programme altogether in the knowledge that they would then be included in the programmes of other Western suppliers. As it turns out, however, there is no convincing evidence that either of these strategies was put into operation.

The fact that the United States excluded former recipients in the late 1960s tends immediately to belie the implementation of the 'uniform reduction' strategy. In addition, the implementation of this same strategy would lead us to expect the variability of US aid allocations to remain more or less stable over the period of contraction. But in reality, their variability increases substantially over the course of the 1960s, which suggests that the 1969 exclusions are the logical consequence not of a uniform decrease across all recipients, but of the United States increasing its aid transfers to some recipients at the expense of others.[11] Finally, this strategy's implementation could be expected to produce stronger relationships over time between the US aid programme and those of the other suppliers as the latter sought essentially to supplement US aid allocations in proportion to the extent of their reduction by the United States. While strong relationships are indeed found for the FRG, Japan and the World Bank in the early 1960s, these, along with those for France and the United Kingdom, become uniformly weaker rather than stronger as the years pass.

An alternative orchestration strategy to maintain the leverage potential of the US aid programme is for the United States to drop a number of its recipients, while keeping them subject to its influence by arranging for them to be 'picked up' in the aid programme of one or more of the other Western suppliers. Again, however, there is little convincing evidence that this strategy was implemented. While it is true that the increase in the proportion of non-recipients of US aid from 1969 onwards is associated with an increase in the proportion of Third World countries receiving aid exclusively from a Western bilateral supplier other than the United States, it is also the case that this latter increase is smaller in size and that the proportion of such countries receiving no Western bilateral aid at all undergoes an increase of similar magnitude. What is more, neither does the multilateral World Bank programme show itself to be any more likely to take under its umbrella the countries rejected by the United States. In short, the failure of either strategy to materialise counsels rejection of the argument of Western co-operation under US leadership in the politics of aid transfers to the Third World.

Indeed, perhaps the strongest evidence against this orchestration argument is independent of the aid programmes of the other Western suppliers. That is, faced with internal pressures to reduce the volume of its aid transfers, the United States might well be forced, albeit reluctantly, to accept the penetration of its aid population as the only effective means of both sharing its aid burden and keeping an ever-growing Third World in the Western sphere of influence generally. These constraints notwithstanding, if the United States were indeed intent on retaining maximum influence for itself under these circumstances, it could simultaneously be expected to seek to perpetuate its own private sphere of influence by preventing the penetration of its relatively highly selective population of military assistance recipients. But there is no support for this hypothesis. In point of fact, the other Western bilateral suppliers' penetration of this population was just as comprehensive as was their penetration of the US aid population. It also followed exactly the same pattern, being sharpest in the early 1960s and all but complete by the early 1970s.[12] This same process equally characterised the expansion of the World Bank's aid programme.[13] The importance of this all-round penetration is simply that it would not be expected had the United States been the overlord of a grand co-operative strategy designed to enhance its own influence to the fullest extent compatible with its sharing of the aid burden with other Western suppliers of the transfer.

If co-operation of this type cannot satisfactorily explain the permeability of US transfer recipients, then it stands to reason that the penetration proceeded regardless, or perhaps even despite, the United States. In other words, it is a penetration that reflects the individual and unco-ordinated efforts of the other Western suppliers to promote their own interests in the Third World through their respective aid programmes. That these programmes overlapped to some greater or lesser extent with the United States' indicates, therefore, not that the other suppliers deliberately promoted US foreign policy interests, but that they had a number of such interests in common with the United States and that certain Third World countries served these common interests better than others.

Particularly convincing support for this 'self-interest' interpretation of the French, FRG, Japanese and UK aid programmes comes from the variation in the pattern of their individual relationship to the US aid programme. This relationship in fact varies substantially with regard to both the number of common recipients and the form that it takes within each of the four pools of common recipients. The important point is that this variation is not random. Rather, it takes precisely the form that we would expect given the larger post-war patterns of foreign policy convergence and divergence between the United States and each of its four allies.[14]

To be more precise, the numbers of common recipients and the inter-correlations between aid programmes rank the allies in the order of the FRG, Japan, the United Kingdom and France, with respect to the degree to which the national foreign policy interests that each pursues through its aid programme coincide with the United States'. This ordering is precisely what we would expect given the post-war relations between each of these four countries and the United States. The FRG and Japan are states that to all intents and purposes were created and sustained by the United States in the aftermath of World War II. Moreover, their rapid and remarkable economic recovery since then has been achieved in good part through massive US assistance and, most importantly, their status as non-nuclear powers leaves them largely dependent on the US nuclear umbrella for their security. The FRG, with an agressive

USSR on its doorstep, has always been particularly sensitive to the extent to which its national security is linked to US foreign policy goals. France and the United Kingdom, in contrast, are less closely tied to, or dependent on, the United States partly because each retained full sovereignty in the period following World War II, partly because each of them has a former colonial empire to take into account in its policy towards the Third World and partly because each has its own nuclear deterrent. Of the two, however, the United Kingdom has shown itself to be the less independent of the United States in foreign policy terms, preferring instead to cultivate its 'special relationship' with this superpower.

All in all, then, our analysis suggests that the interrelationships between the Western suppliers' aid programmes reflect differences in the extent to which the individual allies equate their own national interest with those US foreign policy goals that the superpower pursues through its aid transfers. This conclusion is supported not only by the longitudinal stability in the differential strength of these relationships, but also by a common, although not uniform, decline in their strength, especially over the course of the 1970s. This decline is symptomatic of a larger erosion of unity of vision and purpose within the Western alliance over much the same period.[15]

The cumulative evidence, therefore, clearly suggests that the leverage potential of the US aid programme has been substantially undermined by the expansion of French, FRG, Japanese and UK aid programmes that have become increasingly dominated by the politics of national self-interest. It should be emphasised, however, that while this change may be taken to indicate that these countries follow the US policy lead in the Third World ever less faithfully, it cannot be interpreted to mean that they are increasingly at odds with this same policy. Such an interpretation would require minimally that the allies' aid programmes be correlated negatively and significantly with the United States' and none of them ever is. None the less, the United States' fall from hegemony with respect to the domination of Third World aid transfers does mean that the disutilities accruing to recipients of this transfer have diminished precisely because other sources of supply in the West are now available to them and the loss of supplier exclusivity goes a long way to undermining the leverage afforded by any official transfer. This decline in first-order utilities is probably an important factor in the United States' decision to run down its aid programme and place a greater emphasis on the sale of arms to the Third World.

Arms sales

In direct contrast to its economic aid counterpart, the US arms sales programme expands in terms of both its number of recipients and its dollar volume over the course of the 1970s. Moreover, expanding French, FRG and UK activity in this same market is not associated with quite the same fall from hegemony that it is in the case of economic aid. This difference between the two programmes manifests itself in two ways. Firstly, the United States' share of the dollar value of Western arms sales actually increases a little from the beginning to the end of the decade. Secondly, and more importantly, while the proportion of Third World countries receiving exclusively US arms sales may not increase with the positive change in the absolute number of Third World countries receiving Western arms generally, nor does it decline. Equally, the allies' proportion of exclusive arms recipients remains more or less stable over this same period. But how is this maintenance of exclusivity to be interpreted? Does it mean simply that, unlike with economic aid, the United States has been successful in insulating its small group of exclusive recipients against penetration by the other major arms suppliers? Alternatively, does it mean that, once again unlike with aid, it has successfully enhanced its influence by orchestrating Western arms transfers generally in a co-ordinated Third World security strategy?

At first glance, the maintenance of some degree of exclusivity in the US and allies' arms sales programmes could be taken to indicate a logical division of labour whereby each supplier takes on different clients in pursuit of the common, overriding goal of Western security in the Third World. In other words, co-operation is more pronounced than national self-interest in explaining arms sales patterns. On closer inspection, however, there is little support for this interpretation of the findings. For a start, it has no basis in logic. In stark contrast to aid, arms sales directly boost the domestic economies of suppliers in a number of ways, not the least of which is their contribution to keeping suppliers' balance of payments in credit. Therefore, within the constraints of broad foreign policy considerations, it makes good sense for individual suppliers to seek to maximise their arms sales to 'friendly' countries rather than enter into a co-operative arrangement whose likely effect would be to limit their respective volumes of sales. After all, if the objective is simply to ensure that certain Third World countries purchase their arms from the West, it makes little practical difference from which Western supplier they originate. Indeed, given that recipient countries generally have at best limited resources with which to make such purchases, individual suppliers have every strategic and economic reason to isolate their recipients from the attentions of other Western suppliers since such action can hardly be construed to place general Western security interests at risk.

But it is not only logic that militates against an orchestration interpretation of Western arms sales to the Third World. The simple fact of the matter is that for such an interpretation to be valid, the new purchasers emerging during the 1970s would have to be assigned to either the United States' or the allies' pool of exclusive recipients. No such assignment is made, however. Instead, newcomers, at least in the aggregate, tend clearly to receive arms transfers from both the United States and the other suppliers. In addition, if arms sales were orchestrated, we would expect each supplier to increase its sales within its own previously designated pool of recipients, but the reverse pattern of growth turns out to be the case. All four suppliers in fact sell an increasing proportion of their arms to recipients that they have in common with other suppliers. In other words, perhaps because relatively few Third World countries can actually afford to purchase arms, Western suppliers can generally be seen 'scrambling for' the same limited market so that their exclusive recipients account for a decreasing proportion of their total arms sales. Thus, in the absence of a co-operative strategy whereby markets are divided by prior agreement, it once again stands to reason that the politics of national self-interest dominates arms sales, just as it does aid transfers.

This conclusion is only validated by an examination of the national differences in the overlap between the French, FRG and UK arms transfer programmes on the one hand and the United States' on the other. France proves to be the least reluctant to penetrate the US arms sales population and the FRG the most reluctant; the United Kingdom stands in between the two of them. The same pattern of differences emerges from an examination of how the allies' arms sales programmes are related to the United States' within pools of common recipients. While circumspection is advisable here in view of the small number of cases in each pool, it is highly pertinent that these relationships mirror those found for economic aid. Not only does the number of recipients that the United States has in common with each of the other suppliers vary, but also the correlations between French and US sales are predominantly negative and insignificant, while those for the FRG and the United Kingdom, the two allies having a higher foreign policy consensus with the United States, tend more often to be positive and significant.

The conclusion that inevitably emerges, therefore, is that arms sales offer the United States a more effective means of pursuing its national self-interest than economic aid because of the greater leverage that accrues to them by virtue of the fact that their exclusivity is relatively well maintained despite French, FRG and UK expansionism in the arms sales market.[16]

Nor can this difference between the two transfer programmes be attributed to chance. Rather, perhaps because it does not seek to share an arms sales burden that it finds onerous, the United States appears to take pains to protect the exclusive sphere of influence afforded by its arms transfers. It will be remembered that the US military assistance population is comprehensively penetrated by other Western suppliers' aid transfers, but the same is not true of their arms transfers. The 1969–75 period sees Western arms sales increase massively and the US military assistance programme all but phased out. Despite a decline of almost 25 per cent (from thirty-four to twenty-five) in the number of military assistance recipients, however, the proportion of all Third World countries receiving arms transfers from the United States and from no other Western supplier actually remained constant over these six years.[17] The importance of this difference between the aid and military assistance programmes is that it indicates that the United States withdraws its military assistance only from recipients also receiving arms sales from other Western suppliers. It seems reasonable to conclude, therefore, that US military assistance is distributed, at least in the 1970s, with a view to maintaining the integrity of a pool of recipients that is entirely dependent on the United States for its military hardware and that consequently becomes susceptible to the leverage that such exclusivity bestows on US military assistance and arms transfers.

With the phasing-out of the military assistance programme in the mid-1970s, this characteristic of leverage appears to adhere to the arms sales programme alone and, seen in this light, it becomes no coincidence that the United States increasingly emphasises arms sales at the expense of economic aid as the 1970s wear on. Not only is it a less costly programme in domestic economic terms, but also it affords greater dividends in the form of leverage potential when the United States' foreign policy interests in the Third World do not coincide with those of its allies either individually or collectively. The extent of the programme's leverage potential should not be overstated, however. It needs to be borne in mind that by 1978 exclusive recipients account for only a very small proportion of all US arms sales. The norm for those Third World countries that can afford to buy Western arms, i.e. the more important and powerful countries, seems to be to diversify their sources of supply, probably precisely because they wish to weaken the leverage inherent in this transfer and thereby minimise their own first-order demand disutilities.

Notes

1. Although our analysis only begins in 1960 it is not intended to deny that France, the FRG and the United Kingdom in particular made aid transfers before this date. Our decision to ignore them, however, rests on two grounds. Firstly, the aid transfers that there were are small in volume and, secondly, comparable aid figures, in the form of OECD data, are available only from 1960 onwards. While on this topic, it might also be pointed out that since its focus is a comparison of Western suppliers, this chapter relies entirely on OECD data, even for the USA. Elsewhere in the book, the US figures analysed come from official US publications, but nothing is lost by the switch in this chapter since the two sets of US aid figures correlate almost perfectly (see Chapter 2). The single best source for a comparative evaluation of the bilateral aid transfers of all the major Western suppliers is the annual OECD publication entitled *Development Assistance Review*.
2. Following an admittedly awkward convention, we count Japan as a 'Western' country.
   Another bilateral aid programme that 'came of age' relatively late (i.e. over the decade of the 1970s) is that of the OPEC group of countries. It is not included in this chapter, however, because it is not 'Western' in any sense of the term. None the less, it might be pointed out that OPEC's as a proportion of total OECD aid is 6 per cent in 1970, 45 per cent in 1975 and 33 per cent in 1980. In distributional terms, OPEC aid is enormously concentrated, with Egypt (prior to the Camp David agreement), Jordan

and Syria getting from one half to two-thirds of it between them. The OECD now monitors OPEC aid and its *Development Assistance Review* contains both figures and general descriptive distributional information.

3. The World Bank group is made up of the International Bank for Reconstruction and Development (IBRD), which began allocating aid in 1945, the International Finance Corporation (IFC), which began distributing it in 1957 and the International Development Agency (IDA), which began its allocations in 1961. Our figures for all multilateral agency allocations are taken from the US government publication entitled *US Overseas Loans and Grants*, which is also our principal source for US aid data (see Chapter 2). Just as it does not constitute a comprehensive list of bilateral donors, Table 3.1 does not include all multilateral agencies. Excluded, for example, are the Inter-American, Asian and African Development Banks.

   Some recent studies dealing with the various multilateral agencies are: J. E. Sanford, *US Foreign Policy and Multilateral Development Banks* (Boulder: Westview Press, 1982); E. S. Mason and R. E. Asher, *The World Bank Since Bretton Woods* (Washington D.C.: Brookings, 1973); and J. P. Lewis and I. Kapur, *The World Bank Group, Multilateral Aid and the 1970s* (Lexington: Heath, 1973).

4. Since this chapter deals with the United States in a comparative frame of reference, it uses SIPRI arms sales data for all suppliers. It will also be noticed that military assistance does not figure in this chapter. This is because we have no comparative data for this particular transfer.

5. Japan, while included as one of the four major Western suppliers of aid besides the United States, is excluded from the arms sales analysis since its arms transfers have thus far been negligible in volume.

6. It is not the purpose of this chapter to undertake a systematic analysis comparing the influences structuring these various aid distributions. For such an exercise, see R. D. McKinlay, 'The Aid Relationship: A Foreign Policy Model and Interpretation of the Distributions of Official Bilateral Economic Aid of the US, UK, France and Germany, 1960–70', *Comparative Political Studies*, **11** (1979).

7. In so far as they indicate that total US arms sales to the Third World are £435m in 1965, $343m in 1967 and $837m in 1969, the SIPRI figures show the same growth pattern as US official figures.

8. The US arms sales programme expands in number of recipients as well as dollar volume over the course of the 1970s. The proportion of Third World countries purchasing US arms is 25.0 in 1969, 31.9 in 1971, 22.4 in 1973, 33.0 in 1975, 35.0 in 1977 and 37.0 in 1978. At the same time, the proportion of these countries getting no Western arms at all (i.e. from the USA, France, the FRG or the United Kingdom) generally decreases. The figures are 56.8 in 1969, 49.0 in 1971, 60.8 in 1973, 50.5 in 1975, 47.5 in 1977 and 40.6 in 1978.

9. These figures are not presented in tabular form in the text since the small number of cases involved in many instances makes them potentially misleading. Over the six test years between 1969 and 1978, the USA has a mean thirty countries purchasing its arms, of which it shares a mean twelve with France, four with the FRG and nine with the United Kingdom.

10. The United States' formal commitment to a burden-sharing scheme with other western countries is discussed in J. J. Kaplan, *The Challenge of Foreign Aid* (New York: Praeger, 1967), ch. 14. In confirming that such

a scheme was never implemented, Kaplan validates the interpretation of this chapter to the effect that there is no evidence of an orchestrated Western aid strategy redounding to the political benefit of the United States.

11. Calculated over all cases in each test year, the coefficients of variation (i.e. the standard deviation divided by the mean) for US aid allocations are 1.66 in 1961, 2.34 in 1963, 2.56 in 1965, 2.77 in 1967 and 1969, 2.73 in 1971, 2.55 in 1973, 2.67 in 1975, 3.38 in 1977 and 3.43 in 1978.

12. The actual proportion of Third World countries receiving US military assistance and no economic aid from any of the other Western bilateral suppliers is 21.9 in 1961, 16.3 in 1963, 7.1 in 1965, 5.1 in 1967, 4.2 in 1969, 4.1 in 1971, 2.0 in 1973 and 1.0 in 1975. The correlations between US military assistance and aid from one or other of France, the FRG, Japan or the United Kingdom are based on reasonably sized numbers of cases, but are not reported in detail since every single one of them is insignificant and except in the case of France, when their relationship is negative, they are also inconsistently signed.

13. While not as comprehensively as in the case of the bilateral suppliers, the US military assistance programme is also penetrated by multilateral aid transfers from the World Bank. Following the same pattern of decline as for the bilateral suppliers, the proportion of Third World countries receiving military assistance and no multilateral aid is 32.9 in 1961, 32.5 in 1963, 17.6 in 1965, 21.1 in 1967, 14.7 in 1969, 8.2 in 1971, 8.8 in 1973 and 6.9 in 1975. Nor is there a great deal of evidence to suggest that the United States orchestrates World Bank allocations to reinforce its own military assistance programme. While the two transfers are positively and significantly correlated among common recipients in 1961, 1973 and 1975, they are not related in the intervening years, which is the period in which World Bank penetration proceeds most rapidly before levelling off in the closing years of the military assistance programme.

14. These similarities and differences are among the subjects treated in a good, interpretative account of post-war US foreign policy, J. A. Nathan and J. K. Oliver, *US Foreign Policy and World Order*, 2nd ed. (Boston: Little, Brown, 1981).

15. Most of the literature dealing with the strains in the Western alliance concerns itself with NATO. A broader, if very controversial, treatment of this theme is M. Kaldor, *The Disintegrating West* (Harmondsworth: Penguin, 1978).

16. For some thoughts along these lines, see A. J. Pierre, 'Arms Sales: The New Diplomacy', *Foreign Affairs*, **60** (Winter 1981/82).

17. The actual proportion receiving only US military assistance is 17.9 in 1969, 19.4 in 1971, 18.6 in 1973 and 16.8 in 1975. Also indicating the incompatibility of this US transfer with French, FRG or UK arms transfers is the fact that, while insignificant in all but one case, the correlations between the transfers are negative in all but one test year. It should be borne in mind, however, that these correlations are calculated over very small numbers of cases; a mean of seven for France, of three for the FRG and of eight for the United Kingdom.

4 Power Capabilities

Introduction

Theoretical rationale

The common argument to the effect that the relations between states are all but monopolised by considerations of power has been most forcefully and consistently put forward by those writers who are generally known as 'realists'.[1] Theirs is a school of thought that conceptualises the international system as a hierarchy of sovereign and autonomous nation-states, each of which possesses a central government that is capable of maintaining its internal sovereignty and, from this position, each of which pursues what it perceives to be its own national interest in its relations with other nation-states. In other words, international activity is characterised by each state pursuing its national interest and the central government of each is the agent that is primarily responsible for the articulation and promotion of this interest. In an international system that is constituted of individualistic states, however, sovereignty can be protected and the national interest promoted only through the pursuit and acquisition of power and this is the goal of all states in their international interactions. Power itself resides primarily, although not solely, in so-called power capabilities, a truism that, from the realist perspective, has two consequences. Firstly, since they are the primary resource base from which the national interest can be promoted, each state is obliged always to seek to expand its power capabilities. Secondly, since the international hierarchy of states is by and large determined by power capabilities, the position of individual states in this hierarchy stems principally from the relative size of their power capabilities. Once again, therefore, sovereignty and national interest dictate the aggrandisement of these capabilities.

There have been a number of criticisms—conceptual, empirical and evaluative—of the realist perspective on the nature of international relations, but these are of no concern to us. Our interest in it lies not in the extent to which it is comprehensive, descriptive, ideological or whatever, but in the extent to which it actually does profile a set of beliefs and values that serve as a prescription for state behaviour. Our analysis in no way represents an effort to formalise or test realism. Rather, we use it simply to justify this chapter's analytical focus on power capabilities.

The notion that official transfers can, and indeed should, be used to promote the first-order utilities of the supplier would be readily acceptable to the realist. Logically, therefore, he would accept that the supplier's second-order utilities (although he might not use this particular phrase) would be the pursuit of its national interest, as defined by a set of specific foreign policy goals. That is, since the supplier's own power position is enhanced to the extent its transfers afford some degree of commitment and leverage, the logic of realism leads to the hypothesis that suppliers will structure their transfers in proportion to the power capabilities of recipients. Among the supplier's goals, for example, could be a desire to use its more powerful recipients to influence other Third World countries or to discourage these same recipients from developing ties of allegiance with other suppliers or to 'sew up' potentially large markets for its own goods. In 'other words, while individual recipients may vary in their substantive contribution to the supplier's overall national interest, it would still seem to be the case that the more powerful a Third World country, the greater the volume of official transfers that it is likely to receive, not least because, other things being equal, the greater will be its ability to contribute to the national interest of the supplier. Thus, while we would not suggest that the realist would hold official transfers to be distributed exclusively on the basis of recipient power capabilities, the logic of his position inexorably suggests the hypothesis of a positive relationship between the two.

It would be equally consistent with realist logic that official transfer programmes could be terminated. After all, if their primary *raison d'être* is to enable the supplier to promote its own pursuit of power, then to the extent that they cease to serve this end the programme can be expected to be run down, or even terminated.

Nor need the realist perceive official transfers as being attractive and functional only to the supplier. Their receipt can obviously serve to enhance Third World countries' power capabilities and thereby enable them to pursue their own national interest more effectively, especially *vis-à-vis* countries of similar status in the international hierarchy. The direct enhancement of first-order utilities or the indirect enhancement of second-order ones can thus be as applicable to recipients as to suppliers. In the same vein, the recipient is equally free, at least in principle, to curtail official transfers if it perceives them not to serve its national interest any longer. In short, realism provides a rationale for both demand and supply utilities.

Most importantly, however, the realist position that countries with larger power capabilities are, other things being equal, better able to help suppliers realise their second-order utilities, leads us to hypothesise a positive relationship between official transfers and recipient power capabilities.

Operationalisation

In the analysis, we distinguish power capabilities along two dimensions, the first of which is absolute vs. relative capability. Relative capabilities are simply absolute capabilities standardised to correct for some other absolute capability. Wealth as measured by gross domestic product (GDP) is an example of an absolute power capability, but not of a relative one since wealthy countries with large populations are unlikely to be as powerful as their counterparts with small populations. Thus, GDP per capita is our measure of relative power capability. The second dimension of differentiation relates to the substantive nature of the capability and here we distinguish economic and politico-security capabilities.

This analysis measures absolute economic power capabilities by GDP, gross exports, gross imports and gross international liquidity holdings. Relative economic capabilities are measured by per capita GDP and international liquidity as a proportion of gross imports. Per capita GDP is, as noted previously, a measure of relative wealth and per cent international liquidity of relative liquidity or, more precisely, the ability to finance imports. The variables measuring absolute politico-security capabilities are population size, gross military expenditure and number of diplomatic associations with the other states in our population.[2] These associations are measured by both the number of embassies accredited to each of our countries, an indicator of its ascribed international political status, and the number each accredits overseas, which is an indicator of its perception of its own status and/or aspirations. Our sole measure of relative politico-security capability is military expenditure as a percentage of GDP.

Before embarking on a detailed analysis of the relationship between power capabilities and official transfers, it is worth noting that, while the variables measuring these capabilities are statistically significantly intercorrelated, the degree of their intercorrelation does not seem to be so high as to introduce severe collinearity problems into our analysis. Indeed, if we square the simple correlations, these variables explain for the most part less than 50 per cent of the variance the one in the other. Thus, while there may be statistical overlap between our predictor variables, it none the less remains possible to estimate their relative influence on the dependent variable of official transfers. This observation applies equally to the relative capability variables, which, generally speaking, are significantly correlated neither with each other nor with their absolute capability counterparts.

The differences between these two sets of zero-order intercorrelations highlight the conceptual importance of maintaining the distinction between absolute and relative capabilities. It could become important, for example, to a supplier interested in power politics and in striking a balance between the two types of capability in its population of recipients. After all, countries with large GDPs may be important to it on one dimension of interest and those of high relative wealth important to it on another. Still further subtleties and complexities are potentially introduced by the fact that the relative capabilities are themselves not, in general, significantly intercorrelated. It is, in other words, entirely conceivable that different types of transfer may be more attractive to those recipients with a high relative military expenditure than to those with substantial relative liquidity holdings. It is to the analysis of such possibilities that we now turn.

Findings: distribution

Economic aid

We begin the presentation of our findings by examining, through one-way analysis of variance (ANOVA), the bivariate relationship between the individual capability variables and gross aid receipts where recipients are classified into four categories, zero, small, medium and large (see Appendix B for details of how these categories are defined).

   To take the politico-security variables first, aid increases with population size throughout the period covered by the analysis and, what is more, those countries with very large populations are, in aggregate, disproportionately heavily concentrated in the large recipient category. This same general pattern holds equally for absolute military expenditure until the late 1960s, after which time the positive and linear relationship between the two variables holds only within the population of recipients. The value of non-recipients' military expenditure lies, in general, between the medium and high categories, a value that is higher than would be expected were the linear relationship in the recipient categories to be extrapolated to non-recipients. A similar picture emerges from an examination of relative military expenditure. Prior to the mid-1960s, it shows no systematic relationship with the categories of aid recipient, but afterwards it increases positively and linearly across these categories and, as in the case of absolute military expenditure, non-recipients have a mean value between that found in the medium and high recipient categories. The remaining two variables in the politico-security cluster, diplomatic associations, show no systematic variation with levels of aid receipt until the mid-1960s, from which time both increase linearly and positively across all four categories.

   With regard to recipients' economic capabilities, GDP follows the same developmental path as absolute military expenditure. From being linearly related across all four aid categories until the mid-1960s, it becomes so related only to recipients afterwards and non-recipients have a mean GDP value between the medium and high category values. As for the gross export and import variables, they are unrelated to aid prior to the mid-1960s and linearly related to it among recipients only in subsequent years. In these same years, non-recipients, by contrast, have mean export and import values equal to or greater than those found in the high recipient category. Gross international liquidity conforms to the same general pattern as trade, whereas the two relative economic capabilities, per capita income and per cent international liquidity, show no systematic relationship to aid receipts at all. It is the case, however, that their values do show statistically significant differences between non-recipients and recipients as a single category from the mid-1960s onwards.

   Particularly notable in this set of ANOVA results is that, from the late 1960s, the linearity found in the three recipient categories does not continue into the non-recipient category on many of the capability variables. Examining the

Table 4.1: Results for the discriminant analysis of recipients (R) and non-recipients (NR) of economic aid by power capability variables, 1969–79*

	Actual group	Predicted group			Standardised discriminators†	
		NR	R	(N)		
1969:	NR	2 (8)	23 (92)	25	GDPPC	−0.60
	R	4 (6)	61 (94)	65	PM1tExp	−0.50
					EmbFr	0.79
1971:	NR	2 (9)	20 (91)	18	GDPPC	−0.46
	R	1 (1)	74 (99)	67		
1973:	NR	7 (28)	18 (72)	25	GDPPC	−0.46
	R	2 (3)	65 (97)	67	M1tExp	0.81
					GrEx	−0.86
					PM1tExp	−0.47
					EmbFr	0.54
1975:	NR	6 (29)	15 (71)	21	GDPPC	−0.76
	R	2 (3)	72 (97)	74	GrEx	−0.42
					EmbFr	0.52
1977:	NR	8 (40)	12 (60)	20	GDPPC	−0.51
	R	2 (3)	69 (97)	71	GrEx	−0.80
					EmbFr	0.38
1979:	NR	7 (35)	13 (65)	20	GDPPC	−0.57
	R	3 (5)	63 (96)	66	GrEx	−0.59

* The figures in parentheses represent the row percentages.
† For an explanation of the acronyms see the appendix to this chapter.

discriminant analysis results, we now focus on the question of what it is that differentiates non-recipients and recipients as a single group.

Table 4.1 presents the discriminant analysis results for every odd year from 1969 onwards.[3] The equations turn out to be statistically significant for each of the test years and, as a group, they show per capita GDP to be consistently the single most important discriminator among the range of power capabilities. Almost commensurate in discriminatory power are exports and diplomatic associations. In short, recipients of US aid have lower levels of per capita income and of trade, but higher levels of international diplomatic status than non-recipients. It is noticeable, however, that the power capabilities correctly classify recipients more successfully than non-recipients, an asymmetry that can but qualify the discriminatory power of the capability variables.[4]

The final stage in this section of our analysis presents the results of the multiple regression analyses. These analyses serve to determine, firstly, how well power capabilities explain the overall variation in the distribution of gross

Table 4.2: Standardised coefficients for the regressions of gross aid on the power capability variables, 1951–79*

1951:	(0.60)	Pop	0.74		1967:	(0.70)	Pop	0.63
	(0.27)	PMltExp	0.30			(0.51)	MltExp	0.18
	(0.18)	GrEx	−0.23			(0.18)	GrEx	−0.11
		$R^2 = 49$					$R^2 = 51$	
1953:	(0.20)	Pop	0.35		1969:	(0.72)	Pop	0.72
	(0.59)	PMltExp	0.61			(0.25)	PMltExp	0.25
	(−0.03)	GrEx	−0.24				$R^2 = 58$	
		$R^2 = 43$						
					1971:	(0.62)	Pop	0.63
1955:	(0.20)	Pop	0.33			(0.20)	PMltExp	0.21
	(0.69)	PMltExp	0.69				$R^2 = 43$	
	(−0.11)	GrEx	−0.24					
		$R^2 = 56$			1973:	(0.35)	PMltExp	0.49
						(−0.06)	GDPPC	−0.32
1957:	(0.62)	Pop	0.42			(0.14)	GrIm	0.29
	(0.59)	PMltExp	0.55			(0.00)	EmbFr	−0.23
	(0.14)	GrEx	−0.39			(0.22)	Pop	0.18
		$R^2 = 53$					$R^2 = 27$	
1959:	(0.69)	Pop	0.77		1975:	(0.73)	PMltExp	0.74
	(0.24)	PMltExp	0.26			(0.41)	Pop	0.43
	(0.10)	GrEx	−0.18			(−0.03)	IL	−0.18
		$R^2 = 57$					$R^2 = 73$	
1961:	(0.80)	Pop	0.81		1977:	(0.83)	PMltExp	0.34
	(0.11)	PMltExp	0.16			(0.82)	MltExp	0.72
		$R^2 = 66$				(0.08)	IL	−0.29
							$R^2 = 85$	
1963:	(0.84)	Pop	0.80					
	(0.45)	EmbIn	0.16		1979:	(0.69)	MltExp	0.86
	(0.12)	PMltExp	0.13			(0.14)	GDP	−0.42
		$R^2 = 76$				(0.67)	PMltExp	0.23
							$R^2 = 69$	
1965:	(0.83)	MltExp	0.94					
	(0.20)	IL	−0.23					
		$R^2 = 75$						

* The figures in parentheses represent the zero-order correlation coefficients.

aid and, secondly, which particular capabilities are more influential than others in structuring this distribution over time.

The regression analyses produce a series of equations that are not only statistically significant, but also consistent in the variables that they identify as predicting to gross aid receipt.[5] As shown in Table 4.2, the single most powerful positive estimator is population size, which is followed closely by per cent military expenditure. Relative military expenditure's generally greater importance than its absolute counterpart may initially be thought to be surprising in view of the fact that its bivariate correlation with the dependent variable is lower than is absolute military expenditure's. The key to this apparent paradox, however, is that relative military expenditure's lower correlation with population serves to increase its partial correlation, controlling for population, with gross aid. The overall picture changes from 1973 onwards when one or other of the military expenditure capabilities consistently displaces population size as the most powerful predictor and one of the absolute economic variables, usually exports but sometimes international liquidity, appears as a consistent negative predictor.[6] These economic variables are positively correlated with gross aid, but are also highly correlated with population size and military expenditure so that, after partialling, they appear as negative estimators. Thus, aid allocations are so modelled that the Third World countries receiving them in relatively large volumes tend to be the more populous ones with higher levels of military expenditure. Economic capabilities, on the other hand, are not only of much less importance in structuring its distribution, but also, once account is taken of the principal estimators, actually deter it.

With regard to our second dependent aid variable, per capita aid, its distribution is explained far less successfully by the power political capabilities than is gross aid's. The ANOVAs show the absolute politico-security variables not to be very systematically related to per capita aid, although the general direction of the relationship between them is one of declining absolute capabilities with increasing per capita aid. While not inevitable in the light of our previous findings, these results are not surprising since, having standardised gross aid by population size, the absolute capability variables could only have retained their explanatory power had aid increased at a proportionately faster rate than population. But this does not happen. The results indicate that while large countries get more gross aid than smaller ones, their population size increases proportionately faster than gross aid receipts so that smaller countries receive on average slightly more per capita aid. The aid relationship is stronger, however, in the case of the only relative politico-security capability variable, per cent military spending, which shows a linear increase across the three recipient categories. Particularly from the later 1960s, however, non-recipients once again have military expenditure levels close to or in excess of the high per capita aid category.

For the same statistical reason as with the politico-security variables, absolute economic capabilities generally decrease with rising per capita aid. The relative capability, per capita GDP, generally increases, although not very steeply, across the three per capita aid recipient categories.

Table 4.3 summarises the per capita aid regression analyses and, while identifying a number of significant estimators, it shows that these provide no more than a fluctuating and not especially strong explanation of its distribution among Third World countries.[7] Generally speaking, per cent military expenditure can be seen to be the single most important predictor with per capita income next most important, particularly in the 1970s. The equation also usually include one or more absolute variables that are negatively related to per capita aid.

Table 4.3 Standardised coefficients for the regressions of per capita aid on the power capability variables, 1951-79*

1951:	(0.52)	PM1tExp	0.56		1967:	Not significant		
	(−0.12)	GDPPC	−0.22		1969:	(0.45)	PM1tExp	0.53
		$R^2 = 32$				(−0.22)	GrEx	−0.35
1953:	(0.44)	GDPPC	0.68			(0.19)	GDPPC	0.31
	(0.40)	PM1tExp	0.42			(0.05)	PIL	−0.30
	(−0.08)	Pop	0.42				$R^2 = 36$	
	(−0.21)	GrEx	−0.61		1971:	(0.51)	PM1tExp	0.44
		$R^2 = 56$				(−0.19)	GrEx	−0.32
1955:	(0.39)	PM1tExp	0.28			(0.30)	GDPPC	0.28
	(−0.49)	EmbIn	−0.42				$R^2 = 37$	
		$R^2 = 56$			1973:	(0.71)	PM1tExp	0.70
1957:	(0.27)	PM1tExp	0.25			(−0.19)	EmbIn	−0.26
	(−0.43)	EmbIn	−0.42			(0.34)	PIL	0.22
		$R^2 = 50$				(−0.17)	GrEx	−0.17
1959:	(0.54)	PM1tExp	0.52			(0.35)	GDPPC	0.14
	(0.23)	GDPPC	0.45				$R^2 = 70$	
	(−0.35)	GrEx	−0.46		1975:	(0.62)	PM1tExp	0.66
		$R^2 = 55$				(0.52)	GDPPC	0.53
1961:	(0.45)	PM1tExp	0.49			(0.03)	EmbIn	−0.41
	(0.15)	GDDPC	0.32			(−0.09)	Pop	0.20
	(−0.24)	IL	−0.36			(−0.11)	GrEx	−0.11
		$R^2 = 35$					$R^2 = 68$	
1963:	(0.35)	PM1tExp	0.32		1977:	(0.74)	PM1tExp	0.78
	(0.15)	EmbIn	0.34			(0.35)	GDPPC	0.24
	(−0.13)	GDP	−0.32			(0.10)	EmbIn	−0.23
		$R^2 = 21$					$R^2 = 65$	
1965:	(0.45)	PM1tExp	0.53		1979:	(0.64)	PM1tExp	0.66
	(−0.12)	PIL	−0.23			(0.36)	GDPPC	0.30
	(0.00)	M1tExp	−0.13			(0.05)	EmbIn	−0.24
		$R^2 = 27$					$R^2 = 54$	

* The figures in parentheses represent the zero-order correlation coefficients.

Military assistance

Starting our analysis of the distribution of military assistance with the ANOVA tests, the results indicate that it stands in no systematic relationship to population size either across all four categories or across the three recipient categories only. Clear linear relationships between the two do appear occasionally, but these are both positive and negative in direction so that our overall conclusion can only be that population size has no systematic influence on the distribution of military assistance. Military expenditure, on the other hand, does generally show a positive linear increase across the four categories, although there is an occasional element of non-linearity with the non-recipients. The linear increase across the categories is even stronger in the case of relative military spending, although the non-linearity in the non-recipient category is also more pronounced. The final politico-security variable, diplomatic associations, shows no systematic relation across the three recipient categories, but from the early 1960s onwards non-recipients become clearly differentiated from all recipients by their having a substantially lower number of diplomatic ties.

As for economic capabilities, trade turns out to be unrelated to gross military assistance and much the same holds true for international liquidity, whether it is expressed in absolute or relative form. Nor does the other relative variable, per capita income, vary systematically with the distribution of military assistance.

Our next question is whether power political capabilities differentiate military assistance recipients and non-recipients and, broadly speaking, the answer is affirmative. Table 4.4 indicates that until the late 1950s, relative military expenditure, being approximately 50 per cent higher among military assistance recipients, is the only variable significantly to discriminate between the two groups.[8] Afterwards, however, it is complemented by higher levels of gross military expenditure, trade and diplomatic associations in the recipient group. Military assistance policy would, therefore, appear to have undergone a pronounced shift towards a more generalised focus on power politics at the end of the 1950s.

There is at least the possibility that this shift is, in fact, an artefact of the rapid expansion of independent Third World countries around this time. That is, since many of these new countries were small, the change in policy emphasis that we note could have resulted from the United States continuing to supply military assistance to established recipients and not to newly independent countries. This particular explanation of the change in military assistance policy is not borne out by the evidence, however. To be sure, the new countries were less powerful on average than were the already independent ones, as is indicated by a decrease in the overall means of the capability variables during this 'population explosion', but it is also the case that the United States actually expanded its recipient population over this same period (from twenty-three in 1957 to forty-one in 1963). Futhermore, while the capability means may have decreased across all Third World countries, they increased for the more limited group of military assistance recipients. There is no evidence, therefore, that the increased discriminatory power of the capability variables is an artefact of the changing population of Third World countries in the early 1960s.

Recipients continue to score more highly on the capability variables throughout the 1960s and to be differentiated significantly from non-recipients by their higher diplomatic standing, their larger export volume and their higher level of relative military spending.[9] This picture changes, however, at the turn of the decade. By the 1970s, the two groups differ only insubstantially except, that is, on the dimension of diplomatic associations and on which recipients

Table 4.4 Results for the discriminant analysis of recipients (R) and non-recipients (NR) of military assistance by power capability variables, 1959–69*

	Actual group	Predicted group			Standardised discriminators	
		NR	R	(N)		
1959:	NR	15 (71)	6 (29)	21	PM1tExp	1.03
	R	7 (37)	12 (63)	19	EmbFr	0.56
1961:	NR	16 (73)	7 (27)	26	PM1tExp	0.82
	R	6 (20)	24 (80)	30	EmbFr	1.12
					GDPPC	−0.64
					Pop	−0.61
1963:	NR	23 (68)	11 (32)	34	PM1tExp	0.61
	R	12 (31)	27 (69)	39	EmbFr	0.94
1965:	NR	34 (79)	9 (21)	43	PM1tExp	0.59
	R	16 (46)	19 (54)	35	EmbFr	0.47
					GrEx	0.57
1967:	NR	34 (77)	10 (23)	44	PM1tExp	0.37
	R	16 (46)	19 (54)	35	EmbFr	0.61
					GrEx	0.59
1969:	NR	41 (80)	10 (20)	51	EmbFr	0.71
	R	17 (52)	16 (48)	33	GrEx	0.60

* The figures in parentheses represent the row percentages.

score significantly more highly. Thus, power political capabilities come to discriminate recipients and non-recipients only very weakly in the closing years of the military assistance programme.[10]

Given the general picture outlined in our earlier bivariate results, it is not surprising that the multiple regression analyses are not very successful in explaining the distribution of gross military assistance within the recipient population (see Table 4.5). While all but two of the biannual analyses produce statistically significant equations, percentage military expenditure is the only predictor to appear in them consistently. In the later years of the programme, a highly disproportionate amount of military assistance goes to Vietnam, making it, in statistical terms, an outlier. But whether it is included or excluded, the equations are almost identical in terms of both their explained variation and significant estimators.[11]

The distribution of per capita military assistance is also poorly explained by recipient power capabilities. Other than a directional decline in capabilities with increasing per capita assistance, the ANOVA results show it to stand in no clear or consistent relationship to the absolute politico-security variables. Relative military spending, in contrast, does increase across the recipient categories,

Table 4.5 Standardised coefficients for the regressions of gross military assistance on the power capability variables, 1953-75*

1953:	(0.68)	PM1tExp	0.68	1969:	Not significant		
		$R^2 = 47$		1971:	(0.32)	PM1tExp	0.32
1955:	(0.53)	PM1tExp	0.56			$R^2 = 11$	
	(0.28)	EmbIn	0.34	1971:	(Without outlier)		
		$R^2 = 39$			(−0.30)	EmbIn	−0.53
1957:	(0.60)	PM1tExp	0.60		(0.21)	GrIm	0.48
		$R^2 = 36$				$R^2 = 26$	
1959:	(0.45)	PM1tExp	0.57	1973:	(0.48)	PM1tExp	0.48
	(0.12)	EmbIn	0.57			$R^2 = 23$	
	(−0.14)	GrEx	−0.37	1973:	(without outlier)		
		$R^2 = 39$			(0.46)	PM1tExp	0.46
1961:	(0.38)	M1tExp	0.80			$R^2 = 21$	
	(−0.23)	EmbFr	0.71	1975:	(0.31)	PMltExp	0.31
		$R^2 = 47$				$R^2 = 14$	
1963:	(0.37)	M1tExp	0.66				
	(−0.01)	EmbFr	−0.45	1975:	(Without outlier)		
		$R^2 = 25$			(0.35)	PM1tExp	0.61
					(0.20)	GDPPC	−0.51
1965:	(0.51)	PM1tExp	0.51			$R^2 = 32$	
		$R^2 = 26$					
1967:	Not significant						

* The figures in parentheses represent the zero-order correlation coefficients.

although, once again, the non-recipient category adds an element of non-linearity to the overall relationship. As for the economic capability predictors, neither of the liquidity variables varies systematically across the four recipient categories. Nor, in general, does per capita GDP. Both the trade variables do, however, show some signs of being negatively related to per capita military assistance.

The multiple regression equations are, in general, highly significant and produce for the most part a more satisfactory level of explanation than they do in the case of gross military assistance.[12] Table 4.6 shows that the single most important and consistent estimator is overwhelmingly percentage military spending and, in this respect, a clear parallel with the results for gross military assistance can be drawn. But this parallel should not be overdrawn since this variable's explanatory power is considerably greater in the per capita military assistance regressions than in the absolute ones. The basic reason for this differential prominence is that, while the two military spending variables are more or less equally correlated with gross military assistance, the relative version is much more highly correlated with this transfer in its per capita form. Indeed, in a number of years, relative military spending is the only significant estimator

Table 4.6 Standardised coefficients for the regressions of per capita military assistance on the power capability variables, 1953–75*

1953:	(0.82)	PM1tExp	0.82		1969:	(0.61)	PM1tExp	1.13
		$R^2 = 67$				(−0.10)	PIL	−0.83
							$R^2 = 78$	
1955:	(0.54)	PM1tExp	0.54					
		$R^2 = 29$			1971:	(0.59)	PM1tExp	0.86
						(0.22)	PIL	−0.38
1957:	(0.69)	PM1tExp	0.89				$R^2 = 42$	
	(−0.23)	EmbIn	−0.42					
	(−0.12)	Pop	0.20		1971:	(Without outlier)		
		$R^2 = 82$				(0.69)	PM1tExp	1.31
						(0.03)	PIL	−0.88
1959:	(0.74)	PM1tExp	0.87				$R^2 = 88$	
	(−0.06)	EmbIn	0.46					
	(−0.20)	Pop	−0.36		1973:	(0.60)	PM1tExp	0.65
		$R^2 = 69$				(−0.04)	PIL	−0.20
							$R^2 = 40$	
1961:	(0.79)	PM1tExp	0.79					
		$R = 62$			1973:	(Without outlier)		
						(0.51)	PM1tExp	0.52
1963:	(0.66)	PMltExp	0.66			(−0.12)	M1tExp	−0.30
		$R^2 = 43$				(0.34)	PIL	0.27
							$R^2 = 40$	
1965:	(0.80)	PM1tExp	0.88					
	(0.05)	PIL	−0.17		1975:	(0.50)	PM1tExp	(0.50)
	(−0.13)	GDPPC	0.23				$R^2 = 25$	
	(−0.29)	GrEx	−0.16					
		$R^2 = 72$			1975:	(Without outlier)		
						(0.74)	PM1tExp	0.74
1967:	Not significant						$R^2 = 54$	

* The figures in parentheses represent the zero-order correlation coefficients.

and when other variables do enter the equation, their influence is usually negative. It would seem, therefore, that once it has taken account of relative military spending, the United States is indifferent to other power capabilities when determining the per capita distribution of its military assistance.

Arms sales

The ANOVA results point to there being no systematic relationship between population size and the three arms recipient categories, but they do show non-recipients to have much smaller populations than recipients as a whole. This same observation applies in the case of absolute military spending, although there is the proviso that the small and medium recipients, spending on average about the same as each other, have substantially lower levels of military expenditure than the large arms recipient category. There is, in other words, a positive linear increase in absolute military expenditure more or less across the four categories. The linear increase in relative military spending, by contrast, holds only across the three recipient categories. Non-recipients, while spending less on their military in absolute terms, none the less spend in relative terms at a level comparable to the small recipient group. The same cannot be said of their diplomatic associations, however. Non-recipients have a significantly lower number of diplomatic associations than do arms recipients in all three categories, although there is no systematic relationship between the two variables across these three categories.

The economic capability variables are relatively straightforwardly related to the purchase of arms by Third World countries. Absolute GDP increases linearly across all four recipient categories so that whereas gross economic aid was correlated with population size but not with GDP, the reverse is the case for arms sales. That per capita GDP, trade and gross international liquidity are also positively and linearly related to arms sales serves to emphasise the stronger economic component of this particular transfer. Percentage international liquidity alone is not clearly and consistently related to it.

In general, arms recipients have significantly higher scores than non-recipients on most of the power capability variables. The discriminant analyses consistently and significantly differentiate arms recipients and non-recipients on three main variables.[13] That is, recipients can be seen from Table 4.7 to have higher international status (as measured by the number of embassies accredited to them), higher levels of trade and, to a lesser extent, higher levels of military expenditure.

Table 4.7 Results for the discriminant analysis of recipients (R) and non-recipients (NR) of arms sales by power capability variables, 1971–9*

	Actual group	Predicted group			Standardised discriminators	
		NR	R	(*N*)		
1971:	NR	60 (90)	7 (10)	67	GrEx	0.75
	R	13 (50)	13 (50)	26	EmbFr	0.48
1973:	NR	61 (92)	5 (8)	66	GrEx	0.83
	R	14 (54)	12 (46)	26	EmbFr	0.49
					Pop	−0.45
					PM1tExp	0.26
1975:	NR	56 (90)	6 (10)	62	EmbFr	0.77
	R	16 (47)	18 (53)	34	GrEx	0.53
1977:	NR	47 (89)	6 (11)	53	EmbFr	0.81
	R	11 (31)	24 (69)	35	GrEx	0.30
					PM1tExp	0.24
1979:	NR	51 (88)	7 (12)	58	EmbFr	0.68
	R	14 (37)	24 (63)	38	M1tExp	0.50

* The figures in parentheses represent the row percentages.

Table 4.8 Standardised coefficients for the regressions of gross arms sales on the power capability variables, 1971–9*

	Including outlier			Excluding outlier		
1971:	(0.84)	PM1tExp	0.70	(0.42)	PM1tExp	0.69
	(0.61)	M1tExp	0.16	(0.33)	GrEx	0.70
	(0.46)	GDPPC	0.33	(−0.09)	GDPPC	−0.62
	(−0.10)	PIL	−0.30	(0.12)	Pop	−0.39
		$R^2 = 87$			$R^2 = 62$	
1973:	(0.70)	M1tExp	0.67			
	(0.56)	GrEx	0.61			
	(0.11)	GDP	−0.40			
		$R^2 = 76$				
1975:	(0.88)	M1tExp	0.47	(0.82)	PM1tExp	0.56
	(−0.07)	Pop	−0.35	(0.79)	M1tExp	0.40
	(0.27)	PIL	0.15	(0.06)	PIL	0.26
		$R^2 = 87$			$R^2 = 85$	
1977:	(0.81)	M1tExp	0.90	(0.78)	IL	0.71
	(0.08)	EmbIn	−0.42	(0.62)	PM1tExp	0.47
	(0.63)	IL	0.28	(−0.03)	EmbFr	−0.21
		$R^2 = 87$			$R^2 = 92$	
1979:	(0.76)	GrEx	0.50	(0.77)	M1tExp	0.94
	(0.62)	PM1tExp	0.64	(−0.05)	Pop	−0.42
	(−0.07)	Pop	−0.26		$R^2 = 75$	
	(0.13)	EmbIn	−0.22			
		$R^2 = 90$				

* The figures in parentheses represent the zero-order correlation coefficients.

But while diplomatic ties and trade may crucially determine the recipient population, multiple regression analysis indicates that they play no role in explaining the distribution of arms sales within this population. Instead, it is the military expenditure variables that best predict which countries receive what volume of arms. Moreover, including or excluding the outlier does not alter this basic conclusion.[14] The only difference in the two sets of equations is that absolute military expenditure takes priority over relative military spending when the outlier is included and the reverse is the case when it is excluded.

The ANOVAs for the per capita arms sales variables indicate that, although still larger than the non-recipients, the more preferred countries tend to be smaller in population size. Relative military expenditure increases just as clearly and steeply as it does in the case of gross sales, but this is not so true for absolute military spending. Finally, diplomatic associations, although they continue to be significantly higher in the recipient category as a whole, are not systematically related to per capita arms sales. All the absolute economic variables, by contrast, are positively, related to these sales and there is some evidence of

Table 4.9 Standardised coefficients for the regressions of per capita arms sales on the power capability variables, 1971–9*

	Including outlier			Excluding outlier		
1971:	(0.84)	PM1tExp	0.75	(0.77)	PM1tExp	0.99
	(0.50)	GDPPC	0.40	(0.00)	M1tExp	−0.47
	(−0.06)	PIL	−0.32		$R^2 = 76$	
		$R^2 = 86$				
1973:	(0.90)	PMltExp	0.92			
	(0.15)	GrEx	0.21			
		$R^2 = 86$				
1975:	(0.91)	PM1tExp	0.94	(0.91)	PM1tExp	0.67
	(0.13)	IL	0.13	(0.80)	M1tExp	0.36
		$R^2 = 85$			$R^2 = 91$	
1977:	(0.73)	PM1tExp	0.62	(0.72)	PM1tExp	0.61
	(0.70)	GDPPC	0.54	(0.70)	GDPPC	0.54
	(−0.05)	EmbIn	−0.14	(−0.07)	EmbIn	−0.15
		$R^2 = 83$			$R^2 = 83$	
1979:	(0.76)	GrEx	0.74	(0.76)	PM1tExp	0.68
	(0.55)	PM1tExp	0.37	(0.56)	GDPPC	0.54
	(0.16)	GDP	−0.24	(0.17)	GrEx	−0.23
	(0.61)	GDPPC	0.17		$R^2 = 78$	
		$R^2 = 83$				

* The figures in parentheses represent the zero-order correlation coefficients.

percentage international liquidity being similarly related. The major contrast with the gross sales ANOVAs, however, is the existence of a very clear and consistent relationship between per capita GDP and per capita sales.

The regression equations are all highly significant and, as with gross sales, percentage military expenditure is the single most important and consistent predictor. It is strongly complemented in the late 1970s by per capita GDP, but despite such clear relations with economic capability variables, it is the politico-security variable of relative military expenditure that dominates the distribution of per capita arms sales. The inclusion or exclusion of the outlying case makes no substantive difference to this general conclusion.

Findings: impact

The main focus of this section of our analysis is the investigation of the impact of official transfers on power political capabilities, i.e. of the relationship between the level of official transfers received to changes in individual capabilities over time.

If only because of its unorthodoxy, it is worth recapitulating the methodology of this and subsequent impact analyses before proceeding further. As explained more fully in Appendix C, Third World countries are grouped into zero, small, medium and high categories on the basis of the aggregated volume of transfers that they receive for periods of t to $t + 3$ years (e.g. 1950–3). The change in individual power capabilities is measured for each country over the period t to $t + 4$ (e.g. 1950–4) and is expressed as the mean annual percentage change over the period t to $t + 4$. This procedure is repeated for each power capability on each of the three official transfers in both their absolute and relative forms.

We employ a ranking procedure to summarise these impact analyses. Taking each of the four-year periods 1950–4, 1952–6 through to 1974–8, we assign a rank on the basis of each capability variable's rate of growth in the small, medium and high recipient categories.[15] The category showing the highest rate of growth is scored 1 and that showing the lowest is scored 3. These ranks are then summed across the thirteen five-year periods for tabular presentation. Were there a perfect positive relationship between size of transfer receipt and capability rate of growth, the summed ranks would be 39, 26 and 13 for the small, medium and large categories respectively. If, on the other hand, there were no relationship between the two variables, these same figures would be 26, 26 and 26. We use ranks in preference to averaged scores from the interval-level rate of change measures primarily because an abnormally large rate of change in any one five-year period could distort the overall picture by 'artificially' inflating the value of the mean. With regard to this problem there is, for example, a time effect as the result of larger rates of change in the capability variables in the 1970s. The advantage of ranks is that they overcome such distortions and allow each time period a uniform influence in determining the overall result.[16]

The obvious disadvantage of using ranks, however, is that they do not take account of absolute variations. Thus, the differences in growth rates of, say, 3.3, 3.2 and 3.1 give rise to the same rank ordering as those between 10.0, 6.0 and 2.0. The cost is an undoubted loss of information. There is also the risk of an acute distortion problem if, for example, it were the case that the mean rates of change for consecutive five-year periods were 3.3, 3.2 and 3.1 followed by 2.0, 6.0 and 10.0. The sum of the ranks would be 4 for all three categories, indicating no relationship, whereas the mean interval changes would be 2.7, 4.6 and 6.6, indicating a strong, positive relationship. But it is highly unlikely that such a pattern would extend over a set of thirteen aggregated time periods; it is certainly not to be found in our data. The only cost then, is a loss of information, but this is outweighed by the ranking method preserving an equal influence for each four-year test period.[17]

Economic aid

Table 4.10 presents the summed ranks for the individual capability variables across the three recipient categories of both gross and per capita aid.[18] The only variables whose growth rates show any significant covariation with gross

Table 4.10 Summed ranks for average percentage change in the power capability variables for the small, medium and large recipient categories of gross and per capita economic aid for the thirteen four-year periods, 1950–4, 1952–6 to 1974–8

	Gross aid			Per capita aid		
	Small	Medium	Large	Small	Medium	Large
GDP	25.5	28.5	24.0	27.5	29.0	21.5
GDPPC	26.0	26.0	26.0	28.0	29.5	20.5*†
M1tExp	28.0	26.0	24.0	24.0	28.0	26.0
PM1tExp	24.0	25.5	28.5	23.0	27.0	28.0
GrEx	27.5	29.5	21.0	31.5	30.5	16.0*†
GrIm	26.5	29.5	22.0	24.5	31.5	20.0*
IL	32.5	27.5	18.0*†	33.0	26.0	19.0*†
PIL	35.0	24.0	19.0*†	32.5	25.5	20.0*

* Indicates significance at the 0.05 level or beyond for the chi-square test across all three categories.

† Indicates significance at the 0.05 level or beyond for the cumulative binomial test on the number of highest, or lowest, rank placings for the large category.

aid are absolute and percentage international liquidity. Not only do these variables generate significant chi-square and binomial values, but also both display a linear and progressive reduction in their summed ranks score across the three recipient categories. Thus, while rates of change of national income, trade and military expenditure do not covary with level of aggregated aid receipt, higher volumes of gross aid are associated with the more rapid growth of Third World countries' international liquidity holdings.

The two liquidity variables covary significantly with aggregated per capita aid receipts as well. In contrast to gross aid, however, significant covariation is also found for gross exports and imports, although the relationship is not linear for imports. Finally, there is a significant relationship between per capita aid receipts and per capita income growth rates. Indeed, with the notable exception of military expenditure, higher per capita aid receipts are associated with more rapid growth rates on all the major capability variables.

Since there are only five test periods in which we can compare growth rates across the non-recipient and recipient categories, the findings deriving from such a comparison must necessarily be treated as tentative. Bearing this proviso in mind, we can proceed to an examination of the non-recipient category. In the case of gross aid, the summed ranks for the non-recipient category are close to the value that would be expected were US aid to have no impact. In other words, while international liquidity growth rates may increase with gross aid receipts, US aid itself would not seem to be a prerequisite for achieving these rates of growth.

The per capita aid summed ranks indicate that none of the capability variables that show significant covariation across the three recipient categories also display lower growth rates in the non-recipient category. While based on too few test periods to be treated as definitive, this finding does caution against too ready an acceptance of an interpretation to the effect that the receipt of higher volumes of per capita US aid promotes faster capability growth rates. It can be concluded more certainly, however, that the receipt of aid is not a prerequisite for such growth.

Military assistance

Table 4.11 indicates that there is no significant covariation between level of aggregated military assistance receipt and the national income or international liquidity variables. Military assistance is significantly related to growth rates on the military expenditure and trade variables, however. Showing little variation across the small, medium and large receipt categories, the main source of military spending's significant variation is a non-recipient category whose members consistently display more rapid absolute and relative military expenditure growth rates than recipients as a whole.[19] The significant variation for gross exports and imports, by contrast, is due in good part to the large recipient category experiencing higher rates of trade growth.

Per capita military assistance covaries significantly with both trade variables as well as with gross international liquidity and, once again, there is a tendency for the significance in the variation to stem mainly from the large recipient category.

Table 4.11 Summed ranks for average annual percentage change in the power capability variables for the zero, small, medium and large recipient categories of gross and per capita military assistance for the eleven four-year periods, 1952–6, 1954–8 to 1972–6

	Gross military assistance				Per capita military assistance			
	Zero	Small	Medium	Large	Zero	Small	Medium	Large
GDP	31.5	28.5	22.0	28.0	31.5	30.0	24.5	24.0
GDPPC	34.0	26.0	21.5	28.5	32.5	26.5	26.0	25.0
MltExp	18.5	29.5	31.0	31.0*‡	20.0	29.0	30.0	31.0
PMltExp	15.0	29.0	31.0	35.0*‡	21.0	29.0	28.5	31.5
GrEx	32.0	33.0	29.0	16.0*†	31.0	37.0	27.0	15.0*†
GrIm	30.5	30.0	31.5	18.0*†	32.5	30.5	29.0	18.0*
IL	35.5	23.0	28.5	23.0	37.0	28.0	27.0	18.0*
PIL	32.0	22.0	28.0	28.0	33.0	28.0	25.0	24.0

   * Indicates significance at the 0.05 level or beyond for the chi-square test across all three categories.
   † Indicates significance at the 0.05 level or beyond for the cumulative binomial test on the number of highest rank placings for the large category.
   ‡ Indicates significance at the 0.05 level or beyond for the cumulative binomial test on the number of highest rank placings of the zero category.

Arms sales

Our discussion of the impact of arms sales is especially tentative since it is based on only three test periods. Judging by this limited number of observations, however, the individual power capabilities would appear not to be influenced by the receipt of arms sales. In other words, these variables show no clear directional covariation across the four categories of either gross or per capita arms sales.

This lack of significant overall covariation notwithstanding, it is noticeable that the summed ranks for the non-recipient category are generally lower than those found in the three recipient categories of both gross and per capita aid. Exploring this difference further, Table 4.12 presents the raw (as opposed to ranked) growth rates on the power capability variables for arms sales non-recipients and recipients as a whole. This comparison confirms the general absence of significant relationships. The only exception is military expenditure, the growth rates of which are substantially higher in both its absolute and relative forms among arms sales recipients.[20]

In sum, therefore, it would seem that the growth rates of the capability variables are not generally influenced by either gross or per capita arms sales receipts. Furthermore, there appears to be no substantial difference between recipients and non-recipients as a whole except with regard to military spending. Here, in addition to having substantially higher levels of both absolute and relative military spending, arms sales recipients also display substantially higher growth rates in comparison to non-recipients.

Table 4.12 Average annual percentage change in the power political variables for non-recipients (NR) and recipients (R) of arms sales for the three four-year periods, 1970–4, 1972–6, 1974–8

	NR	R	NR	R	NR	R	NR	R
	GDP		GDPPC		MltExp		PMltExp	
1970–4	15.0	17.2	12.6	15.6	0.6	7.2	−2.8	−0.3
1972–6	15.9	17.2	13.4	15.4	3.6	8.1	0.5	2.5
1974–8	11.8	10.8	9.4	9.2	2.1	4.9	−0.5	4.2
	GrEx		GrIm		IL		PIL	
1970–4	19.1	23.7	19.4	23.0	17.8	21.5	0.9	1.0
1972–6	19.2	21.8	20.3	22.9	14.3	16.9	−6.2	−4.9
1974–8	8.7	7.4	11.7	12.4	9.5	13.2	−0.6	2.2

Interpretation: distribution

Economic aid

Our most general conclusion from the findings presented earlier is that power political considerations have a strong influence on the distribution of both gross and per capita economic aid, although, at least as measured in this analysis, they do not provide a complete explanation of the distribution of either. We can more correctly conclude, therefore, that US aid allocations to Third World countries are very consistently and very significantly structured by considerations of recipients' power political capabilities. Thus, to the extent that these capabilities profile relative importance, US aid is systematically directed towards the more important Third World countries.

Within this general conclusion, there are two more specific ones. The first of these is that power political considerations are more determinative of the distribution of gross, as opposed to, per capita aid. Not only are the bivariate relations less clear in the case of the latter distribution, but also the explained variation scores are lower. These weaker relations have already been explained in terms of the slower proportionate increases in US aid volume in comparison to the increase in the absolute values of the power capability variables. While there may be good economic and political justification, there is no logical reason why the United States could not design an aid policy that would allow the distribution of both gross and per capita aid to be determined equally strongly by recipient power capabilities. That it does not have this policy demonstrates a reluctance to allow power considerations to outweigh all others in its aid decisions.

The second specific conclusion concerns the relative importance that the United States attaches to the different types of power capabilities. Here the evidence indicates that it attaches a higher overall priority to recipients' politico-security capabilities than to their economic ones. Thus, recipients' importance, as measured by military expenditure, diplomatic associations and population size, outweighs their importance, as measured by trade, international liquidity and size of GDP, in the determination of the distribution of gross aid. This conclusion could be questioned on the grounds that we underestimate the importance of economic capabilities, and especially of trade, either because we are looking for the wrong relationship in the first place or because the relationship is not a straightforwardly linear one. It might be argued, for example, that trade is not a determinant of aid, but a surrogate for it. But if such were the case, trade would be expected to be inversely related to aid. It simply is not. Similarly, it might be held that the aid–trade relationship is not linear since aid may increase with trade up to a point, but that it is likely to decline in relative volume among the United States' major trading partners. Once again, however, the simple fact of the matter is that there is no evidence of a quadratic relationship of this kind.

Although not quite to the same degree, a relative emphasis on politico-security considerations also characterises the distribution of per capita aid. Relative military expenditure, for example, is consistently its single most important predictor. That the economic capability of per capita income is also a significant predictor might initially suggest the conclusion that it is a prerequisite of high military spending and, as such, is the more substantively important of the two predictors. This conclusion would be erroneous, however, since not only are the two variables lowly intercorrelated, but also per capita income emerges as a significant estimator after the influence of relative military spending has been controlled.

Our general conclusion, then, is that Third World countries' importance, as profiled primarily by their politico-security capabilities, has a strong structuring effect on the distribution of gross and, to a lesser extent, per capita US aid. This conclusion, however, is potentially open to two major criticisms, which we shall now address.

The first criticism essentially asserts that we have done nothing more than to demonstrate that larger Third World countries receive more US aid than smaller ones. We reject this criticism for two reasons. Firstly, our analysis is preceded by a theoretical justification of why we might expect so-called large countries to be advantaged by the distribution of aid. Secondly, 'large' can be conceptualised in a number of different, and not necessarily synonymous, ways so that, for example, the relationships of aid to 'large' as measure by military expenditure and 'large' as measured by trade are altogether different. A further variant of this first criticism is the charge that the strong association between aid and population size in reality indicates the primacy of humanitarian over power political criteria in US aid policy. After all, it can be argued, it is altogether humanitarian that countries with larger populations get more aid than those with smaller ones since they are in greater need of it. But to make this simple association is to provide far from adequate evidence of humanitarianism at work. After all, two countries with similarly sized populations could none the less differ radically in their respective need for aid for any number of reasons. A more suitable test of the humanitarian perspective is to examine the relationship between per capita income and per capita aid. This perspective would lead us to expect that relatively wealthy Third World countries would get less per capita aid. As it turns out, however, the relationship proves to be positive rather than negative. In other words, the actual distribution of aid flies in the face of humanitarianism in the sense that wealthy countries receive proportionately more per capita US aid than do poorer ones. Finally, it may be added that it is difficult to think of any humanitarian explanation of the strong and consistent relationship between gross aid and absolute military spending.

The second major criticism relates to the distinctiveness of the non-recipients of transfers from the mid-1960s onwards, i.e. to their tendency to have higher power capability scores than many transfer recipients. This distinctiveness

suggests that the power political explanation of aid may work well within
the recipient population, but has little to offer with regard to distinguishing
recipients from non-recipients. This criticism is potentially very damaging since
power political considerations can hardly be held to have a crucial structuring
effect on the distribution of aid if a considerable number of countries with
substantial power capabilities simply fall outside the aid programme's scope.

The problem disappears with further analysis, however. If we divide non-
recipients of US aid into two groups, those receiving US arms sales and those
not receiving them, Table 4.13 shows that the former's individual power capability scores are always higher than the latter's and only in the cases of population size, per capita income and percentage military spending are the intergroup
differences not consistently significant.[21] In short, the non-recipient aid category
is constituted of two quite distinct sub-populations. The first receives arms
sales and has capability scores that match (GDP, military expenditure, diplomatic associations) or exceed (per capita income, trade and international
liquidity) the values on the same variables that are found in the large aid recipient category. The sub-population receiving neither aid nor arms, by contrast, generally has capability scores that are more similar to those found in
the small aid recipient category. Thus, the sub-population receiving arms but
not aid is similar to the large aid recipient category with the notable exception
that it is much wealthier in relative terms, while the sub-population receiving
neither aid nor arms is similar to the small aid recipient category except that
it enjoys a higher per capita GDP and is generally smaller in population size.

We suggest, therefore, that a number of Third World countries do not receive
aid precisely because they are unimportant in terms of the power capability
criteria (population size, diplomatic associations and military expenditure)
employed by the United States to determine its distribution of this transfer.
It goes without saying that this group fits our power political interpretation
of US aid very nicely. But, at least at first glance, the same cannot be said of
the second sub-population of non-recipients of aid. This group scores highly
in both critical areas of military spending and diplomatic associations while,
on average, being smaller in population size than the countries in the large
aid category and, more importantly, being three to four times wealthier than
them. It must be remembered, however, that relative wealth did not turn out
to be a critical determinant of the distribution of US aid. What is more, although excluded from the receipt of aid, this group does receive arms supplies.
The logical conclusion, therefore, is that they are ignored in the aid programme
not because of a weakness in the power political interpretation of the distribution of this transfer, but because, given their relative wealth, they are more
suitably picked up by the US arms sales programme.

This juxtaposition of the two transfer programmes serves to emphasise
that the United States manipulates its individual transfers in a complementary
and flexible manner. Thus, a situation that might be interpreted as a weakness

for the power political interpretation of economic aid is seen not to be a weakness for the same interpretation of official transfers in general. The discontinuity that initially threatened our interpretation, in fact, turns out to enhance it. What we now see is the United States manipulating its different transfer programmes in a manner flexibly tailored to accommodate the diversity of Third World countries, but none the less tailored to pursue a common power political objective.

Military assistance

The principal general characteristic of military assistance is that its distribution is less structured by recipient power capabilities than is economic aid's. The explanation of this relative weakness if best understood by conceptualising military assistance's distribution as a two-stage process, the first involving the selection of recipients and the second the distribution of the transfer within the recipient population.

With regard to the selection of recipients, politico-security considerations take priority over economic ones in determining their identity, just as they did with the economic aid programme. What is more, the importance of politico-security considerations becomes more pronounced with the passage of time. Throughout the 1950s, recipients are distinguishable only by their higher levels of relative military expenditure, but in the early 1960s their distinctiveness becomes more generalised and pronounced. Since this development coincides with the expansion of the military assistance programme in terms of both real dollar value and number of recipients, it would seem to have been the consequence of an explicit change of policy on the part of the United States. That a second policy change occurred in the late 1960s and continued into the 1970s is indicated by the declining ability of power capabilities in general, and politico-security ones in particular, to distinguish military assistance recipients from non-recipients over this period.

This evolutionary pattern might seem to suggest the obligatory conclusion that power political considerations play a decisive role in the selection of military assistance recipients through to the late 1960s, but become substantially less determinative after that time. As is the case with economic aid, however, this conclusion can be seen to be premature if we divide non-recipients of military assistance into two sub-populations, those receiving arms sales and those not receiving them. This division shows arms sales recipients in fact, to have substantially higher scores than non-recipients on all the power capability variables (see Table 4.14). Even more importantly, the sub-population of arms sales non-recipients has capability scores that are generally well below those found in the small military assistance category. In other words, this sub-population has very low levels of population size, diplomatic associations, trade and military expenditure. The arms sales recipient sub-population, by contrast, has capability scores that match or exceed those found in the large military assistance

Table 4.13 Means for power capability variables in non-recipients of economic aid (NR) broken down by non-receipt and receipt of arms sales (NRA and RA) and for the small and high aid recipient categories (SR and HR), 1969–79

	NR		SR	HR	NR		SR	HR
	NRA	RA			NRA	RA		
	GDP				**GDPPC**			
1969	2,341	10,292*	1,824	10,637	533	613	282	222
1971	1,494	13,030*	1,902	12,336	598	967	282	337
1973	3,221	10,392*	3,568	12,620	686	1,313	362	350
1975	7,369	18,476	6,157	15,019	1,366	3,248*	575	629
1977	3,992	33,438*	7,704	20,475	1,793	2,903	750	652
1979	4,916	37,350*	10,118	28,501	2,915	3,510	891	862
	Pop				**M1tExp**			
1969	6.7	15.4	6.3	83.3	75	428*	57	351
1971	5.6	15.3	5.6	74.5	133	273	57	463
1973	6.5	10.0	8.7	73.7	73	393*	123	605
1975	8.6	8.6	8.6	80.7	172	460	138	794
1977	3.3	21.8*	9.5	95.2	113	1,200*	75	904
1979	2.3	18.9*	10.6	103.0	156	932*	93	832
	PM1tExp				**GrEx**			
1969	3.6	6.5	2.5	5.8	295	1,218*	390	581
1971	4.2	4.0	2.4	7.2	399	1,540*	380	804
1973	3.8	5.2	2.6	8.7	498	2,749*	572	1,008
1975	4.3	5.0	2.2	11.1	1,699	9,283*	1,581	1,888
1977	5.6	7.4	2.2	10.2	3,434	10,641*	1,112	2,861
1979	4.8	6.0	2.4	9.3	2,858	11,364*	1,654	3,248
	GrIM				**IL**			
1969	354	1,590	310	816	141	629*	153	224
1971	316	1,915*	317	1,063	129	932*	126	411
1973	436	2,075*	612	1,259	181	1,618*	310	844
1975	1,249	4,020*	1,290	2,167	685	3,162*	841	684
1977	1,361	6,921*	1,448	3,498	965	6,019*	484	1,150
1979	1,764	9,935*	1,978	4,237	1,511	5,657*	950	1,762

Table 4.13 (*cont.*)

	NR		SR	HR	NR		SR	HR
	NRA	RA			NRA	RA		
	PIL				**EmbIn**			
1969	32	54	44	27	17	50*	19	40
1971	36	82	35	33	21	44*	18	45
1973	47	110*	42	61	17	40*	24	39
1975	41	107	45	30	19	37*	25	48
1977	45	81	34	31	17	50*	25	54
1979	65	61	47	39	20	52*	25	58
	EmbFr							
1969	20	38*	22	41				
1971	21	44*	21	40				
1973	18	38*	28	33				
1975	19	36*	27	44				
1977	18	52*	26	48				
1979	20	54*	27	53				

* Indicates a significant difference at the 0.05 level or higher for *t*-test between recipients and non-recipients of arms sales within the non-recipient aid population, i.e. between NRA and RA.

category. The main difference is that this sub-population of countries is substantially wealthier than those receiving large amounts of military assistance.[22]

Thus, if arms recipients are removed from the group of countries receiving no military assistance, a very clear and consistent power capability difference emerges between military assistance recipients and non-recipients. Recipients are larger in terms of population size and have substantially higher levels of military spending, of trade, of international liquidity holdings and of diplomatic associations. They are, in other words, considerably more important than non-recipients in power political terms. Non-recipients whose power capabilities would lead us to expect them to be selected into the military assistance programme are excluded from it precisely because their relatively extreme wealth allows them to be picked up by the arms sales programme instead. Once again, therefore, to take account of the interdependence of the individual US official transfer programmes highlights the importance of power political criteria in determining their individual and joint distributions even when the importance of these criteria is not immediately apparent.

To turn now to the distribution of military assistance within the recipient population, the overall conclusion is that the power political variables do not play an especially important role in structuring it. This observation is particularly apposite with regard to gross military assistance since no variable has an especially marked effect on its distribution. Relative military spending, however,

Table 4.14 Means for power capability variables in non-recipients of military assistance (NR) broken down by receipt and non-receipt of arms sales (NRA and RA) and for the small and high military assistance recipient categories (SR and HR), 1969–75

	NR		SR	HR	NR		SR	HR
	NRA	RA			NRA	RA		
	GDP				**GDPPC**			
1969	1,421	5,791*	6,048	6,777	322	617	380	345
1971	1,118	12,147*	7,570	6,029	320	1,091	406	345
1973	2,859	5,852	10,196	6,220	407	928*	558	215
1975	3,195	19,707*	12,061	12,561	646	1,826*	846	393
	Pop				**MltExp**			
1969	6.4	31.2	37.0	21.0	44	421*	176	345
1971	5.9	34.4	37.0	19.0	60	529*	203	320
1973	16.3	21.0	20.9	22.9	95	1,160*	225	308
1975	7.7	55.9 *	13.4	34.7	113	773*	171	297
	PMltExp				**IL**			
1969	2.5	8.6	3.2	8.5	92	440*	237	401
1971	2.8	8.9	3.2	8.5	95	797*	282	520
1973	2.8	9.0	2.2	8.4	140	1,160*	705	866
1975	3.2	7.0*	2.2	6.4	278	2,727	951	1,330
	PIL				**GrEx**			
1969	31	48	46	44	216	724*	717	610
1971	34	81	40	47	284	1,325*	830	549
1973	46	89	45	58	353	1,969*	1,094	600
1975	32	95*	37	42	788	6,566*	1,940	2,697
	GrIM				**EmbIn**			
1969	254	953*	574	932	15	44*	35	36
1971	260	1,620*	698	1,017	16	44*	40	38
1973	343	1,429*	1,206	1,061	18	39*	39	33
1975	733	2,958*	2,060	3,187	20	44*	38	37
	EmbFr							
1969	19	41*	37	30				
1971	19	38*	41	29				
1973	21	42*	41	27				
1975	22	45*	40	31				

* Indicates a significant difference at the 0.05 level or higher for *t* test between recipients and non-recipients of arms sales within the non-recipient military assistance population.

does crucially influence the relative preference that the United States expresses through its per capita military assistance allocations.

It is conceivable that the US involvement in Vietnam was so intense as to distort the 'true' criteria employed in allocating military assistance and, hence, our identification of these criteria. Generally speaking, we do not set much store by such claims since too many countries receive military assistance for idiosyncratic influences to have a great deal of influence on its overall distribution. This scepticism is only reinforced by the finding that the identity of our estimators as well as the proportion of variance explained by them are similar whether or not Vietnam is included in the military assistance distributional analyses. In sum, our relatively weak explanation of military assistance's distribution, especially in its gross form, among recipients is attributable not to the nature of the distribution, but to the relatively low priority attached to power political considerations by the United States when determining its allocations within the select population of recipients.

Arms sales

In contrast to military assistance, power political considerations play an extremely important role in structuring the Third World distribution of arms sales. What is more, this general observation holds whether we are discussing the selection of recipients or the allocation of this particular transfer among recipients.

In terms of arms recipients vs. non-recipients, the former group is constituted of countries that are militarily, diplomatically and economically the more important in the Third World. Moreover, the more pronounced the power capabilities of these recipient countries, the more arms sales they attract. It is noticeable, however, that the politico-security capabilities of population size and diplomatic associations influence the distribution of arms considerably less than they influence the distribution of economic aid and that economic capabilities enjoy a substantially more marked distributional influence in the case of arms sales than they do in that of either of the other two transfers. But this contrast is not unexpected since we have already argued that a number of countries are excluded from the aid and military assistance recipient populations precisely because their relative wealth enables the United States to bring them under its overall transfer umbrella via an arms sales programme that helps to offset the economic costs of the other two programmes.

Interpretation: impact

Economic aid

The overall conclusion to emerge from our analysis of the relationship between economic aid transfers and capability variable growth rates is that, generally speaking, the relationships that are found to exist are not particularly strong. Before drawing out the implications of this conclusion, however, a number of more specific observations on the findings suggest themselves.

The first of these observations concerns the nature of the relationship between aid and military expenditure, the only politico-security variable to figure in the impact analysis of this chapter.[23] The distributional analysis demonstrated that both gross and per capita US aid are strongly attracted to the larger absolute and relative military spending countries in the Third World. Does this relationship mean that aid promotes military spending? The impact analyses would suggest not since they unequivocally indicate that aid has no systematic influence on military expenditure growth rates. The possibility remains, however, that US aid receipts may, in fact, maintain relatively high levels of such spending by allowing for the diversion of funds to the military that were originally earmarked for some other area of expenditure. But while possibly valid, this argument should not be overstated. In point of fact, the difference in military expenditure levels between high and low aid recipients exceeds the difference in the volume of their respective aid receipts so that even if aid does help to underwrite higher levels of military spending, it cannot be the only factor doing so.

A second specific observation concerns the relationship between trade and aid. Gross aid has no impact on the growth rate of trade, but per capita aid does. In itself, this difference is hardly surprising since, other things being equal, we would expect any effect that aid might have to make itself felt through the per capita programme. After all, per capita aid is the more sensitive measure of the transfer's relative importance to the recipient. It should be noted, however, that the trade effect is confined primarily to the large per capita recipient category. Now since the distributional analysis shows that trade volume generally decreases with per capita aid receipt, it follows that the aid effect is felt primarily in the smaller trading states. This conclusion is directly relevant to the often-voiced argument that trade follows aid. While the covariation of aid and trade cannot be denied, there is, in fact, little in our findings to suggest that this effect is consciously and purposively promoted through the US aid programme. In the first place, the distributional analysis shows that trade does not fundamentally structure aid allocations. What is more, to the extent that it does influence them, its influence is supportive rather than promotional in nature. Secondly, if aid allocations were expressly intended to foster trade growth, then we would reasonably expect them to be directed at the larger, rather than smaller, trading states. Yet the impact analysis indicates that it is the smaller states that display the more rapid rates of growth of trade.

The final specific observation concerns the relationship between aid and international liquidity. The strongest evidence in the analysis is for an aid effect on Third World countries' international liquidity holdings. But is this a 'real' effect? Liquidity holdings can increase in a variety of ways. Generally speaking, we can rule out currency revaluation. An excess of exports over imports is an equally unlikely explanation in the majority of cases since most Third World countries run balance-of-payments deficits. In addition, and more importantly, larger aid recipients tend not only to have larger deficits, but also to show no sign of reducing their deficits more quickly than smaller recipients. It seems likely, therefore, that the expansion of liquidity holdings stems principally from increased loans and it is quite conceivable that aid, by signalling US commitment to, and confidence in, recipients, encourages such loans. In other words, aid could well have an indirect impact on international liquidity holdings in the Third World.

Returning to the overall picture, the conclusion is inevitable that aid does not generally have a pronounced effect on the growth rates of the power capability variables. When it does have an effect, it generally does so, and perhaps not surprisingly, through the per capita programme. Taking a purely covariational perspective, it is clear, therefore, that the United States does not align itself through its economic aid with those Third World countries enjoying higher capability growth rates. But since the distributional analysis demonstrates that its aid flows disproportionately to the more powerful Third World states and since the impact analysis demonstrates that these same states at least match the capability growth rates of the less powerful countries, then it clearly is the case that US aid recipients experience the highest absolute increases in their power capabilities. In this respect, the impact analysis emphasises that the aid programme helps the United States to maintain its existing ties with the more powerful Third World states, i.e. those that are more powerful at the outset and whose capabilities increase at a faster absolute rate. At this point, however, two caveats are in order. Firstly, aid does not cause the variation in capability growth patterns; any relationship that it has to these patterns is spurious. Secondly, when there does appear to be a real aid effect, it is confined by and large to the per capita programme and, therefore, to the less powerful Third World states.

Nor do aid recipients seem to be systematically disadvantaged by their receipt of the transfer. It is apparent, for example, that aid in no way hampers their power capability development. Particularly with regard to countries being granted higher relative priority through the per capita programme, there is even some evidence that aid receipts serve to enhance their capability growth rates. As for gross aid, no matter what the expectations of its recipients, it generally has no impact, positive or negative, on these growth rates.

Military assistance

To an even greater extent than was the case with economic aid, our general conclusion with regard to military assistance is that it does not have a pronounced effect on power capability development. This conclusion does need to be qualified on two counts, however.

The first of them concerns international trade, which covaries positively and significantly with both gross and per capita military assistance. The principal source of significance in these two relationships is the large recipient category and it would seem rash to impute causality to this covariation precisely because there is not a military assistance effect across all four receipt categories.

The second, and more interesting, qualification relates to the finding that military expenditure growth rates do not vary systematically across the three categories of transfer recipient, but that they are significantly higher in the non-recipient category. Before evaluating several potential explanations of this difference, it is worth noting that the results of the impact analysis clearly indicate the need to reject the hypothesis that military assistance directly promotes military expenditure. For this hypothesis to hold, we would minimally need to find a progressive increase in military spending growth rates across the four recipient categories.

Returning to the difference between non-recipients and recipients as a whole, one possible explanation of it is that military assistance has a substitution effect in the sense that its recipients simply do not need to expand their military spending as rapidly precisely because they are in receipt of external assistance. This explanation is not convincing, however, since, taken to its logical conclusion, it would lead us to expect a decrease in growth rates across the three recipient categories and there is not the slightest evidence of such a pattern. Nor is there any evidence of a substitution effect in the distributional analysis, which in fact indicates that as military assistance increases, so too does the commitment to higher military spending in both its absolute and relative forms.

An alternative explanation is that our findings are nothing more than a data artefact. That is, it could be that countries with smaller levels of expenditure display higher growth rates simply because their growth is measured from a smaller baseline. This explanation fails on two grounds, however. Firstly, our method of calculating capability rates of growth controls for the size of the base and would produce artificially high estimates only when its size is extremely small, which it never is in the case of military expenditure. Secondly, the base values for the non-recipient category, although generally slightly lower, are not substantially different from those for the small recipient category, yet the military expenditure growth rates in these categories differ considerably.

The most plausible explanation of non-recipients' higher military expenditure growth rates is that US military assistance has an indirect promotional effect. It may not stimulate higher rates of growth among recipients, but it does do so among non-recipients precisely because they do not receive military assistance while potential adversaries do. Their higher growth rates, in other words, represent an attempt to compensate for the disadvantage at which they are placed by other countries receiving external military assistance. As such, military assistance, by virtue of its being distributed very selectively, has the effect of stimulating relatively high levels of military expenditure in those Third World countries not receiving it rather than in those actually receiving it.

In sum, then, from a narrow power capabilities perspective, it is difficult to see what benefits the United States derives from its military assistance programme.

With the exception of higher trade growth in the large recipient category, this transfer has no direct impacts. What is more, unlike with economic aid, the distribution of military assistance does not serve to align the United States with the progressively more powerful Third World countries. Consequently, it is not as closely aligned with the countries experiencing the greatest absolute increases in their power capabilities. Equally, and on the other side of the coin, it is difficult to see what, if any, capability expansion benefits accrue to military assistance recipients. Indeed, in net terms, this transfer appears to entail only disadvantages as its recipients find themselves in something of a vicious circle as they seek to keep pace with non-recipients whose rate of military spending is growing more rapidly.

Arms sales

Being based on only three test periods, this interpretation of the findings concerning the impact of arms sales is best treated as exploratory and tentative. None the less, it follows the aid and military assistance programmes in producing little evidence of a pronounced effect on capability growth rates. Indeed, the only sign of an arms sales impact is in the area of military expenditure where, in direct contrast to military assistance, transfer recipients display significantly higher military spending growth rates than non-recipients.

The explanation of this relationship that immediately springs to mind is that arms sales stimulate military spending. This explanation is not convincing for two reasons, however. Firstly, arms sales flow to countries whose very high levels of military spending in fact antedate the expansion of the US arms sales programme. Secondly, and more importantly as far as growth rates are concerned, acceptance of the arms sales stimulation hypothesis would require that growth rates increase with volume of arms sales receipt. But this is not the case; growth rates do not vary systematically across the three recipient categories.

The more likely explanation is that the distribution of arms sales is in part structured by recipient demand so that, other things being equal, countries planning relatively high increases in military spending are more likely to make themselves available as clients for arms sales. Since projected growth need in no way be related to extant levels of military spending, growth rates can be relatively uniform across the different levels of arms sales receipts as, indeed, they are. The absolute level of expenditure is important only in so far as it influences the volume of arms purchase, an explanation that accounts for the positive relationship between volume of arms sales receipt and military spending. Thus, while US arms sales can respond to a domestic demand for them and thereby effectively promote higher military expenditure, the higher expenditure growth rates in arms recipient countries would seem to be the result of factors that are independent of the arms transfers themselves.

More generally, however, there is little evidence that US arms sales influence capability growth rates. Thus, the recipients of this transfer may be far more powerful than non-recipients, but they are indistinguishable from them in terms of power capability growth rates. But since recipients do not actually have lower growth rates and since they have substantially higher capability levels at the outset then, as with economic aid, the United States aligns itself through its arms sales programme not only with the more powerful Third World countries, but also with those achieving the greatest absolute, as opposed to relative, increase in their general power capabilities.

Appendix: variables and their acronyms

Acronym	Variable description
GDP	Gross domestic product (in current $US)
GDPPC	Gross domestic product per capita (in current $US)
Pop	Population size
MltExp	Gross military expenditure
PMltExp	Military expenditure as a percentage of GDP
GrEx	Gross exports
GrIm	Gross imports
IL	Gross international liquidity
PIL	International liquidity as a percentage of imports
EmbIn	Total number of embassies that the country has in overseas countries
EmbFr	Total number of embassies accredited to the country by overseas countries

1. As in the previous chapter, we use capital letters in the acronyms to indicate the start of a new word.
2. In order to facilitate the interpretation of the acronyms, we have used the following convention: several variables are expressed in both their gross and percentaged form. These forms are distinguished by the abbreviations Gr and P respectively. The variables that appear in gross and percentaged form in the tables of this chapter are: MltExp (military expenditure); and IL (international liquidity).

Notes

1. The best-known statement of the realist position is H. J. Morgenthau's *Politics Among Nations,* 5th edn (New York: Knopf, 1973). See also J. H. Herz, *Political Realism and Political Idealism* (Chicago: University of Chicago Press, 1951) and, for a more recent version, J. H. Herz, 'Political Realism Revisited', *International Studies Quarterly*, 22 (1978).
2. A diplomatic association, or tie, is defined as the physical presence of a high commission, embassy or legation (collectively called embassy) from country A on the soil of country B, or vice versa.
3. To facilitate the interpretation of the discriminant analysis results in this and the next chapter, the signs of the individual coefficients have, when

necessary, been adjusted so that a positive coefficient always predicts to transfer recipients. This adjustment has sometimes been necessary since the discriminant functions predict to group means, which may be positive or negative. This variability means that the function itself cannot be interpreted until each of the recipient and non-recipient groupings has been identified with one or other mean. Thus, when the recipient group mean is lower in value than the non-recipient group's, i.e. when it is negative, we have simply reversed the signs, a transformation that does no injustice to the data. The result is that a positive value in the discriminant tables in the text always indicates a higher score for recipients and a negative value a lower score for this same group.

4. This qualification is not intended to deny that the discriminant equations as a whole are highly significant. It does explicitly acknowledge, however, that their significance is in part a reflection of the unequal size of the two groups. That is, since significance is achieved essentially by assigning individual cases to the group to which they actually belong, the relatively large size of our recipient group means that statistical significance can be achieved despite the failure to classify correctly the majority of cases in the smaller non-recipient group. That this situation transpires in Table 4.1 is the reason for our reservations in the text about the overall discriminatory power of the capability variables with regard to aid recipients and non-recipients.

On the other hand, it must be pointed out that these results are based on a classification procedure that accentuates the problems arising from the unequal size of the two groups. That is, by drawing the classification line through a point that takes account of this inequality rather than through a point mid-way between the two group means, we have made it more difficult for cases in the smaller group to be classified correctly. Indeed, this choice is an example of the methodological conservatism that will be our strategy throughout the book, i.e. we shall always opt for the methodological alternative generating results that are less supportive of our hypothesis.

5. In this and all subsequent regression analyses, we report only those individual equations that are significant at the 0.05 level or beyond.

6. A change of policy from a US attraction to population size to an attraction to military expenditure seems to account for the unusually low R^2 value in 1973. To confirm that this aberration is not a data artefact, we ran the same regression equation for 1974 (with 1973 predictors) and produced an R^2 value of 40, which is higher than in 1973 but lower than in 1975. The principal estimators for 1974 are PMltExp (0.35), GDPPC (−0.19) and Pop (0.17). In short, the United States does seem to be adjusting its priorities away from population size and towards military expenditure over this three-year period and the lower R^2 values for 1973 and 1974 probably reflect the time lag that it takes for this adjustment to make itself felt in the distribution of this transfer.

7. The only year for which a significant equation is not generated is 1967. An additional regression run for 1968 also failed to produce a significant result. Unlike with the weakening of the gross aid equations in 1973 and 1974, however, no substantive importance should be attached to the 1967 and 1968 per capita aid results. In a general context of not very powerful results, the problem would seem to be that generally significant, but otherwise weak, estimators simply fail to cross the threshold of significance in these two years.

8. The emergence of only one significant discriminating variable in 1953, 1955 and 1957 explains the absence of equations for these years from Table 4.4.
9. Given our earlier qualification of the aid discriminant results, it is worth noting that in Table 4.4 not only are there significant equations until 1969, but also a majority of both recipients and non-recipients is correctly classified in each year.
10. As in note 8, the emergence of only one significant variable, diplomatic associations, in 1971, 1973 and 1975 explains why there are no discriminant equations in Table 4.4 after 1969.
11. There is no general rule or convention governing the identification of outliers. Our rule of thumb is that if one country receives 30 per cent or more of an official transfer in any one year, it qualifies as an outlier to be excluded from the regression analysis for that year. Following this rule, no outliers at all are found in the economic aid distribution, whereas they do figure in the military assistance distribution in 1955 and from 1967 to 1975 inclusive. In these years, we then checked to determine whether there were other outliers after the first one had been removed and found none. In addition, the military assistance regressions for these years were run twice, once including the outlier and once excluding it and the results were then compared. Any important differences that emerged are reported in the text.
12. The only exception is 1967 when no significant equation is generated. An additional regression for 1968 produces a significant equation, but with an R^2 value of 29, which is substantially lower than the comparable values in 1965 and 1969. The principal estimators in 1968 (PMltExp (-0.53), EmbFr (-0.26) and GrIm (0.16)), however, conform to the pattern found in other years. This conformity makes the low R^2 values for 1967 and 1968 more enigmatic and we do not have an explanation for them.
13. It is noticeable in Table 4.7 that not only are significant equations generated, but also very good discrimination is achieved in terms of the correct classification of cases in both the recipient and non-recipient groups.
14. Using the 30 per cent rule outlined in note 10 above, the arms sales distributions yield outliers in 1971, 1975, 1977 and 1979.
15. Strictly speaking, this description applies only to the ranking procedure for economic aid, the only one of the three transfers for which we have the full thirteen four-year test periods. However, because of the small number of non-recipients prior to the late 1960s, we can only examine the zero recipient category from 1966–70. Most of the time, therefore, aid impacts are examined only over the small, medium and large recipient categories. None the less, following the procedure outlined in Appendix C, we compute, but do not report, a zero category for the preceding test periods. In the case of military assistance, by contrast, we can examine impacts across all four receipt categories, but can do so only for the eleven test periods stretching from 1952–6 to 1972–6 inclusive. The volume of military assistance transferred is simply too small for analysis in the remaining two test periods. Finally, all four arms sales receipt categories can be analysed, but only over the three test periods 1970–4, 1972–6 and 1974–8.
16. The ranking procedure involves taking each performance variable in each four-year test period and running a one-way ANOVA across the mean rate

of change within each of the four receipt categories. Rank scores of 1 to 4 are then assigned to the largest through smallest mean change scores.

An obvious alternative method of assessing impact is simply to look for significant results in the individual ANOVA tests for each four-year test period. But we rejected this alternative for several reasons. Firstly, to place an overall interpretation on say, thirteen sets of results for each predictor variable, would be extremely difficult unless none or all were found to be significant. This problem is only aggravated by the fact that we have no a priori theoretical reason to expect to achieve significant outcomes in particular trials. Secondly, as with any significance test, there are limits on the substantive importance that should be attached to its outcome simply because any one of a number of idiosyncrasies, e.g. a quirk in the data or one extreme category out of four, may produce an 'unwarranted' significant result. Alternatively a constant, but moderate, transfer effect could remain entirely hidden. One of the strengths of our ranking procedure is that it is not so subject to such idiosyncrasies; it demands that if a transfer is to be regarded as having an impact, then that impact must manifest continuously over time. As such, it is a suitably conservative methodology.

17. Two tests are used to assess the significance of the differences in the rank scores. The first of them is chi square-based and can be used over either three or four receipt categories. When there are four categories, the mean and variance of the ranks 1 to 4 must always be 2.5 and 1.25 respectively in any test period. Over repeated test periods, the expected summed ranks value for any one category, designated $r + j$, would, following the central limit theorem, be normally distributed with a mean of 2.5 (or $r + j/t$, where $t = $ the number of trials) and a variance of $1/t \times 1.25$. Under a random normal distribution, the summed ranks for each category ($r + 1$ to $r + j$), which are correlated, would equally be normally distributed. The actual distribution of the rank scores can, therefore, be evaluated against the expected distribution by means of the formula $\Sigma(r + j - 2.5t)^2 / (t \times 1.25)$. The resultant chi square statistic has three degrees of freedom. When comparing across only three receipt categories, the mean and variance become 2.0 and 0.67 respectively and the degrees of freedom for chi square are two. We are indebted to Dr Joseph Whittaker of the Department of Mathematics, University of Lancaster for drawing our attention to this test.

The second test is a binomial test and is based on the number of highest, or lowest, ranks accruing to the large recipient category. In the four-category case, the probability of this category achieving the highest rank is 0.25 and, using the binomial test, we can calculate the exact probability of obtaining r outcomes (r being the number of first rank values) over N trials (where each trial is one test period) as:

$$\binom{N}{r} \times (0.25)^r \times (0.75)^{N-r}.$$

In the text, the cumulative probability, or the sum of all the exact probabilities for r plus the outcome values greater than r, is always reported.

18. The two diplomatic variables are deliberately excluded from Table 4.10 since the absolute change in the number of new embassies established in any one five-year test period is very small. Even so, there appears to be no relationship between aid receipt and rate of growth of diplomatic associations.

19. The raw growth rates in absolute military expenditure for non-recipients and recipients as a whole are respectively: 8.8, 5.8 (1952-6); 9.7, 6.0 (1954-8); 8.1, 3.3 (1956-60); 6.2, 5.2 (1958-62); 11.3, 4.5 (1960-4); 8.6, 5.8 (1962-6); 8.8, 7.0 (1964-8); 10.2, 5.4 (1966-70); 8.6, 8.0 (1968-72); 0.6, 3.3 (1970-4); and 3.4, 7.7 (1972-6). For relative military expenditure, the raw growth rates for the same periods are 4.1, −0.4; 6.0, 1.5; 4.7, −0.7; 1.9, −0.2; 6.4, −1.3; 4.8, 0.1; 4.3, 1.4; 5.2, −1.6; 3.6, 1.3; −3.1, 0.5; and 13.5, 18.1.

20. Since they are almost identical to their gross counterpart, the per capita arms sales results are not discussed in the text. Table 4.12 is, of course, exactly the same whether we focus on gross or per capita arms sales impacts.

21. The number of cases in each of the NRA, RA, SR and HR categories in Table 4.13 are respectively: 22, 4, 43, 11 (1969); 15, 7, 46, 14 (1971); 22, 6, 44, 15 (1973); 15, 7, 50, 12 (1975); 13, 10, 51, 11 (1977); 12, 10, 48, 10 (1979). The difference-of-means tests use separate, as opposed to pooled, variance estimates when the variance in the two groups being compared differs significantly.

22. The number in each of the NRA, RA, SR and HR categories in Table 4.14 are respectively: 55, 4, 25, 8 (1969); 55, 5, 27, 8 (1971); 60, 9, 23, 6 (1973); and 58, 15, 17, 9 (1975).

23. Population size is excluded because it is difficult to think of any reasons why official transfers should directly influence population growth rates, especially in the short term. More unfortunately, the diplomatic associations variables have also had to be excluded since the rate of change on them is so small. The closely related bloc preference variable in the next chapter does, however, throw some light on the impact of official transfers on Third World countries' patterns of diplomatic associations.

5 Competition with Communism

Introduction

Theoretical rationale

The theoretical rationale guiding the analysis in this chapter rests on the proposition that the emergence and institutionalisation of the 'superpower' rivalry between the United States and the USSR has been, and continues to be, the dominant cleavage in the international system. It is for basically this reason that we would expect, or hypothesise, that the US transfer programmes are structured so as to reflect a competitive response to the presence of communism in the Third World, whether this presence manifests itself in the form of either or both domestic communism and external ties with the USSR in particular or the communist bloc more generally.

This rivalry has its roots largely in the collapse of the Euro-centric state system both during and, more importantly, after World War II. The importance of this collapse is that it served to bring to the forefront of international politics two states that had previously been relatively insignificant world actors, the United States and the USSR. Their emergence as superpowers was not surprising; rather it represented a correction of the imbalance between each's domestic capabilities and international activity that had been the product of their common preference for isolationism in the inter-war years. Nor was their emergence avoidable. The collapse of the Western European-dominated international hierarchy meant that there was an international power vacuum that had to be filled if international order was to be restored. But from the outset there was no superpower agreement on the form that this 'new' order should take and the history of their relations in the intervening period is one of continuous, albeit variably fierce, competition in an effort to define it to their own advantage. Pitted against each other by ideological hostility and disagreement as to the proper economic and political organisation of the world system, the United States and the USSR came to an uneasy *modus vivendi* that radically altered the character of the established international system. Centres of power shifted and spheres of influence were negotiated so that a new and dominant 'East-West' cleavage was introduced into world politics. The USSR extended its hold on Eastern Europe, the four-power division of Germany was 'rationalised' into East and West Germany and the major states of Western Europe became part of the US sphere of influence through the Marshall Plan and NATO.

The character of superpower competition has changed with the passage of time, however. Initially, the two countries competed on an unequal footing in that the United States was not only economically and militarily superior to the USSR, but also enjoyed a closer relationship with the world's former major powers, most importantly with the United Kingdom and France. These countries may have had their resources dramatically depleted by the war, but they still controlled vast colonial empires. These various advantages allowed the United States to impose an open-door, liberal economic order on a large part of the world so that its own trade and investment could flow relatively freely to like-minded countries. What is more, this order was reinforced by US-initiated organisations like the United Nations Organization (UN), the International Monetary Fund (IMF) and the World Bank, all of which, and especially the last two, were largely controlled and manipulated by their principal founder. The USSR was viewed as a dangerous but inescapable flaw in this grand schema and the United States immediately bent its efforts to ensure the physical containment of the Soviet 'contagion' through a series of security alliances and mutual defence treaties with friendly powers. Moreover, any doubts as to the US commitment to this policy were dispelled early by its actions in Korea and Berlin. The USSR, for its part, strove increasingly hard to reverse its military inferiority in particular so that it could assert itself against its superpower rival. In consequence, East–West tension came to dominate world politics.

US domination has persisted despite a number of changes in its original design for a liberal international economy in that greater part of a bipolar world that it had not ceded to Soviet influence. Not least among these changes has been that a world which, even at the height of the Cold War, was never fully bipolar has become increasingly multipolar. Western Europe and Japan in particular have recovered economically and, while for the most part remaining closely allied with the United States, have nonetheless not always followed its lead, even in security matters. Equally, the burgeoning Third World has not developed as a united, autonomous and uniformly pro-Western bloc, although it has generally looked to the West for trade and investment. Indeed, a number of developments within the Third World, for example the emergence of newly-industrialising countries and, more importantly, of the OPEC (Organisation of Petroleum Exporting Countries) cartel, has altered the international power balance. At the same time, and partly in consequence of these and similar developments in the international system, the United States has clearly fallen from its position of hegemony within the UN and, although to nothing like the same degree, within the World Bank and IMF as well.

The USSR has also experienced a diminution of its hegemony with the erosion of bipolarity in the years since the height of the Cold War. Its Eastern European satellites, for example, have provided it with problems as well as with political support. Still more dramatic has been the transformation of its alliance with mainland China into an antagonistic relationship. On the credit side, however, it has made inroads into the United States' early position of unquestioned pre-eminence in the international system. Not only has it succeeded in breaking down the physical containment barrier that the United States erected in the Cold War, but it has also reached a position of military and strategic, though not economic, parity with its erstwhile pre-eminent superpower rival.

The erosion of bipolarity and the relative rise of the USSR notwithstanding, the superpower status of neither the United States nor the USSR has been seriously challenged in the post-war period. Despite its best efforts, the Third World has not succeeded in replacing East–West with 'North–South' issues on the international political agenda and none of the developments in Western Europe or Japan have moulded a united bloc capable of rivalling either superpower. When all is said and done, it is the United States and the USSR that continue to hold a near monopoly of nuclear capabilities and it is they that are the main protagonists in the confrontation between the NATO and Warsaw Pact powers in Europe and, more generally, in the numerous relatively small-scale confrontations between their allies and satellites in other areas of the world.

In sum, therefore, despite the erosion of bipolarity and despite the rise of doctrines of peaceful coexistence and *détente*, the United States and the USSR have succeeded in perpetuating and effectively institutionalising a mutual rivalry and competition that dominates the international political arena without monopolising its agenda.

Though not intended as a comprehensive exposition of the various forms that superpower rivalry can take, this brief survey does serve to document its international pre-eminence and its development and institutionalisation in the years since 1945. In this sense, it furnishes the basis of the rationale for the general hypothesis that competition with communism exercises a decisive influence on the structuring of US official transfers to the Third World. Given this rationale, the purpose of this chapter is to put the general hypothesis deriving from it to the empirical test. First of all, however, we need to consider what form(s) the US response to communism through its official transfer programme can take. The transfers themselves, of course, provide the United States as their supplier with the first-order utilities of commitment and leverage, i.e. the means by which it can pursue its second-order foreign policy goal of containing communism. But what strategies are adopted to achieve containment? To answer this question, it seems to us that there are three principal containment strategies that the United States can promote through the manipulation of its official transfers. We shall call these strategies aversion, mutual veto and reinforcement and demonstrate that the particular one adopted is a function of the form, if any, that communism takes in the recipient country.

The aversion strategy essentially involves the allocation of transfers, or the promise of them, to discourage the development of domestic communist movements and/or the establishment of close links of one kind or another with the USSR in particular or the communist bloc in general. That is, countries with neither of these characteristics are rewarded by being allocated transfers and those developing one or more of them are punished by being denied transfers.

Resort to the mutual veto strategy, by contrast, is appropriate where countries already display either domestic or external associations with communism. The United States' goal with this strategy is to counter or stalemate the communist influence accruing from these associations. The final containment strategy is reinforcement and its essential method of operation is to reward recipients that manifest some affinity with the United States or its allies and, conversely, some antipathy towards the USSR. It is a strategy that could be pursued, for example, by rewarding trading links or investment ties with the United States or by making relatively large volumes of a transfer to recipients whose political systems conform to liberal democratic standards.[1]

Recipients may take advantage of US competition with communism to achieve utilities of their own and these may be of two types. Firstly, the recipient may independently define its own national self-interest in terms of containing the development and spread of communism within its own borders and/or its spread from neighbouring countries that have or are developing close internal or external communist associations. Its second-order utility of containment can be pursued directly through the enhancement of its domestic power capabilities and/or indirectly through the deterrent value of overt US commitment to the recipients. But whether direct or indirect, official transfers figure centrally, and perhaps crucially, in the recipient's containment strategy. Secondly, official transfers can also have a utility for recipients with no direct interest in the East–West conflict, but who may none the less be perceived by the United States to be important to the success of its overall containment strategy. Such circumstances provide ample opportunity for counter-dependence to accrue to the recipient. Whatever the precise supplier strategy, the recipient can then manipulate its counter-leverage to reduce substantially its own first-order disutilities and simultaneously to increase the supplier's first-order disutilities.

Operationalisation

Reflecting its central role in post-war US foreign policy, a substantial number and range of variables are used to operationalise competition with communism. These variables are treated as a single bloc in our multivariate analyses, but are here divided into a number of discrete sets for the sake of clarity of presentation. The first of them profiles a number of measures of diplomatic associations, which figure in our analysis because the establishment of embassies is an institutionalised means of ceding formal recognition to a country. The measures themselves are the accreditation of an embassy to and from the USSR (each being measured as a dummy variable), the number of embassies to and from the communist bloc as a whole (measured as a simple count), bloc preference for the West and, finally, the percentage of contiguous neighbours' embassies accredited to and from each of the West and the communist bloc. The bloc preference measure is a composite indicator, having a range of both positive and negative values. Positive values indicate some degree of preference in diplomatic terms for the West, while negative values indicate a similar predisposition to the East.[2] The two measures of neighbour's diplomatic associations are included to determine whether US interest in a country is influenced by the level of communist activities in bordering countries.

The second set includes a number of measures of aid and trade associations. They are communist bloc aid, communist bloc gross trade and trade share (the latter being gross trade as a percentage of total trade), US gross trade and trade share and neighbours' gross and percentage trade with both the United States and the communist bloc.[3] The trade variables figure in the analysis partly because of their purely commercial importance and partly because of their ability to foster other, more enduring relations that, at least in the short term, can be terminated only at some considerable cost to both parties to the relationship. Thus, in view of the commercial and political importance of trade, we would expect communist bloc trade to be subjected by the United States to either the aversion or mutual veto strategies and US trade to be encouraged by means of the reinforcement strategy. Measures of trade share are included because, more faithfully than gross trade, they represent the relative domination of one or other transfer supplier. Neighbours' trading patterns are included for exactly the same reason as for their diplomatic associations.

The third set of variables pertains to US security interests in the Third World. The first of these is a dummy variable indicating a country's 'forward defence status'. This status was accorded to countries either bordering on, in the case of an island like Taiwan, or being in close proximity to one or more communist bloc countries and which are consequently perceived by the United States to be crucial to the success of its containment strategy.[4] This variable is excluded from the late 1960s, however, because it was not amended by the United States to take account of the explosion in the number of Third World countries and the expansion of the communist bloc and so loses its initial importance. Other US security indicators are the USSR and communist bloc arms sales in gross and percentage form and neighbours' gross and percentage arms receipts from both the communist bloc and the United States.[5]

The final set of variables consists of two indicators of domestic communism. They are the presence of a legal and active communist party and the presence of extensive left-wing violence, both of which are measured as dummy variables.[6]

In summary then, these four sets of variables tap aspects of Soviet or communist activity to which we would expect the United States to respond through, among other things, its official transfer programmes. But we would not expect its reponse to be either random or unthinkingly uniform. Rather, it should vary with the form that the Soviet or communist activity takes within recipient countries and follow one or more of the aversion, mutual veto or reinforcement strategies.

Findings: distribution

Economic aid

As in the previous chapter, we start by examining the bivariate relations between the range of competition with communism variables, proceeding set by set, and gross aid receipts. Third World countries are divided into zero, small, medium and large recipients on the basis of the volume of their aid receipts.

With regard to diplomatic associations, the United States' virtually comprehensive network of embassies means that there is no variation across the four levels of aid receipt. The same is not true for the USSR, however, and there is, in fact, a general propensity for the number of Soviet diplomatic associations to increase with the level of US aid receipt. This trend is even more marked with regard to communist bloc diplomatic associations. Over the 1950–79 period, high aid recipients average in excess of twice the number of embassies in the communist bloc than do the zero and small recipients. The bloc preference index, by contrast, proves to be more sensitive to change over time. In the 1950s, high aid recipients may have more embassies in the communist bloc, but they also have proportionately more embassies in the West so that there is no systematic variation in bloc preference across the four categories of US aid recipient. But this picture changes between 1960 and 1973. In this period, the growth of Third World diplomatic associations with the communist bloc proceeds more quickly than with the West so that the mean aggregate bloc preference score for all countries drops from 2.7 in favour of the West in 1959 to 0.9 in 1973. This same period also sees the appearance of a systematic and positive relationship between bloc preference for the West and level of US aid receipt. In other words, the United States responds to the communist bloc's diplomatic expansion by complementing its own traditional attraction to recipients having relatively more diplomatic ties with the communist bloc in absolute terms with a simultaneous attraction to those recipients that none the less retain disproportionate ties with the West. From the mid-1970s, the 1950s picture of no relationship between bloc preference and levels of aid receipt reasserts itself as the earlier communist expansion is neutralised by a proportionately similar increase in the number of embassies that the lower categories of aid recipient have in the West. As for the contiguous neighbours' diplomatic associations variable, their proportionate share of embassies in both the communist bloc and the West stands in no systematic relationship to levels of aid receipt.

The set of trade variables also provides a mixed bag of results. Soviet trade with the Third World is on average about one-third of the communist bloc total, although the simple correlations between the two are generally in excess of 0.90. Not surprisingly, therefore, the volume of both stand in much the same relationship to US economic aid, i.e. both show a tendency to increase with the level of aid received. This picture changes somewhat in the late 1970s, however, when non-recipients of aid come to show relatively large volumes of such trade. Soviet and communist bloc trade share also increase with US aid receipts, but the relationship is weaker. There is, on the other hand, no clear relationship between US gross trade and US aid until the 1960s, after which time a positive relationship emerges. From the early 1970s, however, aid non-recipients develop trading volumes close to those in the high recipient category. The relationship between US trade share and US aid follows exactly the same pattern. Finally, US aid receipts generally increase, if only slightly, as do neighbouring countries' gross and percentage trade with the communist bloc.[7]

When we turn to the set of security variables, we find that, unlike with trade, the USSR dominates communist bloc arms sales, generally being responsible for the transfer of over 90 per cent of them. As with trade, therefore, Soviet and communist bloc transfers are effectively synonymous. Soviet arms transfers to the Third World to all intents and purposes begin only in 1957 and for a few years show no systematic relationship to US aid receipts except that none of the high US aid recipients purchase any Soviet arms at all. From 1961 onwards, however, a strong and positive relationship appears between Soviet arms and gross US aid receipts. But, again, this relationship changes from 1969 to take on a 'U'-shaped distribution whereby non-recipients and high recipients of US aid both get a much higher volume of Soviet arms than do the small and medium aid recipients. Soviet arms share follows much the same pattern with the slight exception that non-recipients of aid score higher on this variable than do high aid recipients. As for contiguous neighbours, there is no relationship between their level of aid receipt and gross Soviet or communist bloc arms sales until the 1970s when a generally positive association develops. There is, by contrast, never any sign of a clear relationship between gross aid receipts and the percentage of neighbours' arms transfers coming from the USSR or the communist bloc. Finally, forward defence areas are concentrated in the medium and high aid recipient categories throughout the 1950s. This concentration then weakens progressively over the course of the 1960s.

Left-wing violence and the presence of a legal and active communist party, i.e. the variables profiling domestic communist activity, stand in no clear or consistent relationship to gross US aid receipts.

Having completed the presentation of our bivariate results, we turn to the differentiation, through discriminant analysis, of the aid recipient and non-recipient groups in terms of the range of competition with communism variables.[8] This exercise begins in 1969 since it is only then that the non-recipient group becomes non-trivial in size. Table 5.1 indicates that significant discrimination is achieved in five of the six test years between 1969 and 1979.[9] What is more, the overall picture that emerges is clear and consistent.[10] Thus, through to 1977 (excluding 1975 when there is no significant result), US aid recipients are distinguished from non-recipients primarily by their far more pronounced diplomatic bloc preference for the West and their lower volume of communist bloc arms receipts. Controlling for these two variables also serves to bring into

Table 5.1: Results for the discriminant analysis of recipients (R) and non-recipients (NR) of economic aid by selected competition with communism variables, 1969-79*

	Actual group	Predicted group			Standardised discriminators	
		NR	R	(N)		
1969:	NR	2 (8)	23 (92)	25	BPref	0.96
	R	4 (6)	61 (94)	65	GrArCB	−0.78
					PTrCB	0.75
1971:	NR	3 (15)	17 (85)	20	BPref	0.62
	R	1 (1)	72 (99)	73	LWV	0.49
					GrArCB	−0.60
1973:	NR	8 (30)	19 (70)	27	PTrCB	1.11
	R	3 (5)	62 (95)	65	BPref	1.02
					GrTrUS	−0.77
					PArCB	−0.57
					PTrUS	0.47
1975:	Not significant					
1977:	NR	8 (42)	11 (58)	19	GrTrUS	−1.12
	R	5 (7)	64 (93)	69	PTrCB	0.64
					PTrUS	0.56
					PArCB	−0.46
					AidCB	0.44
					BPref	0.42
1979:	NR	9 (43)	12 (57)	21	GrTrUS	−0.77
	R	6 (9)	64 (91)	70	GrTrCB	−0.70
					AidCB	0.49
					PTrCB	0.46
					PTrUS	0.35

* The figures in parentheses represent the row percentages.

the discriminant equations three other variables that, in bivariate terms at least, are unrelated to the receipt or non-receipt of US aid. These are communist bloc trade share and gross US trade, both of which are negatively related to the dependent variable, and US trade share, which is positively related to it. The picture for 1979 is rather different since bloc preference disappears and aid recipients become distinguished principally by their lower US and communist bloc gross trade and their simultaneously higher US and communist bloc trade shares.

However, too much should not be read into this change since it is as misleading as is the discrimination for earlier years understated. It must be borne in mind that the aid non-recipient population is made up of some countries that do receive US arms transfers and some that do not and, as was seen in the last

Table 5.2: Means on selected competition with communism variables for recipients of US economic aid (R), non-recipients of economic aid (NR), non-recipients of both economic aid and arms sales (NRNR), and non-recipients of economic aid but recipients of arms (NRR), 1969–79

	R	NR	NRNR	NRR	R	NR	NRNR	NRR
	GrTrUS				PTrUS			
1969	215	161	131	426	20	13*	12	16
1971	239	218	47	659†	19	10*	6	17
1973	248	343	191	717†	17	12	11	14
1975	572	997*	621	1,328	16	15	16	11
1977	629	1,918*	791	2,584†	18	17	16	16
1979	893	2,803*	941	4,058†	17	17	16	17
	GrTrCB				PTrCB			
1969	52	68	62	116	5	7	8	4
1971	51	100	92	136	5	9	10	5
1973	71	73	50	168†	6	5	5	4
1975	232	202	143	295	7	5	6	3
1977	240	306	219	417	3	14	3	4
1979	221	464*	279	535	7	4	4	4
	GrArCB				PArCB			
1969	2	13*	14	0	7	26*	32	0
1971	3	23*	27	3	8	20	22	7
1973	6	4	4	0	9	13	14	0
1975	14	8	9	0	9	16*	19	0
1977	4	28	39	1	3	14*	24	4†
1979	20	27	36	8	13	9	21	1†
	BPref				AidCB			
1969	2.1	0.7*	0.2	3.8†	9	9	9	0
1971	1.9	0.6*	0.1	3.0†	12	25	30	0
1973	1.3	0.1*	-0.4	2.4†	26	26	28	0
1975	1.0	0.6	0.2	1.6†	27	54	6	124
1977	0.7	0.5	-0.3	1.2†	13	14	5	117
1979	1.3	1.1	0.3	1.9†	23	14	1	25

* Indicates a significant difference at the 0.05 level or beyond for the difference of means test between R and NR.

† Indicates a significant difference at the 0.05 level or beyond for the difference of means test between NRNR and NRR.

chapter, these two groups of countries differ markedly in their power capabilities. It is entirely likely, therefore, that they will also differ in terms of their associations with communism and Table 5.2 shows that such is indeed the case.[11] The effect of removing arms transfer recipients from the aid non-recipient group is to exaggerate the differences isolated in Table 5.1, particularly in the areas of bloc preference and communist bloc arms receipts. Thus, in all six test years, Third World countries receiving neither US aid nor arms transfers are noteworthy for their very low aggregate bloc preference scores, which even take on a negative value on two occasions and thereby indicate a diplomatic bias towards the East. In addition, these countries have substantially higher communist bloc arms share scores and usually get higher gross volumes of communist bloc arms transfers. In short, there is a systematic difference within the US aid non-recipient population between those Third World countries receiving and not receiving US arms. This latter group is excluded from both transfer programmes precisely because of its closer alignment in diplomatic and security terms with the East.[12]

This important conclusion having been drawn, we now turn to the presentation of the results of our multiple regression analyses, which constitutes the final stage of the analysis of the distribution of gross US aid. The results themselves are presented in Table 5.3 and they confirm the view that competition with communism generally exercises a strong structuring influence on the distribution of gross aid. It is equally the case, however, that the identity of the principal structuring variables changes over time in such a manner as to suggest three major, somewhat overlapping, phases in the US aid programme between 1950 and 1979.

The first phase lasts until the end of the 1950s and in it the single most important predictor of gross US aid is forward defence area status, which indicates the clear preference given to those countries deemed important to the success of physically containing the USSR. But the relatively few countries accorded this status are not the only ones to receive aid. Indeed, three secondary influences of approximately equal importance also characterise this first phase of the aid programme. They are the presence of domestic communist activity and relatively extensive contacts with the USSR through trading or diplomatic links. It is highly pertinent, however, that these secondary characteristics are not clearly important in bivariate terms, but achieve significance only after other variables, and especially forward defence area status, have been controlled. In other words, their independent effects become significant primarily because these characteristics are relatively muted in the forward defence area countries. Thus there seem, initially at least, to be two prongs to the US strategy of containment. On the one hand, the countries that it has selected as forward defence areas function effectively as exclusively US zones of influence and, on the other, other countries are supported with aid to countervail the influence in them of both domestic and Soviet communism. That some importance, albeit relatively marginal, is also attached to direct ties with the United States itself is indicated by the consistent appearance of the US trade share variable.

The second phase in the gross US aid programme runs through most of the 1960s and is characterised by an adjustment of priorities rather than by a radical

Table 5.3: Standardised coefficients for the regressions of gross aid on the competition with communism variables, 1951-79*

1951:	(0.46)	ForDef	0.66		1967:	(0.54)	AidCB	0.34
	(0.36)	CommP	0.63			(0.27)	LWV	0.23
	(−0.04)	PTrCB	−0.48			(0.36)	ForDef	0.17
	(−0.22)	DRInUR	0.42			(0.48)	GrArCB	0.28
	(0.15)	BPref	0.36			(0.28)	PTrUS	0.34
	(−0.03)	GrTrUR	0.24			(0.16)	CNPDRCB	0.26
	(−0.08)	PTrUS	0.23				$R^2 = 58$	
		$R^2 = 67$						
					1969:	(0.60)	GrTrUR	0.70
1953:	(0.70)	ForDef	0.45			(0.35)	LWV	0.36
	(0.56)	CNGrTrCB	0.80			(0.17)	PTrUS	0.35
	(0.45)	LWV	0.39			(0.19)	CNPDRCB	0.32
	(−0.05)	CNGrArUS	−0.47			(−0.04)	AidCB	−0.17
	(−0.08)	PTrUS	0.29			(0.13)	PArCB	−0.13
		$R^2 = 94$					$R^2 = 66$	
1955:	(0.63)	CNPDRDM	0.97		1971:	(0.52)	GrArCB	0.40
	(−0.10)	PTrUS	0.69			(0.50)	LWV	0.22
	(0.63)	ForDef	0.31			(0.25)	PTrUS	0.37
	(−0.29)	CNGrTrUS	−0.23			(0.24)	CNPDRCB	0.47
		$R^2 = 82$				(−0.09)	CNPArCB	−0.33
						(0.21)	CNPTrCB	0.21
1957:	(0.47)	ForDef	0.52				$R^2 = 61$	
	(0.17)	CommP	0.21					
	(0.28)	GrTrUR	0.38		1973:	(0.45)	LWV	0.27
	(−0.07)	PTrCB	−0.32			(0.27)	CNPTrCB	0.35
		$R^2 = 40$				(0.27)	PTrUS	0.47
						(0.14)	CNPDRCB	0.33
1959:	(0.48)	ForDef	0.45			(0.19)	CNPDRDM	0.26
	(0.38)	DRInCB	0.35				$R^2 = 45$	
		$R^2 = 35$						
					1975:	(0.53)	GrTrUR	0.32
1961:	(0.42)	GrArUR	0.68			(0.43)	CNPTrCB	0.47
	(−0.01)	PArCB	−0.56			(−0.01)	CNPDRCB	−0.16
	(0.32)	ForDef	0.33			(0.39)	PTrCB	0.24
	(0.40)	GrTrUR	0.27			(0.17)	CNPTrUS	0.26
		$R^2 = 51$				(0.28)	CNGrArCB	0.18
							$R^2 = 57$	
1963:	(0.63)	GrTrCB	0.90					
	(0.33)	ForDef	0.28		1977:	(0.43)	GrTrUR	0.48
	(0.47)	GrTrUS	0.08			(0.33)	CNPTrCB	0.55
	(0.19)	GrArCB	−0.29			(−0.03)	CNPDRCB	−0.33
	(0.08)	PTrCB	−0.18			(0.08)	GrArCB	−0.27
	(0.20)	PTrUS	0.16			(0.28)	PTrCB	0.16
		$R^2 = 66$					$R^2 = 45$	
1965:	(0.69)	GrTrUR	1.08		1979:	(0.43)	GrTrCB	0.53
	(−0.02)	PTrCB	−0.69			(0.42)	CNPTrCB	0.49
	(0.16)	CNPTrCB	0.47			(0.00)	CNPDRCB	−0.29
	(0.05)	GrArUR	−0.30			(0.05)	AidCB	−0.26
	(0.26)	PTrUS	0.29				$R^2 = 42$	
		$R^2 = 91$						

* The figures in parentheses represent the zero-order correlation coefficients.

break with the past. This adjustment takes the form of an emphasis on responding directly to communist bloc associations so that one particular such association, usually gross trade, becomes the most powerful predictor of the distribution
of gross US aid and is positive in its impact. When these association variables are
in their percentaged form, by contrast, their impact is negative, but not always
significant.[13] In this phase also, forward defence area status recedes to become
a secondary influence and effectively ceases to have any meaningful effect after
1963. US trade share, on the other hand, follows a different path and becomes
a slightly more important positive predictor than it was in the 1950s, a change
which points to the United States developing an interest in supporting its own
associations as well as countervailing communist bloc ones. In short, this second
phase sees US aid flow in greater volume to Third World countries that are
closely tied to the USSR, usually through trade, but whose communist trade or
arms share is simultaneously lower than their US trade share.

A further adjustment characterises the US aid programme in its transition to
a third phase at the end of the 1960s. A gross communist bloc association,
usually in the form of trade, continues to be a principal influence on the distribution of US aid, but it is now more or less equalled in predictive importance by
communist trading activity in and, to a lesser extent, diplomatic associations
with, aid recipients' neighbouring countries. This 'new' importance of neighbours' communist associations is the principal difference between the second
and third phases of the aid programme. There are, however, some relatively
minor differences as well. Not only does US trade share disappear as a significant
estimator after 1973, but also communist bloc trade share simultaneously
becomes a positive predictor of gross aid despite having been a negative one
earlier.

Having completed the presentation of our gross aid findings, we now examine
the bivariate relations of each of the sets of competition with communism
variables to per capita aid. Our first observation is that, unlike with gross aid,
there is no evidence of a positive and linear relationship between Soviet or
communist bloc diplomatic ties and per capita aid. Indeed, if anything, Soviet
diplomatic ties actually decline in the high per capita recipient category. The
pro-West bloc preference indicator, by contrast, follows the same pattern for
aid in both its forms. That is, it shows little systematic variation across the
aid recipient categories in the 1950s, but the relationship becomes strong and
positive in the 1960s and continues in this form, albeit with a reduced slope
to the end of the 1970s.[14] As with gross aid, the contiguous neighbours' diplomatic associations variables show no variation across the levels of per capita
aid receipt.

With respect to the set of trade variables, gross US trade is inversely related
to per capita aid throughout the 1950s. This relationship disappears in the
1960s, but then reasserts itself in the 1970s. In this regard, the relationship
is the mirror image of its counterpart between US gross aid and gross trade.

Per capita aid's relationship to US trade share, on the other hand, follows much the same pattern as that of gross aid. In other words, the two variables are not related in the 1950s, but a relationship emerges in the early 1960s only to disappear again from the mid-1970s. Interestingly, however, the US gross trade pattern is the same as its counterpart for all OECD countries combined, whereas the US trade share pattern differs from its OECD counterpart in that the latter is never systematically related to per capita aid. The difference would seem to indicate that US trade share is, in fact, an independent and meaningful determinant of per capita aid allocations. As for Soviet or communist bloc gross trade, neither is systematically related to per capita aid receipts until the 1970s when both come generally to decline as per capita aid levels themselves decline, which contrasts with the 1960s when the highest per capita aid recipients have a slight tendency to relatively low gross trade values. Soviet or communist bloc trade share, by contrast, never shows any systematic relationship with per capita aid. Nor do the neighbours' gross or percentage trade variables.

But very clear bivariate relations do appear in the security variables. Until the mid-1970s, the vast bulk of Soviet arms sales flows to non-recipients of US aid and it is only after this time that the high per capita aid category is substantially penetrated to give rise to a 'U'-shaped distribution.[15] The Soviet share of Third World arms purchases follows broadly this same developmental pattern, with the exception that it is more negatively and linearly related to per capita US aid throughout the 1970s. Forward defence areas are concentrated, albeit less densely than was the case with gross aid, in the medium and high recipient categories, but this relationship deteriorates to the point of disappearance in the 1960s. As with gross aid, neighbours' Soviet or communist bloc arms receipts are not related, at least in bivariate terms, to per capita aid.

This same conclusion of no bivariate relationship holds with regard to both the variables in the fourth set, the presence of left-wing violence or of an active and legal communist party.

We now progress to our multiple regression analyses, which display some considerable affinity with those for gross aid in that both point to a fusion of continuity and change in emphasis over time. Only in 1961, an apparent time of transition, do we not get a highly significant regression equation. Prior to this time, there are a number of more or less equally important influences on the distribution of per capita aid. The first of these is forward defence area status, but it disappears in 1957 and never reappears, thereby emphasising that it structures per capita aid receipts far less effectively than it does gross aid receipts. A more persistent, and negative, estimator of per capita aid is direct association with the USSR or the communist bloc in the form of either diplomatic or trading links. Equally persistent is the positive influence of neighbours displaying higher levels of association with the communist bloc, initially in the realm of trade and, subsequently, in that of arms supplies.[16] Finally, albeit less

COMPETITION WITH COMMUNISM

Table 5.4: Standardised coefficients for the regressions of per capita aid on the competition with communism variables, 1951-79*

1951:	(0.58)	ForDef	0.69	1967:	(0.39)	PTrUS	0.53
	(-0.07)	PTrCB	-0.32		(-0.06)	GrTrUS	-0.32
		$R^2 = 43$			(0.33)	LWV	0.22
					(0.27)	CNPArUS	0.18
1953:	(0.41)	CommP	0.26		(-0.09)	CNPDRCB	0.17
	(0.30)	DRInCB	0.92			$R^2 = 33$	
	(-0.10)	DRInUR	-0.79				
	(-0.16)	CNGrTrUS	-0.31	1969:	(0.31)	LWV	0.31
	(-0.04)	GrTrCB	-0.47		(-0.26)	DRInUR	-0.21
	(0.16)	CNPDRCB	0.38		(0.23)	CommP	0.39
		$R^2 = 60$			(-0.08)	GrTrUS	-0.38
					(0.27)	PTrUS	0.47
1955:	(0.45)	LWV	0.34		(0.01)	CNPDRCB	0.31
	(-0.36)	CNPTrUS	-0.17			$R^2 = 41$	
	(-0.16)	GrTrCB	-0.24				
	(0.41)	ForDef	0.32	1971:	(0.41)	CNPArUS	0.22
	(0.21)	CommP	0.28		(0.38)	PTrUS	0.65
		$R^2 = 44$			(0.13)	CNPDRCB	0.35
					(0.24)	CNGrArCB	0.24
1957:	(0.40)	CNGrArCB	0.48		(-0.02)	GrTrUS	-0.26
	(0.31)	ForDef	0.53		(0.33)	CNGrArUS	0.21
	(-0.22)	DRInUR	-0.58			$R^2 = 52$	
	(-0.15)	BPref	-0.32				
	(-0.11)	CNPArUS	-0.23	1973:	(0.40)	CNGrArCB	0.61
		$R^2 = 57$			(0.35)	CNGrArUS	0.39
					(-0.22)	DRInCB	-0.33
1959:	(0.53)	CNPArCB	0.47		(-0.12)	PArCB	-0.39
	(-0.20)	DRInUR	-0.46		(-0.08)	GrArUR	0.20
	(-0.27)	CNPTrUS	-0.29			$R^2 = 49$	
		$R^2 = 42$					
				1975:	(0.54)	CNGrArCB	0.44
1961:	(0.26)	CNPArCB	0.26		(0.41)	CNPTrCB	0.47
	(-0.24)	DRInUR	-0.24		(-0.11)	CNPDRCB	-0.35
		$R^2 = 13$			(-0.13)	DRInCB	-0.21
						$R^2 = 51$	
1963:	(0.28)	PTrUS	0.46				
	(0.16)	CNGrArCB	0.19	1977:	(0.52)	CNPTrCB	0.66
	(-0.04)	GrTrUS	-0.29		(-0.03)	CNPDRCB	-0.47
	(0.06)	DRInCB	0.17		(-0.10)	DRInCB	-0.28
		$R^2 = 42$			(0.37)	CommP	0.18
					(-0.09)	CNPTrUS	-0.22
1965:	(0.42)	PTrUS	0.52			$R^2 = 47$	
	(0.31)	LWV	0.30				
	(-0.01)	CNPArUS	-0.15	1979:	(0.48)	CNPTrCB	0.44
	(-0.30)	CNPDRDM	-0.18		(-0.22)	DRInUR	-0.20
	(0.00)	GrTrUS	-0.19		(0.41)	CNGrArUS	0.29
		$R^2 = 37$			(0.31)	BPref	0.17
					(0.28)	CommP	0.22
					(-0.04)	GrArCB	-0.20
						$R^2 = 50$	

* The figures in parentheses represent the zero-order correlation coefficients.

consistently, there is some evidence of US per capita aid preference for recipients confronting domestic communist activity.

In short, then, the phase of the per capita aid programme stretching to the turn of the 1960s sees the United States rewarding those Third World countries that have relatively muted direct communist bloc associations, but whose contiguous neighbours have relatively extensive such associations. An additional, if less consistent, preference is accorded to forward defence areas and recipients confronting domestic communist activity.

The second phase of the programme runs through to the end of the 1960s and in it the pattern of rewarding countries whose neighbours have substantial ties with the communist bloc countries continues. More specifically, the United States responds primarily to neighbours' communist diplomatic ties and only secondarily to their source of arms supply. Also continued is the US support for Third World countries confronted with domestic communist activity, while its proclivity to punish direct associations with the communist bloc is less marked. Instead, this proclivity is overtaken by a strong propensity to support US trade share. Interestingly, the positive impact of US trade share is inevitably accompanied by a strong negative impact for gross trade.[17] This indicates that the US goal is domination rather than building up trade relations for their own sake.

In the second phase then, the US per capita aid distribution favours countries over which it enjoys a substantial degree of domination through trade and whose neighbours have relatively extensive associations with the communist bloc. Some additional favour is shown to regimes confronting domestic left-wing violence.

The third phase of the per capita aid programme, i.e. the 1970s, sees the continuation of a strong preference for countries whose neighbours display communist bloc associations, initially in the realm of arms supplies and, subsequently, in that of trade. It also sees the disappearance of support for US domination through trade and its replacement by the penalisation of direct associations with the communist bloc through diplomatic or arms receipt ties. But the tendency to provide support, albeit less consistently, for countries facing domestic communist activity persists. In short, the influences are similar to those operating in the programme's first phase in the 1950s.

Military assistance

With regard to the set of diplomatic variables, no relationship appears between gross military assistance and diplomatic ties with the USSR or the communist bloc. The same general conclusion holds true for the bloc preference variable as well, although it is the case that recipients, as an undifferentiated group, are clearly more pro-West on this variable, and especially from the 1960s onwards. Equally, the percentage of contiguous neighbours' diplomatic ties that are with the communist bloc is unrelated to military assistance, although it is generally the case that high recipients also have neighbours with the largest number of communist bloc diplomatic associations.

In the trade variables, no systematic relationship emerges until the early 1960s, from which time non-recipients of military assistance come to show much lower levels of gross US trade relative to recipients. As with bloc preference, however, there is little variation in US trade across the three recipient categories. It might be argued that this finding is simply a reflection of the fact that, as was found in the previous chapter, non-recipients of military assistance have lower levels of aggregate trade. But the deficiency of this argument is that, from the early 1960s, the United States enjoys a higher percentage trade share among recipients of military assistance, which indicates that the gross US pattern is not a simple reflection of aggregate trade behaviour. On the other hand, trade share, like gross trade, hardly varies across the three recipient categories. There are some signs that Soviet and communist bloc trade increase slightly within the recipient population until the end of the 1960s, although trade levels in the non-recipient population are higher than a linear projection would lead us to expect. Soviet and communist bloc trade share, in contrast, show little systematic covariation with levels of military assistance.

The security variables play a far more powerful role in structuring the distribution of military assistance. For a start, in only four of the ten test years are Soviet and communist bloc arms transfers not confined to the zero and small assistance categories.[18] Soviet and communist bloc percentage arms sales are, of course, similarly restricted. It is noticeable, however, that while non-recipients receive more arms in terms of dollar value than small recipients, the disparity between the two groups is more pronounced in the case of percentage share. Soviet arms sales do not penetrate the medium and high US military assistance categories, but they are to be found in relatively large absolute and percentage quantities in the neighbours of the countries falling into these two categories. Indeed, generally speaking, gross, but not percentage, arms transfers increase across the three recipient categories.

As for domestic communist activity, it is only for a short time in the first half of the 1960s that the United States includes countries with legal and active communist parties in the medium and high categories of military assistance recipients. On the other hand, it shows a clear propensity to transfer such assistance to countries confronting left-wing violence from the start of the 1960s.

The next stage of our analysis is concerned to differentiate recipients and non-recipients of military assistance in terms of the range of competition with communism variables. The results of the discriminant analyses are summarised in Table 5.5 and they indicate that the analyses have been highly successful in that they achieve a high level of correct classification overall as well as, and more importantly, within the two groups individually.[19] The two principal discriminators in the 1950s are forward defence area status and a pro-West diplomatic bloc preference, but as we move into the 1960s, the bloc preference variable becomes both the more important of the two and the single most

Table 5.5 Results for the discriminant analysis of Recipients (R) and non-recipients (NR) of military assistance by selected competition with communism variables, 1953–75*

	Actual group	Predicted group			Standardised discriminators	
		NR	R	(N)		
1953:	NR	17 (94)	1 (6)	18	ForDef	1.16
	R	3 (30)	7 (70)	10	BPref	0.76
					PTrUS	0.51
1955:	NR	13 (87)	2 (13)	15	ForDef	0.96
	R	4 (29)	10 (71)	14	BPref	0.67
					CommP	−0.55
1957:	NR	14 (93)	1 (7)	15	BPref	1.07
	R	1 (6)	15 (94)	16	CommP	−0.70
					PArCB	−0.64
					ForDef	0.62
					GrTrUS	−0.36
1959:	NR	19 (91)	2 (10)	21	ForDef	1.06
	R	6 (32)	13 (68)	19	BPref	0.68
1961:	NR	23 (89)	3 (12)	26	BPref	1.13
	R	9 (29)	22 (71)	31	ForDef	0.81
					GrTrUS	−0.38
					PTrUS	−0.45
1963:	NR	29 (85)	5 (15)	34	BPref	0.97
	R	8 (21)	31 (79)	39	PTrCB	0.54
					PTrUS	0.50
					ForDef	0.34
					LWV	0.31
1965:	NR	36 (84)	7 (17)	43	BPref	0.65
	R	11 (31)	24 (69)	35	ForDef	0.56
					CommP	0.36
					PTrUS	0.34
					LWV	0.33
1967:	NR	40 (91)	4 (9)	44	BPref	0.90
	R	13 (37)	22 (63)	35	LWV	0.52
					GrTrUS	0.48
					ForDef	0.26
					PTrCB	0.24
1969:	NR	44 (86)	7 (14)	51	BPref	1.07
	R	11 (33)	22 (67)	33	LWV	0.51
					ForDef	0.39
					GrTrCB	0.36
1971:	NR	51 (85)	9 (15)	60	BPref	0.86
	R	14 (38)	23 (62)	37	LWV	0.71

Table 5.5 (*Cont.*)

	Actual group	Predicted group			Standardised discriminators	
		NR	R	(N)		
1973:	NR	54 (84)	10 (16)	64	LWV	0.51
	R	16 (50)	16 (50)	32	BPref	0.50
					PTrUS	0.53
					CommP	0.25
1975:	NR	66 (96)	3 (4)	69	BPref	0.57
	R	26 (93)	2 (7)	28	LWV	0.56
					PTrUS	0.56
					GrTrCB	0.35

* The figures in parentheses represent the row percentages.

important predictor of the receipt of military assistance. Next in importance is domestic left-wing violence, which appears in 1963 and persists as a highly significant predictor right through to the end of the military assistance programme. Another major influence is US trade share. With the exception of an interlude at the close of the 1950s, it is, in bivariate terms, always significantly higher among recipients and emerges as a significant discriminator in the multivariate analysis on a number of occasions. Finally, the presence of a communist party is negatively related to the receipt of military assistance on two occasions in the 1950s and positively related to it in one year of each of the 1960s and 1970s. Its early negative influence is a reflection of the simple difference between recipients and non-recipients. But this difference disappears in later years and it assumes a positive influence only after other variables have been controlled. The one variable of note that is hidden in the multivariate analyses, largely because of its collinearity with the other discriminators, is communist bloc arms sales. Although not figuring in Table 5.5, it will be recalled that the bivariate results consistently indicated that military assistance recipients purchase fewer arms from the USSR and communist bloc.[20]

In short, the United States selects its military assistance recipients on the basis of extremely consistent criteria. They display a clear preference for the West in diplomatic terms, have been designated as forward defence areas, confront domestic left-wing violence and generally show a preference for the United States in terms of trade share.[21]

The multiple regression analyses within the recipient population yield equally decisive, if longitudinally less consistent, results. That is, as with the aid programme, the military assistance programme passes through a number of clearly interlinked and overlapping phases, the first of which lasts until 1957 and appears to be characterised by the US establishment of security spheres of influence. Forward defence area status clearly differentiates recipients from non-recipients of military assistance and, although enjoying the significant simple

Table 5.6: Standardised coefficients for the regressions of gross military assistance on competition with communism variables, 1953-75*

1953:	(0.73)	CNPDRDM	1.13		(0.64)	CNGrArUS	0.43
	(0.08)	PTrCB	−0.63		(0.14)	CNPArUS	−0.27
		$R^2 = 78$			(0.06)	PTrCB	−0.27
1955:	(0.87)	CNGrArUS	1.02		(0.22)	CNPTrCB	−0.27
	(0.06)	DRInUR	−0.35		(−0.27)	CNPTrUS	−0.21
		$R^2 = 87$				$R^2 = 72$	
1955:	(Without outlier)			1969:	(0.51)	ForDef	0.17
	(0.87)	CNGrArUS	0.88		(0.36)	LWV	0.40
	(−0.23)	CNGrTrUS	−0.27		(0.47)	CNPDRCB	0.71
	(0.05)	CNPTrCB	−0.35		(0.04)	PTrUS	0.42
	(0.43)	CNPDRCB	0.27		(−0.16)	DRInUR	−0.22
		$R^2 = 94$				$R^2 = 63$	
1957:	(0.58)	ForDef	0.81	1969:	(Without outlier)		
	(−0.08)	CNPTrCB	−0.67		(0.73)	CNTArUS	0.76
	(0.17)	CNGrArCB	0.58		(0.67)	ForDef	0.14
	(0.45)	CNPArUS	0.40		(−0.03)	DRInUR	−0.45
	(010)	PTrCB	−0.39		(0.35)	CNPDRCB	0.27
		$R^2 = 77$			(0.17)	CNPTrCB	0.21
1959:	(0.57)	ForDef	0.53			$R^2 = 80$	
	(0.35)	CNGrTrCB	0.27	1971:	(0.53)	CNPDRCB	0.75
		$R^2 = 40$			(0.22)	PTrUS	0.56
1961:	(0.66)	ForDef	0.41		(0.37)	CNPArUS	0.30
	(0.56)	CNPTrCB	0.59			$R^2 = 64$	
	(−0.11)	DRInUR	−0.61	1971	(Without outlier)		
	(0.35)	CNGrTrCB	0.38		(0.44)	CNGrArUS	0.55
		$R^2 = 81$			(0.36)	CNPDRCB	0.57
1963:	(0.79)	ForDef	0.66		(−0.01)	PTrUS	0.51
	(−0.29)	CNPDRDM	−0.30		(0.20)	CNPDRDM	0.37
	(0.14)	DRInCB	0.23		(0.17)	CNGrTrCB	0.36
	(0.33)	LWV	0.22		(−0.04)	DRInUR	−0.37
		$R^2 = 73$				$R^2 = 61$	
1965:	(0.67)	ForDef	0.56	1973:	(0.50)	LWV	0.86
	(0.43)	LWV	0.24		(0.05)	CNGrArUS	−0.50
	(0.00)	CNGrTrCB	−0.32			$R^2 = 44$	
	(0.46)	CNPTrCB	0.26	1973:	(Without outlier)		
		$R^2 = 61$			(0.83)	CNGrArUS	1.18
1967:	(0.65)	ForDef	0.23		(−0.15)	BPref	0.57
	(0.29)	LWV	0.29			$R^2 = 95$	
	(0.46)	CNPDRCB	0.55	1975:	(0.60)	LWV	0.34
	(0.32)	CNPArUS	0.32		(0.39)	CNGrArUS	0.30
	(0.07)	PTrUS	0.33		(0.56)	CNPDRDM	0.33
	(0.44)	CNPTrCB	0.18			$R^2 = 51$	
		$R^2 = 71$		1975:	(Without outlier)		
1967:	(Without outlier)				(0.85)	CNGrArUS	0.85
	(0.74)	ForDef	0.67			$R^2 = 72$	

* The figures in parentheses represent the zero-order correlation coefficients.

correlations of 0.55 in 1953 and 0.46 in 1955 is not sufficient to allow the variable to figure in the multiple regression equations for these years. Table 5.6 suggests that this security variable also generally influences the distribution of military assistance within the recipient population. But more important is that such assistance flows in greater volume to countries whose neighbours receive relatively large gross arms transfers from the United States. Its volume is negatively related, by contrast, to contiguous neighbours' trade with the United States, which indicates that the latter is expressly interested in promoting security, rather than trading, spheres of influence. That gross military assistance can also be seen to decline with communist bloc trade share only emphasises US efforts to create exclusive security spheres and this goal is the hallmark of the first phase of the military assistance programme.

The second phase, which runs through to 1965, is marked by a more direct concern to compete directly with communism after it has established itself. If anything, forward defence area status becomes a more important predictor of the distribution of military assistance, but neighbours' US arms transfers are displaced by the positive influence of neighbours' communist bloc arms purchases and, more emphatically, of their communist bloc trade. There is also some evidence of a positive preference for countries confronting domestic left-wing violence.

The third phase represents in many respects a fusion of the distributional criteria employed in the first two. Running from 1965 to 1975, it sees the disappearance of forward defence area status by the end of the 1960s and a dominant emphasis on support for countries that, while themselves displaying a distinct pro-West bias, are surrounded by neighbours receiving relatively extensive US arms transfers. This characteristic is very reminiscent of the first phase of the programme and develops into its sole preoccupation in the programme's final years. Earlier, military assistance also flows to countries whose neighbours display relatively pronounced trading and diplomatic associations with the communist bloc. Finally, there is some evidence that for the first time the United States penalises recipients that have direct trading or diplomatic ties with the communist bloc.[22]

The bivariate analysis of the distribution of per capita military assistance provides no evidence of systematic covariation in the set of diplomatic variables. The only exception is the bloc preference indicator, according to which, especially from the late 1950s, non-recipients of military assistance show themselves to be distinctly less pro-West than do recipients as a whole.

Gross US trade initially shows little variation across the three categories of recipient until a weak negative relationship forms from the early 1960s onwards. At the same time, recipients become more distinctive on this variable vis-à-vis the non-recipient group through their having much higher trading levels. This same conclusion holds for US trade share. As for both recipients' own trade with the communist bloc and their neighbours' trade with it, there is not even significant variation between recipients and non-recipients, let alone across the three categories of recipient.

With regard to the security variables, some per capita military assistance relationships are even stronger than they are in the case of gross assistance. Thus, the communist bloc, through its arms sales programme, scarcely penetrates the medium per capita category and never penetrates the high one.[23] Equally, per capita assistance generally increases with neighbours' communist bloc arms sales, the most preferred per capita recipients generally scoring higher on this variable than their gross assistance counterparts. It is also the case, however, that per capita military assistance receipts increase with US arms sales to neighbouring countries.

The ANOVA profiles for the domestic communist activity variables are essentially the same as they were for gross military assistance, i.e. there is by and large no relationship in the case of the communist party variable and a positive one from the beginning of the 1960s onwards in that of domestic left-wing violence.

The per capita military assistance multiple regression analyses produce a series of highly significant equations that are characterised by a greater consistency over time, a consistency that would seem to be a function of the fact that this programme employs simpler distributive criteria than its gross counterpart. Table 5.7 shows these criteria to be principally forward defence area status and left-wing domestic violence. Initially, it is the former that enjoys the greater predictive power, but it comes to be equalled by the latter at the start of the 1960s and is overtaken by it subsequently. Compared to these two variables, neighbours' associations with the United States or the communist bloc have a very minor impact, but, of these, the receipt of US arms is the more important, a fact that highlights the US promotion of security spheres of influence through its military assistance transfers. Over the long term, this emphasis is more consistent than it is for gross military assistance, but it becomes equally pronounced for the transfer in both its forms in the 1970s.

In this context, it is pertinent to observe that per capita military assistance does not flow to countries whose neighbours trade with the United States. Even the simple correlations between neighbours' US trade and per capita military assistance are either insignificant or negative. That this variable does not appear in Table 5.7 despite the controlling procedure of multivariate analysis only strengthens the earlier conclusion that the United States does not regard trade as a tool for cultivating spheres of influence. Neighbours' communist bloc trade does influence, albeit negatively, the distribution of per capita military assistance, however. What is more, its influence emerges much more strongly after the effects of the other variables have been controlled than it does in the simple correlations. This difference can only be taken to indicate that, other things being equal, the United States distributes military assistance with a view to promoting its exclusivity in territories bordering its favoured recipients.

Table 5.7: Standardised coefficients for the regressions of per capita military assistance on competition with communism variables, 1953–75*

1953:	(0.62)	CNPDRCB	1.02	1965:	(0.65)	LWV	0.62
	(0.04)	BPref	0.91		(0.61)	ForDef	1.05
	(−0.32)	GrTrUS	−0.41		(0.14)	CNGrArUS	−0.60
		$R^2 = 81$			(0.30)	CNPTrCB	−0.47
					(0.40)	CNGrArCB	0.30
1955:	(−0.43)	CNPTrUS	−0.80			$R^2 = 84$	
	(−0.05)	DRInUR	−0.67				
	(0.37)	CNGrArUS	0.52	1967:	(0.57)	ForDef	0.22
	(−0.27)	CNGrTrCB	−0.46		(0.47)	LWV	0.50
		$R^2 = 84$			(0.41)	CNPArUS	0.46
					(0.32)	CNPDRCB	0.38
1957:	(0.51)	ForDef	0.86			$R^2 = 69$	
	(−0.18)	CNPTrCB	−0.82				
	(0.44)	CNPArUS	0.26	1969:	(0.53)	ForDef	0.33
	(−0.09)	DRInCB	−0.50		(0.49)	LWV	0.45
	(−0.07)	PTrUS	−0.39		(−0.16)	CNGrTrCB	−0.17
	(0.04)	CNGrArCB	0.29		(0.43)	CNPDRCB	0.36
		$R^2 = 81$			(0.09)	DRInUR	−0.23
						$R^2 = 62$	
1959:	(0.64)	CNGrArCB	1.22				
	(−0.13)	DRInUR	−0.92	1971:	(0.50)	CNPArUS	0.40
	(−0.08)	CNPDRDM	0.42		(0.48)	CNPDRCB	0.68
	(0.01)	CommP	0.34		(0.15)	PTrUS	0.58
		$R^2 = 89$			(−0.09)	BPref	−0.26
						$R^2 = 64$	
1961:	(0.60)	ForDef	0.58				
	(0.43)	LWV	0.29	1973:	(0.70)	LWV	0.63
	(−0.22)	DRInUR	−0.28		(−0.12)	DRInUR	−0.35
		$R^2 = 54$			(0.35)	CNPDRCB	0.32
						$R^2 = 60$	
1963:	(0.76)	ForDef	0.86				
	(0.56)	LWV	0.46	1975:	(0.70)	LWV	0.80
	(−0.04)	CNGrTrCB	−0.68		(−0.15)	CNPTrCB	−0.66
	(0.01)	CommP	0.23		(−0.23)	CNPTrUS	−0.39
	(0.00)	CNGrTrCB	0.36			$R^2 = 76$	
	(−0.27)	CNGrTrUS	0.20				
		$R^2 = 90$					

* The figures in parentheses represent the zero-order correlation coefficients.

Yet it is not always able to pursue this goal comprehensively. That the neighbours' communist bloc arms transfers variable also figures in Table 5.7 indicates that the United States is willing to ignore or, perhaps more accurately, postpone its aspirations to territorial exclusivity in order to provide military assistance to countries whose security it perceives to be threatened by communist expansion.[24]

Any summary of our findings about the distribution of per capita military assistance must be prefaced by a reiteration of the need to view them in conjunction with our earlier discriminant analysis results. Thus, within a minority population of selected recipients generally displaying a distinct pro-West bias, the United States distributes its military assistance in proportion to the communist threat facing Third World recipients. This threat stems principally from their strategic location as forward defence areas and, especially in later years, from the presence within them of left-wing violence. Secondary importance is attached to the promotion of exclusive US influence in countries whose neighbours already show a marked bias towards the United States although military assistance is also granted to countries whose neighbours fall within the communist bloc's sphere of influence, i.e. that receive communist bloc arms transfers. It is noticeable, however, that these last two considerations are accorded lower priority in the distribution of per capita military assistance than they are in the distribution of the transfer in its gross form.

Arms sales

The diplomatic variables show the number of Soviet and communist embassies to decline slightly over the small, medium and large categories of US arms sales recipients, but their number is clearly lowest in the non-recipient category. While sharing this marked discontinuity between recipients and non-recipients, the bloc preference indicator, on the other hand, generally increases across the levels of US arms sales receipt and the pro-West diplomatic bias of recipients becomes more marked. In contrast, there emerges no relationship between this transfer and the contiguous neighbours' diplomatic representation variables.

In the trade variables, gross US trade generally increases with volume of arms receipt, while its trade share tends to decline across the small, medium and high categories, albeit with a discontinuity in a non-recipient category that enjoys values on a par with those found in the high category. Soviet and communist bloc gross trade show a more complicated relationship in that both variables increase and decrease in different years across the three recipient categories. There is, however, a consistent and substantial gap between US arms non-recipients and recipients as a whole; the latter have much higher levels of gross trade with one or the other communist entity. Soviet and communist bloc trade share follow much the same pattern except for the non-recipient value on these variables being higher relative to the recipient category than it was in the case of gross trade. Contiguous neighbours' trade with the communist bloc increases systematically in both gross and percentage terms with US arms sales receipts.

With regard to the security variables, gross Soviet and communist bloc arms sales behave much as they did in the case of military assistance, i.e. they are concentrated in the zero and small transfer recipient categories.[25] The percentage share figures follow the same pattern. Contiguous neighbours' gross and percentage communist bloc arms receipts, on the other hand, increase very systematically with US arms transfers. In other words, Third World recipients of higher levels of US arms sales do not in general receive arms from the communist bloc, but their contiguous neighbours certainly do.

Finally, the variables profiling domestic communist activity do not stand in any systematic relationship to US arms sales, although there is some indication of a slight tendency for communist parties to be relatively more prevalent in the population of arms sales recipients.

The next stage of our investigation, the discriminant analyses, yields a very powerful and consistent set of results.[26] Recipients of US arms sales are found to be differentiated from non-recipients by four variables that are roughly equally powerful in their discriminatory power. Recipients have higher levels of trade with both the United States and the communist bloc, have higher levels of diplomatic bias towards the West and have lower levels of communist bloc arms receipts. Additionally, US trade share has a negative discriminatory influence

Table 5.8: Results for the discriminant analysis of recipients (R) and non-recipients (NR) of arms sales on selected competition with communism variables, 1971–9*

	Actual group	Predicted group			Standardised discriminators	
		NR	R	(N)		
1971:	NR	61 (95)	3 (5)	64	BPref	0.95
	R	6 (25)	18 (75)	24	GrTrUS	0.74
					PTrUS	−0.67
					GrTrCB	0.67
					GrArCB	−0.67
					PArCB	0.32
					LWV	0.28
1973:	NR	65 (94)	4 (6)	69	BPref	0.95
	R	11 (48)	12 (52)	23	GrArCB	−0.77
					PTrUS	−0.70
					GrTrUS	0.64
					GrTrCB	0.60
					AidCB	0.55
1975:	NR	60 (97)	2 (3)	62	GrTrUS	0.77
	R	17 (50)	17 (50)	34	BPref	0.67
					PTrUS	−0.45
					GrTrCB	0.40
1977:	NR	47 (89)	6 (11)	53	GrTrUS	0.96
	R	11 (31)	24 (69)	35	PTrUS	−0.42
					BPref	0.35
					GrArCB	−0.32
					GrTrCB	0.30
1979:	NR	49 (93)	4 (8)	53	GrTrCB	0.79
	R	15 (41)	22 (60)	37	PArCB	−0.56
					GrTrUS	0.42
					BPref	0.41

* The figures in parentheses represent the row percentages.

in four of the five test years despite not being related to the dependant variable in simple terms. It is the case, however, that it is significantly correlated with gross US trade (generally at a value of about 0.50) so that, given its zero relationship to the receipt of arms, it assumes a significant negative value once gross trade has been controlled.[27] Thus, in direct contrast to the selection of military assistance recipients, the United States emphasises absolute rather than relative trade share in its selection of arms sales recipients. Otherwise both groups of recipients display lower communist bloc arms supplies and a pronounced pro-West diplomatic bias.

The multiple regression equations are not as powerful as their discriminant analysis counterparts. Table 5.9 indicates that the 1971 analysis produces no significant regression equation and the 1979 one produces an equation that is significant at only the 0.10 level. The intervening three test years, however, provide highly significant results in that they show the distribution of arms sales within the recipient population to be dominated by two overriding considerations, both of which relate to communist bloc influence. Firstly, US arms sales increase with neighbours' level of trade with the communist bloc, which is itself significantly related to their communist bloc arms receipts. In this context, it might be noted that neighbours' trade with the United States is either unrelated or negatively related to US arms sales. Secondly, US arms recipients are penalised for direct associations, especially in the form of

Table 5.9: Standardised coefficients for the regressions of gross arms sales on competition with communism variables, 1971-9*

1971:	Not significant			1977:	(0.45)	CNPTrCB	−0.12
					(0.40)	CNGrTrCB	1.05
1973:	(0.46)	CNPTrCB	0.59		(−0.12)	CNGrArUS	−0.74
	(−0.14)	GrArUR	−0.36		(0.22)	CNGrTrUS	−0.49
	(0.09)	CNGrArUS	0.38			$R^2 = 57$	
	(−0.18)	PTrCB	−0.54				
	(0.28)	GrTrUR	0.43	1977:	(Without outlier)		
		$R^2 = 58$			(−0.49)	DRInUR	−0.46
					(−0.29)	CNPTrUS	−0.34
1975:	(0.53)	CNPTrCB	0.47		(0.18)	CommP	0.15
	(0.22)	CNGrTrUS	0.65		(0.37)	CNGrTrCB	0.40
	(0.46)	CNPArCB	0.26		(−0.06)	CNGrArUS	−0.31
	(−0.12)	DRInUR	−0.29			$R^2 = 53$	
	(−0.23)	CNPTrUS	−0.32				
		$R^2 = 63$		1979:	Not significant		
1975:	(Without outlier)						
	(0.67)	CNPTrCB	0.54				
	(−0.36)	DRInUR	−0.35				
	(0.45)	CNGrTrCB	0.34				
		$R^2 = 65$					

* The figures in parentheses represent the zero-order correlation coefficients.

diplomatic ties, with the communist bloc. But overall there are not the signs of the promotion of US spheres of influence that were found with military assistance.

As for per capita US arms sales, its individual bivariate relationships to the diplomatic variables are essentially the same as those for gross sales with the exception that the bloc preference indicator shows a little less variation across the three recipient categories.

In the trade variables, the per capita transfers show both a lesser tendency to increase with gross US trade and a slightly greater propensity to decrease with trade share than in the case of gross arms sales. Neither communist bloc gross nor percentage trade shows much variation with levels of per capita arms receipts, while contiguous neighbours' trade with the communist bloc is positively related to the per capita transfer, but not as steeply as it is to gross US arms sales.

The set of security variables affords essentially the same results for both gross and per capita US arms sales. That is, in both cases, Soviet and communist bloc arms transfers are concentrated in the zero and small recipient categories, whereas neighbours' communist bloc arms transfers increase systematically with per capita US arms sales receipts.[28]

The regression results for per capita arms sales are generally more powerful than for gross sales, although relatively weak results are once again produced in 1971 and 1979 and, what is more, the distributional criteria in these two years differ from those in the intervening three test years (see Table 5.10). In these two years, the primary predictor is neighbours' levels of US arms transfers, which is positive in its impact. But it is complemented in 1971 by a negative influence for neighbours' pro-West diplomatic bias. That this diplomatic variable

Table 5.10: Standardised coefficients for the regressions of per capita arms sales on competition with communism variables, 1971–9*

1971:	(−0.40)	CNPDRDM	−0.36		1977:	(0.56)	CNPTrCB	0.90
	(0.35)	CNGrArUS	0.30			(−0.08)	CNPDRCB	−0.82
		$R^2 = 26$				(−0.19)	PTrUS	−0.34
						(−0.35)	DRInCB	−0.21
1973:	(0.68)	CNPTrCB	0.95			(−0.06)	LWV	0.23
	(−0.09)	GrArUR	0.44				$R^2 = 70$	
	(−0.14)	CNPArUS	0.32					
	(0.32)	CommP	0.27		1979:	(0.58)	CNGrArUS	0.55
		$R^2 = 74$				(−0.28)	DRInCB	−0.30
						(0.17)	CommP	0.26
1975:	(0.72)	CNPTrCB	0.99				$R^2 = 45$	
	(0.08)	CNPDRCB	−0.61					
	(−0.32)	CNPDRDM	−0.38					
	(0.37)	CNGrTrCB	0.18					
		$R^2 = 86$						

* The figures in parentheses represent the zero-order correlation coefficients.

is strongly collinear with neighbours' communist bloc arms transfers, however, implies that a continued major concern for the United States is the promotion of security spheres. In the mid-1970s, US attention switches to a more immediate concern with the communist bloc associations of recipients' neighbours; the higher their neighbours' level of communist bloc trade in particular, the greater are recipients' per capita arms sales receipts. The negative influence of neighbours' communist bloc diplomatic ties is entirely a function of this variable's positive simple correlation with the neighbours' communist bloc trade variable.[29]

Findings: impact

Economic aid

Generally speaking, our findings, as summarised in Table 5.11, indicate that the receipt or otherwise of gross aid has little systematic impact on the pattern of change over time in the variables profiling competition with communism.

To take the set of trade variables first, the rate of growth of gross US trade, in fact, shows little variation across the different categories of recipients within any single four-year period. Indeed, if we aggregate the individual rank scores over all four-year periods, change in gross US trade shows an almost perfectly random variation across these categories. Moreover, this random variation is not the product of mutually cancelling patterns of systematic variation over shorter periods of time. Over the whole 1950–79 period, therefore, there is no evidence that the receipt of gross US aid has any effect on the rate of change of Third World countries' trade with the United States. This conclusion contrasts somewhat with the matching distribution analysis, which found US aid and trade to be unrelated in the 1950s, but positively correlated in the 1960s.

More or less the same results hold for US trade share, although perhaps the more interesting characteristic of this variable is not so much its absolute level but its general decline in value over time. From a figure of some 39 per cent in the early 1950s, the US share of Third World trade falls to about 15 per cent in the late 1970s. But this decline notwithstanding, the distribution of US aid has no systematic impact on the general rates of decay. Indeed, if anything, the receipt of aid is associated with more rapid decay of US trade share. For the five four-year periods in which our data allow us to analyse zero aid recipients, we find that this category manifests the highest rate of growth on the trade share variable (or the lowest rate of decay) in four of them. Thus, while this finding does not constitute sufficient grounds for arguing that US aid actually inhibits the growth, or even maintenance, of US trade share, the larger pattern of results does underscore that aid is assuredly not a means for promoting US trade growth or even for maintaining its trading status quo.

We do find significant covariation across the three recipient categories in the case of Soviet gross trade. But any conclusion that US aid is associated

Table 5.11: Summed ranks for average percentage change in the competition
with communism variables for the small, medium and large
recipient categories of gross and per capita economic aid
for the thirteen four-year periods, 1950-4, 1952-6 to
1974-8

	Gross aid			Per capita aid		
	Small	Medium	Large	Small	Medium	Large
GrTrUS	25.0	30.0	23.0	22.0	29.0	27.0
PTrUS	23.0	28.0	27.0	21.0	25.0	32.0
GrTrUR	29.0	30.0	19.0*†	22.0	27.0	29.0
GrTrCB	24.5	22.5	31.0	23.0	28.0	27.0
PTrUR	28.0	25.0	25.0	23.5	27.0	27.5
PTrCB	24.0	22.0	32.0	22.0	28.0	28.0
CNGrTrCB	23.5	27.5	27.0	24.0	26.0	28.0
CNPTrCB	24.5	24.5	29.0	25.5	28.0	24.5
CNGrTrUS	21.0	28.0	29.0	24.0	25.0	29.0
CNPTrUS	24.0	26.0	28.0	28.0	25.0	27.0
GrArUR	22.0	19.0	19.0‡	18.5	18.0	23.5‡
GrArCB	23.0	20.0	17.0‡	20.0	18.5	21.5‡
PArUR	21.0	21.5	18.5‡	18.0	20.5	21.5‡
PArCB	21.0	21.0	18.0‡	22.0	17.5	20.5‡
CNGrArUS	28.5	25.5	24.0	27.0	24.0	27.0
CNPArUS	29.0	23.0	26.0	26.0	26.0	26.0
CNGrArCB	22.0	21.0	17.0‡	21.0	16.0	23.0‡
CNPArCB	22.0	20.0	18.0‡	20.0	18.0	22.0‡
BPref	28.0	25.0	25.0	33.0	22.0	23.0
CNPDRCB	28.0	24.0	26.0	30.0	25.0	23.0
CNPDRDM	31.5	22.5	24.0	26.0	30.0	22.0

 * Indicates significance at the 0.05 level or beyond for the chi-square test across all three
categories.
 † Indicates significance at the 0.05 level or beyond for the cumulative binomial test on
the number of highest, or lowest, rank placings for the large category.
 ‡ Indicates summed ranks over only ten four-year periods.

with increased rate of growth of Soviet trade should be treated with some circumspection. For a start, the summed ranks for each recipient category are not
evenly and progressively distributed so that our results cannot indicate a progressive increase in Soviet trade growth across the three recipient categories. Nor
does even this limited relationship show up for communist bloc trade as a whole.
Furthermore, no significant relationships of any kind show up for either Soviet
or communist bloc trade share. The logical conclusion, therefore, is that the
USSR targets countries receiving relatively large amounts of US aid and seeks
to counter the influence afforded by this transfer through the promotion of its
own trading ties with them.

The final observation in the set of trade variables is that there is no indication that aid triggers differential growth rates in contiguous neighbours' trade
with either the United States, the communist bloc in general or the USSR

in particular. Thus, while in distributional terms, communist bloc trade with contiguous neighbours may generally increase with aid receipts, there is no indication that rates of growth on this variable do likewise.

The security variables are also notable for their 'non-findings'. Level of aid receipt shows itself to have no consistent impact on either Soviet or communist bloc arms sales, whether these be measured in gross or percentage terms. Were US aid to immunise recipients against communist penetration, however, we would expect these growth rates to be inversely affected by aid receipt levels so that our 'non-findings' can be taken to indicate some degree of success in communist penetration of the Third World. But, on the other hand, it is equally the case that communist growth rates are not disproportionate in countries that the United States considers to be more important (importance being measured by volume of aid transfer over several years) so that the United States could equally be argued to have experienced some success in staving off communist expansion.

Although still not strong, US aid receipts do have a slightly more systematic impact on the growth rates of neighbours' communist bloc arms transfers. This impact becomes most apparent when we compare aid non-recipients with recipients as a single group. The latter displays higher growth rates in four of the five time periods (starting in 1966–70) for which our data allow this comparison to be made. There is some consistent, if slight, evidence, therefore, that the communist bloc achieves higher arms sales growth rates in Third World countries sharing a border with US aid recipients.

Turning our attention to the diplomatic variables, we come across the same phenomenon as occurred in the case of US trade share, i.e. a steady and substantial decline in the mean value of the pro-West diplomatic preference variable over the period of our analysis. This decay, however, appears to have been unaffected by level of aid receipt. In other words, despite a very clear distributional switch to reward a pro-West diplomatic bias from 1960 onwards, there is no indication that volume of economic aid in fact reversed the erosion of this same bias. Nor do rates of change in neighbours' communist bloc diplomatic associations vary systematically across levels of aid receipt. None the less, it is the case that non-recipients have lower growth rates on this variable than recipients in four of the five test periods in this impact analysis. Interestingly therefore, the communist bloc has achieved higher arms sales and diplomatic representation growth rates in those Third World countries sharing a border with recipients of US economic aid.

Aggregated per capita aid is related to the trade variables in much the same way as is gross aid, the only real difference being its tendency not to vary systematically with Soviet trade. Overall, therefore, we can find no evidence that per capita aid has any systematic impact on the individual trade variables.

This uniform conclusion does not apply equally to the security variables, however. While there is no generalized effect across all three recipient categories, there is some evidence that high levels of per capita aid depress the growth rate of Soviet or communist bloc arms transfers. Firstly, high per capita aid recipients begin with no Soviet arms transfers in eight of the ten test periods and end up the same way in five of these same eight periods. Secondly, in the remaining five periods, the Soviet arms growth rates among high recipients do not differ significantly from those found among small and medium recipients. Finally, in four of the five test periods over which we are in a position to compare aid recipients and non-recipients, it is the non-recipient group that has higher Soviet arms transfer growth rates. On the other hand, it must be noted that non-recipients show no propensity to expand the Soviet or communist bloc's share of their total arms imports disproportionately quickly. As for the growth rate of neighbours' arms from the communist bloc, these are not systematically related to per capita aid receipts, although there is some weak evidence that they are higher among the neighbours of aid recipients.

Finally, we come to the diplomatic variables. Here there is more evidence of a systematic per capita aid impact in so far as the medium and high recipient categories show more pronounced pro-West (or less pronounced pro-East) bloc preference growth rates than the small category. Indeed, of the three recipient categories, it is the small one that displays the lowest growth rate in nine of the thirteen test periods. The non-recipient category, for its part, shows still weaker growth rates on this variable, but its score does not differ significantly from that for the recipient categories. There are also some signs that neighbours' diplomatic associations with the communist bloc grow more rapidly across the recipient categories, although the difference between them is not significant. Furthermore, in four of the five test periods in which we are able to compare non-recipients and recipients, it is non-recipients that have the lowest growth rates on this variable.

Military assistance

Since essentially exactly the same results transpire for the impact of both gross and per capita military assistance we shall not treat the two forms of the transfer separately.

Each of the gross and per capita military assistance variables do vary with the rate of growth of some of the trade variables, but it is difficult for the most part to discern a meaningful pattern in this variation. Thus, the rate of growth of US trade turns out to be unrelated to either form of military assistance. US trade share, on the other hand, has a significant chi-square value across the four receipt levels of both forms of the transfer, yet there emerges no intuitively meaningful pattern across the three recipient categories. The major source of significance in the chi-square value is a non-recipient category in which the growth rate of US trade share is consistently and significantly higher than among recipients. While we would hesitate to interpret these findings as indicating that military assistance purposively inhibits the growth of US trade share,

Table 5.12: Summed ranks for average percentage change in the competition with communism variables for the zero, small, medium and large recipient categories of gross and per capita military assistance for the eleven four-year periods 1952–6, 1954–8 to 1972–6*

	Gross military assistance				Per capita military assistance			
	Zero	Small	Medium	Large	Zero	Small	Medium	Large
GrTrUS	26.0	32.5	31.0	20.5	24.0	31.0	34.0	21.0
PTrUS	18.5	33.5	32.0	26.0†‡	19.0	26.0	35.0	30.0†‡
GrTrUR	22.0	35.0	23.0	30.0*†	24.0	32.0	26.0	28.0
GrTrCB	29.0	27.0	22.0	32.0	24.5	27.0	24.0	34.5
PTrUR	21.0	31.0	24.0	34.0*†	23.0	29.0	23.0	35.0
PTrCB	26.0	26.0	22.0	36.0	23.0	24.5	24.5	37.0†‡
CNGrTrCB	25.0	31.0	27.0	27.0	25.0	23.0	32.0	30.0
CNPTrCB	26.0	28.0	28.0	28.0	28.0	25.0	32.0	25.0
CNGrTrUS	21.0	31.0	29.0	29.0	25.0	32.5	21.0	31.5
CNPTrUS	27.5	29.5	25.5	27.5	25.5	26.5	30.5	27.5
CNGrArCB	26.0	23.5	21.5	19.0‡§	22.0	24.0	23.0	21.0§
CNPArCB	26.0	23.0	22.0	19.0‡§	28.5	19.5	19.0	23.0§
CNGrArUS	24.0	30.0	31.0	25.0	25.0	28.0	35.0	22.0
CNPArUS	25.0	29.0	30.0	26.0	25.0	27.0	32.0	26.0
CNPDRCB	28.0	22.0	30.0	30.0	26.0	25.0	27.0	32.0
CNPDRDM	32.0	24.0	25.0	29.0	34.0	19.5	29.5	27.0†
BPref	29.0	25.0	28.0	28.0	29.0	30.0	25.0	26.0

* Due to the number of zeros, the ranks for Soviet and communist bloc arms transfers are not included in this table but are dealt with in the text.

† Indicates a chi-square significance value greater than 0.05.

‡ Indicates significance at the 0.05 level or beyond for the cumulative binomial test on the number of highest, or lowest, rank placings either for the zero or large category.

§ Indicates summed ranks for only nine four-year periods.

we would certainly not hesitate to conclude that military assistance in either form fails to foster US trade domination.

Other significant variations that emerge are gross military assistance with absolute and percentage Soviet trade and per capita military assistance with communist bloc trade. The problem with the growth of absolute Soviet trade, however, is that our impact analysis points to the existence of no clear linear or, for that matter, comprehensible non-linear, relationship. With percentage Soviet trade, by contrast, although no strong, generalised effect (i.e. a linear relationship across all four categories of recipient) emerges, there is none the less some indication that high aggregated receipts of gross military assistance inhibit the growth of both Soviet and communist bloc trade share. Finally, the trade variables give no indication that the receipt of either form of military assistance is related to the growth rate of neighbouring countries' trade with the communist bloc.

The security variables, in contrast, reveal very clear and systematic relations between military assistance receipts and the growth rates of Soviet and communist bloc arms transfers. To be precise, the growth rates of these variables decline as assistance levels increase. Non-recipients begin all nine test periods by receiving communist bloc arms transfers and end six of them experiencing a positive rate of growth on this variable. The picture alters slightly in the small recipient category where two of the nine periods begin and end with no communist bloc arms receipts and four of the remaining seven periods witness positive rates of growth. The medium category sees five periods begin with no communist bloc arms transfers and four of them end up in the same way, while only two of the remaining four periods display positive growth rates. Finally, in the high military assistance recipient category, all nine periods begin with zero receipts and seven of them terminate likewise. Moreover, exactly the same pattern of diminishing growth rates across assistance levels is found for the Soviet and communist bloc percentage arms share variable.[30]

With regard to both gross and percentage communist bloc arms sales to recipients' contiguous neighbours, the growth rates of these variables do appear to increase somewhat across the gross military assistance recipient categories. While neither relationship is significant, the large recipient category is, at least in binomial terms, significantly different from the others, indicating that neighbours of this category of gross military assistance recipient display the highest rate of growth of communist bloc arms imports significantly more frequently than average. The same pattern prevails, although less strongly, in the case of per capita military assistance.

Moving on to the set of diplomatic variables, level of military assistance receipt has no impact on rates of growth of diplomatic bloc preference. This same general conclusion holds for neighbours' communist bloc diplomatic associations.[31]

Arms sales

As with military assistance, the findings for gross and per capita arms sales are virtually identical and are consequently presented together. It should be borne in mind, however, that these findings are best treated as tentative since they are based on only the three test periods running from 1970 to 1974.

The trade variables show arms sales to have no systematic impact on any variable, a conclusion that holds across all levels of recipient as well as for non-recipients as opposed to recipients as a whole.

In the set of security variables, the relationship between levels of US arms sales receipt and rate of growth of communist bloc arms transfers is perhaps more interesting for what it does not show than for what it does show. Table 5.13 indicates that US arms sales do not immunise recipients against increasing communist bloc arms transfers or, more precisely, any early signs of immunity have disappeared by the last test period. Indeed, we find in this period a positive association over the three recipient categories between level of US arms sales and the rate of growth of communist bloc arms sales. Non-recipients of US arms, by

Table 5.13: Means and average annual percentage change in Soviet arms sales and arms sales share across zero, small, medium and large recipients of US gross and per capita arms transfers, 1970-4, 1972-6, 1974-8

	US gross arms sales				US per capita arms sales			
	Zero	Small	Medium	Large	Zero	Small	Medium	Large
Mean in 1970 of GrArUR	6.4	9.8	2.7	0	6.4	10.0	0	2.3
Growth 1970–4 of GrArUR	−0.3	−2.8	−3.7	0	−0.4	−6.9	0	3.3
Mean in 1972 of GrArUR	5.7	0.1	0	0	5.9	0.1	0	0
Growth 1972–6 of GrArUR	0	3.3	0	0	0	3.1	0	0
Mean in 1974 of GrArUR	14.3	5.0	0	0	14.6	5.0	1.3	0
Growth 1974–8 of GrArUR	0.9	5.5	0	10.0	0.9	4.0	5.8	8.3
Mean in 1970 of PArUR	8.7	10.9	7.1	0	8.9	12.2	0	4.8
Growth 1970–4 of PArUR	−0.8	−2.5	−6.0	0	−0.8	−6.7	0	1.2
Mean in 1972 of PArUR	7.9	1.7	0	0	8.1	1.6	0	0
Growth 1972–6 of PArUR	−0.8	3.2	0	0	−0.8	3.1	0	0
Mean in 1974 of PArUR	9.9	5.0	0	0	10.0	3.5	5.4	0
Growth 1974–8 of PArUR	0.8	2.8	0	10.0	0.8	2.7	1.0	8.3

contrast, have rates of growth on this variable that are no different than are those for recipients as a whole. There are no signs of any relationship between either gross or per capita US arms sales and growth rates in neighbours' communist bloc arms purchases.

The individual diplomatic variables are unaffected by US arms sales receipts. In other words, diplomatic bias towards the West may increase as US arms sales receipts do, but the level of US arms sales receipt does not influence the rate of growth or decay of this diplomatic variable. Similarly, recipients' neighbours do not experience higher rates of growth of diplomatic associations of any kind than do the neighbours of non-recipients.

Interpretation: distribution

The findings of our various distribution analyses all lead to the conclusion that competition with communism has a very direct and important structuring effect on the distribution of all three US official transfers. To state this conclusion another way, the pursuit of the second-order utilities of competing with communism in the Third World is an integral part of the United States' official transfer programme. But it is also the case that our findings are complex and, therefore, potentially confusing. There are two keys to the simplification and ordering of this complexity, however.

The first of them involves taking account of the growing Soviet presence in the Third World during the period covered by this study. At the beginning of the chapter, we made the point that the reshaping of the international system in the aftermath of World War II both resulted from, and was fed by, the increasingly apparent rivalry between the United States and the USSR. What is more, this reshaping was, initially at least, asymmetrically skewed in favour of a United States that was not slow to take advantage of its superiority. Indeed, Truman's 1950 'Point Four' speech laid the foundations for the spread of US influence throughout the Third World at the same time that his country was heavily involved in the rebuilding of Western Europe. The USSR was in no position at the time to match US expansionism, partly because it had far fewer resources, partly because it had to cope with the effects of substantial war-time damage on its own soil and partly because it had not expanded overseas during the war itself. Over and above these disadvantages it also, of course, found itself encircled by the United States and its allies in the early and most successful phase of the US containment enterprise so that it is hardly surprising that the expansion of its activities in the Third World lagged behind that of the United States. But the USSR did eventually penetrate the Third World (see Table 5.14). The US strategy of physical containment may have discouraged Soviet expansionism into contiguous territories, but it proved ineffectual against the 'leap-frog' expansionist strategy that the USSR actually adopted. Moreover, the success of this strategy is a major factor explaining the dynamic, adaptive chapter of the US official transfer programmes.

The second key to the simplification and ordering of our findings involves categorising into general strategies the various responses to communist expansionism open to the United States through its official transfer programmes. It seems to us that there are three such strategies: aversion, reinforcement and mutual veto. The aversion strategy is appropriately employed in the case of communist bloc associations and involves penalising these associations in the distribution of transfers. An example of an aversion deployment of, say, US aid would be the existence of an inverse relationship between it and a communist bloc association like diplomatic ties. Reinforcement is the other side of the coin to the aversion strategy in that it rewards US or Western ties. It

Table 5.14: The growth of Soviet and communist bloc arms sales, trade and
diplomatic activity in the Third World, 1950–78

	GrArUR as % GrArUS	GrTrUR as % GrTrUS	GrTrCB as % GrTrUS	DRInUR	DRFrUR	BPref
1950	–	1	5	36	47	2.3
1952	–	1	5	35	42	2.6
1954	–	2	9	34	39	2.7
1956	24	2	12	34	39	2.7
1958	28	5	19	40	50	2.7
1960	26	6	21	40	48	2.3
1962	100	8	18	39	50	1.8
1964	60	8	41	44	49	1.6
1966	106	12	35	49	58	1.5
1968	86	9	29	52	60	1.6
1970	75	7	29	56	61	1.5
1972	100	9	28	56	61	1.0
1974	112	8	35	56	64	0.9
1976	48	6	30	63	67	0.6
1978	44	5	21	65	70	1.0

also differs in that it can take two forms. The first of them is supportive
reinforcement and it would lead us to expect a positive relationship between,
say, US aid and US trade. In its second form, promotional reinforcement, we
would expect a quadratic relationship, either positive or negative, since the
transfer in question would be deployed so as to stimulate associations with the
United States or its allies rather than passively to reward associations that
already exist. Mutual veto is our third strategy and it can take either of two
forms, mutual veto within or mutual veto across. Unlike reinforcement, but like
aversion, mutual veto is directed at communist associations. But unlike aversion,
which is a strategy that discourages such associations by penalising potential
transfer recipients that cultivate them, mutual veto in both its forms is directed
at stalemating extant communist associations. The within and across variants
of the strategy are differentiated by whether US transfers are oriented towards
the communist associations of recipients themselves (within) or towards the
communist associations of recipients' neighbours (across). The mutual veto
within strategy would therefore manifest itself through a positive relationship
between a US transfer like economic aid and its recipients' ties with the communist bloc or experience of domestic communist activity. The mutual veto
across strategy would crystallise in the form of a positive relationship between,
say, US aid and the communist bloc ties of its recipients' neighbours.

Set against this background of over-expanding communist activity in the
Third World eliciting a number of different US response strategies, our findings
can now be more easily and cogently interpreted.

Economic aid

With gross aid being channelled principally to forward defence areas, the first phase of this transfer programme runs through the 1950s and is predominantly characterised by the supportive variant of the reinforcement strategy. Albeit much less saliently, there is also some reinforcement of US trade share, but more of gross trade. The mutual veto within strategy also manifests itself, although less strongly, in that aid flows to Third World countries with domestic communist activity and, to a lesser extent still, with communist bloc trading or diplomatic ties.

The pre-eminence of the reinforcement strategy in this first phase is a direct product of the US resort to the physical containment of communism. What is more, that US aid rewards official more than private associations can be explained by the fact that, at a time of its unquestioned international economic dominance, its own trading patterns did not figure in the key US consideration of the time, namely, support for countries deemed strategically significant in the overall containment enterprise. Nor is it certain that any US administration, no matter how determined, could redefine the US pattern of trade to make it coincide with official foreign policy goals. None the less, an administration could actively promote US trade through its transfer programmes and the failure to deploy a promotive reinforcement strategy to this effect is more difficult to explain. Perhaps, quite simply, the United States does not regard trade as an instrument of foreign policy. The difficulty with this explanation, however, is that the United States had previously used trade as such an instrument and had very quickly come to regard communist bloc trade as an official transfer. A more likely explanation, therefore, is that, firstly, the United States did not anticipate the need for a trade promotional strategy simply because it would have been unnecessary had containment succeeded and, secondly, it underestimated the potential longer-term benefits of such a strategy, i.e. trade could be both an instrument of foreign policy and a credit on its balance of payments.

The failure to include diplomatic bloc preference considerations in the reinforcement strategy may be partly a function of the effectively blanket coverage of US diplomatic ties and partly a function of the then generally high levels of pro-West preference anyway. None the less, there is still variation in the strength of this preference and the failure to accord it greater importance probably indicates that the United States failed to anticipate the rapidity of the expansion of communist bloc diplomatic activity. The insular nature of communism at this time also helps to explain why the mutual veto within strategy is characterised only by a US response to domestic communist activity. It is only in the late 1950s that it starts to respond directly to communist bloc activity in a wider context.

The aid programme's second phase lasts from the early 1960s to the start of the 1970s and it testifies to a number of changes of emphasis. The supportive reinforcement of forward defence areas continues, but it becomes much less salient, whereas the reinforcement of trade becomes more pronounced. This reinforcement, however, raises the possibility of a spurious relationship. To be more specific, in Chapter 4 we already noted the strong relationship between US aid and recipients' gross, or total, trade over this same period so that the US trade–US aid link may be no more than a reflection of the US aid–gross trade link. Given this possibility, it would seem advisable to test for an independent US trade effect by expressing its gross trade as a percentage of the total trade in each of the four aid recipient categories. If it is to have an independent effect, we would expect the US percentage figure to increase across these same categories. Table 5.15 shows that there is indeed such an increase in the years from 1963 to the early 1970s and this finding suggests that a genuine supportive strategy was applied to US trade. But we find no evidence for a similar strategy being deployed for bloc preference.

Table 5.15: US trade as a percentage of total trade across the small, medium and large aid recipient categories for alternate years, 1959-73

	Small	Medium	Large
1959	39	13	25
1961	32	25	24
1963	16	30	28
1965	15	30	31
1967	17	26	31
1969	19	28	25
1971	19	25	26
1973	17	17	23

A further change of emphasis in this second phase of the aid programme is signalled by a greater US reliance than previously on the mutual veto within strategy. What is more, there is also a change of emphasis in this strategy. Aid continues to flow to Third World countries experiencing domestic communist activity, but this variable has now taken second place to external communist bloc activity in the form of trading ties and, to a lesser extent, of arms sales. The final change witnessed in this second phase is the appearance, although in a relatively weak form, of an aversion strategy that is directed principally at communist bloc trade or arms share.

All the changes of emphasis in the second phase can be attributed to the expansion of communist bloc activity on all fronts in the Third World. Essentially, oriented as it was to direct physical containment, the supportive reinforcement of the 1950s was ill-suited to cope with this mode of expansionism and its continued emphasis would only have risked losing substantial areas of the Third World to communist influence. The United States was therefore obliged to redefine its priorities. This redefinition has already been noted in the last chapter to include from the late 1950s an increased emphasis on recipients' gross power political capabilities. That the United States simultaneously attaches greater importance to the mutual veto strategy in face of Soviet expansionism suggests not only that it redefines its aid programme somewhat to favour more powerful countries, particularly in military and diplomatic terms, but also that these are the same countries at which the USSR also directs its activities. The outcome of this common focus of attention and concern is that the superpowers become locked into a reciprocal mutual veto strategy so that the United States is compelled by the logic of the situation to increase its aid the more closely its recipients become linked to the communist bloc. What is more, in order to give itself some advantage over the USSR in the Third World, the United States complements its mutual veto strategy with supportive reinforcement for both US trade and pro-West diplomatic bias. Finally, that there is also some evidence of the hesitant deployment of the aversion strategy during this phase would seem to indicate that there are limits beyond which the United States will not persist with a mutual veto strategy—which only serves to underline the success of communist expansionism in the 1960s.

The third phase of the aid programme gets under way at the end of the 1960s and is most immediately characterised by its exclusion of an unprecedentedly large proportion of potential recipients. The actual selection of those countries which receive aid and those which do not turns out to be based on all three strategies for competing with communism. Pre-eminent among them is supportive reinforcement through rewarding pro-West bloc preference and US trade share. Second in structuring influence is aversion, directed principally against communist bloc arms transfers, and third is mutual veto within, directed against communist bloc trade share. But when we turn to consider the distribution of aid within the recipient population, we find it determined almost entirely by a mutual veto strategy deployed in both its within and across forms.

Our first priority must be to deal with the question of why the United States chooses to ignore a substantial pool of potential recipients from 1969 onwards. Our findings thus far suggest at least three reasons for this decision. In the first place, and as is indicated by the decline in the total volume of US aid distributed from this time (see Table 2.1), a clear financial constraint comes into operation so that the contraction of the programme's scope affords the United States a means of either maintaining or expanding its allocations to those recipients remaining in its orbit. In the second place, the previous chapter has identified a very consistent rationale for exclusion. The simple fact of the matter is that some of those excluded are US arms sales recipients and the remaining non-recipients of aid are generally relatively unimportant in power political terms. Finally, this chapter has shown that non-recipients are more oriented than recipients to the communist bloc in terms of arms transfers and show no distinct preference in diplomatic terms for the West. In short, the aid non-recipient category consists of a group of countries which are relatively firmly in the communist bloc sphere of influence and which, even if it were possible, could be 'won back' by the United States only through a mutual veto strategy that would be financially punitive.

The US decision to exclude these countries from the aid programme marks an important development in superpower relations in the Third World; it is the culmination of an expansionism on the part of a USSR that, over time, has cultivated a relatively exclusive communist sphere of influence and the US isolation of this group through its aversion and reinforcement strategies is but the logical consequence of this development. In other words, when we take account of both the financial constraints on the aid programme and the relative unimportance of non-recipients in power political terms, then it appears that the United States has employed a very coherent and consistent logic of exclusion.

Having dealt with the selection of recipients, our second question concerns why the United States should rely almost exclusively on the mutual veto strategy in the distribution of its gross aid in the recipient group of countries. In this regard, it is easy to understand why it should avoid the aversion strategy. After all, the successful deployment of this strategy entails the risk of encouraging yet more Third World countries to place themselves more firmly in the communist camp, which is, of course, counter-productive from the US point of view. Equally, the resort to mutual veto is easily understood. Communist bloc arms sales may be concentrated in the aid non-recipient category, but they are far from exclusive to it. In addition, the bulk of communist bloc trade is conducted with recipients of US aid so that there is, in both respects, substantial communist bloc activity to be countered and the mutual veto strategy is, in principle, ideally suited to this task. The avoidance of the reinforcement strategy, however, is less easily understood, at least initially. In contrast to aversion, its deployment would be unlikely to entail the risk of being counter-productive so there must be other reasons why it is not used. Two such reasons immediately spring to mind. In the first place, it would seem that US trade patterns do not correspond closely to official foreign policy objectives so that trade is not necessarily rewarded by official transfers. In the second place, it would again seem that the US goal of containing communism is more curative than preventive in character. In other words, it channels its efforts more towards a direct response to communist expansionism than towards an attempt to prevent it in the first place.

With regard to the distribution of per capita aid, we see the same strategies as with gross aid, but in different combinations for the same three periods or phases. The first phase of the programme is characterised by aversion and mutual veto in that order, the second by mutual veto and reinforcement and the third, as with the first, by aversion and mutual veto. This overall picture gives rise to the following observations.

Firstly, and perhaps most importantly, the per capita aid allocations display a much greater degree of aversion than do their gross aid counterparts and understanding this difference necessitates a brief recapitulation of our conceptualisation of the transfer in its two forms. To state the difference simply, the variation in gross, or absolute, allocations reflects the variation in preference among recipients, i.e. the larger the receipt, the greater the preference. The variation in per capita allocation, by contrast, is a measure of relative preference. Holding constant the gross transfer, the country with the larger per capita receipt would have greater relative preference bestowed on it. There would seem to be several reasons why the aversion response is more pronounced in the context of relative, as opposed to absolute, preference. Firstly, aversion is itself more of a manifestation of preference than is mutual veto and so cannot but be more compatible with the special preference inherent in the distribution of per capita aid allocations. Secondly, as has already been noted, aversion is a less conservative strategy than mutual veto or reinforcement since its deployment risks pushing those countries that it penalises further into the communist camp. Gross aid allocations, however, have been shown to minimise this risk by avoiding the aversion strategy. Under these circumstances, aversion can become an attractive strategy in the context of per capita allocations since its deployment can combine the potential benefits of the more active discrimination inherent in the aversion strategy with the minimisation of risk inherent in the other two. In short, by co-ordinating its gross and per capita aid allocations, the United States can seek to 'have the best of both worlds'.

A second general observation is that US per capita aid allocations betray a more consistent and enduring longitudinal deployment of the mutual veto strategy exercised in the context of recipients' neighbours, i.e. mutual veto across, than do gross aid allocations. Other things being equal, we would fully expect the United States to respond to expanding communist activity in the Third World by taking account of the bloc proclivities of its recipients' neighbours in its aid transfer and this response is exactly what characterises gross aid transfers in the 1970s. It should come as no real surprise, therefore, to discover that the United States was, in fact, responding to recipients' neighbours' communist bloc associations at a much earlier stage in its per capita aid programme.

Our final observation is that, once again, there is relatively little emphasis on the reinforcement strategy. But we can throw no further light on this finding other than to repeat that it can probably be explained, at least in part, by the failure of US official transfers blindly to follow private sector trading patterns. In general, therefore, gross and per capita aid allocations clearly reveal that the United States follows parallel and complementary strategies in its overall response to competition with communism in the Third World.

Military assistance

The selection of military assistance recipients is dominated by supportive reinforcement directed at forward defence areas, US trade share and pro-West diplomatic bias. There is, in addition, an element of mutual veto within, which is directed at domestic communist activity. Finally, aversion also manifests itself implicitly in so far as the volume of communist bloc arms sales is significantly lower among military assistance recipients than non-recipients. It is the case, however, that such arms sales do not figure in the discriminant analyses since it is a variable that is collinear with some of the significant reinforcement variables. This is why we describe the aversion strategy as implicit.

It is eminently clear, then, that the selection of military assistance recipients is strongly and consistently influenced by considerations of US competition with communism. This consistency in selection criteria and response strategies means that the recipient selection process has not been unduly disturbed by the expansion of communist bloc activity in the Third World. This is not to suggest, however, that it is a process that has not changed at all. The progressive increase in the salience of the bloc preference indicator at the expense of forward defence area status reflects a growing US acceptance of the shortcomings of its physical containment enterprise, shortcomings to which we have already called attention. None the less, the very pronounced continuity over time in the recipient selection process must be taken to reflect the consistency of the response to communism adopted by the United States in its military assistance programme. The primacy of the reinforcement strategy indicates that this response is relatively conservative and passive. It appears to have been chosen to avoid the direct confrontation with the communist bloc implicit in the mutual veto strategy, preferring instead to support countries already showing a pronounced predisposition to the West and a marked indifference to the East. In short, at least with regard to its selection of military assistance recipients, the United States pursues a reinforcement strategy that rewards Third World countries for aligning themselves with the West.

As for the distribution of gross military assistance within the recipient population, three phases can once again be identified. The first phase lasts until 1957 and is characterised by an emphasis on supportive reinforcement directed principally at forward defence areas and contiguous neighbours' US arms transfers. Both variables indicate the promotion of US security spheres. This early emphasis on reinforcement probably reflects the relatively low level of communist bloc activity at the time, a situation that would make the deployment of the aversion or mutual veto strategies redundant. In an international system in which it enjoyed unquestioned hegemony, it is easy to appreciate why the United States would prefer to emphasise its support for recipients that it deems critical to its foreign policy goals. On the other hand, it is still perhaps surprising that, after employing passive and conservative criteria in the initial selection of military assistance recipients, the United States did not adopt a more ambitious promotional reinforcement strategy in distributing its military assistance within this relatively small recipient population.

In the second phase, which lasts until 1965, the reinforcement strategy persists, although in a more muted form since it is now directed solely at forward defence area status. But complementing it is a mutual veto across strategy directed at recipients' neighbours' communist bloc arms purchases. This switch of emphasis can, in our opinion, be attributed to the rising levels of communist bloc activity in the Third World. That is, the expansion is occurring primarily outside the territory of the most preferred military assistance recipients, thereby obviating the need for the United States to adopt an aversion or mutual veto within strategy. But it can, and does, respond to communist expansionism by seeking to stop it spreading further by allocating military assistance to countries whose neighbours display relatively strong communist bloc associations.

The final phase sees the continuation of the mutual veto across and reinforcement strategies, but the latter now reverts to being directed at neighbours' US arms transfers. Being a reversal to an earlier focus of concern, this change is not at all radical and is best interpreted as underlining the consistency of the United States' definitions of its interests in territorial terms.

The criteria determining the distribution of per capita military assistance within the population of recipients are broadly similar. The programm's twin emphases are reinforcement directed at forward defence areas and mutual veto directed at domestic communist activity. Additionally, there are elements of mutual veto across and reinforcement directed at promoting US exclusivity.

In the aggregate, then, competition with communism has a highly pronounced influence on the structure of the military assistance programme. The recipient selection criteria determine in many respects the nature of the larger programme since, in addition to defining the population of recipients, it also effectively delimits the strategies that the United States can follow in the second, allocation phase. That is, since inclusion is based largely on the absence of communist ties, the deployment of either the aversion or mutual veto within (except, of course, when directed at domestic communist activity) strategies effectively becomes unnecessary. As for the allocation of military assistance, the United States' failure to deploy either supportive or, more especially, promotional reinforcement to foster US trade makes this stage of the overall programme seem passive and unambitious. But, while accurate in its own right, the impression of passivity disappears when the military assistance and economic aid programmes are evaluated jointly. In fact, the distribution of economic aid is generally more versatile and responsive to changing levels of communist bloc activity and, as such, it encourages a pronounced level of balanced stagnation, or veto and counter-veto. Worse still from a US perspective, the exclusion of a substantial number of Third World countries from the aid programme after 1968 provides the communist bloc with its own relatively exclusive sphere of influence. Against this background, military assistance becomes the means by which the United States can escape the generalised action-reaction syndrome of the mutual veto within strategy. While this observation does not itself alter the relatively passive image of military assistance allocations, it does highlight that these allocations can be seen as the means, within a larger framework of countervailing mutual veto pursued through economic aid, whereby the United States displays its particular preference and support for a more restricted number of Third World countries that have shown themselves relatively immune to the communist bloc. Thus, the economic aid and military assistance programmes complement each other in the United States' competition with communism in the Third World.

Arms sales

Our findings indicate that arms sales recipients are very clearly selected on the basis of reinforcement and mutual veto response strategies, the former manifesting itself through the US trade and pro-West preference variables and the latter through the communist bloc trade variable. While the interpretation of bloc preference in terms of reinforcement is not problematic, the relationship between US arms sales and both US and communist bloc trade, at least as these relations are interpreted within the context of reinforcement and mutual veto strategies, could be somewhat problematic and does need to be looked at more carefully.

The main problem arises from the finding in Chapter 4 that the selection of arms sales recipients is strongly related to total, or aggregate, trade volume, i.e. recipients have substantially higher levels of total trade than non-recipients. The question inevitably arises, therefore, as to whether the United States chooses its arms recipients directly on the basis of their trading links with itself and the communist bloc or on the basis of their aggregate trade levels. In the latter case, the apparent relationships between US arms sales and US and communist bloc trade would be an artefact of a US attraction to recipients gross trade. If this were indeed the case, since the larger trading countries are also likely to have higher levels of trade with both the United States and the communist bloc, we would almost certainly find a relationship between selection into the arms sales recipient population and each of US and communist bloc trade. This relationship, however, could be spurious. The very fact that these three variables are interrelated presents us with an apparent dilemma of interpretation.

But it is a dilemma that can be resolved satisfactorily. The three variables may be positively and significantly correlated with each other, but they are far from perfectly collinear and their interrelationship should vary under different hypothetical conditions. Thus, should the selection of US arms recipients be directly structured by its own or the communist bloc's trade with the Third World, then minimally the US or the communist bloc share of recipients' total trade should be higher than their respective share of non-recipients' total trade. But if their trade shares are relatively constant across the two groups of Third World countries, we can reject the hypothesis that the United States reacts directly and explicitly to its own or communist bloc trading patterns in the selection of its arms sales recipients. Table 5.16 shows that this hypothesis can indeed be rejected.

US arms sales recipients undoubtedly have higher levels of trade with the

Table 5.16: US and communist bloc trade as percentage of total trade in the
non-recipient (NR) and recipient (R) categories of US arms
sales, 1971–9

	US trade percentage		CB trade percentage	
	NR	R	NR	R
1971	16	22	8	4
1973	21	18	8	3
1975	19	17	8	5
1977	21	18	6	5
1979	27	19	7	4

United States and the communist bloc, but it now seems the case that the
United States does not manipulate its arms sales directly to promote its trade
volume. These two recipient trading links would seem to be simply a reflection
of the US concern with power political considerations in its transfer programmes.
What is more, the interrelationships between the US arms sales receipt and US
and communist bloc trade variables can now be seen to indicate that the USSR
has a very similar concern in its relations with the Third World. These findings
also indicate that while the United States may not explicitly pursue either the
reinforcement or mutual veto strategies with regard to trading links when
selecting its arms recipients, it none the less achieves them precisely because of
its preoccupation with recipients' power political capabilities. Its only direct
strategy, as far as selection is concerned, is reinforcement directed at pro-West
diplomatic preference.

The allocation of arms sales within the recipient population is dominated
principally by the strategies of mutual veto across and aversion, both of which
are directed mainly at diplomatic ties. The results for the per capita distributions
are essentially the same, although they do also include hints of the use of a
reinforcement strategy to promote US security spheres. That there is no sign of
this strategy being directed at US trade ties only provides support for our interpretation of Table 5.16. The allocation stage's emphasis on mutual veto across
over mutual veto within is a function of there being a level of communist bloc
activity among recipients, especially in the area of arms imports, that is similar
in magnitude to that found in the non-recipient population. Given this similarity,
it seems logical for the United States to switch its attention to the level of
communist bloc activity in recipients' neighbours and generally to supply more
arms to those recipients whose neighbours display relatively high levels of such
activity.

In sum then, the US arms sales programme is not its military assistance programme under another name. There are certainly some similarities between
them, particularly with respect to their rewarding of a pro-West diplomatic
bias, but the countries receiving US arms are by and large not as exclusively

oriented towards the West in general and the United States in particular as are those receiving military assistance. In this respect, the arms sales programme is the less clientelist of the two, which implies a recognition on the part of the United States of the need to respond to communist bloc expansionism by means other than trying to make it stop before it starts, i.e. by aversion. This is not to argue that the United States simply goes to the other extreme, however, and channels its transfers into countries already characterised by relatively high levels of communist bloc associations. Instead, it seems to divide the Third World into three parts. Some countries are simply allowed to be 'annexed' by the communist bloc, some are equally exclusive to itself, while others, usually characterised by their more substantial absolute power capabilities, are attractive to, and 'courted' by, both it and the communist bloc.

Interpretation: impact

The interpretation of the findings from our distribution analysis centered around the three US response strategies of reinforcement, aversion and mutual veto. With the exception that they now refer to outcomes rather than to response strategies, these same three categories can be equally fruitfully employed to order and interpret our impact findings.

It is important to note at the outset that reinforcement, aversion and mutual veto as strategy in the distribution analysis are not necessarily related to their respective counterparts as outcome in the impact analysis. To be sure, a supplier may view strategy and outcome as but opposite sides of the same coin so that for it to pursue, say, an aversion strategy without achieving an aversion outcome could be tantamount to the failure of that strategy. Yet it could equally be the case that a supplier achieves an aversion outcome although it did not deliberately pursue an aversion strategy. The supplier might, for example, be concerned to reinforce its own Third World ties through its aid programme, but this strategy could have the side-effect of discouraging the formation or consolidation of similar ties between its recipients and its competitors.

A reinforcement outcome in the impact analysis would be signalled by a positive association between level of US official transfer receipt and rate of growth on variables tapping recipients' direct links with the West or the United States, for example, US trade. A reinforcement outcome has an opposite, counter-reinforcement, but, while logically possible, the latter is highly unlikely to manifest itself in our analysis since it would involve an inverse relationship between, say, level of aid receipt and rate of growth of US trade. An aversion outcome is constituted by an inverse relationship between level of US transfer receipt and growth rate on one or other variable profiling Third World countries' ties with the communist bloc. Like reinforcement, aversion also has its obverse, but counter-aversion is, in fact, far more likely to develop since it seems entirely possible that a US transfer could stimulate a positive rate of growth in, say, communist bloc arms sales as the USSR seeks to neutralise, or stalemate, the advantage accruing to the United States by virtue of its transfer. Finally, a mutual veto outcome would take the form of there being no systematic relationship between the level of the US transfer and growth rate on individual communist bloc variables. Obviously, since this outcome denies the existence of a relationship, a counter-mutual veto outcome is a logical impossibility.

Impact outcomes can be usefully evaluated in terms of gains and losses. From the perspective of a supplier like the United States, a reinforcement outcome indicates a clear gain in the sense that a positive relationship develops between its transfers and the growth rate of its own, or other Western, associations with the recipients of the transfer. Conversely, counter-reinforcement is an outcome that represents a loss for the supplier in that its transfers prove unable to structure favourable growth rates in these same US and Western ties.

The remaining outcomes, aversion and mutual veto, explicitly calculate US gains and losses against the growth or otherwise of Soviet or communist bloc associations in the Third World. An aversion outcome is a gain for the United States in that its transfers are associated with decreasing rates of growth of communist associations among their recipients. Inevitably, what is a successful outcome for the United States is a loss for the USSR since its own growth rates have thereby been inhibited. Logically, therefore, a counter-aversion outcome is a gain for the USSR and a loss for the United States since its occurrence means that, despite the receipt of relatively large volumes of a transfer, recipients display relatively high growth rates in their communist bloc associations. When these growth rates are examined in the context of recipients' neighbours, by contrast, a counter-aversion outcome signifies a no gain and no loss outcome for both superpowers.[32]

The mutual veto outcome also represents essentially a no gain and no loss outcome for both the United States and the USSR. In other words, the United States does not experience the loss that goes along with a counter-aversion outcome but, equally, it does not enjoy the gain afforded by an aversion outcome.[33]

Any one outcome then, can be evaluated in terms of the gains and losses accruing by virtue of it to the United States (and, conversely to the USSR in the cases of the aversion and mutual veto outcomes). But given that each US transfer programme embraces a large number of performance variables, an overall perspective on any one of them requires that they be viewed as collections or aggregations of outcomes. Thus, if the United States experiences a matching number of aversion and counter-aversion outcomes in, say, its economic aid programme, the overall characterisation of that programme would be one of matching gains and losses, i.e. of a mutual veto outcome. To take a still broader perspective, these same considerations apply between transfer programmes as well as within them.

This gain and loss calculus can be applied equally to transfer recipients.[34]

Other things being equal, the reinforcement and aversion outcomes that are gains for the United States are losses for the recipients of its transfers since they mean that these transfers effectively delimit the range of development options open to them.[35] On the other hand, counter-reinforcement and counter-aversion outcomes amount to gains for recipients since it means that high levels of transfers have flowed from the United States despite their not having structured the growth pattern of associations with either the communist bloc or the West. In addition, counter-aversion means that Third World countries can simultaneously attract high levels of transfers from both the East and West, thereby undermining the first-order utilities of both transfer sources and reducing their own first-order disutilities.[36] Finally, a mutual veto outcome indicates that there has been no gain and no loss in the sense that receipt of the transfer entails neither the gains of counter-aversion and counter-reinforcement nor the losses of aversion and reinforcement outcomes.[37]

Economic aid

The United States could be expected to seek a reinforcement outcome in its aid transfers with respect to rates of growth of its own trade and of diplomatic bloc preference for the West. In general terms, our findings provide no evidence of such an outcome in the area of trade growth and no more than limited evidence of it in that of bloc preference trends.

With regard to US trade growth, aid could be expected to reinforce it in either of two ways. On the one hand, aid could be manipulated to promote domestic and economic political developments that serve to stimulate recipients' gross trade. As was demonstrated in the previous chapter, however, there is no evidence that such a stimulation has, in fact, taken place. On the other hand, even if US aid were not to stimulate recipients' trade directly, it could none the less promote higher trade growth rates with the United States by discouraging recipients from trading with other partners. In other words, the relationship would be based not on a direct expansion of volume of trade, but on a shift in trading patterns. There is, however, no evidence that this association in fact exists and so we can only conclude that there is no support for the view that trade follows economic aid.[38] If the United States ever anticipated that its aid programme could promote its trade with the Third World, it is an expectation that has not been met in practice.

The substantial decay in the value of the bloc preference variable from the early 1950s to the late 1970s indicates a marked decline in Third World countries' diplomatic attraction to the West in preference to the East (see Table 5.14). But while of interest in its own right, this trend cannot be taken to constitute evidence of the aid programme's failure to put a brake on communist bloc diplomatic expansionism. This argument would be convincing only if aid were the sole determinant influence on this expansionism. Since it clearly is not, it can just as convincingly be argued that but for aid, the expansionism would have progressed at a still more rapid pace. Indeed, that a bias towards the West persists even into the late 1970s could superficially be interpreted to indicate the programme's success.[39] On the grounds that aid is intended to insulate recipients against communist bloc ties, any argument as to the programme's failure in this respect would lead us to expect rates of bloc preference decay actually to increase across levels of aid receipt. As it turns out, however, decay rates in fact diminish with increases in per capita aid. This relationship points to a reinforcement outcome that is strong enough to suggest that per capita aid does inhibit bloc preference decay. No similarly strong outcome characterises the gross aid programme. Yet, it is still the case that large gross aid recipients not only enjoy higher bloc preference scores from the early 1960s onwards, but also fail to display higher decay rates. In this limited sense, therefore, the gross programme visits neither gain nor loss upon the United States.

The only indication of an aversion outcome occurs in the relationship between per capita aid receipts and Soviet arms sales. Again, the aggregate trend is for these sales to increase over time to the point where they achieve parity with the United States' from the early 1960s (see Table 5.14). Again, therefore, the United States has proved unable to contain communist expansionism in the Third World but, as argued above, this failure cannot be 'blamed' solely, if at all, on the US aid programme. Indeed, there is evidence that, as with bloc preference, Soviet arms sales grow less quickly as per capita, but not gross, aid increases. This relationship indicates an aversion outcome. But is the effect of aid on the growth rate of Soviet arms sales spurious? While not conclusive, the evidence in fact points to aid having a real inhibition, or aversion, effect on this variable. One potential source of spuriousness, for example, is that the United States simply selects countries as large per capita aid recipients on the basis of their low levels of Soviet arms imports. But since our aid aggregations are based on only four-year periods, it is very unlikely that a spurious result would appear consistently over the much longer period of three decades. It might also be that the lower growth rates on the performance variable are caused not by per capita aid receipts, but by some other variable. While entirely possible, this unidentified variable would minimally have to covary with aid receipt, as does, for example, bloc preference. The exact nature of this three-way relationship is not important, however. Countries with a high pro-West bloc preference score may be relatively little inclined to import Soviet arms and be reinforced in this proclivity by relatively high per capita US aid receipts or, alternatively, it may be that these receipts inhibit the importation of communist arms which, in turn, strengthens the already existing pro-West bloc preference. Whatever the precise pattern in the relationship, per capita aid could still be argued to have generated a real aversion outcome.[40]

The most prevalent aid outcome is mutual veto. In aggregate terms, communist bloc trade again expands disproportionately over time, although, unlike arms sales, it never reaches the level of its US counterpart. Rather, it rises to reach about 35 per cent of US total trade around the mid-1960s and remains at this point thereafter. But since there is no evidence at any time of a systematic impact of US aid, gross or per capita, receipts on the rate of growth of communist trade, we cannot but conclude that the US aid programme does not have a structuring influence on Third World countries' rate of growth of trade with the communist bloc. In short, a mutual veto outcome prevails, just as it does in the cases of the impact of gross aid on the rates of growth of the bloc preference and communist bloc arms sales variables.

Switching attention to the communist bloc associations of recipients' neighbours rather than of recipients themselves, we find the mutual veto outcome to be predominant once again, although there are signs that it is complemented by a counter-aversion outcome in the later years of the study. The counter-aversion outcome itself becomes most apparent when non-recipients are compared to recipients as a single group.[41] It is worth remembering that, in the context of the aid programme, such a comparison can only meaningfully be made in each of the five test periods from 1966-70 so that conclusions deriving from the comparisons should be treated with circumspection. Furthermore, the conclusions that do present themselves hold only for gross, and not per capita, aid and, in addition, are based only on the performance variables of neighbours' arms transfers from, and diplomatic associations with, the communist bloc. Bearing these provisos in mind, it turns out that US aid recipients have neighbours with higher growth rates on both the communist arms and diplomatic variables than the neighbours of non-recipients. In this respect, a paradoxical feature of the US aid programme is that its incorporation of Third World countries into its recipient population only serves to stimulate a tendency on the part of their neighbours to expand their communist bloc associations more rapidly, particularly in the areas of arms receipts and diplomatic ties. In short, it could be argued that the US aid programme is self-defeating in that it encourages a 'spiral of insecurity' rather than security itself.

This overview of the overall impact of the US aid programme leads to two main conclusions and one less important one. First, and most importantly, to the extent that our analysis shows mutual veto to have been its dominant outcome, this programme's aggregate impact over time is best characterised as no gain and no loss. Over the 1950-79 period, communist bloc activity in the Third World expands enormously, although it never attains complete parity with that of the United States and, indeed, remains substantially below it in the area of trade in particular. This expansion itself, however, should not be taken to indicate the failure of US aid; it is probably more accurately viewed as the predictable redressing of the asymmetrical influence that the United States enjoyed in the Third World immediately after the onset of the Cold War. What could be considered a failure, by contrast, is the programme's general inability with one or two notable exceptions in the case of per capita aid, to structure the actual pattern of communist bloc expansion in any pronounced way. In short, the distribution of aid may well have been strongly influenced by communist bloc activity, but its impact on structuring this activity has been relatively negligible. It is in this sense that the aid programme has experienced very little gain. But, on the other hand, the prevalence of the mutual veto outcome indicates that the communist bloc has hardly impaired US Third World priorities either so that the aid programme overall might equally be said to have shown very little loss. Indeed, it is possible that, without it, the pattern of communist bloc expansion could have been detrimental to US interests in the Third World.

In summary then, if by containment we understand a condition of mutual veto, the United States can be concluded overall to have realised its second-order utilities *vis-à-vis* communist expansion. But if we understand this term to mean a condition of confinement (a condition that would be characterised essentially by our aversion outcome), then the US aid programme has clearly failed to achieve its second-order utilities.

Our second main conclusion concerns the countries that receive US aid. US competition with communism is clearly an important determinant of the distribution of this aid, but our impact analysis indicates that the receipt of aid does not turn out by and large to prejudice the developmental pattern of Third World countries *vis-à-vis* the communist bloc. It seems very likely therefore that, at least in this area, recipient countries incur relatively few first-order disutilities in accepting US aid. Indeed, the superpower rivalry leaves substantial scope for recipient countries, especially those with higher power capabilities, to exercise counter-leverage. But this advantage notwithstanding, Third World countries cannot be argued to have achieved their most favourable outcomes, counter-reinforcement and counter-aversion. In this respect, it appears that the superpowers have institutionalised a relatively stable equilibrium in their mutual veto positions.

A third, and less general, conclusion concerns those relatively few instances where an aid impact is in fact detected. In the first place, it is per capita, and not gross, aid that has the impact, which is not surprising since, other things being equal, the preference inherent in the per capita programme affords it greater leverage potential. In the second place, it is noticeable that it is diplomatic bloc preference and communist bloc arms sales rather than US or communist bloc trade that are structured to some extent by aid receipts. In other words, as in the previous chapter, we cannot escape the conclusion that the aid programme is oriented more to US politico-security concerns than to economic ones.

Military assistance

There is no evidence that the receipt of military assistance generates a reinforcement outcome in either of the areas in which we might expect it to occur, i.e. US trade and diplomatic bloc preference. Indeed, in so far as US trade share actually grows more rapidly among non-recipients, there would seem to be some evidence of a counter-reinforcement outcome. Since there is no immediately obvious explanation of why military assistance transfers should undermine US trade, however, this finding probably reflects that, against a background of general decay of US domination of Third World trade, the non-recipients of the transfer started off with very much lower levels of trade with the United States so that their relatively less precipitous decline is not overly surprising. Furthermore, if counter-reinforcement really were taking place, we would expect a progressive increase in the value of US trade's summed ranks across all three recipient categories, i.e. we would expect variation among aid recipients and not only between non-recipients and recipients as a whole. But, as Table 5.12 shows, this expectation is not met. In any event, perhaps puzzling as it may be, this finding serves minimally to emphasise that the United States does not achieve any trade reinforcement through its military assistance transfers.

Nor does the bloc preference variable provide any evidence of a reinforcement outcome, but it will be recalled from the distribution analysis that military recipients score much more highly on this variable than non-recipients. Thus, while military assistance transfers may not promote higher rates of growth on this variable (or, more accurately, lower rates of decay), it does seem conducive to the maintenance of a substantially greater pro-West diplomatic bias in the recipient population. Otherwise, the difference between the two groups would be expected to have narrowed substantially in the face of communist diplomatic expansionism.

Military assistance appears to have a very pronounced aversion effect on the growth of communist bloc arms sales. There is, in general, a progressive decline in communist ability to increase arms sales as the level of US military assistance receipt grows. But is this a real effect or is it a confounded one resulting from one or other variable's happening to be collinear with military assistance? A number of such variables have already been identified in this analysis and perhaps the most important among them is bloc preference. Thus, it might be argued that countries with high pro-West bloc preference scores are less inclined to import communist arms and that since these countries also receive US military assistance, the apparent importance of military assistance is an artefact and the 'real' inhibiting effect comes from bloc preference. This argument cannot be proved in any meaningful sense, but nor can it be falsified since we have no cases of low bloc preference and high military assistance, or vice versa, on which it could be tested. None the less, there is a clear, logical reason as to why we can expect US military assistance to inhibit communist bloc arms purchases and it is that they can act as a quid pro quo for not making such purchases or can displace them if they are already being made. In addition, the transfer's inhibiting effect grows stronger as its volume increases. For both these reasons, we feel confident in concluding that military assistance exercises a genuine aversion effect on the growth rates of communist bloc arms transfers to the Third World.

Per capita military assistance also has a significant aversion effect on the growth of communist bloc, but not Soviet, trade share. What is more, while the

Soviet trade share relationship may not be significant, it does show the direction-
ality that we would expect from an aversion outcome. As for communist bloc
and Soviet gross trade growth rates, the impact of per capita military assistance
is unequivocally one of mutual veto. Thus, this transfer does appear to inhibit
the growth of communist bloc trade share in the Third World, but not of communist bloc or Soviet gross trade.

Although weaker, there are signs that gross military assistance also has an
inhibiting effect, but on Soviet gross and percentage trade share. There are two
reasons why this apparent aversion outcome is probably better viewed as a
mutual veto outcome. In the first place, the significant chi-square value notwithstanding, there is no clearly linear relationship across the three transfer
recipient categories. Secondly, while non-recipients have the highest growth
rates on average, these are not significantly different from those for recipients
as a whole. In other words, the initial indication of an aversion outcome when
non-recipients are compared to recipients as a whole is hardly founded on strong
evidence so that the impact of gross military assistance on the growth rates of
Soviet gross and percentage trade share would seem to be more safely interpreted in terms of a mutual veto outcome.

Mutual veto also characterises the impact of both forms of military assistance
on the growth of neighbours' diplomatic and trading ties with the communist
bloc. Their effect, and particularly that of gross military assistance, on neighbours' communist bloc arms purchases, by contrast, indicate a counter-aversion
outcome. In other words, US military assistance recipients have neighbours that
display higher growth rates on communist bloc arms imports. As in the case of
economic aid, therefore, there is some evidence of a self-defeating escalation in
the competition between the two superpowers.

This overview of the outcomes of the military assistance programme suggests
two conclusions. The first of them is that, from the perspective of the United
States, the net outcome of this programme is again one of no gain and no loss,
an outcome that is seen most clearly with respect to US and communist bloc
trade. In the area of communist bloc arms sales, by contrast, it might seem
that the aversion outcome signals a clear US gain. In one sense this conclusion
is altogether accurate; in a group of Third World countries that it has presumably
identified as important, the United States has proved consistently able to forestall the development of arms ties with the communist bloc. But the price of this
'success' has been a recipient selectivity that has opened the way for the communist bloc to develop its own aversion outcome in countries either rejecting
or not favoured by the United States. These countervailing aversion outcomes
mean that, in a global sense, the military assistance programme, like the economic
one, is best characterised as having promoted no gain and no loss in terms of the
United States' competition with communism in the Third World. This conclusion is only strengthened by the counter-aversion outcome that characterises
communist bloc arms sales. That is, since this outcome derives from the

behaviour patterns of recipients' neighbours and not recipients themselves, it also indicates a no gain and no loss outcome, albeit of a self-defeating nature, for both superpowers. Finally, that neither the United States nor the USSR makes any overall net gain or loss is testified to most vividly by the various mutual veto outcomes that characterise the impact of military assistance.

Our second conclusion is that, what are from the perspective of the Third World the most favourable outcomes of any transfer programme, i.e. counter-reinforcement and counter-aversion, do not fully materialise from military assistance transfers. Furthermore, its least advantageous outcome, i.e. aversion, materialises only in the area of communist bloc sales. In other words, part of the development of Third World countries is structured by a US transfer programme, but it is only a small part. To be sure, these countries may have to meet certain criteria if they are to be included in the US recipient population, but it is also the case that there are alternative sources of assistance to which they can turn if excluded and, constraints notwithstanding, recipients still appear to enjoy substantial latitude in their development of associations with the East or West except in the area of arms purchases from the communist bloc. In short, it is difficult to escape the conclusion that the first-order disutilities accruing to the Third World as a result of the US military assistance programme are not at all substantial.

Arms sales

Again, there turns out to be no evidence whatsoever of any reinforcement outcome in the areas of US trade and diplomatic bias. While these two variables were critical determinants of the receipt and distribution among recipients of arms sales, neither the volume nor even simple receipt of arms has any influence on their subsequent behaviour patterns. Thus, although the United States has not lost in the sense of experiencing lower trade and pro-West diplomatic growth rates among the recipients of its arms transfers, it has equally not achieved any gain in the sense of promoting higher growth rates on either of these two variables.

As for aversion, in marked contrast to its economic aid and military assistance counterparts, there is no sign of this outcome in the arms sales programme. As such, the US arms sales programme is unique in the sense of having exercised no inhibiting or deterrent effect on the development of Third World countries' ties with the communist bloc. A US aversion to communist bloc arms receipts might well be apparent in the context of the distribution of US arms sales, but it is entirely absent in the context of their impact. The absence of an aversion outcome clearly separates the arms sales programme from its economic aid and military assistance counterparts and the difference is probably attributable to the lower level of leverage that is inherent in arms sales simply because, being conducted on a commercial basis, they are more likely to contain no concessionary element. Thus, while the United States may well have reduced some of its disutilities by shifting its emphasis to commercial transfers, it has also commensurately sacrificed some of the first-order utilities afforded by its concessionary transfer programmes.

As with the economic aid and military assistance programmes, then, the predominant outcome of the arms sales programme is one of mutual veto. Our overall conclusion, therefore, cannot but be that the United States and communist bloc find themselves in a position of balanced stalemate, a position that suggests two conclusions.

In the first place and from the US perspective, the impact of its arms sales programme is to promote a perfect outcome of no gain and no loss. Although unable to stimulate developments in the Third World that would redound to its own advantage at the expense of the USSR, the impact of the US arms sales programme has been to forestall developments that would be favourable to the USSR at the expense of the United States. In terms of the original US goal of containment, therefore, there is no sign of its successful realisation when this goal is conceptualised in terms of geographical confinement, but there is every sign of its realisation when it is conceptualised more diffusely in terms of countervailment. In this latter sense, we find the two superpowers containing each other via their respective networks of ties with Third World countries.

The second general conclusion takes the perspective of Third World countries and it is that while they do not realise their most advantageous outcomes, they none the less enjoy an outcome that is in their net favour. While the issue of whether or not they actually get arms from either or both superpowers is to some extent determined by their ties with the East and West, the development of their ongoing associations with either the United States or the USSR (at least of those profiled in this chapter) is immune to the receipt of US arms sales. In other words, the arms sales programme has established a condition of mutual veto under which Third World countries can minimise a number of potential first-order and second-order disutilities. On the other hand, the ability of the two superpowers to maintain a mutual veto rather than a counter-aversion outcome does serve to inhibit the development of any substantial counter-leverage potential among the recipients.

Appendix: variables and their acronyms

Acronym	Variable description
Diplomatic set	
DRInUR	Presence of diplomatic representation in the USSR
DRFrUR	Presence of diplomatic representation from the USSR
DRInCB	Number of embassies accredited to the communist bloc
DRFrCB	Number of embassies accredited by the communist bloc
BPref	Bloc preference

| CNPDRCB | Percentage of neighbours' total embassies accredited by the communist bloc |
| CNPDRDM | Percentage of neighbours' total embassies accredited by the West (developed market economies) |

Trade set

AidCB	Economic aid from the communist bloc
GrTrUR	Gross trade (exports + imports) with the USSR
GrTrCB	Gross trade (exports + imports) with the communist bloc
PTrUR	Percentage of total trade conducted with the USSR
PTrCB	Percentage of total trade conducted with the communist bloc
GrTrUS	Gross trade (exports + imports) with the USA
PTrUS	Percentage of total trade conducted with the USA
CNGrTrCB	Contiguous neighbours' gross trade (exports + imports) with the communist bloc
CNPTrCB	Percentage of contiguous neighbours' total trade conducted with the communist bloc
CNGrTrUS	Contiguous neighbours' gross trade (exports + imports) with the United States
CNPTrUS	Percentage of contiguous neighbours' total trade conducted with the United States

Security set

ForDef	Status as designated forward defence area
GrArUR	Gross arms purchases from the USSR
GrArCB	Gross arms purchases from the communist bloc
PArUR	Percentage of total arms purchases from the USSR
PArCB	Percentage of total arms purchases from the communist bloc
CNGrArCB	Contiguous neighbours' gross arms purchases from the communist bloc
CNPArCB	Contiguous neighbours' percentage of total arms purchases from the communist bloc
CNGrArUS	Contiguous neighbours' gross arms purchases from the United States
CNPArUS	Contiguous neighbours' percentage of total arms purchases from the United States

Domestic communism set

| CommP | Presence of legal and active communist party |
| LWV | Presence of extensive left-wing violence |

1. As in previous chapters, we use capital letters in the acronyms to indicate the start of a new word.
2. In order to facilitate the interpretation of the acronyms, we have used the following conventions:
   a. If a variable represents a flow from one or a set of countries, we place the abbreviation for the country name at the end of the acronym. The abbreviations themselves are: US (USA), UR (USSR), DM (developed market economies or the West) and CB (communist bloc).

b. Several variables are expressed in both their gross and percentaged form. These forms are distinguished by the abbreviations Gr and P respectively. The variables that appear in gross and percentaged form in the tables of the chapter are: Tr (trade), Ar (arms sales) and DR (diplomatic representation or embassies).

c. These variables of trade, arms and diplomatic representation are measured not only for each Third World country, but also for each's contiguous neighbours. The acronyms for the latter group of variables always begin with CN (contiguous neighbours').

Notes

1. We can illustrate the logic of official transfer strategies with reference to the Marshall Plan. Devised against a background of intense US–Soviet rivalry, the Marshall Plan perfectly illustrates how the aversion and reinforcement strategies were employed by the United States to effect the general containment of communism. Through the 'carrot and stick' potential of official transfers, a manifest aversion to communism could be made a precondition of inclusion in the Plan. The promotion of reconstruction also promised to enable Western European countries to fend off Soviet incursion, to help to forestall the emergence of domestic communist movements and, finally, to provide investment and trading partners for the United States rather than the USSR. As things turned out, the Marshall Plan proved to be an outstanding success on all these fronts. Thus, when it began to channel official transfers to the Third World, the United States could only be optimistic about their role in containing communist expansion there.

2. The bloc preference index is constructed as follows: $BP_{DM} = O_{DM} - E_{DM}$ where BP_{DM} is bloc preference for developed market countries (or the West), O_{DM} is the observed number of embassies in developed market economies, and E_{DM} is the expected number of embassies in the West. $E_{DM} = *(O_{DM} + O_{CB})$, where O_{CB} is the observed number of embassies in the communist bloc, * is a constant equal to the total number of countries in the West divided by the sum of countries in the West and the communist bloc. Since the number of countries in the West remains unchanged, the value of this constant figure differs slightly depending on the number of countries in the communist bloc (see Appendix D). To illustrate: if a Third World country has 12 embassies in the West and 4 in the communist bloc, then $BP_{DM} = 12 - [(26/40)(12 + 4)] = 1.6$. Had we calculated the index the other way round, i.e. bloc preference for the communist bloc, the value obtained would be identical except for its sign having changed. Thus, $BP_{CB} = 4 - [(14/40)(4 + 12)] = -1.6$.

3. The communist bloc aid figures are not directly comparable with OECD ones, not least because they come from a different source, i.e. *The United Nations Statistical Yearbook* and are available only from 1962. In the context of our analysis, this lack of direct comparability is not a problem since we use the UN figures only to indicate an association with the communist bloc and not, for example, to assess the explanatory power of communist, as opposed to OECD, aid. Of course, had the figures been directly comparable, we would have been able to extract much more information from the communist bloc aid variable.

4. The forward defence areas are: Greece, Iran, Laos, Pakistan, Philippines, South Korea, South Vietnam, Taiwan, Thailand and Turkey.
5. Since suppliers other than just the United States now figure in our analysis, we use SIPRI arms sales data.
6. The left-wing and non-left-wing violence variables were collected from newspaper sources, principally *Keesing's Contemporary Archives*. These variables measure violence within, and not between, Third World states. Working on an annual basis, individual states are scored '0' if there is no evidence of the existence of such violence or if its occurrence, when it does occur, is both sporadic and involves ten or fewer deaths. While essentially only a rough benchmark, these criteria were adopted on the assumption that if they were not in fact met, it is unlikely that the incidence of violence would even reach the United States' attention. But if, on the other hand, the violence that does occur is persistent and/or widespread, i.e. if it is relatively large-scale, a score of '1' is given to the state for the year in which this extensive violence occurs.

   It is obvious that a distinct judgemental element enters into this scoring procedure. While accepting both this observation and its implications of the potential for measurement error, we would like to make two observations on this issue. Firstly, every effort was made to ensure that individual Third World states were given the 'correct' score on this variable. Secondly, precisely in order to minimise measurement error, we limit ourselves to conceptualising this variable in a dummy format. For these reasons, we feel that it is a substantively important and meaningful variable in the context of this analysis.
7. Because of its insignificance in later analyses, we do not mention communist bloc aid in the text. Initially, however, it tends to covary positively with US aid, but their relationship fades in the late 1960s and after.
8. A list of the full title and acronym of every variable used herein can be found in the appendix at the end of this chapter.
9. As in Chapter 4, we have adjusted the signs of the standardised variables to facilitate the interpretation of the tables summarising the outcome of the discriminant analyses. In other words, we have reversed the signs of all variables when the group mean for recipients is negative and that for non-recipients is positive.
10. Our major reservation about the discriminant results concerns the competition with communism variables' relatively low level of success in correctly allocating actual non-recipients to the predicted non-recipient cell. Ideally, the individual countries would be allocated primarily to the top left and bottom right cells of each discriminant table, but we generally do not locate 'correctly' the majority of actual non-recipients. This problem is partly a function of the convention set in Chapter 4 whereby we draw the line between the means of the recipient and non-recipient populations on the basis of their relative size rather than at the simple mid-point between the two means. This procedure in fact makes it more difficult for the discriminating variables to assign cases correctly, but we think it preferable to err on the side of conservatism. None the less, it must be acknowledged that the low level of success in correctly assigning actual non-recipients remains a weakness in our results.
11. In examining Table 5.2, it should be borne in mind that the NRNR and NRR categories together comprise the NR category in Table 5.1. In addition,

some caution needs to be exercised in interpreting the significance values. When the variances of the compared groups differ significantly, we use the separate, as opposed to pooled, variance estimates in the t-tests. This practice is not uncommon, especially when, as in the NRNR and NRR comparisons, one or both of the groups being compared is small in size. Its disadvantage, however, is that it makes it more difficult to obtain significant values for the t-tests. An additional problem is that categories contain zero variance in a number of cases so that a t-test cannot be executed at all. For these reasons, the t-test significance level should be treated somewhat cautiously and attention should be paid to the actual mean scores.

The number of cases in the four categories of R, NR, NRNR and NRR differ marginally by variable depending on missing data. The actual numbers for the full data set across years are: 68, 26, 22, 4 (1969); 75, 22, 15, 7 (1971); 73, 28, 22, 6 (1973); 80, 22, 15, 7 (1975); 78, 23, 13, 10 (1977); and 79, 22, 12, 10 (1979).

12. The way to interpret Table 5.2 is to examine first of all the difference on individual variables between recipients (R) and non-recipients (NR) of economic aid and then to look for substantial change when the distinction is made within the non-recipient population between those countries not receiving US arms sales (NRNR) and those receiving them (NRR). To take gross US trade as an example, the difference between the R and NR groups progressively erodes over time, but when non-recipients are disaggregated into the NRNR and NRR sub-populations, a far more complex picture emerges. Recipients come gradually to have about the same gross trade with the United States as those Third World countries receiving neither aid nor arms sales (i.e. NRNR), but far less than those not receiving aid, but receiving arms sales (i.e. NRR). While this exercise may lead us to qualify the discriminant results for gross US trade in Table 5.1, it also accentuates the importance of bloc preference and communist bloc arms sales. That is, the difference between R and NR on bloc preference appear to erode over time, but once arms sales recipients are removed from the non-recipient sub-population, the difference between recipients and non-recipients, i.e. between R and NRNR, becomes very pronounced.

13. Since Soviet gross and percentage transfers are positively correlated, the weaker association between US aid and the Soviet percentage share variables transforms the latter's influence into a negative one. In effect, what this transformation means is that the United States is attracted to certain gross Soviet transfers, but once this attraction is controlled, it actually reacts against situations of high Soviet percentage share.

14. It might be thought that the smaller number of communist bloc embassies among the larger per capita aid recipients is simply a reflection of this group's tendency to have relatively few embassies abroad. It is the case, however, that this group of Third World countries displays proportionately fewer diplomatic ties to the East than to the West so that they do manifest a very real pro-West bias in their diplomatic orientation.

15. Indeed, it is not until 1961 that Soviet arms transfers are found at all in the high per capita aid category.

16. The US trade ties of recipients' neighbours actually assume a negative influence on US aid allocations in 1953 and 1955, but this influence is broadly analogous to, and easier to understand as, a positive influence for neighbours' communist bloc ties. In other words, when the contiguous US

variables are introduced into the analysis, the partial correlations for the contiguous Soviet variables are almost identical except for having the opposite sign.

17. US gross and percentage trade share are moderately highly correlated, although the latter enjoys a significant simple correlation with per capita US aid and the former an insignificant one. It is this difference that explains why the gross trade variable takes on a negative sign when both variables are included in the regression equation.

18. Soviet arms transfers are to be found in the medium recipient category in 1961 and 1963 and in the large category in 1963, 1965 and 1969.

19. This statement means that not only do we achieve significant results in the discriminant analysis as a whole, but that we also succeed in correctly classifying a majority of the cases in each of the military assistance recipient and non-recipient groups, something that the economic aid discriminant analyses proved unable to do. The only 'unsuccessful' year in this respect is 1975, but given that the military assistance programme had all but been run down by this time, we attach no substantive importance to this exception to the rule.

20. A number of other variables appear sporadically, but they owe their influence to their qualifying effect on more important variables. Gross US trade, for example, has a negative influence on selection into the military assistance recipient population in both 1957 and 1961, but its appearance as a discriminator is primarily the result of its positive relationship with bloc preference. When this relationship is controlled for, the US trade variable's weak positive influence becomes a stronger negative one.

21. Unlike with economic aid, the inclusion of US arms sales recipients in the military assistance non-recipient population does not affect our overall results. All that the re-definition of the non-recipient population to exclude arms recipients does is to exaggerate the differences that have already been identified. It on no occasion introduces a dimension of differentiation that had not already appeared. By way of illustration, we might note that re-definition produces its most pronounced exaggeration effect in the case of bloc preference. Thus, t-tests between recipients and non-recipients of arms within the population of non-recipients of military assistance produce differences that are significant at the 0.05 level or greater in each of the years from 1969 to 1975. The mean values for arms recipients and non-recipients are respectively 3.3, 0.6 (1969); 2.5, 0.7 (1971); 2.3, 0.0 (1973); and 1.4, 0.1 (1975). When recipients are compared to non-recipients as a whole, however, this pattern is barely disturbed. In fact, the values become 2.9, 0.9 (1969); 2.8, 0.9 (1971); 2.3, 0.3 (1973); and 2.2, 0.3 (1975).

22. The regression results presented in Table 5.6 also include the results of the runs excluding the outlying case in those years in which it claims 30 per cent or more of total US military assistance, i.e. 1955, 1967, 1969, 1971, 1973 and 1975. The equations in which the outlier is included produce essentially the same results until 1973 and 1975. It should be noted, therefore, that Vietnam does have a disturbing effect in these last two years of the military assistance programme.

23. Communist bloc arms transfers are found in the medium recipient category in only three years and are trivial in volume in two of them.

24. Considerations of space have obliged us not to present the regression results for 1955, 1967, 1969, 1971, 1973 and 1975 when the outlier is excluded.

Up to and including 1971, however, these equations produce essentially the same R^2 values and variable loadings as do those including the outlier. As with gross military assistance (see note 22 above), to include the outlier has a disturbing effect in 1973 and 1975 when it helps to produce lower R^2 values and to give left-wing violence greater explanatory power. As usual, we have opted for the conservative alternative and presented the weaker equations.

25. The medium category of US arms sales recipients displays communist bloc arms transfers in 1969, 1977 and 1979 and the high category in 1979 only.

26. It is worth noting that, as in the case of military assistance, the competition with communism variables correctly classifies a majority of both recipients and non-recipients of US arms sales.

27. When assessing the relative importance of the principal discriminating variable, account needs to be taken of the fact that the negative qualifying influence of US trade share inflates slightly the power of gross US aid.

28. It is only in 1969 and 1971 that communist bloc arms transfers penetrate the medium US arms sales cateogy and in 1973 and 1979 that they penetrate the high category.

29. The equations presented in Table 5.10 exclude the outlier. Those including the outlier contain basically the same predictors with the same loadings. Generally, however, their R^2 values are higher, which explains why we report the equations excluding the outlier.

30. To take gross military assistance and the growth rate of Soviet arms share, for example, the zero US transfer recipient category begins all nine periods with Soviet arms transfers and positive rates of growth occur on five of these nine occasions. The small recipient category sees seven periods begin with positive values and four of them experience positive growth rates. What is more, in two of the remaining periods, the Soviet arms share variable both begins and ends at zero. In the medium category, only four of the nine periods begin with positive values and positive growth rates occur in no more than two of the four. The remaining five periods see the Soviet variable begin and end with a value of zero. Finally, all nine periods in the high category begin with zero share and seven of them end the same way.

31. Although Table 5.12 shows a significant chi-square value for the West's diplomatic associations with recipients' neighbours, we disregard this 'finding' as there is no intuitively meaningful pattern to the variation across the four transfer categories.

32. While a supplier loss in the context of recipients alone, counter-aversion is a no gain and no loss outcome in the larger context of recipients' neighbours because recipients are accorded greater preference by the United States at the same time that their neighbours are accorded it by the USSR. Neither controlling the whole area, therefore, the superpowers find themselves in a 'stand-off' position. What is more, this position cannot be attributed to the failure of the transfer programme in question since, at least in theory, transfers to recipients afford the United States no leverage over the communist bloc associations of their neighbours.

33. Because mutual veto sees the same growth rates in all Third World countries regardless of volume of transfer received, it is an outcome that is probably more accurately seen as lying on the loss side of no gain and no loss for a supplier like the United States. This qualification notwithstanding, however, the mutual veto outcome remains essentially a no gain and no loss one.

34. The fact that gains and losses are evaluated in terms of second-order utilities makes their calculation more troublesome for Third World recipients precisely because we know so little about what their utilities are either individually or collectively. This uncertainty forces us to evaluate their gains and losses against the benchmark of non-alignment with either superpower. Given the importance attached to non-alignment by Third World states generally, it does not seem unreasonable for this analysis to assume that they actively pursue it in their relations with both the United States and the USSR. For this reason, any transfer structuring effect will be considered a loss for the recipient simply because it erodes its non-aligned status. The absence of such an effect is, conversely, considered to be a gain.

35. Here we must emphasise the importance of our evaluation benchmark, i.e. non-alignment. If, however, a particular Third World country in fact wished to be allied exclusively to the United States, then it is obvious that aversion and reinforcement outcomes would constitute a gain in its eyes.

36. The only exception is counter-aversion in the context of recipients' neighbours. To the extent that US recipients found their own increasing ties being matched by their neighbours' increasing ties with the communist bloc, counter-aversion would be a no gain and no loss outcome for the recipients of US transfers.

37. The recipient's position is on the gain side of no loss and no gain since the absence of any structuring effect of the type inherent in aversion and reinforcement outcomes is accompanied by the receipt of transfers.

38. This result is not altogether unexpected. Not only does the distribution indicate at best a weak relationship between US aid and trade, but also the reinforcement of which we find signs in the 1960s is of the supportive rather than promotional variety. It is also the case that if we examine US trade rates of growth over this reinforcement period, they do not differ in magnitude from the rates over the remainder of the period of the analysis. When considering this last point, however, it is worth bearing in mind that a reinforcement outcome is not necessarily predicated on a reinforcement distribution strategy.

39. Parity would be indicated by a bloc preference score of zero. But this score would not mean equality in an absolute sense since the measure controls for the very different number of countries in the communist bloc and the West.

40. The relationship between gross aid and gross Soviet trade could be taken to indicate a counter-aversion outcome. For reasons discussed in the Findings section of this chapter, however, we attach no substantive importance to this relationship.

41. The summed ranks for the zero, small, medium and large categories on the growth rates of neighbours' communist diplomatic association growth rates are respectively 18, 13, 8, 11. These same figures for gross communist bloc arms imports are 17, 11, 11, 11 and they are 15, 10, 11, 14 for neighbours' percentage communist bloc arms imports.

6 Economic structure and performance

Introduction

Theoretical rationale

To a greater extent than in the previous two chapters, the reasons as to why we would expect a relationship between official transfers and economic considerations do not form a single, all-embracing rationale. There are, in fact, five major rationales which, while overlapping, are none the less clearly distinguishable.

The first of them is identified by recipient development needs and it holds that the principal objective of official transfers is the alleviation of Third World countries' development needs. Accordingly, one would anticipate that transfers flow in largest volume to those countries whose development needs are most pronounced.[1] Given the supplier description of the three transfers, development needs criteria are likely to be especially pronounced, if at all, in the distribution of economic aid since the logic of this transfer is essentially that, acting as an investment supplement, it promotes development.[2] This logic need not apply only in the context of the aid programme, however. To the extent that official transfers can be substituted for each other, then the receipt of say, military assistance, could well free resources that were originally earmarked for military expenditure and allow them to be redirected for economic development purposes. In other words, there is no necessary reason why military assistance and arms sales should be excluded from this development needs rationale. Still, given the explicitly security-oriented focus of military assistance and arms sales, the distribution of these two transfers is unlikely to be structured by development needs criteria. Where a relationship might be found, on the other hand, is in the impact analysis. Here the receipt of say, military assistance might foster growth on some economic variable precisely because transfer substitution does take place. Should development needs be found to structure the distribution of official transfers, it would undermine our security-based supply utility conceptualisation of transfers, whereas the discovery of an impact relationship would be compatible with this conceptualisation.[3]

The second rationale also concerns recipient development, but concentrates on development prospects rather than on development needs. Since this rationale holds that official transfers reward prospects and since countries with the most chronic and persistent needs also have the worst development prospects, it would lead us to expect such transfers to stand in the opposite relationship to prospects that they do to needs.[4] Thus, while a supplier may be concerned, as in the case of needs, to promote development in the Third World, this concern does not derive from the humanitarian impulse to alleviate need. Rather, it is a concern that exists either because suppliers deem it both useful and desirable to be associated with the more viable Third World states (viability itself being a function of development potential) or because development is itself seen as the means to other ends, which may include, for example, political stability (i.e. countries with better development prospects may be deemed more likely to achieve stability) or trading and investment opportunities (i.e. countries displaying higher growth rates may be deemed more promising trading partners).

The third rationale is essentially a variant, or extension, of the development prospects argument. According to this, official transfers can be expected to be distributed so as to promote trading and investment opportunities for the supplier, opportunities which can themselves be seen as second-order utilities. These opportunities may be valued for the immediate benefits they are likely to bring to the supplier or for the longer-term benefits that are likely to accrue to it as a result of its transfers having contributed to recipient economic growth and infra-structural development or to recipient integration into a Western-oriented inter-national economic system. In short, official transfers can redound to both the short-term and long-term economic self-interest of the supplier by providing it with a forum for trading and investment opportunities.

The fourth rationale takes the logic of this argument still further and holds that the purpose of official transfers is actively to promote the economic dependence of recipients. Again, it is a rationale whose principal foci are trading and invest-ment considerations, but the supplier's objective is seen to be the stimulation of recipient dependence on foreign, Western, high-income production rather than the carving out of opportunities for itself in countries experiencing economic develop-ment. Official transfers, it is held, foster such dependence to the extent that they stimulate Third World countries to participate in an international economy in which their relative backwardness places them at a distinct disadvantage or that they serve to incorporate these same countries into an international economic division of labour that is self-interestedly dominated by the West.

The final rationale is not so clearly tied to the notion of supplier economic self-interest because it derives from the already demonstrated US attraction to the Third World countries' power political capabilities. It is obviously the case that economic characteristics are no more than a subset of these more general capabilities, but just as states can be ordered when their importance is measured in terms of say, military expenditure, so too can they be ordered with respect to their economic capabilities. For this reason, we would expect these capabilities to structure to some extent the US official transfer programmes.

From the perspective of the supplier then, we can identify several rationales as to why economic considerations can be expected to be construed as second-order utilities to be pursued through the commitment and leverage potential in-herent in its official transfers. Although interrelated to some extent, it is obviously the case that the rationales that have been identified can be differentiated along a number of dimensions, including the particular interests being promoted (e.g. recipient development or supplier trading and investment opportunities), and the direction and strength of the relationships between the transfer and supplier economic interests. We shall speak to such relatively detailed issues when we interpret our findings later in this chapter. For the moment, however, we shall simply reiterate our observation that these several, somewhat complementary rationales lead us to expect there to be a relationship between official transfers and economic considerations, whether these considerations be conceptualised in terms of development, trade and investment, dependence or power politics. Having identified the supplier economic interests pursued, the impact analysis will then enable us to determine whether or not its second-order utilities are, in fact, promoted by its transfers.

Since official transfers are not a one-way phenomenon, we might also reasonably expect economic considerations to play some role in stimulating Third World demand for them. After all, the recipient first-order utilities inherent in these transfers could lead to the receipt of them being viewed as the means whereby Third World countries would be able to pursue a number of their own second-order utilities, for example, growth or closer incorporation into the world economy. It is equally conceivable, however, that the official transfers could be associated with recipient disutilities. The impact analysis in this chapter will indicate whether Third World countries experience either or both utilities and disutilities as a result of receiving US official transfers.

Operationalisation

The variables tapping supplier economic interests can, for the sake of clarity of presentation, be divided into three sets that are not independent of each other in conceptual terms. We shall call these sets 'production structure', 'trade structure' and 'investment and banking structure'.

The first set is designed to profile Third World countries' basic production structures and it comprises the following individual variables: real per capita income, gross domestic fixed capital formation as a percentage of GDP (GDFCF) and agricultural and industrial production as a percentage of GDP.[5] These variables are especially pertinent to the development rationale and to assessing recipient utilities and disutilities in the impact analysis. The 'needs' rationale, for example, would anticipate a larger volume of transfers to Third World countries with relatively low levels of per capita income or GDFCF, while its 'prospects' counterpart would anticipate exactly the opposite relationship. In the same vein, if transfers are associated with higher growth rates on say, real per capita income then, other things being equal, it cannot but be concluded that the transfer does not visit a second-order disutility on its recipients in this regard. This conclusion itself then becomes centrally relevant to a development vs. dependence interpretation of the official transfer in question.

The second set of variables profiles recipients' trade structure. Among its more obvious constituent variables are exports and imports, each being expressed in absolute terms and as a percentage of GDP. The percentaged variables are taken to measure Third World countries' relative commitment to international trade. What is more, when examined over time, these variables also afford measures of sectoral change in the larger economy, just as do the agricultural and industrial production variables. Exports are also examined when they have been disaggregated into agricultural, mining and manufacturing components, each of which is again measured in absolute terms and as a percentage of total exports. The reason for this disaggregation is to determine whether it is a particular type of trade or trade in general that attracts official transfers from the United States. Finally, this set includes three variables that profile recipient diversification. They are export diversification by commodity, export diversification by destination and import diversification by source.[6] These three variables are central above all to the dependence explanation of official transfers, whereas the trade structure variables as a set play a prominent role, although not always the same one, in each of the rationales. In particular, the different rationales hypothesise marked dissimilarities in the nature of the relationship between the trade variables and official transfers.

The final set of variables profiles the international banking and investment activities of Third World countries. The first investment variable is net factor income from abroad in both its gross and percentaged forms and it summarises the balance of production by foreign nationals in a country's economy relative to that country's own production in overseas economies. The second investment measure is investment income from abroad, which represents the repatriated returns on foreign investments by the country overseas. Again, it is expressed in both its gross and percentaged forms in this analysis. The third, and similar, investment variable is the balance on direct foreign investment. Loans to the Third World country by the Export–Import Bank (ExIm) are the final investment variable. The banking sector variables are the foreign assets and liabilities of commercial banks measured in gross and percentaged form. Liabilities are loans received from foreign sources, whereas assets are loans made by domestic commercial banks to foreigners. Collectively, this set of variables profiles the external investment and banking activities of Third World countries, activities that are directly relevant, albeit to varying degrees and in different forms, to each of the rationales. Moreover, they are of substantial pertinence and interest to the utilities evaluation in the impact analysis of this chapter.

Findings: distribution

Economic aid

Taking the variables profiling production structure first, GDP increases, although not very steeply, across the three gross aid recipient categories. Non-recipients have generally low values until the late 1960s, after which time their GDP value becomes similar in magnitude to that found in the large recipient category. Per capita GDP, on the other hand, assumes a consistent relationship with level of aid only from the late 1960s when the non-recipient category comes to display consistently higher scores on this variable than any and all of the recipient categories. GDFCF shows little variation across the four aid categories and the same is true of both agricultural and industrial production across the three recipient categories. It is the case, however, that non-recipients of aid have substantially larger industrial sectors and smaller agricultural sectors than do recipients. GDP apart, therefore, there is little linear covariation between gross aid and the various aspects of production structure within the population of Third World countries receiving US aid. The systematic differences that do appear are between non-recipients on the one hand and recipients as a whole on the other.

With regard to the cluster of trade variables, our earlier analysis of power political capabilities has already indicated that gross exports and imports covary positively with volume of aid receipts from the early 1960s onwards, although the high scores in the non-recipient category create non-linearities beginning in the late 1960s. Exports and imports as a percentage of GDP generally decline over all four aid categories, a decline that is most abrupt in the transition from the zero to small recipient category. In other words, non-recipients tend to have relatively high levels of both gross trade and commitment to trade. Within the aid recipient population, by contrast, gross trade increases with aid, but the commitment to trade declines with it.

Our next step is to examine the principal components, or types of trade, in the export structure of Third World countries. These components are agricultural, extractive and manufactured exports and the examination of their relation to aid follows from the argument that since potential aid recipients do vary in their export mix, the United States could manipulate its aid programme to encourage and promote one or other type of export rather than exports in general.

Albeit not very steeply, agricultural exports generally increase with economic aid from the early 1960s, but the increase is not as pronounced as it is for total trade so that there emerges a small decline in agriculture as a percentage of total exports across the three recipient categories, and especially in the large recipient category. But the lowest scores are still found among non-recipients. Within the three recipient categories, there is no systematic relationship between level of aid and extractive exports in either their gross or percentaged form. Non-recipients, on the other hand, have higher levels of both types of extractive exports. Manufactured goods, by contrast, show a much more consistent pattern, generally increasing across all four aid categories over the whole 1950-79 period. What is more, their gross value increases a little more rapidly than do total exports so that there is also a small, positive increase from one recipient category to the next in the value of manufactures as a percentage of total exports. Manufactured imports also increase somewhat with aid, although they have especially high values in the non-recipient category. But this pattern more or less matches that of total imports with the result that, when percentaged, manufactured imports show no systematic variation across levels of aid receipt.

The investment and banking cluster shows, among other things, that net factor income from abroad develops a systematic relationship with aid only in the three recipient categories and then only in the 1970s when it increases slightly and positively from one aid category to the other. But since GDP increases more substantially, net factor income, expressed as a percentage of this same GDP, declines across the recipient categories, although this negative relationship weakens in the 1970s. Even taking account of their relatively high GDPs, however, it is non-recipients that have the highest levels of gross and percentaged net factor income. Net foreign direct investment, by contrast, shows no pattern of systematic variation over the four categories. As for the variable of investment income, it is not related to aid within the recipient categories until the 1970s when it tends to increase across them. But it is an increase that is insufficient to offset the increase in GDP so that, when standardised by the latter, investment income comes to decline slightly with aid levels. Standardisation by GDP also serves to eliminate the discontinuity created by the non-recipient category's having scored highest on this variable in absolute terms. Both the foreign assets and liabilities of commercial banks covary with aid receipts only in the 1970s when a weak, positive relationship develops. None the less, this relationship is strong enough to match the increase in GDP so that, from 1970, assets and liabilities as a proportion of GDP in fact show some increase across the three aid recipient categories. Non-recipients generally boast high assets and liabilities scores but, as is evident from the similarity of their percentage score with those of the recipient categories, their higher absolute assets and liabilities are a reflection of their relatively large GDPs. Finally, loans from the ExIm Bank are confined almost entirely to aid recipients and covary positively with their level of aid recipt until the mid-1960s. Thereafter, non-recipients of aid become moderately large recipients of ExIm loans and the systematic variation across the three categories of aid recipient all but disappears.

In the previous two chapters, our analysis has proceeded at this point to the differentiation of the recipient and non-recipient groupings of Third World countries by means of discriminant analysis. But since the operational mode of this particular technique is to exclude any case showing missing data on one or other independent variable and since a number of our cases have data missing on certain economic structure variables, we resort in this chapter to differentiating recipients and non-recipients through bivariate difference-of-means tests. While this strategy may deprive us of discriminant analysis' power of controlled differentiation, it effectively achieves the same results and, at the same time, avoids the bias and distortion that the problem of missing data would otherwise have introduced into our results.

The difference-of-means tests identify a number of pronounced differences in the production structure cluster of variables. Most immediately noticeable is that non-recipients of aid consistently display signficantly higher levels of per capita income (GDP) and significantly larger industrial sectors than recipients.[7] The inter-group differences in GDFCF, in contrast, are not significant. In the early years, absolute GDP likewise tends to be similar in value across the two group-ings, but non-recipients' GDP values become larger in later years. Significant differences in the trade cluster of variables are found in the areas of percentage exports and imports when, once again, non-recipients prove to have higher values. This grouping tends to have higher levels of gross exports and imports also, but its superiority in terms of dollar value becomes significant only in the later years of analysis. In general, the magnitude of the differences between reci-pients and non-recipients of aid is less pronounced in the investment and banking cluster of variables. With the exception of ExIm loans, which enjoy similar values in both groupings, there is none the less a tendency for the variables in this cluster to score more highly in the non-recipient population of countries. What is more, the differences sometimes achieve significance, but only when the variables are in their gross, and not relative, form.

In sum therefore, it appears that the Third World countries selected to receive US aid from 1969 onwards tend to be less wealthy, to have a smaller industrial base, to have a lower commitment to trade and a lower absolute, but not rela-tive, involvement in international investment and banking.

It could be, however, that this overall picture will change when, as in previous chapters, we take account of the fact that certain potential aid recipients do not in fact receive the transfer because they are tied to the United States by virtue of being included in its arms sales programme. And, as it turns out, excluding this set of countries from the non-recipient population does indeed substantially alter the nature of the criteria determining inclusion or otherwise in the US aid programme.

The production structure variables now show that while per capita GDP and in-dustrial sector size remain significantly larger in the truncated non-recipient popu-lation, the magnitude of the per capita income difference is none the less reduced.[8] Absolute GDP changes even more markedly in that it is now consistently lower among non-recipients. The trade cluster duplicates, broadly speaking, this differ-ence between the gross and relative forms of its constituent variables. That is, rela-tive commitment to trade, as measured by percentage exports and imports, remains significantly higher among non-recipients of aid, whereas absolute commitment, i.e. gross trade, is generally lower in this same group of countries. As for the investment and banking variables, the differences between aid recipients and non-recipients on these variables are reduced substantially once arms sales recipients are excluded from the latter population. Indeed, in a number of areas, the indepen-dent variables assume values that are lower among the remaining non-recipients.

Thus, excluding arms sales recipients means that the remaining non-recipients differ from the recipient population principally in the relative aspects of their pro-duction and trade structures. That is, non-recipients are wealthier, have relatively

Table 6.1: Means on selected economic variables for non-recipients of economic aid (NR), recipients of economic aid (R) and non-recipients of both economic aid and arms sales (NRNR), 1969–79

	GDP			GDPPC			GDFCF		
	NR	R	NRNR	NR	R	NRNR	NR	R	NRNR
1969	3,613	3,610	2,341	545*	285	533†	18	16	17
1971	5,164	4,058	1,494	716*	298	598†	20	17	19
1973	4,814	5,278	3,221	826*	362	687†	21	18	20
1975	11,072	8,246	7,369	1,993*	554	1,366†	19	19	18
1977	18,014*	8,969	3,992	2,321*	705	1,792+	24	22	23
1979	21,133	12,071	4,917	3,221*	800	2,915†	24	22	22

	Indust			GrEx			PEx		
1969	26*	18	25†	437	430	295	27*	18	28†
1971	32*	19	30†	761	489	399	29*	18	27†
1973	31*	19	28†	980	624	497	32*	16	29†
1975	41*	22	34†	4,112*	1,524	1,699	66*	22	65†
1977	45*	20	52†	6,416*	1,335	2,575	61*	21	78†
1979	41*	21	43†	6,909*	1,825	2,857	59*	19	77†

	NFI			InvInc			ForDrInv		
1969	−156	−69	−156	129	87	107	33	23	26
1971	−155	−65	−86	171	92	46	68	23	20
1973	−329*	−54	−247†	145	114	78	5*	33	−13
1975	−780*	−151	−531	372	187	268	−165	54	41
1977	−1,450*	−152	−475	428	228	129	−53	64	−49
1979	−1,079*	−207	−504	537	357	119†	−120	92	−55

	CBFA			ExImLn					
1969	89	39	72	4	6	4			
1971	213*	42	138†	7	6	0†			
1973	126	138	106	13	16	5			
1975	283	27	87	25	18	13			
1977	567	343	115	17	23	3†			
1979	947	546	238	20	27	12			

* Indicates a significant difference at the 0.05 level or higher between NR and R.
† Indicates a significant difference at the 0.05 level or higher between NRNR and R.

large industrial sectors and display a relatively greater commitment to trade. The previous differences in the areas of investment and banking and in gross production and trade structure, on the other hand, now largely disappear.

Finally, our analysis of the distribution of gross US aid moves on to the regression phase, the results of which are presented in Table 6.2. While significant, the equations generated for the first half of the 1950s make little sense and appear to be no more than artefacts of other, more important considerations. Thereafter and through the 1960s, however, the results are both stronger and more readily

Table 6.2: Standardised coefficients for the regressions of gross aid on the economic variables, 1951–79*

Year				Year			
1951:	(0.59)	GrMfEx	1.68	1969:	(0.59)	GDP	1.27
	(0.00)	CBFL	−0.89		(0.17)	GrAgEx	−0.47
	(0.05)	ForDrInv	−0.68		(0.01)	NFI	0.58
	(−0.30)	PMfIm	0.40		(0.08)	CBFL	−0.47
		$R^2 = 80$			(0.25)	IL	0.28
						$R^2 = 73$	
1953:	(0.49)	PEx	0.49				
		$R^2 = 24$		1971:	(0.52)	GDP	0.70
					(0.02)	NFI	0.26
1955:	(−0.49)	PEx	−0.75		(−0.24)	PAgEx	−0.39
	(0.23)	PMnEx	0.36		(−0.15)	Indust	−0.35
	(−0.14)	PForDrInv	−0.30			$R^2 = 51$	
	(0.00)	PIm	0.23				
		$R^2 = 50$		1973:	(−0.28)	PEx	−0.30
					(−0.16)	PAgEx	−0.19
1957:	(0.57)	GDP	0.43			$R^2 = 12$	
	(−0.54)	PEx	−0.48				
	(0.16)	PMnEx	0.28	1975:	(0.43)	PMfEx	0.44
		$R^2 = 56$			(−0.30)	PMfIm	−0.23
					(−0.10)	PMnEx	0.23
1959:	(0.63)	GDP	1.21		(−0.25)	PEx	−0.21
	(−0.18)	ForDrInv	−0.93		(0.15)	GDPPC	0.17
		$R^2 = 94$				$R^2 = 32$	
1961:	(0.68)	GDP	0.93	1977:	(0.27)	CBFA	0.47
	(0.00)	CBFL	−0.68		(−0.04)	PInvInc	−0.33
	(0.32)	PMfEx	0.40		(−0.20)	PAgEx	−0.17
		$R^2 = 77$				$R^2 = 17$	
1963:	(0.76)	GDP	1.06	1979:	(0.33)	CBFA	0.79
	(0.36)	GrEx	−0.27		(0.00)	PInvInc	−0.49
	(0.18)	CBFL	−0.22		(−0.26)	PAgEx	−0.19
		$R^2 = 67$			(0.14)	GrMfEx	−0.48
					(0.30)	PMfEx	0.30
1965:	(0.72)	GDP	1.33			$R^2 = 34$	
	(0.04)	ForDrInv	−0.48				
	(0.34)	GrEx	−0.48				
	(0.06)	CBFL	−0.38				
	(0.02)	GDFCF	0.32				
	(−0.15)	PMfIm	−0.24				
		$R^2 = 80$					
1967:	(0.56)	GDP	1.21				
	(0.00)	ExImLn	−0.42				
	(0.01)	NFI	0.68				
	(0.00)	CBFL	−0.50				
	(0.00)	PIL	0.31				
	(0.01)	CBFA	0.26				
	(−0.02)	PMnEx	0.24				
		$R^2 = 70$					

* The figures in parentheses represent the zero-order correlation coefficients.

interpretable. The consistently predominant estimator of aid allocations in this period is GDP and its influence is so dominant that the other estimators appearing in the final equations do little more than qualify it. Typically, they have low simple correlations with the dependent variable and it is their positive or negative relationship with GDP that brings them into the equation once GDP itself has been controlled. While, in principle, there is no reason why such secondary influences should not be interesting and substantively important in their own right, their failure to fall into either a coherent or consistent pattern would seem to incidate that, in this particular instance, they possess neither of these characteristics. The results for the 1970s are, as in the early 1950s, very weak and no clear or coherent pattern is apparent in them.[9]

As for the per capita aid, the bivariate ANOVAs show it to decline with GDP and to increase with per capita GDP. The remaining production structure variables (GDFCF and agricultural and industrial production structure), however, are not systematically related to level of per capita aid receipt.

The trade structure variables show both gross exports and imports to decline as per capita aid increases. Relative commitment to trade, i.e. trade as a percentage of GDP, declines slightly across the recipient categories in the 1950s, shows little variation in the 1960s and generally increases in the 1970s. The agricultural, mining and manufactured exports variables, in contrast, show no sign of a systematic relationship with the dependent variable. Thus, apart from those instances where relationships are only to be expected (as, for example, when absolute aggregates like GDP or gross trade are arrayed over a relative aggregate like per capita aid), we find no systematic relationships between per capita aid and the individual trade structure variables.

Much the same general conclusions hold with regard to the international investment and banking variables. Gross net factor income from abroad decreases with level of per capita aid receipt, whereas its relative counterpart varies hardly at all across the categories of the dependent variable. This same picture characterises the investment income and net foreign direct investment variables. A slight difference appears in the case of commercial banks' foreign assets and liabilities. In their absolute form, these variables stand in no clear or consistent relationship to per capita aid, whereas, when expressed as a percentage of GDP, they generally covary positively with it. ExIm loans, in contrast, generally covary negatively with it. In sum, therefore, the bivariate results suggest that, with the slight exception of commercial banks' foreign assets and liabilities, the range of investment and banking variables have little or no influence on per capita US aid allocations.

The multiple regression results for per capita aid are presented in Table 6.3 and at least initially, they seem difficult to understand and interpret. For a start, their R^2 values drop sharply after the 1950s, a drop that could reflect a US policy change or that could be an artefact of the data. The latter would seem to be the more plausible explanation, not least because of the enigmatic role of the percentage

Table 6.3: Standardised coefficients for the regressions of per capita aid on the economic variables, 1951-79*

1951:	Not significant			1967:	(−0.23)	NFI	0.36
					(−0.13)	Agric	−0.36
1953:	(0.51)	GDFCF	0.99		(−0.13)	PMfEx	−0.23
	(−0.17)	GMnEx	−0.27			$R^2 = 16$	
	(−0.23)	PMfIm	−0.55				
	(−0.23)	PCBFL	−0.41	1969:	(−0.28)	Agric	−0.47
	(−0.16)	IL	−0.37		(−0.24)	NFI	0.53
	(0.04)	Indust	−0.37		(0.10)	PMnEx	0.33
		$R^2 = 82$				$R^2 = 30$	
1955:	(−0.41)	PEx	−0.76	1971:	(0.34)	CBFL	0.50
	(0.24)	GDFCF	0.98		(−0.04)	GMfIm	−0.57
	(−0.24)	GDP	−0.64		(−0.26)	Agric	−0.34
	(−0.28)	PMfIm	−0.44		(−0.18)	PEx	−0.32
	(−0.01)	GDPPC	−0.47		(−0.17)	PAgEx	−0.27
		$R^2 = 85$				$R^2 = 40$	
1957:	(−0.49)	PEx	−0.73	1973:	(0.42)	PIm	0.50
	(0.21)	PIm	0.23		(−0.06)	PEx	−0.39
	(−0.25)	PCBFL	−0.22		(0.34)	GDPPC	0.34
	(−0.32)	GrIm	−0.44		(−0.21)	PAgEx	−0.27
	(−0.16)	GDFCF	0.37		(−0.17)	GrEx	−0.24
		$R^2 = 68$				$R^2 = 46$	
1959:	(−0.44)	PEx	−0.71	1975:	(0.52)	GDPPC	0.75
	(−0.44)	PIm	0.56		(−0.01)	Indust	−0.62
	(0.23)	GDPPC	0.35		(0.32)	PIm	0.27
	(−0.26)	GMfIm	−0.18		(−0.12)	PAgEx	−0.27
	(0.29)	PCBFL	0.17		(0.03)	PInvInc	0.20
	(0.04)	PMfEx	−0.17			$R^2 = 53$	
		$R^2 = 74$					
				1977:	(0.35)	GDPPC	0.35
1961:	(0.59)	PCBFA	0.71			$R^2 = 13$	
	(−0.32)	PEx	−0.42				
	(0.04)	CBFA	−0.29	1979:	(0.35)	GDPPC	0.49
	(−0.29)	Agric	−0.31		(0.28)	PIm	0.26
	(−0.22)	CBFL	−0.32		(0.02)	Indust	−0.42
	(0.04)	PAgEx	−0.25		(0.27)	PMfEx	0.34
		$R^2 = 70$			(0.06)	PMnEx	0.21
						$R^2 = 35$	
1963:	(−0.39)	Agric	−0.56				
	(0.33)	PNFI	0.69				
	(0.30)	PCBFA	0.28				
	(−0.07)	PMnEx	0.26				
	(−0.10)	GrIm	−0.22				
		$R^2 = 55$					
1965:	(−0.31)	Agric	−0.69				
	(−0.17)	PInvInc	−0.56				
	(−0.13)	GrAgEx	−0.32				
	(−0.06)	CBFA	−0.27				
		$R^2 = 38$					

* The figures in parentheses represent the zero-order correlation coefficients.

trade variable. It is a critical estimator throughout the 1950s (except for 1951 when no significant equation is generated), but what is troublesome on the face of the matter is that its influence is negative.[10] The problem is that it is difficult to see why the United States should use its per capita aid allocations to reward Third World countries with a relatively low commitment to trade. The likely explanation of this puzzle, however, is that the United States is in fact attracted to characteristics that do not appear in this chapter, but that happen to covary with percentage exports. Given this circumstance, together with the fact that the variables appearing in this chapter are at best relatively weakly related to per capita aid, percentage exports emerges as a significant estimator. In essence, though, its relationship to the dependent variable is spurious in an explanatory sense, if not in a predictive one as well.

A further interpretational problem with Table 6.3 is that the regression equations collectively embrace a large number of variables, many of which appear at most infrequently and irregularly. Two observations should allow us to keep this problem in perspective, however. Firstly, much of the variety stems from the trade variables, none of which are strongly related to per capita aid in bivariate terms so that marginal changes in their respective zero-order correlations can cause these variables to move in and out of the regression equations. Secondly, there is some basic and explainable pattern to many of the positive and negative signs. In general, predictor variables expressed in gross form are negatively signed and those expressed in relative form are positively signed. This rule is broken only when a variable enters the equation in a qualifying role, i.e. when it has a zero simple correlation with per capita aid but a significant correlation with a variable already in the equation.[11]

Despite these problems, Table 6.3 does suggest a number of important and interesting conclusions. Firstly, it indicates that purely economic considerations play at best a secondary role in explaining US per capita aid allocations. Secondly, per capita aid flows in greater volume to what would commonly be held to be the more developed Third World countries. Thus, per capita income, GDFCF and a relatively small agricultural sector positively influence the volume of per capita aid received. Thirdly, investment and banking considerations do not generally structure allocations. Finally, particular combinations of export and import patterns are unimportant influences. While there is some evidence of a sporadic US attraction to a commitment to import, no substantive importance should be attached to this finding, not least because we have already dismissed its exports counterpart as essentially spurious.[12]

Military assistance

The ANOVA results indicate that, generally speaking, the individual production structure variables show little systematic variation across the four recipients categories of gross military assistance. The only exception to this generalisation is GDP, which usually increases across the categories until the late 1960s, after which time the relationship disappears. Its value does, however, remain larger among recipients as a whole.

Much the same picture of at best weak relationships characterises the trade structure variables. Both gross exports and gross imports show little covariation with level of gross military assistance receipt, whereas percentage trade shows a slight tendency to decline with it. Equally no marked relationships emerge when the exports variable is broken down into its agricultural, mining and manufactured components, although there is a slight decline in the relative importance of primary exports with gross military assistance received.

Although still limited in their strength, more substantial relationships characterise the banking and investment set of variables. Net factor income from abroad decreases consistently across level of military assistance receipt, although its value in the non-recipient category is generally higher than a simple linear decrease would project. This negative relationship becomes still stronger when the net factor income variable is expressed in relative form. The same pattern holds for gross and percentaged investment income. Foreign direct investment, on the other hand, shows no sign of a relationship of any kind, although it is the case that non-recipients of military assistance tend to have higher relative scores on this variable. Commercial banks' gross foreign assets and liabilities tend to be positively related to gross military assistance, but the pattern of the relationship approximates to that of GDP so that when the assets and liabilities variables are standardised against it, all sign of a relationship disappears. Finally, ExIm loans do not vary systematically across the three recipient categories. Over time, however, non-recipients do come to display somewhat lower values on this variable than do recipients.

The t-test results in Table 6.4 indicate that, with the exception that recipients have markedly larger GDPs from the early 1960s onwards, the production structure variables do not discriminate very successfully between military assistance recipients and non-recipients.[13] This observation holds whether the individual variables are measured in gross or relative terms and the only slight departure from it is that industrial production is significantly higher among recipients of the transfer for three tests years in the 1960s.

The trade variables prove to be more powerful discriminators in that recipients score more highly than non-recipients on gross exports, gross imports and international liquidity from the early and mid-1960s onwards. Prior to this time, the two groups can scarcely be differentiated on these variables. What is more, even when differences between them do emerge, they are of the magnitude of 2 to 1 and are not as great as recipients' 3 or 4 to 1 advantage in terms of GDP. Thus, when exports and imports are expressed as a percentage of GDP, recipient values are lower, but not always significantly so. (Relative international liquidity is not lower in the recipient category, however, since it is standardised by gross imports rather than GDP.) In short, it is Third World countries' absolute, and not relative, commitment to trade that attracts US military assistance transfers.

Table 6.4: Means for non-recipients (NR) and recipients (R) of military assistance by selected economic variables, 1953–75

	NR	R	NR	R	NR	R	NR	R
	GDP		GDPPC		GDFCF		INDUST	
1953	3,330	2,891	233	178	14	12	15	16
1955	3,416	2,690	254	195	15	14	15	19
1957	3,518	3,054	253	210	16	14	15	18
1959	2,976	3,083	257	207	15	14	17	20
1961	2,747	3,304	246	212	15	14	18	19
1963	1,304	3,903*	315	224	14	15	15	20*
1965	1,347	5,499*	319	296	15	15	16	22*
1967	1,338	6,507*	354	343	16	16	19	23*
1969	1,722	6,833*	342	380	16	17	18	24
1971	2,037	7,994*	385	405	17	17	21	23
1973	3,255	9,186*	476	512	19	18	22	22
1975	6,635	14,510	906	731	19	19	26	25
	GrEx		PEx		NFI		InvInc	
1953	296	346	18	13	−42	−24	38	24
1955	348	293	18	14	26	−41	47	30
1957	385	275	18	13	−54	−42	56	40
1959	358	281	18	12*	−50	−46	51	43
1961	355	337	19	12*	−72	−44	78	52
1963	194	390	16	14*	−76	−65	51	71
1965	206	540*	19	15	−61	−78	56	84
1967	241	606*	21	16	−43	−105	52	115
1969	252	720*	22	17	−53	−121	63	149*
1971	377	818*	25	14*	−78	−96	79	150
1973	580	1,023*	25	13*	−153	−60	93	177
1975	2,062	2,307	37	19*	−307	−214	199	292
	ForDrInv		CBFA		ExImLn			
1953	14	26	18	28	0	8*		
1955	9	17	17	31	0	0		
1957	44	19	18	37*	3	4		
1959	20	25	26	43	9	7		
1961	−2	27	25	26	4	5		
1963	19	9	30	28	2	3		
1965	26	14	42	41	2	6		
1967	21	24	54	43	1	6		
1969	21	29	52	54	3	9		
1971	35	26	58	113	1	14		
1973	18	39	82	252*	4	39*		
1975	−19	57	181	525*	12	38*		

* Indicates a significant difference at the 0.05 level or higher.

The international investment and banking variables turn up no consistent patterns of significant differences. Net factor income from abroad and particularly investment income tend to be higher among recipients, but this observation does not hold for net foreign direct investment. Commercial banks' foreign assets and liabilities and ExIm loans prove to be significantly higher among recipients in the 1970s, but not beforehand. As would be expected given that they are standardised against GDP, the relative measures of all these variables tend to show higher values among non-recipients, although the differences are rarely significant.

Unlike in the previous two chapters, the redefinition of the military assistance non-recipient population to exclude those countries actually receiving US arms sales does little to alter the substance of these findings. Indeed, this exercise in redefinition has no consequence other than to accentuate the differences already discussed; no new ones are thrown up. To illustrate this point, we can look at the two most powerful discriminating variables, GDP and volume of trade. As things turn out, the differences between military assistance recipients and non-recipients do nothing but become slightly larger when recipients of US arms are excluded from the non-recipient population. In general, arms sales recipients are among the wealthier Third World countries, but the inclusion of a number of them in the non-recipient category is not sufficient to prevent military assistance recipients from scoring more highly on those variables, like GDP and trade, on which significant differences do appear. All that happens, therefore, is that the exclusion of these countries from the non-recipient population simply serves to exacerbate the differences that we have already noted.

In sum, the range of economic variables covering production, trade and international banking and investment prove unable, at least in bivariate terms, to differentiate recipients and non-recipients of military assistance in the 1950s. Starting in the early to mid-1960s, however, pronounced differences between the two groups of Third World countries do emerge, but these are limited primarily to the production and trade areas and, in addition, to absolute rather than relative measures. In other words, US military assistance would seem to be attracted to larger countries, 'large' itself being defined principally in terms of GDP and trade volume.

As would be expected given the ANOVA outcomes, the multiple regression results are weak overall (see Table 6.5). Other than in 1953, the economic variables prove unable to generate a significant regression equation until 1961. The 1953 result, therefore, is best regarded as an aberration rather than as a phenomenon to be explained and interpreted. From 1961 onwards, significant but weak equations are generated in all years but 1973 when, once again, there are no results.[14] Against this background, percentage exports turns out to be the most consistently important estimator of gross military assistance allocations and its influence is negative. But the prominence of this variable can easily be misinterpreted. We have already called attention to the fact that GDP increases more steeply with volume of military assistance than does gross exports. Inevitably,

Table 6.5: Standardised coefficients for the regressions of gross military assistance on the economic variables, 1953–75*

1953:	(0.42)	PCBFA	0.85	1967:	(0.35)	PNFI	0.66
	(0.35)	PNFI	0.62		(0.14)	PMnEx	0.39
	$R^2 = 78$				(0.14)	PIL	0.29
					$R^2 = 33$		
1955:	Not significant						
				1969:	(0.37)	PNFI	0.65
1957:	Not significant				(0.16)	PMnEx	0.52
					$R^2 = 28$		
1959:	Not significant						
				1971:	(−0.29)	PAgEx	−0.48
1961:	(−0.38)	PMfIm	−0.52		(−0.28)	Indust	−0.48
	(−0.34)	PEx	−0.39		$R^2 = 28$		
	(−0.24)	PIm	−0.49				
	(−0.18)	CBFL	−0.52	1973:	Not significant		
	(−0.19)	PForDrInv	−0.34				
	$R^2 = 62$			1975:	(0.32)	GrMfEx	0.66
					(−0.25)	GDPPC	−0.54
1963:	(−0.38)	PEx	−0.49		(−0.02)	ExImLn	−0.48
	(0.06)	PMnEx	0.26		(0.31)	GDFCF	0.40
	$R^2 = 21$				$R^2 = 49$		
1965:	(−0.34)	PEx	−0.73				
	(−0.15)	PAgEx	−0.48				
	(−0.04)	GrMfEx	−0.25				
	(0.02)	PIL	0.26				
	$R^2 = 34$						

* The figures in parentheses represent the zero-order correlation coefficients.

therefore, exports as a percentage of GDP will covary negatively with military assistance so that it would be erroneous to conclude that particular US transfer is attracted to countries with relatively small export sectors when what we are in fact seeing is a US preference for GDP size relative to volume of trade.

On the other hand, it would be equally erroneous to assume that the results in Table 6.5 are altogether without value. For a start, they indicate that, unlike in the process of selection into the military assistance recipient population, none of the three sets of variables enjoys primacy in determining the transfer's distribution within this recipient population. Secondly, they confirm that a relatively large number of purely economic variables enjoys roughly equally weak relationships with the dependent variable. Finally, and most importantly, purely economic factors, again in contrast to the selection process, are not important influences on the distribution of gross military assistance to recipients.

The per capita military assistance ANOVAs generate weak results. The individual production structure variables show little systematic covariation with the dependent variable except for a slight decrease in GDP from the early 1960s onwards. Trade is also somewhat negatively related to the dependent variable, a relationship that is, in fact, generally more marked in the case of percentage trade. No relationships emerge, on the other hand, for trade type. Finally, there are no strong or consistent patterns of covariation between per capita military assistance and the investment and banking variables, although there is some evidence that both net factor income and investment income decrease as the dependent variable increases.

Although a little stronger than for its gross counterpart, the multiple regression results for per capita military assistance are still weak overall. Generally speaking, they demonstrate that the larger recipients of the transfer in its relative form have smaller trade sectors (see Table 6.6). But while largely uninteresting in themselves, these results will, later in this chapter, prove important in enabling us to reject a number of potential explanations of the distribution of per capita military assistance.

Table 6.6: Standardised coefficients for the regressions of per capita military assistance on the economic variables, 1953–75*

1953:	(0.62)	PCBFA	1.12	1967:	(0.40)	PNFI	0.78
	(0.00)	PIm	0.74		(0.17)	PMnEx	0.44
		$R^2 = 70$			(0.23)	PIL	0.36
						$R^2 = 47$	
1955:	(−0.63)	PMfIm	−0.63				
		$R^2 = 40$		1969:	(0.36)	PNFI	0.70
					(0.24)	PMnEx	0.62
1957:	Not significant					$R^2 = 41$	
1959:	(−0.45)	PMfIm	−1.12	1971:	(−0.32)	PAgEx	−0.53
	(−0.15)	CBFL	−0.80		(−0.30)	Indust	−0.52
	(−0.12)	GDP	−0.56			$R^2 = 33$	
		$R^2 = 70$					
				1973:	(−0.44)	PEx	−0.84
1961:	(−0.31)	PMfIm	−0.53		(0.19)	PIm	0.76
	(−0.35)	PEx	−0.30		(−0.06)	PCBFA	−0.52
	(−0.24)	CBFL	−0.49		(0.24)	PMnEx	0.34
	(−0.12)	PIm	−0.38		(−0.04)	PIL	−0.33
		$R^2 = 49$				$R^2 = 65$	
1963:	(−0.37)	PEx	−0.37	1975:	(−0.39)	PEx	−0.69
		$R^2 = 14$			(−0.36)	PAgEx	−0.68
					(0.27)	GDFCF	0.41
1965:	(−0.33)	PEx	−0.74			$R^2 = 64$	
	(0.08)	PMnEx	0.49				
	(−0.29)	GrEx	−0.47				
	(−0.01)	Agric	−0.49				
	(−0.11)	PCBFL	−0.31				
		$R^2 = 47$					

* The figures in parentheses represent the zero-order correlation coefficients.

Arms sales

The ANOVA results show that the production structure variables of GDFCF and GDP increase slightly across the three categories of arms recipient, whereas per capita income follows the same developmental pattern, only more strongly.[15] The relative size of the industrial sector also increases with gross arms sales receipt and, concomitantly, the size of the agricultural sector decreases.[16]

In the trade area, gross exports and gross imports both increase steeply across the three recipient categories, while percentage trade shows little systematic variation across these same categories. No clear relationships emerge for the particular types of exports, although there are signs in the late 1970s that arms sales flow to countries with high levels of manufactured as opposed to agricultural exports. Finally, gross international liquidity increases over the three recipient categories at about the same rate as the gross trade variables.

The investment and banking variables, and particularly the former, are not as strongly related to gross arms sales for the most part. Foreign direct investment, whether it be measured in gross or relative terms, shows no sign of a relationship. Investment income, on the other hand, increases slightly across the three recipient categories, but its rate of increase is about the same as GDP's so that any sign of a relationship disappears when it is standardised against GDP. Gross net factor income also increases slightly, particularly in the late 1970s, whereas its percentage variant actually decreases as gross arms receipt increases. On the whole, stronger relationships emerge in the field of international banking. ExIm loans, for example, increase very steeply with arms sales volume and the same observation holds for commercial banks' foreign assets and liabilities regardless of whether they are measured in gross or relative terms.

Turning now to the *t*-tests comparing non-recipients and recipients as a whole, significant differences appear on all the production structure variables except GDFCF.[17] In other words, arms sales recipients have substantially larger industrial sectors, higher per capita incomes (in the ratio of about 2 to 1) and massively larger GDPs (in the ratio of about 7 to 1). Similarly, stark differences also characterise the trade structure variables. Arms recipients have significantly larger volumes of exports and imports (about five times larger on average), although they do not differ significantly from non-recipients in their relative commitment to trade. The differences in the banking and investment variables, measured in gross terms, are of roughly the same magnitude. Arms sales recipients have significantly higher levels of investment income, ExIm loans and commercial bank foreign assets. Moreover, while the differences on the net factor income and foreign direct investment variables are generally insignificant, both these variables always have higher values in the recipient population. When standardised by GDP however, the magnitude of the difference on all these variables shrinks to insignificance, indicating that while arms recipients may differ very markedly from non-recipients across a whole range of economic variables measured in gross

Table 6.7: Means on selected economic variables for non-recipients (NR) and recipients (R) of arms sales on selected economic variables, 1971-9

	NR	R	NR	R	NR	R	NR	R
	GDP		GDPPC		GDFCF		Indust	
1971	1,542	11,866*	304	632*	17	19	19	28*
1973	2,794	11,869*	382	788*	18	20	20	27*
1975	2,991	20,193*	617	1,323*	18	20	22	31*
1977	2,389	26,427*	858	1,394*	22	22	22	29*
1979	4,952	27,332*	1,034	1,725*	22	24	22	28*
	GrEx		PEx		NFI		InvInc	
1971	278	1,260*	21	20	−39	−168*	46	256*
1973	350	1,743*	21	22	−85	−164	54	292*
1975	730	4,693*	33	30	−119	−456	107	441*
1977	900	5,092*	34	24	−111	−768	85	556*
1979	1,149	5,698*	31	25	−207	−555	164	738*
	ForDrInv		CBFA		ExImLn			
1971	24	48	46	156*	2	18*		
1973	7	72	68	320*	3	49*		
1975	28	−35	66	677*	6	46*		
1977	4	89	218	688*	4	54*		
1979	16	210*	272	1,182*	20	35		

* Indicates a significant difference at the 0.05 level.

terms, they are not similarly distinctive in their relative commitment to international economic activity.

In sum then, if we conceptualise importance in terms of domestic economic size and absolute international economic activity, US arms sales recipients are very clearly the most important Third World countries.

The multiple regression analysis produces highly signficant equations that do not add a great deal to the insights already provided by the bivariate analyses. The 'problem' is basically that the multivariate analysis does not perform its primary function of ordering and simplifying the overall picture. Not only do a large number of different variables figure in Table 6.8, but also there is little apparent overlap between the equations including and excluding the outlier. This obfuscation can be explained, however. With regard to the number and variety of variables figuring in the table, the bivariate analyses show there to be a large number of strong dependent–independent variable relationships which, in turn, means a large number of relatively strongly intercorrelated predictor variables. When this circumstance combines with a stepwise regression procedure using a high tolerance value, it becomes very easy for a particular variable to appear

Table 6.8: Standardised coefficients for the regressions of gross arms sales on the economic variables, 1971-9*

	Including outlier			Excluding outlier	
1971:	(0.46) GDPPC	0.61		(0.52) InvInc	0.71
	(−0.10) PIL	−0.36		(−0.10) GDP	−0.59
	$R^2 = 32$			(0.19) ExImLn	0.68
				(−0.08) IL	−0.40
				$R^2 = 64$	
1973:	(0.68) InvInc	0.74			
	(0.28) GDPPC	0.11			
	(−0.10) GrAgEx	−0.36			
	(0.22) CBFL	0.29			
	$R^2 = 65$				
1975:	(0.47) IL	0.58		(−0.37) ForDrInv	−0.53
	(−0.06) NFI	0.38		(0.17) GDFCF	0.65
	(0.38) PMfIm	0.17		(0.30) GDPPC	0.32
	(0.14) GrAgEx	−0.39		(0.00) PIm	−0.32
	(0.43) ExImLn	0.43		$R^2 = 41$	
	$R^2 = 56$				
1977:	(0.66) GrMnEx	0.27		(−0.83) NFI	−0.85
	(0.66) GrMfIm	0.56		(−0.23) PCBFL	0.27
	(−0.18) GrAgEx	−0.26		$R^2 = 77$	
	$R^2 = 60$				
1979:	(0.83) GrMnEx	0.84		(0.59) GrMfIm	0.99
	(0.08) ExImLn	0.13		(0.30) NFI	0.87
	$R^2 = 72$			(0.04) PIL	0.37
				$R^2 = 86$	

* The figures in parentheses represent the zero-order correlation coefficients.

as a significant predictor in one year but not another, despite its relationship to the dependent variable having changed very little.[18] The differences in the outcome of the equations including and excluding the outlier are equally more apparent than real. These differences reflect both the above circumstance and the skewing effects of Iran's disproportionately large oil exports.

These statistical provisos notwithstanding, Table 6.8 does give rise to two important and cumulative conclusions. Firstly, it demonstrates unambiguously that there is substantial covariation between a range of economic considerations and US arms allocations within the recipient population. Secondly, and perhaps more importantly, it shows that there are no clearly pre-eminent economic estimators of these allocations. It is for this reason that we would argue that, at least on this occasion, the multivariate analysis adds little or nothing to the understanding provided by the bivariate analyses.[19]

Examining the ANOVA results for the per capita arms sales distributions, the production structure variable that is most strongly and positively related to the dependent variable is per capita income. The larger arms recipients also tend to have smaller agricultural and bigger industrial sectors. There is, on the other hand, no relationship between arms transfers and GDP.

In the trade area, larger per capita arms recipients have more pronounced absolute and relative commitments to trade and, while no relationship characterises their sectoral imports, they also show a bias towards mining and agricultural exports. Finally, both gross and percentage international liquidity covary positively with per capita US arms sales.

A number of relationships can be found in the international investment variables, but they are not as strong. Thus, foreign direct investment does not vary systematically with arms sales, while investment income is positively related to them, but at best weakly. Both the absolute and relative measures of net factor income are positively and somewhat more strongly related to per capita arms transfers. The strongest relationships of all, however, emerge with the international banking variables. These relationships are all positive and are particularly strong for commercial banks' foreign assets and liabilities and, to a lesser extent, ExIm loans.

In general, therefore, while there may be differences of emphasis in the case of individual variables, the overall picture afforded by the ANOVA analyses of the distribution of per capita arms transfers does not differ substantially from that for gross arms transfers.

As for the multiple regression results, they are less decisive in a number of respects than are those for gross transfers. Thus, Table 6.9 indicates that for the first three of the five test years of the 1970s, the R^2 values for the equations are significant, but low. It even proves impossible to generate an equation for 1975 once the outlier is removed. Stronger results emerge in 1977 and 1979. On the credit side, however, while there is some variability in the identity of the principal estimators both over time and across the equations excluding and including the outlier, this variability is lesser in scale than it is for gross arms transfers. Two variables in particular, percentage investment income and especially per capita income, emerge as the most consistent and significant estimators.

On balance, however, Table 6.9 is most useful for its overall emphasis on the fact that while recipient economic characteristics and per capita US arms receipts are undoubtedly related, the relationship is not particularly strong or powerful. The table also highlights the fact that there is no clear hierarchy of estimators, especially among the more powerful ones. These two somewhat negative observations apart then, the regression analysis adds little to what we already know from the bivariate analyses, i.e. that larger per capita US arms transfers flow to the more developed and internationally active Third World countries.

Table 6.9: Standardised coefficients for the regressions of per capita arms sales on the economic variables, 1971-9*

	Including outlier			Excluding outlier		
1971:	(0.50)	GDPPC	0.62	(0.56)	PInvInc	0.56
	(0.06)	IL	−0.54		$R^2 = 32$	
	(0.31)	CBFL	0.38			
		$R^2 = 47$				
1973:	(0.49)	GDPPC	0.45			
	(0.36)	PInvInc	0.32			
	(0.17)	PMfEx	0.42			
		$R^2 = 43$				
1975:	(0.31)	GDPPC	0.59	Not significant		
	(0.19)	GDFCF	0.62			
	(−0.11)	PForDrInv	−0.50			
	(0.04)	PEx	−0.41			
		$R^2 = 34$				
1977:	(0.70)	GDPPC	0.65	(0.70)	GDPPC	0.65
	(0.40)	PInvInc	0.30	(0.44)	PInvInc	0.34
		$R^2 = 58$			$R^2 = 65$	
1979:	(0.85)	GrMnEx	1.00	(0.55)	GDPPC	0.87
	(0.22)	PCBFL	0.27	(0.13)	NFI	0.72
	(0.49)	GrMfIm	−0.23	(0.62)	PCBFL	0.32
		$R^2 = 81$		(0.04)	PIL	0.29
					$R^2 = 80$	

* The figures in parentheses represent the zero-order correlation coefficients.

Findings: Impact

Economic aid

Some of the individual production structure variables do show signs of higher growth rates with the receipt of larger volumes of economic aid (see Table 6.10). This relationship is strongest with regard to the growth rates of real per capita income following upon the receipt of both gross and per capita economic aid. There is also significant variation in GDFCF growth rates across levels of gross aid receipt, although the pattern is not linear. None the less, the cumulative binomial probability for the large aid recipient category in comparison with the other two together indicates a growth rate that is significant beyond the 0.05 level. The industrial sector variable, in contrast, shows no significant or systematic covariation at all.

The trade variables provide evidence of stronger transfer impacts. Chapter 4 has already shown that both gross and percentaged international liquidity grow more quickly across both the gross and per capita aid categories, whereas export and import growth rates increase only across per capita aid categories (see

Table 6.10: Summed ranks for average percentage change in the economic
variables for the small, medium and large recipient categories
of gross and per capita economic aid for the thirteen four-year
periods 1950–4, 1952–6 and 1974–8

	Gross aid			Per capita aid		
	Small	Medium	Large	Small	Medium	Large
CGDPPC	30.0	28.0	20.0*†	30.5	28.5	19.0*†
GDFCF	25.0	34.0	19.0*†	22.0	31.0	25.0
Indust	25.0	30.0	23.0	25.0	29.0	24.0
PGrEx	28.0	25.0	25.0	29.5	29.5	19.0*†
PGrIm	23.0	32.0	23.0*	21.0	29.0	28.0
TrDfct	25.0	30.0	23.0	32.0	19.0	27.0*
ExDvC	27.5	26.5	24.0	27.0	23.5	27.5
ExDvD	31.0	26.5	24.0	21.5	28.0	25.5
ImDvS	31.0	26.0	21.0†	27.0	25.0	26.0
GNFI	31.0	28.0	19.0*†	26.0	27.0	25.0
InvInc	36.0	25.0	17.0*†	33.0	29.0	16.0*†
PInvInc	31.0	30.0	17.0*†	29.5	27.5	21.0*†
ForDrInv	25.0	23.0	30.0	26.0	22.0	30.0
PForDrInv	25.0	21.0	32.0*	23.0	27.0	28.0
CBFA	28.0	33.0	17.0*†	22.0	31.0	25.0
PCBFA	27.0	32.0	19.0*†	21.0	30.0	27.0
CBFL	26.0	25.5	26.5	25.0	28.0	25.0
PCBFL	21.0	28.5	28.5	25.5	27.5	25.0
ExImLn	25.0	28.5	24.5	23.0	28.0	27.0

* Indicates significance at the 0.05 level or beyond for the chi-square test
across all three categories.
† Indicates significance at the 0.05 level or beyond for the cumulative
binomial test on the number of first rank placings for the large category.

Table 4.10). Table 6.10 now complements these earlier findings and shows that
trade deficit growth rates differ significantly, but not linearly, across the three
levels of per capita aid receipt. Finally, Third World countries' overall trading
patterns are not substantially affected by the receipt of US economic aid. In
other words, their growth rates on export diversification by both destination and
commodity and on import diversification by source are not related to the level
of either gross or per capita aid received.

Impact relationships do characterise certain of the international investment
and banking variables. Gross net factor income, for example, grows more quickly
as gross, but not per capita, aid increases. It should be noted, however, that since
this variable is usually negative in value (and our scoring of its growth rates takes
account of this characteristic), this finding means basically that the rate of growth
of foreign production in a country relative to that country's own production overseas increases as gross aid receipts go up. Absolute and relative investment income
growth rates also covary positively with gross aid, and with per capita aid as well.
The balance of foreign direct investment, by contrast, stands in no systematic

relationship to the receipt of either form of the transfer. Finally, while a significant relationship emerges between commercial banks' foreign assets and gross aid receipts, the relationship is not linear in that asset growth rates are lower in the medium aid category than in the small one. Otherwise, no significant relationships appear in the banking variables.

Military assistance

Table 6.11 shows that the rate of growth of several individual production structure variables covaries positively and significantly with one or both forms of military assistance. The rates of growth of real per capita income are positive and significant across the per capita, but not gross, military assistance categories. Moreover, its growth is most marked in the large per capita category. It is also worth noting that, while this variable's overall relationship to gross military assistance is not significant, the cumulative binomial test shows that large recipients experience significantly higher growth rates than the other categories combined. On the other

Table 6.11: Summed ranks for average annual percentage change in the economic variables for the zero, small, medium and large recipient categories of gross and per capita military assistance for the eleven four-year periods 1952-6, 1954-8 to 1972-6

	Gross military assistance				Per capita military assistance			
	Zero	Small	Medium	Large	Zero	Small	Medium	Large
CGDPPC	33.0	27.0	30.0	20.0†	32.5	29.0	30.0	18.5*†
GDFCF	25.5	33.0	28.0	23.5	25.5	35.0	25.5	24.0
Indust	20.0	32.0	29.0	29.0†	19.0	32.5	31.0	27.5*
PGrEx	27.5	29.5	30.0	23.0	29.5	32.0	26.5	22.0
PGrIm	28.0	32.0	36.0	14.0*†	27.5	37.0	23.0	22.5*
TrDfct	26.0	25.0	30.0	29.0	27.0	28.0	28.0	27.0
ExDvC	23.5	24.0	29.0	33.5	22.5	33.5	23.0	31.0
ExDvD	30.0	29.5	28.0	22.5	30.5	27.5	27.0	25.0
ImDvS	34.5	25.5	30.0	20.0*†	32.5	32.0	28.5	17.0*†
GNFI	24.0	30.0	35.0	21.0*	24.5	30.5	32.0	23.0
InvInc	37.0	27.0	33.0	13.0*†	38.0	31.0	30.0	11.0*†
PInvInc	36.0	26.0	36.0	12.0*†	36.0	31.0	29.0	14.0*†
ForDrInv	21.0	28.0	33.0	28.0	18.0	31.0	22.0	29.0
PForDrInv	20.0	33.0	30.0	27.0	17.0	34.0	21.0	28.0
CBFA	36.0	31.0	28.0	15.0*†	34.0	28.0	32.0	16.0*†
PCBFA	31.0	32.0	34.0	13.0*†	32.5	26.0	31.0	20.5†
CBFL	34.0	31.0	22.0	23.0	28.0	24.0	29.0	19.0
PCBFL	33.0	31.0	21.0	25.0	28.5	21.5	29.0	21.0
ExImLn	29.0	24.5	30.5	26.0	29.0	29.0	28.0	24.0

* Indicates significance at the 0.05 level or beyond for the chi-square test across all three categories.

† Indicates significance at the 0.05 level or beyond for the cumulative binomial test on the number of first rank placings for the large category.

hand, the growth rates for the industrial sector and GDFCF do not vary significantly across the three recipient categories. The industrial sector variable, however, does appear to expand more rapidly in those Third World countries not receiving military assistance.

With regard to the trade variables, Chapter 4 has already indicated that the rate of growth of gross trade covaries positively and significantly with the receipt of both gross and per capita military assistance, although their growth tends to be particularly pronounced among large transfer recipients (see Table 4.11). Table 6.11 suggests that this transfer significantly influences sectoral activity as well in that the receipt of military assistance covaries positively with the growth in both exports and imports as a percentage of GDP. In other words, Third World countries' relative commitment to trade increases as their volume of military assistance received goes up. This relationship is especially clear in the case firstly of imports and secondly of the high transfer recipient category. This same category is characterised by its members also having relatively substantial trade deficits, although they are not deficits that are growing disproportionately quickly. The trade diversification variables give rise to mixed results. The rates of growth of export diversification by either commodity or destination show no sign of covarying with either form of military assistance. Import diversification by source, on the other hand, covaries negatively and significantly with both gross and per capita forms of the transfer. In other words, larger recipients are less prone to diversify the countries from which they import goods and services.

As for the investment and banking variables, the strongest transfer covariation is seen in investment income growth rates, although the higher rates are generally restricted to large recipients of gross military assistance. No relationship emerges in the case of foreign direct investment and net factor income growth rates vary systematically with the gross transfer only. The growth rates of commercial banks' foreign assets, in contrast, covary positively and significantly with the transfer in both its forms. In other words, the growth of investment income cannot be explained by military assistance's stimulating foreign direct investment. It could be explained, however, by the transfer's encouraging larger commercial bank loans to foreign enterprises, loans that are themselves underwritten to some extent by outside loans to these same banks, i.e. their liabilities. These bank loans could then stimulate the expansion in foreign production, measured by net factor income from abroad, which could in turn foster higher investment income growth rates.

Arms sales

Arms sales receipts do not seem to exercise any systematic influence on the growth rates of the individual production structure variables. What is more, this conclusion holds true whether potential relationships are sought across all four receipt categories or simply across non-recipients and recipients as a whole.

It is also a conclusion that, generally speaking, applies to the trade variables as well. To be sure, there are some signs that arms recipients experience higher rates of growth on the relative commitment to trade variable, but the relationship is not especially strong. In general, larger recipients display more pronounced export and import diversification by destination and source, but the growth rates on these variables do not covary with receipt levels. Export diversification by commodity, on the other hand, shows no sign of covariation by either absolute level or rate of change.

Finally, the investment and banking variables' individual rates of growth are all unrelated to the receipt or otherwise of arms sales. The only indication of an impact of any kind stems from the fact that arms recipients would appear to experience slightly higher growth rates across the whole array of investment and banking variables than do non-recipients of the transfer.

Interpretation: distribution

Interpreting this chapter's findings poses a problem that, while present in any exercise in interpretation, is more acute in the context of this particular chapter. This problem stems essentially from the validity, or more accurately multi-validity, of some of our important estimators, which is itself primarily a function of the multiple rationales guiding the analysis of this chapter. More explicitly, because these rationales are all economic in character, they are not conceptually independent of each other so that a number of key estimators play a prominent role in the testing of more than one of them. There are, however, two devices that we shall use to keep the rationales distinct. The first of them is simply to use different operational variables whenever possible. The development needs rationale, for example, relies principally on per capita income and GDFCF and does not encompass the various trade and investment variables that form the core of the investment rationales. The second device is the explicit recognition that the different rationales are profiled by different patterns of relationships, even though these patterns may be constituted of similar variables. Thus, the development needs and development prospects rationales contain many of the same variables, but the former postulates their being negatively related to transfer receipts and the latter positively related to them.

The real interpretational difficulties arise when different rationales are found to contain the same variables and, at least in directional terms, the same relationships. For example, the finding that economic aid covaries positively with trade is potentially highly confusing since it is a finding that is consonant with all of the commercial interest, dependence and power politics rationales. This is what we call the multi-validity problem and it is a predicament that undoubtedly raises a number of interpretational difficulties. We are not helpless before these difficulties, however. Even, for example, in those cases where distinct rationales contain common variables and directional relationships, differences in terms of other variables remain. If only for this reason, we interpret patterns of findings rather than single-variable relationships, especially in our multiple regression analyses. In other words, gross trade may figure equally legitimately in the commercial interests, dependence and power politics rationales, but its being accompanied by trade share or trade diversification would be supportive more of a dependence interpretation than a power politics one. Another means of attenuating these validity problems is to evaluate the findings of this chapter against those for Chapters 4 and 5. A final strategy is to focus on our level of explained variation. The trade and investment rationale, for example, would anticipate a high level of explained variation since it is relatively narrow in scope, whereas the expectation of the power politics model would not be so great for the simple reason that trade is only one of several important capability measures that is likely to attract US official transfers.[20]

In sum then, the existence of these problems cannot be denied, but their severity is not at all sufficient to invalidate our efforts to interpret the findings of this chapter.

Economic aid

There can be no question but that our analysis leads to the conclusion that a number of individual economic considerations influence the distribution of US aid. Broadly differentiating between economic and power political considerations, however, its more emphatic conclusion is that economic factors assume explanatory importance only through their affinity with, or enhancement of, the recipients' power capabilities. The importance of this particular conclusion is that it enables us firstly to falsify a number of purely economic interpretations of the purposes of the US aid programme and secondly to incorporate the findings of this chapter into a broader perspective that is consonant with the conclusions of earlier chapters concerning the security bias of economic aid.

The purely economic rationales that are least supported by our findings are the development needs and development prospects ones. The former holds that aid is distributed on the basis of the humanitarian criterion of assisting the most needy. Initially, the strongest support for this argument comes from the characteristics of the non-recipients of the transfer; these are, in fact, the Third World countries with the highest per capita incomes, the largest industrial sectors and the most substantial international trading and investment networks. Caution is advised however, by the fact that these countries do not become non-recipients until the late 1960s so that the question inevitably arises as to why recipient selection was not guided by these apparently humanitarian criteria prior to this time. The brief answer to this question is that in reality these criteria operate neither before nor after this time. Their apparent explanatory importance is an artefact of a change of policy whereby, in an effort to reduce its own first-order economic disutilities, the United States dropped a number of the more advanced countries from its concessionary aid programme and picked them up in its ever-expanding, and relatively profitable, arms sales programme. To be sure, even after excluding these arms sales recipients from the aid non-recipient population, the latter remains relatively privileged by Third World standards. But this privilege notwithstanding, Chapters 4 and 5 have demonstrated that these countries receive neither aid nor arms from the United States because they are relatively unimportant in power political terms or because they are clearly and preferentially aligned with the communist bloc.

Further evidence as to the explanatory impotence of the humanitarian argument is that if such criteria did indeed guide the US selection of recipients from the late 1960s, then we would only expect that they also guided the distribution of aid within the recipient population. Yet, there is not the slightest evidence that they do. While it may be the case that the distribution of per capita aid in particular does not support the opposing view, i.e. that most aid flows to the more developed countries, it is unequivocally true that neither does it support a development needs interpretation of this transfer.

The development prospects argument holds that the more developed Third World countries may not stand in the same relative need of aid, but that those receiving it do so in proportion to their development prospects. In other words, it holds that aid is distributed with a view to helping recipients 'take off' into economic development. We cannot reject this argument outright since our findings do in fact indicate that per capita aid allocations do increase with a number of measures that can be used to assess development prospects, for example per capita income, size of industrial sector and GDFCF. None the less, these relationships are only weak and while they do not lend themselves to the rejection of the rationale, they provide only a very limited, or partial, explanation of the transfer's distribution.

Next there are two purely economic interpretations of the purposes of aid and they posit essentially that the transfer is linked to general international investment interests. Two distinct arguments are put forward. The first is that aid is used to promote or support investment and banking ties. Both the promotional and supportive elements of this argument are consonant with the existence of higher investment and banking scores in the aid non-recipient category. More specifically, however, the promotional hypothesis would imply a quadratic relationship that simply does not emerge in our findings. The supportive hypothesis, on the other hand, would require only a positive linear relationship in order to be accepted. Such a relationship is present to some extent so that the hypothesis cannot be rejected, but the relationship is very weak and hardly constitutes convincing evidence that US aid is so modelled as to support recipients' international investment and banking ties.

The second investment interpretation hypothesises a more Machiavellian role for aid. According to this, the purpose of the transfer is to ensure the economic dependence of its recipients and it achieves this goal by acting as a surrogate for investment. Taken to its logical conclusion, this hypothesis holds that aid itself becomes redundant once economic control has been institutionalised by investment patterns in the Third World. It is, however, a hypothesis that is not supported by the evidence of our findings. In the case of foreign direct investment, there is no significant difference between recipients and non-recipients of aid in four of the six test years after 1969. What is more, there are contradictory outcomes in the other two; recipients score significantly higher on this variable in one year and significantly lower in the other. On the other hand, since the non-recipient figures are negative (it will be recalled that the direct investment variable represents a balance) in two periods, it could be argued that supplier control manifests itself through a counter-flow of investment. It seems to us, however, that this finding is more accurately interpreted as indicating interdependence rather than control. Furthermore, it is highly unrealistic to dichotomise the Third World into those countries controlled through overseas investment and those requiring to be controlled through aid transfers because of a lack of such investment in them.

Investment is, in fact, a continuous phenomenon that does not take the form of being channelled to some countries rather than to others; it is transferred in different amounts to different countries. In other words, if aid were indeed a surrogate for investment, we should expect to find not only significantly higher investment values in the non-recipient category, but also an inverse relationship between the two variables among recipients of the transfer. But there is no sign of such a relationship. Nor is either of these prerequisites met in the case of investment income, a variable that would seem to be a more sensitive test of the surrogate hypothesis because it affords a measure of the actual product of the investment rather than of the size of the investment itself. Net factor income from abroad is a third variable that can be used to test this hypothesis and it appears to satisfy the first prerequisite of support for it, i.e. the variable enjoys values that are significantly higher among non-recipients in four of the six test years and higher in the remaining two. The values in the non-recipient category, however, drop substantially when arms sales recipients are excluded and the fact that the group receiving neither aid nor arms transfers fails to have the highest investment scores is, to say the least, incompatible with the hypothesis that aid is a surrogate for investment. Moreover, the two variables are negatively related among aid recipients so that there turns out to be no support at all for the hypothesis.

Finally, we come to what seems to us to be the most viable and convincing interpretation of our findings, namely that, while complementary, economic factors are subordinate to power political considerations in explaining the distribution of economic aid. The main grounds for this conclusion are the weak influence of many of the economic factors and the fact that GDP is the single most powerful estimator of gross aid allocations. Admittedly, GDP hides other indicators like trade and international liquidity, but it does so for the very sound reason that it is more important than them. The only potential weakness of this observation occurs with respect to trade where it is conceivable that US aid is attracted to one or other particular type of trade rather than to trade in general.

In other words, even if GDP is a more powerful estimator than gross trade, trade in, say, agricultural products could be more important than either of them. But as it is, a particular trade influence emerges only when GDP is excluded from the analysis and, even then, there are no clear and consistent relationships between type of trade and gross aid receipts. If anything, therefore, US aid is attracted to gross trade and not to any particular type of it. Furthermore, the United States is less interested in gross trade than it is in GDP and, in turn, it is less interested in GDP than it is in other power capabilities.

The complementary effect of economic factors is somewhat more pronounced in the case of per capita aid, which, over time, is increasingly channelled a little disporportionately to the more economically developed Third World states. It must be borne in mind, however, that the most developed among these states are restricted to the receipt of arms transfers, a restriction that is altogether rational from the power politics perspective since it keeps these important states in the US sphere of influence at little direct economic cost.

Military assistance

The single most important conclusion to arise from the military assistance findings is that economic considerations, at least as profiled by our range of production, investment and trade variables, have no more than a minor influence on the distribution of this transfer. Moreover, to the extent that it does exist, it is an influence that is subsumed by the power politics model that we have already developed.

More specifically, it is only in the selection, or identification, of military assistance recipients that economic considerations exercise a systematic influence and here it is GDP and gross trade that by and large define the recipient population. Two important conclusions follow from this observation. Firstly, this is not the first time that these economic capability variables have played a prominent role in our findings. We have already assessed their importance in the context of a power politics model that showed them to be subordinate in explanatory power to recipients' politico-security power capabilities (see Chapter 4). For this reason, it would be misleading, even erroneous, to conclude from this chapter alone that recipients are selected into the military assistance programme purely, or even primarily, on the basis of their economic characteristics. Secondly, the relative lack of importance of purely economic considerations is highlighted by the fact that despite this chapter's using a larger number of economic variables than the more general power politics analysis, the economic capability variables still subsume the additional measures.

The distribution, as opposed to selection, stage of the military assistance programme is another story in that it produces no substantively important relationships. The one estimator to appear consistently is percentage trade, but it has no meaning in this particular context. In the case of gross military assistance, its appearance is an artefact of the joint relations of GDP and trade to the dependent variable. In the case of per capita military assistance, its relationship is negative and while it is possible to think of several plausible reasons why percentage trade should attract per capita transfers, it is impossible for us to think of any reason as to why the relationship should be negative in direction. It can only be concluded, therefore, that the relationship is coincidental rather than causal. Thus, on balance, the evidence recommends the rejection of the set of hypotheses positing that US military assistance is deployed for developmental or trade and investment purposes. Obviously, this rejection extends to the more specific scenarios variously placing the transfer in a surrogate, promotional or supportive role.

Since the influence of economic considerations on military assistance allocations is slight, is confined primarily to the selection stage of the programme and is overwhelmingly dominated by recipients' economic power capabilities, this analysis can be concluded to have added little, if anything, to the power politics interpretation of official transfers developed earlier in this book. Yet the analysis of this chapter had not been redundant. By allowing for the rejection of a number of rival interpretations of the transfer that are couched in terms of more immediate goals like the promotion of, or support, for, developmental or trading and investment interests, it has served to substantiate the validity of this power politics interpretation.

Arms sales

Economic considerations structure the distribution of arms sales more effectively than they structure that of economic aid, yet the evidence still suggests that theirs is not a primary and independent structuring role. As with military assistance, their influence is most pronounced in the selection of recipients, but weakens markedly when it comes to structuring the distribution of arms sales within the recipient population. None the less, it is generally the case that the variables differentiating recipients and non-recipients continue to covary, albeit relatively weakly, with the volume of arms transfers so that the importance of economic considerations cannot be dismissed out of hand. But to recognise their importance is not to gainsay that the evidence still does not uphold a purely economic interpretation of the US arms sales programme.

There are three such explanations and they are modelled after our three clusters of variables. Working on the premise that to dismiss them individually can only serve to enhance the validity of our power politics model, we shall now evaluate each of them critically.

The first of these economic interpretations holds that arms are distributed with a view to supporting or promoting international investment interests. That recipients of this transfer do indeed enjoy higher levels of investment income, commercial bank foreign assets and liabilities and ExIm loans than non-recipients constitutes evidence in support of this interpretation, but it is support that is ambiguous. For example, there are for the most part no significant inter-group differences on foreign direct investment and net factor income from abroad. In addition, those significant differences that are found on other variables characterise them in their gross, and not in their relative, form. While this complexity clearly cannot be taken to negate the principal hypothesis of a relationship between arms sales allocations and international investment interests, it does falsify a variant of it to the effect that arms transfers are attracted to Third World countries with higher levels of foreign capital penetration. But even the principal hypothesis is not strongly supported by the evidence. If arms transfers are indeed intended to promote international investment, then the two phenomena should stand in a quadratic relationship to each other, yet they do not. Furthermore, while the direction of the linear relationship between them can be taken to substantiate the hypothesis that arms sales support investment interests, it should be remembered that this relationship is not very strong. Thus, while not denying an association, it none the less seems reasonable to conclude that this association is hardly strong enough to uphold the claim of a substantial and independent connection between arms transfers and international investment and banking patterns.

A second purely economic interpretation contends that arms sales are deployed to promote or support trading ties. This hypothesis has been thoroughly reviewed in previous chapters where it is once again concluded that there is some evidence of a supportive relationship, but none of a promotional one. In addition, the support that there is turns out to be directed mainly at gross trade and not at specifically US trade. This distinction clearly indicates that the United States is attracted to trade as a power capability rather than to its own narrow trading interests *per se*.

The third, and final, economic interpretation is the most important of the three in theoretical terms and it centres on the production structure of recipients. Its central claim is that arms are transferred in greater volume to the wealthier and more developed Third World countries for no other reason than that these are the ones that are best able to afford them. The importance of this hypothesis is that it holds arms sales to be nothing more than a form of trade and, as such, it runs directly counter to the security-based conceptualisation of official transfers elaborated in the opening chapter of this book.

The evidence undoubtedly affords a degree of support for this hypothesis. Recipients of the transfer do, for example, boast significantly higher levels of GDP and per capita income and have larger industrial sectors than non-recipients. These same characteristics also covary with the volume of arms sales within the recipient population. But the case against the hypothesis is more compelling. In the first place, the production structure variables are far more successful in defining the recipient population than they are in explaining the distribution of arms sales within this population, whereas if this transfer were but trade in another guise, then its regression on the production variables should minimally be expected to yield a high R^2 value. It should also give rise to a strong partial correlation between per capita income (our single best indicator of wealth) and arms sales allocations controlling for GDP. As it turns out, however, neither of these expectations materialises since significant equations, never mind high R^2 values, are not generated. Secondly, although far from sufficient evidence in itself to reject the arms-as-trade hypothesis, it is none the less worth pointing out that the hypothesis does contradict US government statements on its arms sales policy. Finally, particularly in the context of US competition with communism, a power politics interpretation of arms sales has already been developed that is both compatible with the arms-as-trade hypothesis and substantially more powerful than it in explanatory terms.

Our argument then, is not that the relatively strong economic component of arms sales can, or should, be denied, but that it can readily and fruitfully be incorporated into our existing power politics interpretation of official transfers. What is more, this is an argument that can be defended on a number of grounds. Most fundamentally, the stronger explanatory influence of economic considerations on the selection, as opposed to distribution, stage of the programme is only to be expected given the nature of arms sales, i.e. they have to be paid for. If economic considerations were the only ones guiding this programme, we would expect them to exercise a similarly powerful influence on both the distribution and selection stages of the arms sales programme. If, on the other hand, foreign policy considerations also influence the programme, we would expect them to come into play in structuring arms sales allocations among those Third World countries whose relative wealth enabled them to surmount the hurdle of being able to afford to purchase the arms in the first place. And to the extent that the influence of purely economic factors weakens in the distributional stage of the programme, the emergence of such considerations would seem to be precisely what happens. In this respect, it must be remembered that distribution is a function of supply and demand and while the latter cannot be explained solely in terms of wealth, a prerequisite of the demand being satisfied is still the possession of adequate wealth. It is self-evident, therefore, that the supplier discretion that is founded on the concessional nature of economic aid and military assistance will not be available to the same degree in the case of arms sales so that the latter will inevitably contain a stronger commercial, or trading, element. The fallacy of the arms-as-trade hypothesis is to transform this truism into a total and comprehensive explanation of the US arms sales programme.

In conclusion then, it would seem that while the relatively prominent influence of purely economic considerations in determining arms sales allocations cannot be denied, there is no reason for overstating their importance. This prominence can be attributed to two related factors, neither of which contradicts a power politics interpretation of this transfer programme. Firstly, to have crossed a threshold of wealth is an absolute prerequisite for the purchase of arms by Third World countries and, secondly, the more explicitly and overtly commercial nature of arms transfers makes them better suited to the pursuit of suppliers' explicitly economic foreign policy interests. The cumulative evidence suggests, however, that economic interests do not reign supreme in the realm of official transfers, otherwise economic aid and military assistance would not be concessional in character. Rather, their relative importance in the context of arms sales would seem best interpreted as indicating a US concentration through its arms sales programme on the economic dimension of a more generalised attraction to relatively powerful Third World countries.

Interpretation: impact

Economic aid

There are four main observations to be made on the subject of the impact of economic aid and the first of them concerns the finding that the growth rate of real per capita income increases positively across the categories of both gross and per capita aid receipts. In interpreting this finding, the two forms of aid are treated separately.

In the case of gross aid, this covariation is best seen as indicating nothing more than that large aid recipients enjoy higher real per capita income growth rates. The fact that this covariation juxtaposes a gross variable, aid, with a relative one, per capita income, cautions against imputing causality in this and similar instances. The problem is that if aid were indeed to influence growth patterns, then, in any one country, the receipt of this transfer would produce growth. Over a larger number of countries, however, there is the methodological problem of controlling for the effects of the variation in their size. That is, if aid is really to influence growth rates, then, other things being equal, it should produce an effect that is proportionate to its importance to recipients' economies. Thus, it is entirely conceivable that aid contributes less crucially to the economies of larger recipients than smaller ones simply because of the difference in the absolute size of their respective economies. This being the case, the higher income growth rates among the larger recipients is probably due to something other than the aid transfer so that it becomes unwise to impute causation to relationships of this type. None the less, this particular relationship is still substantively important because it signals that the United States consistently allies itself through its gross aid transfers with those Third World countries achieving the highest rates of development (as measured by real per capita income).

The problem of controlling for size disparities ceases to exist when the two relative variables, per capita aid and rates of per capita income growth, are juxtaposed. Indeed, that the two covary positively is itself an indication that aid promotes economic growth. What is more, this indication becomes firmer when we evaluate the relationship in the light of the three conditions that need to be satisfied before a causal inference can be made. These are temporal asymmetry, the control of other potential explanatory factors and the specification of the causal mechanism. The time lag built into our analytical procedure satisfies the first of these conditions, while the bivariate character of our impact methodology makes it impossible to satisfy the second of them in any rigorous manner.

However, there are a number of potential explanatory factors, such as per

capita GDP, size of industrial sector and size of GDFCF, that are effectively controlled by virtue of their being unrelated to per capita aid levels. Thus, our confidence in having unearthed a 'real' relationship can only be strengthened. This
same conclusion holds for a related potential criticism that can also be dismissed
and it is the claim that higher growth rates are principally a function of previous
growth rates rather than of aid. This observation may well be accurate in principle,
but it does not jeopardise or confound our findings since the countries comprising
the recipient categories in our analysis change over time even if the relationship
between per capita aid receipts and real per capita income growth rates do not.
Once again, therefore, the causal inference appears eminently plausible. Finally,
there is the third condition, the specification of the mechanism whereby aid can
be expected to promote economic growth and here a plethora of likely candidates
suggest themselves. One such candidate is trade deficits, which unlike, say,
GDFCF, increase significantly as per capita aid receipts get larger.

In sum, therefore, while we certainly would not wish to argue that the receipt
of US aid is a prerequisite of economic growth for Third World countries, our
evidence does suggest that it contributes to it.

Our second observation pertains to the positive relationship between aid
receipts and expanding international economic activity. It was seen in Chapter 4
that both export and import growth rates increase with the volume of either
gross or per capita US aid received. The covariation achieves significance,
however, only in the case of per capita aid. There are, on the other hand, no
significant relationships between either form of aid receipt and percentage trade
growth rates, which means that recipients' expanding volume of trade cannot be
attributed to their enjoyment of an expanding trade sector in their domestic
economies. Any aid effect that exists, therefore, is indirect, working perhaps
through the expansion in production that is apparent in recipients' increasing
real per capita income or, more straightforwardly, through a heightened sensitivity
to international economic interaction. The disproportionate increase in net
factor income among larger aid recipients might well also be the result of greater
international economic activity brought about by the transfer. In direct contrast,
there is no covariation between aid receipts and growth rates of either foreign
direct investment or ExIm loans, which are two findings that tend to falsify the
hypothesis that aid is distributed so as to create a sound infrastructure on which
foreign investment can then capitalise. Finally, aid is positively related to the
rate of growth of investment income, a covariation that is most readily explained
by an expansion of foreign direct investment except for the fact that there is no
evidence of such expansion actually having taken place. Being more likely to be
responsive to aid injections, an alternative source of expansion that might
explain this relationship is a rapidly growing foreign production sector, as
profiled by net factor income.

To summarise then, there are many instances in which larger aid recipients
display higher growth rates on their various dimensions of international economic

activity, although particularly noteworthy exceptions to this generalisation occur with regard to foreign direct investment and commercial bank activities. If nothing else, these exceptions signal caution in imputing causation in those instances where aid receipts are clearly associated with higher growth rates. On the other side of the coin, however, the need for caution should not be exaggerated since, working through either intervening variables or the creation of a more generalised and heightened sensitivity to international economic activity, the effect of aid might be indirect where a relationship does not manifest itself at the bivariate level. On balance, therefore, it seems reasonable to conclude that aid receipts do have an impact on a number of aspects of international economic activity.

Our third observation relates to the question of what our analysis has to say about the argument to the effect that official transfers promote the external economic dependence of their recipients.[21] This argument contends minimally that aid and various measures of economic dependence covary positively and maximally that aid is an instrument that is explicitly designed and manipulated to promote the economic dependence of recipients. The testing of such claims against our findings is seriously hampered, however, by the need to identify valid measures of dependence. There is, in fact, no widely accepted range of such measures and, to make things even more difficult, the same measure does not always mean the same thing to different sides in the argument. To take an example, some analysts would interpret a growth in foreign direct investment as signalling increased dependence, whereas others would see it, other things being equal, as a means of escaping dependence. Stated differently, the opposing paradigms, like structuralism and liberalism, through which the international system is generally viewed, often evaluate the same phenomenon in radically different ways and thereby create validity problems for the researcher. This 'fact of life' serves to complicate any exercise in interpretation, but it need not deter us from testing the dependence model against a number of relatively uncontroversial measures of this phenomenon.

For a start, there is positive covariation between aid and the rate of growth of trade and, for a number of reasons, it is difficult to see how this particular relationship could be interpreted as being indicative of recipient dependence. Firstly, while trade deficits increase with aid, the rate of growth of these deficits does not, which means that trade imbalances are not a function of imports growing more quickly than exports. In other words, aid does not trigger uncontrolled imports that then visit substantial deficits on its recipients. Secondly, it is not altogether clear that larger trade deficits are necessarily associated with deleterious consequences from the point of view of economic development. Indeed, many argue that, under certain circumstances, they are actually beneficial to this process. An alternative dependence argument focuses on trade share and claims that, by virtue of bringing about a structural change in the relative size of recipients' trade sectors (e.g. primary as opposed to industrial sectors), aid fosters dependence. The immediate problem with this argument is that there is no evidence that aid covaries with change in the relative size of trade sectors. A related argument takes as its focus trade diversification rather than trade share. That is, commodity diversification is commonly viewed as being beneficial to Third World countries since it provides them with some insurance against adverse developments that are beyond their control, for example, a sharp drop on the international market in the price paid for their primary commodity.[22] Continuing this logic, commodity concentration is seen as undesirable since it indicates growing dependence. But as it turns out, level of aid receipt is not related to the rate of increase of export commodity diversification. What is more, this conclusion holds equally for the diversification of imports by source and exports by destination. In short, none of the diversification indices provide any evidence that aid promotes dependence. In the area of international investment and banking, aid varies in its relationship to individual rates of growth. Some indicators, such as commerical banks' foreign activities and foreign direct investment, show no sign of covarying with aid, whereas others, like investment income and net factor income from abroad, are related to it. While both these last variables, the repatriation of profits on investment and the expansion of foreign domestic production, can be conceptualised as measures of external economic dependence, they do not appear, given our income growth rate findings, to have an adverse effect on economic growth.

Generally speaking then, the evidence of this analysis provides little or no support for the blanket assertion that aid receipts promote external economic dependence.

Our fourth, and final, observation has a broader interpretational focus than the other three and it is that the most general conclusion to emerge from this analysis is that economic factors play a relatively minor role in structuring the distribution of economic aid, yet the receipt of aid does appear to influence recipients' performance on a number of these economic factors. Thus, there may be no evidence that US aid is distributed so as to promote economic growth in the Third World, but the receipt of this transfer none the less contributes to this process. But even if economic factors do not figure prominently as second-order supplier utilities, the United States still finds itself allied through the aid programme to countries that display significantly better performance rates on a number of economic dimensions. From the perspective of recipients as a whole, therefore, aid would appear to be both a worthwhile and desirable commodity since, at least in narrowly economic terms, its receipt does not entail any pronounced costs, or disutilities. Indeed, the reverse is the case in so far as the transfer actually visits benefits, or utilities, on its recipients.

Military Assistance

This interpretation of our military assistance impact findings follows the same four-observation organisational format as for economic aid.

The first of these observations again concerns the positive relationship between gross military assistance receipts and real per capita income growth rates. Following the logic outlined in this same situation for economic aid, our conclusion here is simply that larger recipients of the transfer have higher rates of growth: no causal inference is implied. The interpretation of this same relationship when military assistance is in its relative form is more complicated, however. The basic problem is that while military assistance may well promote economic growth through a substitution effect, it is difficult to determine how this effect actually works. A number of candidates can be dismissed at the outset. That is, since the transfer is not systematically or strongly related to per capita income, size of industrial sector or GDFCF, its covariation with economic growth cannot be held to be the spurious outcome of one or more of these relationships. To elaborate this point with specific reference to GDFCF, if military assistance takes the place of previously planned military expenditures and thereby frees resources for economic goals, these freed resources would be expected to take the form not of larger absolute levels of GDFCF, but of higher growth rates of it. The simple fact that no such effects manifest themselves means that the substitution hypothesis must be rejected. Suffering the same fate and for the same reasons is the hypothesis to the effect that military assistance fosters more rapid industrial sector growth and, in consequence, higher per capita income growth. A final possible explanation of military assistance's apparent impact on economic growth is that the transfer flows disproportionately to Third World countries already experiencing higher growth rates so that, reflecting nothing more than an existing state of affairs, its effect is, in fact, spurious. This explanation is implausible for two reasons. Firstly, it implies that economic factors play an important role in structuring the distribution of military assistance, whereas this has already been shown not to be the case. Secondly, since the individual countries comprising each recipient category change over time, performance would seem to follow the receipt of military assistance and not be independent of it.

Partly because of the failure of these explanations, it seems that the most likely causal mechanism relating military assistance and economic growth is trade. It has already been established that larger recipients have bigger trade deficits and higher export and import growth rates. What is more, their relatively vigorous trading activity is manifested not only in absolute terms, but also, and perhaps more importantly, in their rapidly expanding trade sectors. It is entirely possible, therefore, that their trading activity has been stimulated by the increased international activity that follows from the receipt of military assistance and that, through this nexus, the transfer works to enhance real per capita income growth. Once again, however, it must be emphasised that our argument is not that military assistance is a prerequisite of economic growth. Nor, in such a complicated web of relationships, is it possible to conclude categorically that military assistance stimulates growth. Less ambitiously, however, there does seem to be reasonable grounds for tracing a causal path from this transfer to economic growth through increased trading activity. The transfer itself is, of course, likely to be no more than one of several factors that are responsible for the growth, but it does seem to make a contribution. It must also be emphasised that to the extent that military assistance does have an impact on growth, it is restricted for the most part to larger recipients so that the evidence for there being a generalised military assistance effect is weak at best.

Our second observation pertains to the interpretation of the positive relationship between military assistance and international economic activity growth rates. Larger recipients have both higher rates of growth of trade and more rapidly expanding trade sectors. This is a pattern of growth that leaves these recipients with bigger trade deficits, although they grow no more quickly than the deficits of smaller recipients. With regard to the explanation of this relationship, it might well be that being one of the favoured few to receive military assistance from the United States convinces Third World countries to take more risks on the assumption that there will be external support to finance their trade deficits or, more simply, it may be that receipt of the transfer encourages trade expansionism by heightening recipients' sensitivity to international economic activity. Such sensitivity is certainly apparent with respect to investment income, commercial banks' foreign activities and foreign production. On the other hand, however, military assistance does not seem to encourage foreign direct investment and this finding alone cautions against too readily imputing a causal relationship in the case of the important finding of covariation between level of receipt of the transfer and investment income. None the less, a plausible causal mechanism indirectly linking these phenomena is that commercial banks make bigger loans to foreign producers, which in turn stimulates more rapid rates of growth of investment income. What makes this scenario even more likely is that the receipt of US military assistance will serve as an indication to foreign producers that their investments are relatively safe. In other words, the military assistance programme implicitly acts as a kind of investment insurance scheme.

The third observation concerns the economic dependence argument. Again, following the logic outlined for economic aid, the increase in rate of growth of trade that is associated with military assistance receipts does not seem plausibly interpreted to signal economic dependence. In contrast to economic aid, though, this transfer is also associated with a change in the sectoral nature of trade, i.e. with an increase in trade as a proportion of total production. Even if due only in part to military assistance, this change raises the question of whether this disproportionate growth in commitment to trade can be taken as a valid indicator of economic dependence. Two overlapping arguments would suggest an affirmative answer to this question. In asserting that dependence necessarily follows from a greater reliance on international trading partners, the first of these arguments verges on the tautological. The second of them, perhaps because it is less tautological, is more convincing in its claim that an increasing commitment to trade promotes dependence because it constrains the development options open to

Third World countries and simultaneously leaves them vulnerable to the substantial fluctuations that can occur in international markets. Given the other evidence available to us, however, this argument is neither persuasive nor convincing. While it cannot be denied that an increased resort to trade structures development options to some greater or lesser extent, this delimitation of choice can be considered deleterious only if it is accompanied by lower exportation growth rates, and in fact it is not. Furthermore, international markets can fluctuate, but so too can domestic ones so that there would seem to be no overwhelming reason to concentrate on one at the expense of the other.

Finally, and perhaps most pertinently, it needs to be recognised that this increased commitment to trade is not achieved by resorting to greater commodity concentration. Indeed, although the relationship is not significant, this commitment goes along with more, rather than less, export commodity diversification. It must also be recognised, however, that this picture of no dependence is not without its qualifications. Levels of military assistance may not covary significantly with export diversification by either commodity or destination, but it is the case that larger recipients of this transfer are significantly less likely to diversify their imports by source and this relationship is compatible with an economic dependence interpretation of official transfers.

Our fourth observation is essentially a reiteration of the points made at this same stage of the economic aid impact interpretation. Economic considerations play a relatively minor role in structuring the distribution of military assistance, yet the transfer apparently has an impact on a number of dimensions of recipients' economic performance. To a greater extent than with economic aid, however, these impacts characterise only the large transfer recipient category, a difference that probably reflects nothing more than the considerably greater selectivity and concentration of the military assistance programme. Thus, as with aid, the United States, while not pursuing second-order economic utilities, does find itself being allied to those Third World countries whose economies perform better. This means that if costs are again defined in narrowly economic terms, military assistance recipients incur very few costs, or disutilities. There is certainly little evidence that recipients become increasingly economically dependent on the United States. Indeed, granting the assumption that at least some of the performance indicators employed in this analysis are perceived by Third World countries as desirable and positive utilities, the receipt of military assistance would seem to afford them a net balance of utilities over disutilities.

Arms sales

The only real conclusion that can be drawn form the arms sales impact analysis is that there is little sign of this transfer having an impact on any of the economic performance indicators. The obvious qualification to this conclusion, of course, is that it applies only to those indicators figuring in the analysis; arms sales may well have very real effects on dimensions of economic performance that we have overlooked or not investigated.

While rejecting that it amounts to an 'economic' explanation, we do find that economic considerations influence the distribution of arms sales more effectively than those of either economic aid or military assistance. Unlike with these other two transfers, however, we also find that arms sales entail fewer systematic impacts. Thus, although the United States allies itself through this programme to the larger Third World economies, it does not align itself with the more dynamic ones—but nor does it align itself with the less dynamic ones. Certainly, therefore, any expectation that the United States might have had about promoting its second-order economic utilities is not realised. From the perspective of the recipient, the lack of covariation between levels of arms sales receipt and economic performance means that while the transfer does not visit any disutilities on them, equally it does not afford them any utilities.

Appendix: variables and their acronyms

Acronym	Variable description
Production structure	
GDP	Gross domestic product
GDPPC	Per capita gross domestic product (current prices)
CGDPPC	Per capita gross domestic product (constant prices)
GDFCF	Gross domestic fixed capital as a percentage of GDP
Indust	Industrial production as a percentage of GDP
Agric	Agricultural production as a percentage of GDP
Trade structure	
GrEx	Gross exports
PEx	Exports as a percentage of GDP
GrIm	Gross imports
PIm	Imports as a percentage of GDP
GrAgEx	Gross agricultural exports
PAgEx	Agricultural exports as a percentage of total exports
GrMnEx	Gross mining exports
PMnEx	Mining exports as a percentage of total exports
GrMfEx	Gross manufacturing exports
PMfEx	Manufacturing exports as a percentage of total exports
GrMfIm	Gross manufacturing imports
PMfIm	Manufacturing imports as a percentage of total imports
TrDfct	Current account trade deficit as a percentage of total exports
ExDvC	Export diversification by commodity
ExDvD	Export diversification by destination

ImDvS	Import diversification by source
IL	International liquidity
PIL	International liquidity as a percentage of imports

Investment and banking structure

NFI	Net factor income from abroad
PNFI	Net factor income from abroad as a percentage of GDP
InvInc	Investment income
PInvInc	Investment income as a percentage of GDP
ForDrInv	Balance on foreign direct investment
PForDrInv	Balance on foreign direct investment as a percentage of GDP
CBFA	Commercial banks' foreign assets
PCBFA	Commercial banks' foreign assets as a percentage of GDP
CBFL	Commerical banks' foreign liabilities
PCBFL	Commercial banks' foreign liabilities as a percentage of GDP
ExImLn	Export–Import bank loans (current prices)

As in previous chapters, we use capital letters in the acronyms to indicate the start of a new word.

Notes

1. This is the classic humanitarian rationale and it was especially prevalent in the literature of the 1960s. Its best-known statement is the Report of the Commission on International Development, L. B. Pearson, Chairman, *Partners in Development* (New York: Praeger, 1969). Albeit more weakly, the rationale persists today and we would see it as being inherent in some of the Brandt Commission proposals. See *North–South: A Programme for Survival* (London: Fontana, 1980). The Brandt Report, however, adds an interesting twist to the rationale in that, while maintaining that those countries with the greatest needs deserve the most assistance, it also argues that it is in the self-interest of high-income countries to be guided by humanitarian considerations. Certainly, this rationale underlies the assistance patterns of non-governmental agencies like Oxfam. It was also one of the factors leading to the establishment of the IDA as a distinctive branch of the World Bank.
2. The term 'supplier description' encompasses both the official and academic definitions of the transfer in question. Since economic aid is the only transfer to contain a definitional element of assistance for development purposes, we would expect neither military assistance nor arms sales to be allocated for explicitly developmental purposes.
3. The humanitarian rationale seems to us to be incompatible with our utility conception of official transfers since, altruism apart, there seems to be no good supplier-oriented reason as to why the supplier should progressively align itself with the countries experiencing the most chronic needs. After all, the rationale is premised purely on recipient needs and takes no account of supplier interests, especially as it was articulated before the Brandt Report.

4. By way of illustration of this point, it should be noted that development needs and development potential indicators can be identical. Per capita income, for example, could function as an indicator of either, differing only in the direction of its relationship to the transfer. Under the needs rationale, aid would be inversely related to income and under the potential rationale, the relationship would be positive.

5. Since aid is measured in current prices, current per capita GDP is used in the distributional analysis. The need to control for price inflation means that real per capita GDP is used in the impact analysis.

6. The diversification measures are computed by means of the Gini-Hirschman index. For export diversification by destination and import diversification by source, it entails the following computational stages: (a) the exports to and imports from each country are expressed as a proportion of total exports and imports for each recipient; (b) each proportionate value is squared; (c) the resultant values are summed for all exports and imports separately; (d) the square root of this sum is multiplied by 100. The result is that each recipient is given a score ranging from 0 to 100 with 100 indicating total concentration. In the case of export diversification by commodity, the 'unit' around which the extent of diversification is calculated is the Standard International Trade Classification in the UN *Yearbook of International Trade Statistics*.

7. The main results are reported in Table 6.1.

8. The number of countries in each of the NR, R and NRNR categories for the biannual observations are respectively: 25, 67, 21; 22, 75, 15; 27, 73 21; 21, 79, 14; 21, 78, 11; 20, 74, 10 (for GDP and GDPPC); 19, 61, 15; 20, 65, 13; 21, 63, 15; 18, 66, 11; 18, 66, 8; 17, 64, 7 (for GDFCF); 22, 62, 18; 19, 67, 12; 21, 66, 15; 16, 69, 9; 15, 65, 5; 15, 22, 5 (for Indust); 26, 65, 22; 22, 71, 15; 28, 68, 22; 22, 74, 15; 21, 71, 11, 21, 70, 11 (for GrEx and PEx); 14, 55, 10; 16, 52, 9; 15, 55, 9; 14, 58, 7; 15, 55, 6; 14, 51, 5 (for NFI); 21, 59, 17; 18, 66, 12; 23, 65, 17; 19, 70, 13; 19, 70, 9; 18, 69, 8 (for InvInc); 14, 57, 10; 15, 64, 9; 22, 61, 16; 19, 65, 13; 18, 67, 8; 17, 68, 7 (for ForDrInv); 22, 67, 17; 18, 66, 11; 25, 66, 20; 18, 72, 12; 17, 67, 9; 18, 72, 9 (for CBFA); and 26, 68, 22; 22, 75, 15; 28, 73, 22; 22, 79, 15; 23, 78, 13; 22, 79, 12 (for ExImLn).

9. The results for the 1970s could well have been disturbed by the economic changes within OPEC. As a safety measure, we ran the regressions for the 1970s including a dummy variable for OPEC membership, but the variable did not figure in any of the final equations.

10. The critical role of percentage trade in these equations is especially apparent in 1955 and 1977 when excluding this variable results in no significant equation being generated.

11. Under these circumstances an absolute variable may have a positive sign and, conversely, a relative variable a negative sign.

12. The positive influence of percentage imports simply qualifies the negative influence of percentage exports to which it is positively related.

13. In Table 6.4, the number of cases in the NR and R categories are: 22, 11; 18, 20; 19, 22; 24, 23; 27, 31; 36, 41; 46, 36; 49, 36; 58, 34; 60, 37; 68, 32; 72, 28 (for GDP and GDPPC); 15, 11; 12, 16; 14, 16; 17, 18; 21, 28; 26, 37; 34, 35; 37, 36; 46, 34; 50, 35; 54, 30; 58, 26 (for GDFCF); 21, 11; 17, 18; 17, 20; 20, 21; 21, 30; 24, 38; 34, 35; 39, 36; 50, 34; 51, 35; 57, 30; 59, 29 (for Indust); 28, 12; 21, 22; 22, 24; 24, 25; 26, 31; 35, 41; 45, 36; 47, 38;

56, 35; 56, 37; 64, 32; 68, 28 (for GrEx and PEx); 16, 11; 13, 16; 15, 16; 17, 19; 19, 26; 15, 37; 25, 34; 31, 36; 36, 34; 35, 33; 40, 30; 46, 26 (for NFI); 25, 12; 19, 20; 22, 21; 24, 23; 20, 28; 16, 38; 24, 35; 34, 36; 47, 33; 49, 35; 58, 30; 62, 27 (for InvInc); 24, 10; 18, 17; 19, 20; 21, 20; 18, 27; 13, 35; 21, 31; 30, 35; 39, 32; 45, 34; 54, 29; 58, 26 (for ForDrInv); 21, 9; 17, 14; 19, 16; 23, 19; 24, 24; 32, 34; 43, 32; 46, 34; 52, 31; 52, 32; 63, 28; 65, 25 (for CBFA); 28, 12; 21, 22; 22, 24; 24, 25; 27, 31; 36, 41; 46, 36; 49, 38; 59, 35; 60, 37; 69, 32; 73, 28 (for ExImLn).

14. On three of the occasions on which the outlier is excluded (1955, 1967 and 1975), there is no signficant equation generated. The same equations for 1969, 1971 and 1973 are respectively: GDFCF 0.56, NFI 0.53, PAgEx −0.30 (R^2 = 43); GDFCF 0.64, NFI 0.53, PAgEx −0.29, PCBFA −0.29 (R^2 = 52); PAgEx −0.47, PInvInc −0.52, GDPPC −0.60, GDFCF 0.58 (R^2 = 58). These three equations show some difference from their counterparts including the outlier, but the differences are more apparent than real. This is because we are in a situation in which there is no clear hierarchy of variables and no strong relationships so that even small changes in simple correlations can result in the generation of apparently quite different equations.

15. We focus the presentation of results here only on the small, medium and large recipient categories since our analysis deals very shortly with the t-test results for the comparison of non-recipients and recipients as a whole.

16. For those variables on which significant differences between non-recipients and recipients as a whole are found, the difference between these groups is far more pronounced than any of the increases found across the three categories of recipient.

17. In Table 6.7, the number of cases in the biannual NR and R categories are: 71, 26; 74, 26; 66, 34; 64, 35; 56, 38 (for GDP and GDPPC); 59, 26; 58, 26; 50, 34; 49, 35; 45, 36 (for GDFCF); 60, 26; 61, 26; 51, 34; 47, 33; 43, 34 (for Indust); 67, 26; 70, 26; 62, 34; 57, 35; 54, 37 (for GrEx and PEx); 43, 25; 45, 25; 39, 33; 36, 34; 30, 35 (for NFI); 59, 25; 63, 25; 57, 32; 54, 35; 52, 35 (for InvInc); 55, 24; 59, 24; 53, 31; 50, 35; 48, 35 (for ForDrInv); 59, 25; 67, 24; 59, 31; 58, 32; 55, 35 (for CBFA); 71, 26; 75, 26; 67, 34; 66, 35; 63, 38 (for ExImLn).

18. Throughout the study a tolerance value of 0.50 has been used in the regression analyses. This value means that no variable is allowed to enter the equation if 50 per cent or more of its variance is explained by estimators that already figure in the equation.

19. To ascertain whether the OPEC countries exercise a disturbing effect on the regression outcomes, these same regressions are run inclusive of a dummy variable for OPEC membership. This variable, however, does not enter any of the equations.

20. It might initially seem that one way of attenuating these problems is to control for the power politics rationale by running the equations both including and excluding the variables tapping it and then comparing the results. But this is, in fact, not a satisfactory strategy for several reasons. Firstly, some of the power politics variables are not unique to that rationale, but figure in others of them as well. Secondly, a number of other variables are collinear with the power politics ones so that to exclude one of them simply allows a collinear variable to enter the equation as its surrogate. Many of the trade aggregates (i.e. agricultural, mining and manufacturing trade), for example,

correlate highly with gross trade. Thirdly, we wish to evaluate the rival rationales comparatively and this can only be done when all the variables are used together. Thus, even if the economic dimension of recipient power capabilities could be isolated (which it cannot), little would be gained from running an analysis excluding it. If power politics variables are not important, they simply will not enter the equation in the first place. If, on the other hand, they are critically important, to exclude them will lead only to a weaker explanation. What is more, if their exclusion were still to produce significant results, we would risk an erroneous interpretation since it would be a subordinate and possibly (though not necessarily so) spurious by-product of 'hidden' power political considerations. Finally, we have employed ANOVA analyses to offset the charge that if power political considerations are dominant, they may disguise other, albeit weaker, relationships in the regression analyses.

21. The strongest version of the dependence argument is called dependency and it asserts that capitalism creates and maintains underdevelopment in the Third World. As mentioned in Chapter 1, we accept that dependency theory contains a variety of interesting observations, but it is not explicated in terms that allow it to be tested by behavioural social science and so it is excluded from our analysis.

22. One caveat has to be made about the benefits of commodity diversification and it is that it is highly unlikely that an increased concentration would be seen as disadvantageous, at least in the short term, if there was an inelastic demand for the commodity in question.

7 Political Structure and Performance

Introduction

Theoretical rationale

It should be pointed out at the outset that the expectation of a direct relationship between recipients' political structure and official transfers is perhaps the most debatable of the four substantive hypotheses tested in this book. The reason for this particular hypothesis' relatively moot status is the argument to the effect that since the United States views social and political change as a by-product of economic development, it contents itself with the promotion of economic change and assumes that social and political reform will follow more or less automatically.[1] Two considerations, however, caution that this argument be treated sceptically and that the hypothesis of a relationship between political structure and official transfers be tested empirically. The first of them is that the argument's validity is seriously questioned by the last chapter's demonstration that purely economic factors exercise little influence on the distribution of official transfers. The second is that it is entirely conceivable that experience could well indicate that social and political change is more easily manipulated than are national economies so that, declarations of intent notwithstanding, the United States actually keeps social and political criteria distinct from economic considerations in its transfer allocation decisions.

The rationale for expecting a relationship between political structure and official transfers falls into two parts. Firstly, and perhaps less importantly, is that official US pronouncements consistently insist that there is such a relationship and, secondly, it would seem to be in the United States' own self-interest that it should exist. To take these reasons in turn, since the onset of the Cold War the United States has held that a primary purpose of its overall foreign policy, including its official transfer programmes, is to build a world that is 'safe for democracy'. A fine example of this commitment is the 1961 Alliance for Progress between the United States and some twenty friendly Latin American states; the Preamble to the Charter of this Alliance sets forth the intention to pursue such goals as 'personal liberty', 'representative democracy' and the improvement and strengthening of 'democratic institutions'.[2] Nor does it seem justifiable to dismiss such statements as empty rhetoric unworthy of further examination, not least because it can reasonably be argued that the achievement of such goals would be in the United States' own self-interest. That is, given its post-1945 efforts to create a new international order congenial to the pursuit of its own interests, then the consummation of these efforts would be made easier to the extent that Third World countries shared the same liberal economic and political values and, hence, accepted the United States' leadership of the 'free world' that it was pre-eminent in creating and sustaining.

The assumption underlying this rationale is that liberal democracy goes hand in hand with political stability and social reform, but there is no necessary reason why it should. Failing democracy, US official transfers could still, for example, be deployed to promote social reform in, say, autocratic military regimes.[3] In this regard, it is certainly the case that US official pronouncements lead us to expect an independent humanitarian dimension in its transfer allocation decisions. The Point Four programme, for instance, promises to 'aid the efforts of the people of economically underdeveloped countries to develop their resources and improve their living conditions.'[4] Thus, a derivative rationale posits a relationship between official transfers and regime social and political characteristics irrespective of political structure. To be more specific, when taken together with the proven US attraction to recipients' power political capabilities, these two rationales suggest a positive relationship on three particular socio-political dimensions, the humanitarian one of social development and the more explicitly political ones of stability and power capabilities.

Operationalisation

In line with the theoretical justification for it, there are basically two clusters of variables in this analysis; the first taps the political structure of Third World countries and the second their social and political aspects that may or may not be related to this political structure.

The political structure cluster is intended to profile the governmental structure of the regime and it comprises the following variables: the presence of a functioning central assembly (measured in a dummy variable format), the number of political parties,[5] the presence of a military regime (measured in a dummy variable format) and the proportion of the governing body's (called 'cabinet' for the sake of simplicity and convenience) membership that is drawn from the military establishment. These variables are appropriate for determining whether the United States discriminates in favour of one or other type of regime in its official transfer allocations. In particular, they speak to the issue of whether these transfers flow disproportionately to regimes showing liberal democratic characteristics. From the perspective of the impact analysis, this cluster also allows us to address the question of whether US transfers actually encourage, or promote, the growth of these same characteristics.

The second cluster of variables comprises three sub-sets, the first of which measures social development and is made up of the following variables: educational expenditure as a percentage of GDP, health expenditure as a percentage of GDP, the national budget as a percentage of GDP and the mean number of people (in 1,000s) per medical doctor. The humanitarian thesis would lead us to expect the volume of official transfers to be related negatively to the first three of these variables and positively to the last of them. Negative relationships should characterise the second sub-set measuring political instability and which is made up of two variables: the incidence of left-wing and non-left-wing violence (both measured in a dummy format).[6] The third sub-set measures power political capabilities and comprises two variables: gross military spending and military spending as a percentage of GDP. The explanatory power of these particular variables has already been established in Chapter 4 and their inclusion herein is not meant simply to reiterate their substantive importance. Rather, their inclusion is designed to determine whether the other variables in the analysis independently structure the distribution of official transfers or whether they influence it only indirectly through their affinity with the apparently overriding foreign policy consideration of power politics.

Findings: distribution

Economic aid

Taking the power politics variables first, both gross and relative military spending have already been shown in Chapter 4 to be linearly and positively related to level of gross aid over all but the first four years of the 1950-79 period. None of the political structure variables, however, prove to be significantly related to level of gross aid receipt, at least in simple bivariate terms. Statistical significance apart, the military regime, per cent military in the cabinet and operating central assembly variables do not even show a consistent pattern, no matter how weak, across the four categories of aid receipt. In slight contrast, the remaining variable, number of parties, has its greatest value in the large recipient category most of the time, but no systematic or consistent pattern emerges across the remaining three categories.

The general picture for the stability variables is not very different. For both left-wing and non-left-wing violence, no consistent or strong relationship with level of aid manifests itself, although there is some tendency for both forms of violence to be more prevalent in the higher recipient categories. As for the social development variables, the proportion of Third World countries' GDP spent on education presents something of an opposite picture. It is never significantly related to gross aid receipt, but its value is consistently at its minimum in the large aid category while no consistent pattern emerges over the other three. Health expenditure as a percentage of GDP displays a similar relationship, although while still weak, it stands in a more linearly negative relationship to aid across the three lowest categories. The related variable of population per doctor is again insignificant and is also non-linear from the early 1960s onwards in that its highest values are found in the zero and large aid recipient categories. The final development variable is budget size and it stands in no significant or systematic relationship to level of aid receipt throughout the 1950s and 1960s. In the 1970s, however, the relationship of these two variables becomes consistently significant and non-linear with the highest values occurring, once again, in the zero and large aid categories.

With regard to the differentiation from 1969 onwards of aid recipients and non-recipients on the basis of the range of socio-political variables, missing data problems oblige us, as in the previous chapter, to use bivariate difference-of-means tests rather than the more powerful and multivariate discriminant analysis. Table 7.1 shows that, as it turns out, these tests identify none of the variables

Table 7.1 Means on socio-political variables for non-recipients of economic aid (NR), recipients of economic aid (R) and non-recipients of both economic aid and arms sales (NRNR) 1969–79

	NR	R	NRNR	NR	R	NRNR	NR	R	NRNR
	MltExp			PMltExp			MltReg		
1969	130	128	75	4.1	3.2	3.6	19	19	18
1971	182	146	133	4.2	3.6	4.2	32	23	33
1973	150	213	73†	4.1	3.7	3.8	36	18	32
1975	263	237	172	4.5	3.7	4.3	18	28	20
1977	631	205	114	6.5*	3.6	5.6	22	31	23
1979	588	210	156	5.5	3.7	4.8	18	30	20
	PMltCab			Parties			CenAss		
1969	11	12	10	1.2	1.4	1.3	69	84	73
1971	15	14	13	0.9*	1.5	0.8†	59	76	60
1973	13	12	12	1.1	1.4	1.1	46*	79	50†
1975	10	17	13	1.2	1.2	1.2	59	70	60
1977	13	19	8	1.1	1.2	1.1	61	67	54
1979	10	18	19	1.1	1.4	0.9	59	68	50
	Budget			Educ			Health		
1969	20	18	20	3.0	2.7	3.1	1.2	1.1	1.2
1971	24*	19	26†	3.0	2.9	3.1	1.3	1.1	1.3
1973	25*	19	25†	3.3	3.0	3.3	1.4	1.1	1.3
1975	26	20	26†	3.1	2.7	3.4	1.4	1.0	1.5
1977	32*	24	36†	3.2	3.2	3.0	1.6	1.2	1.7
1979	29	24	29	4.0	3.1	3.9	1.8	1.2	2.0
	Doctors			NLWV			LWV		
1969	13	15	15	12	6	14	12	7	14
1971	6*	16	8†	5	11	6	5	11	6
1973	11	14	13	4	8	5	4	5	5
1975	3*	14	3†	9	8	13	9	4	7
1977	4*	13	4†	0	9	0	4	4	8
1979	2*	13	3†	5	9	0	5	5	0

* Indicates a significant difference at the 0.05 level or higher between NR and R.
† Indicates a significant difference at the 0.05 level or higher between NRNR and R.

as consistently and significantly differentiating the two groups, although they do identify clear and consistent patterns in the data.[7] Again, to take the power political variables first, gross military expenditure is marginally higher among non-recipients of aid until 1975, after which time it becomes two to three times greater. Relative military expenditure, by contrast, is generally slightly higher among non-recipients, but the differences are far from significant. The mid-1970s also witnesses a change in the inter-group pattern of the military regime and per cent military in the cabinet variables. From enjoying higher values among non-recipients in the early years of the decade, these two variables score more highly in the recipient category from 1975 onwards. The number of parties and central assembly variables on the other hand, score a little more highly in the recipient category throughout the decade.

Consistent patterns rather than significant bivariate relationships also char-acterise the stability and development variables. There is no evidence that violence of either the left-wing or non-left-wing type is systematically related to the receipt or non-receipt of gross aid, whereas the scores for budget, educa-tion and health as a percentage of GDP are consistently higher, even if most often not significantly so, among non-recipients of the transfer. In sharp con-trast, the number of people per doctor is equally consistently higher among recipients of it. Indeed, apart from budget size this relationship is the only one to prove to be significant on anything like a regular basis.

When we restrict our non-recipient population to that group of Third World countries receiving neither aid nor arms sales from the United States, we find that, as in the previous chapter, this exercise in redefinition does little to change our results. With the single notable exception that gross military expenditure now becomes higher in the non-recipient category, this redefinition exercise by and large does little to alter either the outcome of the t-tests or the direction of the relationships whose strength is summarised by them.

The next stage of our analysis involves the regression of gross aid on the complete range of socio-political variables. The results are presented in Table 7.2 and they demonstrate that, in terms of explanatory power, military spending and left-wing violence dwarf the other socio-political variables to the point of reducing them to the status of being inconsequential influences on the Third World distribution of gross aid throughout the 1950–79 period. The measure of their relative unimportance is that only four of them appear in the fourteen significant regression outcomes, none of them is ever the most powerful estimator and no more than one of them, non-left-wing violence, appears in more than one year and on the two occasions that it is present, it is inconsistently signed.

We turn now to the distribution of per capita US aid. The bivariate ANOVA analyses produce much the same results as they did for gross aid, the major difference being that both military spending variables now consistently turn out not to be significantly related to level of per capita aid receipt. As for the remaining socio-political variables, again the pattern of relationships that emerges

Table 7.2 Standardised coefficients for the regressions of gross aid on the socio-political variables, 1951–79*

Year				Year			
1951:	Not significant			1969:	(0.64)	MltExp	0.67
					(0.35)	LWV	0.44
1953:	(0.59)	PMltExp	0.54		$R^2 = 52$		
	(0.45)	LWV	0.51				
	(−0.04)	NLWV	−0.37	1971:	(0.56)	MltExp	0.45
	$R^2 = 56$				(0.50)	LWV	0.41
					$R^2 = 46$		
1955:	(0.69)	PMltExp	0.80				
	(0.61)	LWV	0.64	1973:	(0.45)	LWV	0.41
	$R^2 = 84$				(0.28)	MltExp	0.23
					(−0.30)	Educ	−0.26
1957:	(0.59)	MltExp	0.71		$R^2 = 34$		
	(0.16)	CenAss	0.28				
	$R^2 = 46$			1975:	(0.73)	PMltExp	0.74
					(0.30)	NLWV	0.33
1959:	(0.57)	MltExp	0.54		$R^2 = 65$		
	(−0.19)	PMltCab	−0.36				
	$R^2 = 43$			1977:	(0.83)	PMltExp	0.66
					(0.82)	MltExp	0.40
1961:	(0.71)	MltExp	0.71		$R^2 = 79$		
	$R^2 = 50$						
				1979:	(0.69)	MltExp	0.47
1963:	(0.82)	MltExp	0.82		(0.67)	PMltExp	0.43
	$R^2 = 68$				$R^2 = 62$		
1965:	(0.84)	MltExp	0.84				
	$R^2 = 70$						
1967:	(0.51)	MltExp	0.91				
	(0.02)	PMltExp	−0.56				
	(0.27)	LWV	0.34				
	$R^2 = 55$						

* The figures in parentheses represent the zero-order correlation coefficients.

does not differ sharply from that for gross aid. Indeed, the overall impression to be gained from this set of ANOVAs is that the distribution of per capita aid is explained less successfully by socio-political structure than is that of gross aid.

The bivariate relationships then, suggest that the socio-political criteria governing the distribution of per capita aid will not necessarily be the same or as powerful in their impact as they are for gross aid. Table 7.3 shows that such is indeed the case; its three most striking features are firstly that no significant equation is generated on two occasions; secondly that the R^2 values are on average much lower than for gross aid, and, finally, that military spending is a less consistent predictor than it is in Table 7.2 when, in one or other of its forms, it ranked first in explanatory importance in all but one of the test years.

Table 7.3 Standardised coefficients for the regressions of per capita aid on the socio-political variables, 1951–79*

1951:	(0.52)	PMltExp	0.90		1965:	(0.45)	PMltExp	0.45
	(0.30)	Educ	1.17				$R^2 = 20$	
	(−0.15)	Health	−1.06					
	(0.09)	CenAss	−0.42		1967:	(0.33)	LWV	0.33
		$R^2 = 88$					$R^2 = 11$	
1953:	Not significant				1969:	(0.46)	PMltExp	0.45
						(0.27)	Parties	0.26
1955:	(0.45)	LWV	0.45				$R^2 = 28$	
	(0.39)	PMltExp	0.45					
	(−0.16)	MltExp	−0.27		1971:	(0.51)	PMltExp	0.32
		$R^2 = 43$				(0.37)	LWV	0.36
						(−0.09)	NLWV	−0.30
1957:	Not significant						$R^2 = 38$	
1959:	(0.54)	PMltExp	0.52		1973:	(0.71)	PMltExp	0.49
	(−0.34)	PMltCab	−0.50			(0.54)	Budget	0.42
	(−0.30)	Parties	−0.40			(0.02)	Educ	−0.34
	(−0.06)	Doctors	−0.30				$R^2 = 59$	
	(−0.13)	Health	−0.31					
		$R^2 = 61$			1975:	(0.62)	PMltExp	0.43
						(0.60)	Budget	0.41
1961:	(0.55)	Budget	0.84				$R^2 = 51$	
	(0.05)	Health	−0.55					
	(−0.10)	MltExp	−0.35		1977:	(0.74)	PMltExp	0.74
	(−0.11)	MltReg	−0.26				$R^2 = 54$	
		$R^2 = 50$						
					1979:	(0.64)	PMltExp	0.64
1963:	(0.35)	PMltExp	0.35				$R^2 = 41$	
		$R^2 = 13$						

* The figures in parentheses represent the zero-order correlation coefficients.

But while it enjoys this position in only ten of the thirteen equations in Table 7.3, if for no other reason than that left-wing violence is the most powerful predictor in another two of them, the substantive importance of this apparent 'fall from grace' should not be overstated. Thus, despite the perhaps somewhat unexpected emergence of budget size as the most powerful predictor in one of the remaining two equations, and second most powerful in another two, the regression outcomes can, in fact, be seen not to be radically different from those for gross aid. Health expenditure is the only other variable to appear more than once and to be consistently signed.

Military assistance

Starting our analysis of the military assistance programme with the simple ANOVA results, the military expenditure, or power politics, variables turn out once again to be more strongly and consistently related to the gross transfer than any of the other socio-political variables.[8] The political structure variables, by contrast, do not show the same systematic relationship to level of military assistance receipt. While no relationship emerges across the three recipient categories, military regimes turn out to be somewhat less prevalent among non-recipients in the 1950s and 1960s, but even this small difference disappears in the 1970s. This same broad pattern also characterises the military percentage in the cabinet variable, while the relationship between number of political parties and level of military assistance receipt also changes over time, but in the opposite direction. Prior to 1969, there is little variation in the number of parties across the four recipient categories. Thereafter, however, the relationship assumes a certain linearity, the most systematic difference being that parties are least numerous among the zero recipients and most numerous among the large ones. Finally, the presence of an operating central assembly is linearly, if not significantly, related to the dependent variable in the 1950s when all medium and large recipients boast such an assembly. Any sign of a systematic relationship then disappears in the 1960s and 1970s.

As for the stability variables, the incidence of domestic left-wing violence is the more consistent and systematic in its relationship to level of gross military assistance receipt. But even here, there is no relationship at all prior to the early 1960s when a strong and positive one emerges and persists until the end of the programme in the mid-1970s. What is more, a strong element of non-linearity is introduced into the relationship during this period by virtue of the fact that left-wing violence is particularly prevalent in those Third World countries receiving most military assistance. A contrasting picture characterises the incidence of non-left-wing violence, however. Generally speaking, there is no systematic pattern in its incidence across the four recipient categories, although there is a clear tendency for it to be more prevalent in the zero and small military assistance categories than in the medium and high ones.

The social development sub-set shows that budget size is not at all systematically related to gross military assistance receipt until the late 1960s, from which time its greatest values are almost invariably found in the zero and high recipient categories. Health expenditure as a proportion of GDP is, by contrast, generally negatively and linearly related to the dependent variable, but the relationship is rarely significant and is most notable for the lowest health expenditure scores being found among high military assistance recipients in virtually every year. Educational expenditure as a percentage of GDP and population per doctor are systematically related to gross military assistance receipt only to the extent that the highest values for both variables are found almost invariably in the non-recipient population and neither displays any kind of consistent linear relationship across the remaining three recipient categories.

The next stage of our analysis involves the differentiation of military assistance non-recipients and recipients (as a single group) on the basis of the full range of socio-political variables. As with economic aid in the previous section of this chapter, missing data problems oblige us to use bivariate difference-of-means tests to achieve this differentiation.

To take the power politics variables first, both forms of military spending are invariably higher among the recipients of military assistance and the difference is sufficiently pronounced to be significant about half of the time for each of them.[9] With regard to political structure, the presence of a military regime and military percentage in the cabinet variables also generally score more highly in the recipient population, but the difference is rarely great enough to be significant. Nor can the two groups be differentiated before 1969 on their mean number of parties. Afterwards, however, recipients boast a greater number of parties than do non-recipients and the difference is usually significant. Finally we come to the operating central assembly variable and here recipients and non-recipients of military assistance cannot be meaningfully or consistently differentiated at any point in the 1953–75 period.

While consistent patterns do emerge in the data, the stability and social development variables are on the whole less successful than their political structure counterparts in discriminating the recipient from the non-recipient population. Left-wing violence is almost always more prevalent among recipients but the difference is rarely significant. Non-left-wing violence, by contrast, stands in no systematic relationship at all to the dependent variable and the budget size, health and educational expenditure variables are generally marginally higher in the non-recipient population, although the difference is rarely significant. Finally, we come to the population per doctor variable and it turns out to be unrelated to the receipt or otherwise of military assistance in the 1950s, but to be higher in the non-recipient category throughout the 1960s and 1970s. Indeed, it is significantly higher in all but two of the eight time points comprising these two decades in our analysis.

In sum, therefore, the Third World countries selected as military assistance recipients are, perhaps not surprisingly in the light of our earlier findings, most distinctive from those not selected for having relatively substantial power capabilities and for experiencing domestic left-wing insurgency. They tend also to have a slightly more military complexion in terms of their political leadership and institutions, although this characteristic is offset in the closing years of the programme by their having more political parties as well. Finally, recipients are less intrusive in their countries' societies and economies in so far as their governments tend to dispose of a smaller proportion of their GDP, to spend relatively less of the national wealth on education and health, though they generally have significantly more medical doctors per head of population.

Table 7.4 Means for non-recipients (NR) and recipients (R) of military assistance by the socio-political variables, 1953–75

	NR	R	NR	R	NR	R	NR	R
	MltExp		PMltExp		MltReg		PMltCab	
1953	101	145	2.2	4.1*	15	8	11	18
1955	96	133	2.1	3.8*	19	14	14	16
1957	107	134	3.1	3.6*	14	17	10	13
1959	99	152	2.5	5.1*	4	8	9	12
1961	66	132	2.2	5.3*	11	13	10	14
1963	37	137*	2.2	4.6*	6	12	4	12*
1965	40	173*	2.2	4.0*	7	22*	4	16*
1967	58	232*	2.5	3.8	16	24	11	17
1969	70	222*	2.9	4.3	19	20	10	15
1971	100	236*	3.3	4.2	23	27	11	19
1973	164	263	3.7	4.1	22	25	11	16
1975	247	229	4.0	3.5	26	25	14	20
	Parties		CenAss		Budget		Educ	
1953	1.7	1.8	90	100	13	11	1.3	1.1
1955	1.7	1.7	81	95	13	13	1.5	1.1
1957	1.6	1.7	82	96	15	13	1.6	1.1
1959	1.8	1.7	92	100	17	14	2.0	1.5
1961	1.7	1.5	89	81	16	15	2.3	1.6*
1963	1.5	1.5	83	83	15	16	2.3	2.1
1965	1.5	1.5	93	78*	16	16	2.4	2.0
1967	1.4	1.4	84	82	18	16	2.8	2.4
1969	1.3	1.5	80	80	18	18	2.9	2.5
1971	1.1	1.6*	70	76	21	18	3.0	2.7
1973	1.1	1.7	67	78	22	19	3.2	2.7
1975	1.1	1.5*	67	68	22	18	2.8	2.5
	Health		Doctors		NLWV		LWV	
1953	0.6	0.4	7	5	7	0	4	8
1955	0.7	0.5	8	10	10	0	0	5
1957	0.7	0.6	9	8	5	0	5	0
1959	1.0	0.7	7	13	4	12	4	0
1961	1.0	0.9	14	13	4	10	0	10
1963	1.0	0.9	27	10*	8	13	0	8
1965	1.0	0.9	23	9*	10	14	0	8*
1967	1.1	1.0	20	9*	11	11	0	16*
1969	1.3	1.0	18	8*	8	6	5	14
1971	1.3	1.0	18	8*	8	11	2	22*
1973	1.3	1.0	16	6*	7	6	1	13
1975	1.1	1.9	13	8	8	7	3	11

* Indicates a significant difference at the 0.05 level.

Like in Chapter 6 and unlike in Chapters 4 and 5, to redefine the non-recipient population to consist of Third World countries getting neither military assistance nor arms sales does little to alter this basic picture. Once again, the only consistent change is that this 'new' non-recipient population exhibits lower gross military expenditure scores than do non-recipients as an undifferentiated group. In general, arms sales recipients are among the larger military spenders in the Third World, but the inclusion of a number of them in the non-recipient category does not serve to prevent military assistance recipients from having generally higher levels of military expenditure. All that happens, therefore, is that the exclusion of arms sales recipients from the military assistance non-recipient population exacerbates the differences in military spending that have already been noted.

Turning to the multiple regression results presented in Table 7.5, the most immediately obvious and general observation to be made about them is that the socio-political variables do not provide a very powerful or coherent explanation of gross military assistance allocations over the period of our analysis. Four of the twelve regression equations turn out to be insignificant and the remaining eight do not on the whole generate markedly powerful or consistent results. The order that characterises the table owes its presence to the military

Table 7.5 Standardised coefficients for the regressions of gross military assistance on the socio-political variables, 1953–75*

1953:	(0.68)	PMltExp	0.68	1965:	(0.51)	PMltExp	0.54
		$R^2 = 46$			(−0.33)	Health	−0.35
					(−0.05)	NLWV	−0.29
1955:	Not significant					$R^2 = 41$	
1957:	(0.60)	PMltExp	0.70	1967:	Not significant		
	(−0.36)	Health	−0.70				
	(−0.01)	Educ	0.59	1969:	(0.41)	PMltExp	0.41
		$R^2 = 66$				$R^2 = 17$	
1959:	Not significant			1971:	Not significant		
1961:	(0.71)	PMltCab	0.72	1973:	(0.54)	LWV	0.43
	(0.24)	PMltExp	0.27		(0.36)	Budget	0.45
		$R^2 = 58$			(−0.15)	Educ	−0.33
						$R^2 = 44$	
1963:	(−0.40)	Health	−0.38				
	(0.37)	MltExp	0.61	1975:	(0.60)	LWV	0.49
	(0.34)	LWV	0.57		(−0.45)	Health	−0.56
	(0.05)	NLWV	−0.57		(−0.01)	Budget	0.42
	(0.31)	MltReg	0.25			$R^2 = 55$	
		$R^2 = 54$					

* The figures in parentheses represent the zero-order correlation coefficients.

spending and left-wing violence variables. Between them, they comprise nine of the twenty-one variables appearing in the table and health expenditure is the only other one to figure reasonably prominently in the table and to be consistently signed.[10]

Next we come to the ANOVA results for the distribution of per capita military assistance. Gross military expenditure stands in no systematic relationship to the distribution of this variable, but its relative counterpart generally increases across the three recipient categories and its relatively high value in the zero category adds an element of non-linearity to the overall relationship. The political structure variables, on the other hand, rarely give any indication of standing in any reasonably consistent and patterned relationship to level of military assistance. As a group, however, the stability and development variables fare better in this regard. Left-wing violence tends to increase linearly and positively across the four recipient categories, especially in the 1960s and 1970s. Health expenditure and non-left-wing violence, by contrast, tend, in fact, to decrease across these same categories, with the latter being especially prevalent among zero and small military assistance recipients. Budget size, on the other hand, shows some tendency to take on higher values in the zero and large recipient categories. Finally, population per doctor is not related to the dependent variable in the 1950s, but always scores highest among non-recipients in the subsequent two decades while showing no systematic variation across the three recipient categories.

Focusing our attention once again only on recipients, Table 7.6 presents the results of regressing per capita military assistance on the range of socio-political variables. Immediately noticeable is that, as well as producing more significant equations than the gross military assistance regressions (eleven as opposed to eight), this set of results is also more consistent and decisive in so far as the equations as a whole are more uniformly dominated by the military spending and left-wing violence variables. In fact, one or other of them is the principal estimator in all eleven equations in the table.[11] More interesting perhaps is that left-wing violence is more prominent than in the per capita aid regressions, while budget size is somewhat less prominent.

Arms sales

Generally speaking, the arms sales ANOVAs produce no surprises given our economic aid and military assistance results. Gross military spending increases linearly and highly significantly across all four categories of arms sales receipt, whereas its relative counterpart follows this pattern only across the three recipient categories. That is, non-recipients spend less in absolute terms, but spend in relative terms at a level comparable to that found in the small recipient category. The political structure variables, in contrast, are not systematically or significantly related to the level of gross arms sales receipts over the course of the 1970s.

Table 7.6 Standardised coefficients for the regressions of per capita military assistance on the socio-political variables, 1953–75*

1953:	(0.82)	PMltExp	0.82			(−0.16)	Health	−0.33
		$R^2 = 67$				(−0.13)	NLWV	−0.46
						(−0.07)	PMltCab	−0.62
1955:	Not significant					(0.06)	PMltExp	0.38
							$R^2 = 70$	
1957:	(0.69)	PMltExp	0.69					
		$R^2 = 48$		1969:		(0.58)	PMltExp	0.45
						(0.50)	LWV	0.32
1959:	(0.75)	PMltExp	0.71				$R^2 = 42$	
	(−0.33)	Health	−0.33					
	(−0.19)	Doctors	−0.24	1971:		(0.59)	PMltExp	0.57
		$R^2 = 68$				(0.43)	LWV	0.38
						(−0.09)	NLWV	−0.41
1961:	(0.79)	PMltExp	0.79				$R^2 = 52$	
		$R^2 = 62$						
				1973:		(0.70)	LWV	0.53
1963:	(0.66)	PMltExp	0.90			(0.60)	PMltExp	0.30
	(−0.26)	Health	−0.37				$R^2 = 55$	
	(0.05)	NLWV	−0.65					
		$R^2 = 65$		1975:		(0.71)	LWV	0.83
						(0.18)	Budget	0.40
1965:	(0.81)	PMltExp	0.40			(0.14)	Parties	0.43
	(0.66)	LWV	0.75			(−0.08)	NLWV	0.29
		$R^2 = 68$					$R^2 = 69$	
1967:	(0.48)	LWV	0.78					
	(0.31)	Budget	0.46					

* The figures in parentheses represent the zero-order correlation coefficients.

The incidence of both left-wing and non-left-wing violence is concentrated in the zero and small receipt categories and is all but non-existent in the medium and large ones. The social development variables, by contrast, are more varied in their bivariate relationship to arms sales. Budget size generally enjoys higher values, although not always significantly so, in the medium and large arms sales recipients, whereas educational and health expenditure are more or less invariant across the four receipt categories. On the other hand, a mostly significant and always positive relationship emerges between the number of people per doctor and level of arms sales receipt.

When recipients are aggregated into a single group and compared, through difference-of-means tests, with non-recipients, the ANOVA results are replicated faithfully except for there now being no systematic relationship between either left-wing or non-left-wing violence and the receipt or non-receipt of arms transfers. Table 7.7 shows that, averaging out at a difference of about 8 to 1, recipients have significantly higher levels of gross military spending; their

Table 7.7 Means on socio-political variables for non-recipients (NR) and recipients (R) of arms sales, 1971–9

	NR	R	NR	R	NR	R	NR	R
	MltExp		PMltExp		MltReg		PMltCab	
1971	75	361*	3.2	4.9	24	27	12	19
1973	95	474*	3.2	5.9	21	27	11	17
1975	100	516*	3.3	5.0	27	24	15	16
1977	49	736*	3.0	6.3*	30	26	16	19
1979	61	616*	3.1	5.6*	27	29	15	19
	Parties		CenAss		Budget		Educ	
1971	1.2	1.5	72	73	20	21	2.9	2.9
1973	1.2	1.5	68	77	20	23	2.9	3.4
1975	1.2	1.3	67	68	21	22	2.7	2.8
1977	1.1	1.3	62	71	25	25	3.2	3.1
1979	1.2	1.4	63	71	24	26	3.3	3.3
	Health		Doctors		NLWV		LWV	
1971	1.2	1.1	17	4*	7	15	7	15
1973	1.2	1.2	16	5*	10	0	5	4
1975	1.1	1.0	14	8	6	11	4	6
1977	1.3	1.2	13	8	6	9	5	3
1979	1.3	1.3	15	5*	8	8	5	5

* Indicates a significant difference at the 0.05 level.

relative military expenditure is also inevitably higher, but not always significantly so.[12] With regard to the political structure variables, although the difference is never significant, recipients always have higher values on the military in the cabinet and number of parties variables.

The social development variables are even less successful than the political structure ones in discriminating between arms sales recipients and non-recipients. While non-recipients tend to have bigger budgets, they also have significantly fewer doctors per head of population. No other systematic relationships emerge.

In short, then, arms sales recipients are differentiated from non-recipients principally by their higher levels of absolute and relative military spending. It is also the case, however, that arms transfers flow in significantly greater volume to Third World countries with a relatively favourable ratio of doctors to population.

To the extent that the military expenditure variables enjoy an absolutely uncontested primacy in all five test years, Table 7.8 indicates that they structure arms sales allocations within the recipient population even more overwhelmingly

Table 7.8 Standardised coefficients for the regressions of gross arms sales on the socio-political variables, 1971–9*

	Including outlier			Excluding outlier		
1971:	(0.84)	PMltExp	0.77	(0.42)	PMltExp	0.60
	(−0.13)	NLWV	−0.31	(−0.14)	NLWV	−0.50
	(0.61)	MltExp	0.31	(0.23)	MltExp	0.39
		$R^2 = 86$			$R^2 = 41$	
1973:	(0.71)	MltExp	0.71			
		$R^2 = 50$				
1975:	(0.88)	MltExp	1.17	(0.82)	PMltExp	0.82
	(0.10)	Educ	0.41		$R^2 = 67$	
	(0.31)	Budget	−0.47			
		$R^2 = 87$				
1977:	(0.81)	MltExp	1.02	(0.62)	PMltExp	0.62
	(0.35)	Health	0.33		$R^2 = 39$	
		$R^2 = 74$				
1979:	(0.67)	MltExp	0.62	(0.77)	MltExp	0.75
	(0.51)	Educ	0.36	(0.22)	Educ	0.43
		$R^2 = 61$			$R^2 = 67$	

* The figures in parentheses are the zero-order correlation coefficients.

than do the differentiation of recipients and non-recipients. Against this background, the table has three other interesting features. The first is that military expenditure is initially dominant in its relative form and then in its absolute form as US arms sales rapidly grow in volume over the course of the 1970s. The second is that, in stark contrast to its economic aid and military assistance counterparts, left-wing violence structures the distribution of arms sales not at all, never mind prominently. The third feature is that, unlike with the discrimination of arms sales recipients and non-recipients, no other variable can be conceived of as having substantial importance. The only variable other than military spending to appear more than once is education, but its lack of underlying importance is suggested by its disappearance in 1975 when the outlier is excluded from that year's regression analysis.

The per capita arms sales regressions produce a set of results that are very similar to those for the transfer in its gross form. That is, military expenditure is by far the dominant estimator once again and left-wing violence again fails to figure in any of the regression equations. At the same time, the socio-political variables in general lose some of their ability to structure per capita arms sales allocations; this decline is reflected in the lower R^2 values for 1977 and 1979.

Table 7.9 Standardised coefficients for the regressions of per capita arms sales on the socio-political variables, 1971–9*

	Including outlier			Excluding outlier		
1971:	(0.84)	PMltExp	0.80	(0.77)	PMltExp	0.53
	(0.06)	Parties	0.18	(−0.59)	Parties	−0.48
		$R^2 = 76$		(−0.16)	MltReg	−0.33
					$R^2 = 75$	
1973:	(0.92)	PMltExp	0.92			
		$R^2 = 84$				
1975:	(0.91)	PMltExp	0.91	(0.91)	PMltExp	0.91
		$R^2 = 83$			$R^2 = 83$	
1977:	(0.73)	PMltExp	0.73	(0.72)	PMltExp	0.72
		$R^2 = 53$			$R^2 = 52$	
1979:	(0.55)	PMltExp	0.19	(0.76)	PMltExp	0.76
	(0.54)	Educ	0.39		$R^2 = 57$	
	(0.47)	MltExp	0.31			
		$R^2 = 46$				

* The figures in parentheses represent the zero-order correlation coefficients.

Findings: impact

Before proceeding to the enumeration of the impact analysis findings for the socio-political variables, it should be noted that this section of the chapter includes a variable that does not figure at all in the preceding distributional analysis. The variable in question measures whether or not individual Third World countries engage in arms racing and it is not part of the distributional analysis because we can find no reason to hypothesise that the United States deliberately encourages arms racing through its official transfer programmes.[13] It none the less remains entirely possible that its transfers, if only because of their substitutability, can inadvertently promote arms racing and it is our explicit aim to determine whether they do, in fact, have this effect.

Economic aid

The findings summarised in Table 7.10 indicate that the receipt of whatever volume of either gross or per capita US economic aid generally stands in at best a weak relationship to the pattern of change over time in the individual socio-political variables. To be sure, there is a number of significant chi-square results in the table, but only one of them, the covariation between level of gross aid receipt and the rate of growth of population per doctor, is both linear and significant. On the remaining occasions, significance is achieved by one of the recipient categories, usually the medium one, being substantially higher or

Table 7.10 Summed ranks for average percentage change in the political structure variables for the small, medium and large recipient categories of gross and per capita economic aid for the thirteen four-year periods, 1950–4, 1952–6 to 1974–8

	Gross aid			Per capita aid		
	Small	Medium	Large	Small	Medium	Large
MltExp	28.0	26.0	24.0	24.0	28.0	26.0
PMltExp	24.0	25.5	28.5	23.0	27.0	28.0
MltReg	24.0	25.0	29.0†	25.0	24.5	28.5
PMltCab	23.0	28.0	27.0	25.0	21.0	32.0*†
Parties	27.0	25.5	25.5	24.0	28.5	25.5
CenAss	27.5	29.5	21.0†	23.5	30.5	24.0
Budget	30.0	26.0	22.0	24.0	32.0	22.0*
Educ	25.0	28.0	25.0	23.0	29.0	26.0
Health	27.0	22.0	29.0	22.0	33.0	22.0*
Doctors	22.0	24.0	32.0*†	23.0	25.0	30.0
NLWV	25.0	27.0	26.0	27.5	22.0	28.5
LWV	26.5	20.0	31.5*†	27.5	21.0	29.5
Racing	24.0	24.0	30.0†	23.0	24.5	30.5†

* Indicates significance at the 0.05 level or beyond for the chi-square test across all three categories.
† Indicates significance at the 0.05 level or beyond for the cumulative binomial test on the number of highest, or lowest, rank placings for the large category.

lower in value than the other two, which themselves enjoy roughly equal summed rank scores. The very irregularity of this pattern cautions against reading substantive importance into their achievement of statistical significance.

The binomial tests also generate a variety of significant results, all of which show large aid recipients to follow a growth pattern that differs from those found in the small and medium recipient categories. To take gross aid first, military regimes, population per doctor, left-wing violence and arms racing all increase less rapidly among large aid recipients, whereas central assemblies become significantly more numerous in this same group. Budget size just fails to cross the threshold of statistical significance, yet it is worth noting that it is linearly and positively related to the volume of aggregated gross aid receipt, i.e. the larger its volume, the more rapid the rate of growth of budget as a proportion of GDP. As for per capita aid, only two variables generate significant bivariate results. These are the proportion of military personnel in the cabinet and, once again, arms racing, and both of them experience slower growth rates in the large recipient category. While just failing to achieve significance, the left-wing violence variables also follows this pattern. Budget size, on the other hand, increases most rapidly in this category, but it too falls just short of being significant.

The overall effect of the United States changing its aid policy to create a relatively large pool of habitual non-recipients in the last five test periods is to nullify these relationships. While five test periods are hardly an adequate number to generate a robust impact relationship, it is still the case that this effect is not too surprising since the relationships were weak in the first place. The most suitable conclusion, therefore, is the conservative one to the effect that the pattern of variation across the four categories (the three recipient categories plus the zero one) becomes uniformly more random without entailing a change of direction. In short, the relationships become non-relationships.

Military assistance

The military assistance impact findings presented in Table 7.11 encompass fewer significant results than those for economic aid. In only three instances is a significant chi-square result generated; two of these relationships, gross military assistance and absolute and relative military spending are linear as well, while the third, that between the transfer in its gross form and budget size, is decidely non-linear.

The absolute and relative military spending variables also provide significant

Table 7.11 Summed ranks for average percentage change in the political structure variables for the zero, small, medium and large recipient categories of gross and per capita military assistance for the eleven four-year periods, 1952–6, 1954–8 to 1972–6

	Gross military assistance				Per capita military assistance			
	Zero	Small	Medium	Large	Zero	Small	Medium	Large
MltExp	18.5	29.5	31.0	31.0*‡	20.0	29.0	30.0	31.0
PMltExp	15.0	29.0	31.0	35.0*‡	21.0	29.0	28.5	31.5
MltReg	24.5	23.0	30.0	32.5†	26.0	23.0	26.0	35.0†
PMltCab	24.0	24.0	28.0	34.0†	25.0	26.0	23.0	36.0†
Parties	34.5	27.5	27.0	21.0	33.5	26.5	29.5	20.5
CenAss	26.0	30.0	31.0	23.0	25.0	30.5	32.5	22.0
Budget	27.0	30.0	27.0	26.0	21.0	37.0	24.0	28.0*
Educ	30.0	21.0	25.0	34.0†	29.0	26.0	27.0	28.0
Health	22.0	29.0	27.0	32.0	24.0	24.0	30.0	32.0
Doctors	25.0	27.0	27.0	31.0†	21.0	32.0	30.0	27.0
NLWV	29.5	24.5	27.0	29.0	30.5	30.0	22.0	27.5
LWV	27.0	33.5	21.0	28.5	29.0	29.0	26.5	25.5
Racing	24.5	30.0	29.5	26.0	21.5	31.0	28.0	29.5

* Indicates significance at the 0.05 level or beyond for the chi-square test across all four categories.
† Indicates significance at the 0.05 level or beyond for the cumulative binomial test on the number of highest rank placings for the large category.
‡ Indicates significance at the 0.05 level or beyond for the cumulative binomial test on the number of highest rank placings for the zero category.

binomial results, with the small recipient categories having the fastest growth rates on the two of them. On the other hand, it is the large recipients of the transfer in both its forms that experience the lowest growth rates on the military regime and military cabinet personnel variables. Relatedly, it is also worth noting that, although the difference is not significant, large recipients actually enjoy the fastest growth rate on both the central assembly and number of parties variables. Finally, the only other significant binomial outcomes are once again to be found in the large recipient category, but only in its gross form. This category is characterised by the lowest growth rates on the educational expenditure and population per doctor variables; it also has the lowest growth rate of health expenditure, but the difference between it and the other categories is not quite significant.

Arms sales

Our discussion of arms sales' impact, if any, must be treated as especially tentative since it rests on three test periods only. Even bearing this proviso in mind, however, the growth rates of the individual socio-political variables would appear not to be influenced by the receipt of US arms sales.

The differences that are to be found in these growth rates characterise not the small, medium and large recipients but non-recipients as compared to recipients as a whole. Table 7.12, therefore, presents the raw (as opposed to ranked) growth rates on the socio-political variables for these two groups only. Comparing them confirms the general absence of relationships that are both significant and directionally consistent. The only exceptions to this observation are military expenditure in both its absolute and relative forms and arms racing, which is itself a derivative military expenditure variable.

In sum then, it would seem that the growth rates of the socio-political variables are generally not influenced by either gross or per capita arms sales receipts. Furthermore, there appear to be no substantial and directionally consistent differences between non-recipients and recipients as a whole except with regard to military spending and to a variable that is closely related to it, arms racing.

Interpretation: distribution

Economic aid

From the perspective of the political development of the Third World, the most frequently voiced objective of US foreign policy is the promotion of liberal democracy. There are basically two strategies open to the United States in pursuit of this goal. The more immediate and short-term of them is simply to reward Third World countries with functioning democratic institutions like central assemblies and political parties by transferring larger volumes of official transfers to them. The longer-term strategy can be either complementary to, or independent of, this one and it involves building the social and political

Table 7.12 Average annual percentage change for non-recipients (NR) and
recipients (R) of arms sales for the three four-year periods,
1970–4, 1972–6, 1974–8

	NR	R		NR	R		NR	R		NR	R
	MltExp			PMltExp			MltReg			PMltCab	
1970–4	0.6	7.2		−2.8	−0.3		2.9	−3.4		3.6	−3.5
1972–6	3.6	8.1		0.5	2.5		5.7	−3.3		5.5	3.9
1974–8	2.1	4.9		−0.5	4.2		−0.8	4.2		−0.5	−0.7
	Parties			CenAss			Budget			Educ	
1970–4	−3.2	1.7		−2.2	−1.7		0.5	1.9		−1.4	−1.1
1972–6	−1.7	−6.6		−2.9	−1.7		3.9	3.6		1.5	−0.8
1974–8	3.3	1.4		0.0	−1.4		3.9	4.3		3.4	5.1
	Health			Doctors			LWV			NLWV	
1970–4	−2.1	−0.3		−3.4	−3.1		0.0	−5.1		−0.7	−1.7
1972–6	0.5	0.7		−3.1	−3.9		0.0	0.0		−0.7	1.7
1974–8	2.3	4.5		−0.9	−2.1		0.0	0.0		0.0	0.0
	Racing										
1970–4	−1.8	0.0									
1972–6	−1.9	4.0									
1974–8	−8.3	6.5									

infrastructure that is commonly perceived to be a prerequisite of a viable liberal democracy. In other words, the United States would deploy its official transfers, and especially economic aid, to encourage social reform and political stability. This second strategy has the added advantage of merging the humanitarian goal of giving economic aid to the countries that need it with the political one of encouraging democracy.

Against this background of a US commitment to democracy, the principal conclusion to be drawn from our distributional analysis is that there is little convincing evidence that either of these strategies, never mind both of them, guides US gross or per capita aid allocations. To elaborate by taking the 'institution building' strategy first, to the extent that large aid recipients have most political parties on average and that aid recipients in general are a little more likely than non-recipients to have an assembly and a larger number of parties, the bivariate analyses indicate that this strategy does inform US aid policy. The only problem is that the composite picture emerging from the regression analyses belies the ultimate relevance or importance of these institutional variables since their effect is comprehensively 'drowned out' by the power politics measures in particular. What is more, this conclusion applies equally to institutional variables measuring a military bias in the political make-up of Third World countries. In other words, the United States would appear to display a systematic indifference to the political structural characteristics of potential recipients of its economic aid. Nor is this conclusion affected by excluding the dominant military spending and left-wing violence variables from the regression analyses. All that this exercise achieves is to raise budget size to a position of unchallenged explanatory pre-eminence; the institutional variables still find themselves structuring aid allocations intermittently and weakly at best. We shall return to the interpretation of the budget size variable presently.

Negative results also characterise the social, as opposed to stability, dimension of the alternative 'infrastructural' strategy. Again the bivariate evidence is marginally favourable in that aid non-recipients tend to have significantly fewer people per doctor and marginally higher proportionate expenditures on health and education. But once account is taken of the power politics and left-wing insurgency variables, none of the social development variables directly influences gross aid allocations in any meaningful sense. The picture is slightly different for the per capita aid programme, however, where budget size is a prominent estimator in several years despite the presence of the military spending and left-wing violence variables. Moreover, the exclusion of these dominant variables serves only to elevate budget size to a position of unchallenged primacy in the explanation of the distribution of per capita, as well as gross, economic aid in every test year. Again, we shall return presently to the interpretation of this finding. Suffice it for the moment to note that the explanatory impotence of the social development variables reinforces the last chapter's conclusion to the effect that there is little evidence of a distinct humanitarian dimension in the US aid programme.

At first glance, the stability dimension of the 'infrastructural' strategy holds out greater promise of positive findings with regard to the question of the United States' commitment to democratic development. The source of this promise is the strong and persistent structuring influence of left-wing violence on both the gross and per capita aid distributions. On closer inspection, however, this promise proves to have been false from the outset; the relationship in fact reflects the US antipathy to communism rather than its commitment to creating the stability necessary for a viable democracy. There are two reasons to interpret the relationship in this way. Firstly, if aid were deployed to reward stability, it would, in fact, be negatively and not positively related to left-wing insurgency, which is measured '0' if it is not present and '1' if it is. As it is, the relationship is invariably positive in direction. Secondly, if the United States were opposed in principle to instability because of its adverse effect on democratic development, then we would expect it to react in like manner, i.e. negatively, to both left-wing and non-left-wing violence. But the regression results clearly indicate that both its gross and per capita aid allocations are altogether insensitive to the incidence of non-left-wing insurgency. What we would seem to have, therefore, is a problem of conceptualisation. Left-wing violence is simply not a suitable measure of instability in this context. Rather, it is a measure of US competition with communism and should be interpreted as such. None the less, such an interpretation does not undermine the more general conclusion of a US indifference to the question of stability, otherwise it would be possible to think of a persuasive explanation of why its aid allocations do not react adversely to non-left-wing violence that is subversive of democratic development.

Thus, our overall conclusion can only be that the US commitment to fostering democracy through its aid transfers barely goes beyond rhetoric. The simple fact of the matter is that such considerations do not directly structure its aid allocations; any effect that they might have is indirect and operates through their affinity with the overriding foreign policy goals of power politics and competing with communism.

There is still a loose thread in this interpretation, however, and it is the unexplained prominence of budget size, especially in the per capita aid programme.[14] We now turn to this matter.

This variable is unquestionably of secondary explanatory importance so that, being correlated with relative military expenditure at a mean value of around 0.5 over the period of our analysis, the immediate temptation is to dismiss it as nothing more than a surrogate measure of power politics. The extent of their collinearity, however, does not warrant such presumptive action and cautions a more careful consideration of its meaning.

Taken at immediate face value to indicate Third World countries' degree of commitment to a free market economy characterised by minimal governmental interference in social and economic affairs, the strong and positive influence of budget size can only be taken to confirm the last chapter's conclusion that the aid programme, at least in its per capita form, does not respond to purely economic considerations. But while pertinent and gratifying, this observation still leaves unanswered the question of what it is that attracts US aid to Third World countries whose governments dispose of proportionately large budgets. By treating budget size and military spending as equivalent indicators of power political capabilities, a summary answer to this question would summarily dismiss the former variable as a relatively weak indicator of this phenomenon. This recourse would have the advantage of focusing our attention on budget size as an indicator of some aspect of state power, but it does not take us beyond our earlier observation that the correlation between the two variables is weak enough to suggest that they do not tap the same phenomenon.

A more constructive interpretation of budget size's empirical importance flows most logically from a conceptualisation of state power that explicitly recognises the interrelated, yet analytically distinct, external and internal dimensions of state sovereignty. Hitherto, our analysis has concerned itself only with the relations between states and has consequently emphasised the external, or international, dimension of state sovereignty. But just as states can vary on this dimension, so too can they vary in their degree of internal sovereignty and one valid measure of this internal variation would seem to be the extent to which governments determine the allocation of the resources within a state. Thus, the larger a government's disposition of a state's total wealth (GDP), the more likely is that government to be in control of its domestic environment and, hence, the more likely it is that political stability will prevail within the state's boundaries. In other words, budget size is reasonably conceptualised as a measure ultimately of political stability in the broad sense of internal sovereignty.

Political stability then, complements, albeit in a subordinate role, external power capabilities and competition with communism in structuring US aid allocations. Its influence, however, is not uniformly strong across the gross and per capita programmes. To be sure, both of them most reward powerful Third World countries experiencing domestic communist insurgency, but the relative prominence of budget size in the per capita programme points suggests a division of labour between it and the gross aid programme. That no considerations other than power politics and competition with communism structure the latter programme can be taken to indicate that gross aid allocations react sensitively to change, be it in the short or long term, in the Third World distribution of these characteristics. But while the per capita programme conforms to this same general response pattern, it does so less deterministically in the sense that it also manifests a long-term concern to tie the more stable of these countries to the United States by granting them slightly more aid in relative terms, i.e. by showing preference towards them.

The problem with this interpretation of budget size is that it places us on the horns of a dilemma in so far as it appears flatly to contradict the earlier conclusion that political stability plays no role in determining the distribution of US aid. This contradiction is more apparent than real, however, and two points need to be made to resolve it. Firstly, it is necessary to distinguish between political stability in the sense of violent, perhaps short-lived, insurgency and in the more profound sense of a commodity that is relatively rare in the Third World, namely, internal sovereignty. The two are clearly distinguishable in conceptual terms and it is entirely possible that any supplier of aid, the United States included, could generally respond favourably to one form and be indifferent to the other. The second point is that the substantive importance of stability as internal sovereignty in fact reinforces the United States' indifference to rewarding democratic advance among its recipients. If it were concerned to reward it, we could reasonably expect its focus on long-term stability to be complemented by one on sustaining and rewarding the presence of democratic political institutions and the promotion of social development. That there is no such complementarity can only mean that while we may have to revise our earlier conclusion about a systematic indifference to the question of political stability, it none the less has to be recognised that its concern is with stability for its own sake and not with it as a means of, or even prerequisite for, democratic development more generally.

Military assistance

In contrast to economic aid, military assistance is granted to only a minority of Third World countries so that the programme must be explicitly recognised as comprising two stages. The first stage involves the selection, or identification, of countries to receive the transfer, and the second the distribution of the total military assistance budget among this select group of countries.

To a far greater extent than with economic aid, the selection stage of the military assistance programme is dominated by considerations of power politics and competition with communism, and especially the latter. In other words, recipients are starkly and consistently differentiated from non-recipients by their comparatively high levels of absolute and relative military expenditure and of left-wing (but not non-left-wing) violence. Moreover, this pattern of differentiation becomes even more pronounced when the military assistance non-recipient population is redefined to exclude Third World countries tied to the United States by their arms purchases from it. The effect of this redefinition is to create a 'purer' group of relatively powerless Third World countries that, by virtue of this very characteristic, appear to be deemed unworthy of inclusion in a military assistance programme that is overwhelmingly oriented to recipients whose power capabilities are attractive to the United States both in their own right and for their importance in its perpetual struggle against communist preponderance in the Third World.

The remaining socio-political variables afford even less evidence of a US commitment to liberal democracy than they do in the case of economic aid. To take the 'institution-building' strategy first, military assistance recipients certainly tend to have more political parties than non-recipients, but they are also more likely to be military regimes and to have larger proportions of military personnel in their cabinets. Stated differently, the military assistance programme is overwhelmingly orientated to promoting US security and shows little evidence, even at a bivariate level, of any commitment to the sustenance of democratic political institutions. What is more, this conclusion is even more apposite to the United States' commitment to social development, whether this be interpreted in humanitarian terms or in terms of building the infrastructure of democracy. Whereas aid recipients have significantly more people per doctor, military assistance recipients have significantly fewer. In other words, at least from a humanitarian perspective, this latter group of recipients is less in need of external financial support. It can only be concluded, therefore, that the selection of military assistance recipients is all but unaffected by democratic criteria.

Turning to the interpretation of the distributional findings, the need to maintain a distinction between the gross and per capita military assistance programmes becomes immediately apparent since, as with economic aid, the gross allocations are less successfully explained by the socio-political variables than are the per capita allocations. To be sure, both distributions are dominated by the same military spending and left-wing violence variables but, as is evident from the R^2 values, they are so to differing degrees. Per capita allocations are explained the more successfully of the two because, being standardised by population size, they more sensitively measure supplier preference and it stands to reason that any supplier, including the United States, will disproportionately reward Third World countries with characteristics that it deems attractive and important. This reasoning applies equally to the per capita aid programme in comparison to its gross aid counterpart.

It is at this point that it becomes counter-productive to draw further parallels between the economic aid and military assistance programmes. Both may be dominated by the same considerations of power politics and competition with communism, but it is only in the military assistance programme that the remaining socio-political variables exercise to all intents and purposes no independent influence on the distribution of the transfer in either its gross or per capita form. Furthermore, while neither programme betrays any attraction to the promotion of political democracy, per capita military assistance allocations are more strongly related to left-wing violence, whereas per capita aid allocations do at least show an independent, if subordinate, tendency to reward the long-term political stability that is conducive to democracy.[15] It can only be concluded, therefore, that to the extent that the political structure, social development or stability variables do influence either selection into the military assistance programme or the distribution of the transfer, they do so by way of their affinity with the short-term, general security goals of attracting relatively powerful Third World countries into the US camp and containing domestic communism, especially within these same states.

Of course, even if weighted differently, these same goals characterise the economic aid programme, but there they are complemented by the secondary goal of rewarding internal sovereignty. Once again, therefore, it would seem that the two transfer programmes complement each other within the context of the United States' overall foreign policy design. The most important 'positive' conclusion to be drawn from this analysis, however, is that the promotion of political democracy is not a goal that figures at all prominently in this design.

Arms sales

Like its military assistance counterpart, the arms sales programme involves a relatively small number of recipients and so must be treated in two stages, selection and distribution.

With regard to the first of these stages, there is once again not the slightest evidence that considerations of liberal democracy condition selection into the arms sales programme. While recipients may have marginally more parties on average, they also have a slightly larger proportion of military personnel in their cabinets. What is more, the only significant difference to be found in the social development variables shows recipients in fact to have a far more favourable ratio of doctors to population, which suggests that, if anything, this programme has a bias against social development, or humanitarianism. Given that these relationships are only bivariate, however, the safest conclusion is the conservative one that the United States is systematically indifferent to democratic criteria when choosing its arms sales recipients.

This relationship holds equally unequivocally for the criteria governing the distribution of this transfer within the recipient population. The only democratic institutional variable to appear more than once is number of parties and it is inconsistently signed. In addition, the social development variables that figure in the final regression equations are all positively signed, which is the opposite sign to that which the democratic development, or humanitarian, strategy would lead us to expect. But even so, these variables are marginal in their influence and lack substantive importance. Once again, therefore, the conclusion is inescapable that there is little evidence of a US commitment to the promotion of democracy through an arms sales programme that turns out to be but exclusively dominated by the power political variables.[16] It is noticeable, however, that as the US arms sales programme expands in volume in the late 1970s, even these characteristics come to structure arms sales allocations less successfully, a development that probably reflects a somewhat greater readiness on the part of a United States increasingly beleaguered by Western and Soviet competition to sell arms to any Third World country able to afford them. This being the case, though, it is a change of emphasis that is rooted in economic self-interest and not in a concern to further liberal democracy among the transfer's recipients.

Interpretation: impact

Economic aid

Viewed from the perspective of promoting democracy, the impact findings do initially indicate that, at least when forthcoming in large amounts, US economic aid does make a positive contribution to this process even if it is distributed without an explicit view to doing so. After all, covariation characterises the relationship between large aggregated aid receipts and low growth rates of non-democratic political structures like military regimes or military-dominated cabinets. In addition, these same receipts are positively associated with high growth rates on what is generally taken to be a characteristically democratic political institution, a functioning central assembly.

But the interpretation of this covariation needs to be approached carefully since there is no matching evidence that aid transfers, whatever their volume, promote the social development that is generally accepted as being an infrastructural prerequisite of healthy liberal democracies. Indeed, what evidence there is suggests that the United States is at best indifferent to such development and at worst actively hostile to it. The simple fact of the matter is its aid transfers are not related to growth rates on the social development variables as a whole and the only exception to this generalisation actually points to there being a negative association between social, or humanitarian, need and volume of aid receipt. That is, the growth rate of population per doctor is, in fact, highest in the small recipient category and lowest in the large one, which means that those Third World countries most in need of external economic assistance on humanitarian grounds are granted it, at least from the United States, in smallest volume. To make this observation, however, need not imply a direct causal inference. The more likely explanation of it is that the relationship is spurious because US aid allocations are simply not directed at alleviating immediate human need. In other words, the most plausible interpretation of this relationship is that it is the wealthiest and most powerful Third World countries that get the largest amounts of aid and it is their inherent wealth rather than US aid receipts that explains their relatively favourable growth rates of doctors in proportion to population. Still, we cannot escape the larger, and more pertinent, conclusion that there is no evidence that US aid receipts serve to promote the social infrastructure that the United States itself believes to be the precondition of a healthy democracy. To be sure, it does not discourage such development, but, more importantly, nor does it encourage it.

This conclusion necessarily casts serious doubt on the existence of a US commitment to the democratic development of the Third World and, as such, appears flatly to contradict our previous observation that large aid receipts covary with the growth of political democracy, at least in institutional terms. But does it? The resolution of this apparent contradiction would seem to lie in the answer to the question of whether US aid allocations independently foster the growth of these institutions or whether their growth is recipient-initiated and occurs precisely to attract large amounts of aid from a United States that would undoubtedly like to see evidence of the existence of democratic political structures even if it itself places their encouragement low on its list of priorities. Of course, the nature of our data will not allow us to proffer a definitive answer to this question, but the cumulative evidence does suggest that it is the second of these processes that in fact best accounts for apparent growth of institutional democracy in those Third World countries that persistently receive large amounts of US aid.

We have already presented two pieces of evidence that at a minimum seriously question the United States' commitment to the promotion of political democracy; these are the unimportance of what might be called democratic considerations in determining the distribution of its economic aid and its failure to show any sign of encouraging the social development that underpins democracy. What is important, however, is that this evidence is not necessarily contradicted by the high growth rates of central assemblies and low growth rates of military personnel in the cabinets of large aid recipients since both these relationships can reasonably and credibly be explained by the practice of 'institutional engineering' on the part of Third World governments anxious to attract the maximum possible economic assistance from the United States. The positive growth rate of the central assembly variable is more difficult to ·'explain away', yet it is very noticeable that it is not accompanied by a similar growth rate in that other common feature of liberal democracies, the number of parties. In other words, essentially authoritarian governments may, again for the sake of appearances, sanction the existence of central assemblies because these are more easily controlled and dictated to than a proliferation of political parties that mobilise various factional interests in society. The archetypal example of this institutional pattern is, of course, the USSR.

The absence or presence of a military regime is far less easily controlled by governments whose very fate is often reflected in this variable. None the less, the relatively low increase in this type of regime should be interpreted cautiously if only because it is simultaneously the case that large aid receipts also covary, albeit not quite significantly, with the growth of internal political stability, or sovereignty (as measured by budget size). The importance of this observation is that, given this relative stability, we would probably find low levels of turnover in any type of regime in this particular recipient category. In short, precisely because it is only logical to expect relatively infrequent regime change in stable polities, substantive importance should not be attached to this particular relationship.

In sum then, there turns out to be little or no unequivocal evidence that US economic aid in any sense causes Third World countries to become more democratic, whereas there is relatively plentiful and convincing evidence that aid allocations are indifferent in both a distributional and impact sense to recipients' democratic political development. There remain, however, two relationships that are at least potentially interpretable as indicating that the United States none the less displays a humanitarian concern to promote the general, even if not democratic, welfare of the Third World. The relationships in question are those between large aid recipients and low growth rates of arms racing and left-wing violence.

Once again, however, this humanitarian interpretation does not stand up well to close inspection. In the first place, neither relationship is linear across all three recipient categories so that it immediately becomes less plausible to make causal inferences. In the second place, there are intuitively more convincing interpretations of the two relationships, interpretations that have the added advantage of being consonant with our earlier conclusion about the relationship between economic aid and democratic development. In the particular case of arms racing, the relationship is best interpreted as being spurious. That is, large aid recipients are also high military spenders so that their accumulated reservoir of military personnel and weaponry means that their rate of expenditure does not have to increase proportionately in order to keep pace with, or stay ahead of, the consequences of a faster spending growth rate in the small and medium recipient categories.

As for left-wing violence, this relationship is manifestly misinterpreted if taken to indicate a generalised concern to discourage the spread of domestic violence in the Third World. If the United States had such a concern, it would show itself to be just as responsive to the incidence of non-left-wing violence, but it simply is not. What the relationship in fact signals is the at least partial success of an economic aid programme that has always been overwhelmingly preoccupied with stopping the spread of communism; here we have some evidence of its doing so, even if only among large transfer recipients. Thus, this is the only relationship in the chapter to which we would seem justified in directly imputing causality and its existence can only lead to speculation about the Third World's course of political development had the United States chosen to maintain, or even expand, its aid programme rather than run it down from the early 1960s onwards.

By way of summary then, the aid impact relationships are uniformly restricted in scope and weak in magnitude and the cumulative evidence is that, with the exception of left-wing violence, they are all best interpreted in terms of chance covariation rather than causation. Against this background, therefore, it can only be concluded that the US economic aid programme has met with slightly more success in containing the spread of communism than it has in promoting political democracy.

Military assistance

Chapter 4 has already addressed the question of the nature of the relationship between military assistance transfer receipts and military expenditure growth rates and, broadly speaking, it has argued that US military assistance accelerates the military spending of those Third World countries not benefiting from it.

More interesting and pertinent from the perspective of this chapter, however, is the consistently negative relationship between the receipt of large amounts of military assistance and what might be called the militarisation of the Third World. When combined with the somewhat weaker tendency for this same category of recipients also to enjoy the highest growth rates on the institutional democratic variables of central assemblies and number of parties, the conclusion would seem inescapable that, to a greater extent than economic aid, large amounts of military assistance encourage the growth of political democracy in the Third World. The only fly in the ointment of this argument, however, is that the transfer is not similarly associated with the social development that the United States has always accepted as being a prerequisite of a healthy democracy. Indeed, in so far as these same large military assistance programmes simultaneously have the lowest growth rates of educational and health expenditure and of population per doctor, the evidence indicates that, if anything, large amounts of this transfer actually discourage its recipients' social development.

Once again, therefore, the question of how to interpret this contradictory evidence is raised and it seems to us that a number of factors lead inexorably to the conclusion that the impact relationships that do exist do not result from a firm and overriding US commitment to the promotion of liberal democracy in the Third World. In the first place, these relationships are uniformly weak and restricted to the large recipient category, whereas it would minimally take a strong and linear relationship if the inference of a firm commitment were to be supported. Secondly, the democratic development that can be argued to have taken place is always institutional in character and is clearly stronger and more uniform across the relevant structural variables for military assistance than for economic aid, which would hardly be expected were the United States in fact to have a blanket commitment to democracy in its official transfers. Indeed, the likely explanation of this difference is that precisely because Third World governments seek military assistance rather than the more benign-sounding economic aid, the United States is especially concerned that large recipients of the transfer in particular should not be seen as unchanging and undemocratic military dictatorships. This being the case, our final point is that the United States may be committed to the institutional trappings of democracy, perhaps to legitimise its official transfer programmes at home and in the eyes of the Third World, but it shows no similar concern for its social infrastructure. In one sense, therefore, its official transfers may loosely be said to cause institutional democracy in the Third World, but a commitment to the firm and long-term implantation of these institutions in a hospitable and fertile social infrastructure is at best absent, especially from the military assistance programme. In addition, large military assistance recipients show no sign of disproportionately acquiring the internal political stability without which effectively functioning democracy is all but impossible to achieve.

Arms sales

It is worth repeating at the outset that, being based on no more than three test periods, this interpretation of the arms sales impact findings is best treated as exploratory and tentative. The only clear relationships to emerge are those between the receipt of arms sales and rate of growth of military spending and, hence, arms racing. Chapter 4, however, has already elaborated the argument that these relationships are more accurately interpreted in terms of covariation rather than causation. That is, US arms sales may certainly respond to a domestically induced demand for them and thereby effectively promote faster military expenditure growth rates, but the domestic factors leading to the initial recipient demand for arms precede and are independent of the transfers themselves.

Far more interesting and pertinent from the perspective of this chapter, however, is the lack of a relationship between the receipt of arms sales and democratic growth, whether it be conceptualised in institutional, stability or social developmental terms. This pervasive absence of relationships can only strengthen this chapter's general, if hitherto implicit, conclusion that it is the concessional element in economic aid and military assistance that induces large recipients of these transfers to encourage at least the institutional trappings of democracy in their polities. But once this element is removed, as in the more explicitly economically oriented arms sales, the United States loses any implicit or explicit leverage that its transfers provide with regard to encouraging the growth of even these trappings.

In the case of all three transfers, by contrast, there is no evidence of a similar US commitment to promoting the long-term evolution of a healthy democracy by encouraging both political stability and social development in addition to the institutional basis of this form of government. For this reason, there can but remain a serious question about how profound and genuine is the United States' oft-voiced pledge to promote liberal democracy in the Third World.

Appendix: variables and their acronyms

Acronym	Variable description
Political structure	
CenAss	Presence of a functioning central assembly
Parties	Number of political parties
MltReg	Presence of a military regime
PMltCab	The proportion of the cabinet that is military personnel
Social development	
Budget	National budget as a percentage of GDP
Doctors	Population per medical doctor
Educ	Educational expenditure as a percentage of GDP
Health	Health expenditure as a percentage of GDP
Political stability	
LWV	Presence of extensive left-wing violence
NLWV	Presence of extensive non-left-wing violence
Power politics	
MltExp	Gross military expenditure
PMltExp	Military expenditure as a percentage of GDP
Arms racing	
Racing	Engagement in arms racing

Notes

1. This argument is articulated clearly in R. A. Packenham, *Liberal America and the Third World* (Princeton: Princeton University Press, 1973).
2. Quoted in Packenham, *Liberal America*, p. 20. A good general treatment of the political uses of economic aid is J. M. Nelson, *Aid, Influence and Foreign Policy* (New York: Macmillan, 1968), ch. 5.
3. As in the last chapter, we would expect US political democratic objectives to be pursued most forcefully through the transfer of economic aid since it is less security-oriented than military assistance and less commercially-oriented than arms sales. It is still the case, however, that to the extent that transfers are substitutable, there is no necessary reason why the other transfers should be excluded from the 'political structure' rationale of this chapter.
4. Quoted in A. Sampson, *The Money Lenders: The People and Politics of the World Banking Crisis* (Harmondsworth: Penguin, 1981), p. 114.
5. The coding for the number of parties is '0', '1' and '2 or more'. If greater than two, the actual number of parties is not coded in order to avoid distorting the regression outcomes by having outliers on this variable.
6. The measurement of left-wing and, by implication, non-left-wing violence is described in note 7 of Chapter 5 where left-wing violence functions as one of several measures of US competition with communism. In this chapter, the same variable is used as a measure of political instability. The issue of how the variable is best interpreted is addressed in our interpretation of the distribution findings later in this chapter.
7. In Table 7.1, the number of cases in each of the NR, R and NRNR categories for the biannual observations is respectively: 26, 66, 22; 20, 74, 13; 25, 72, 19; 19, 78 13; 21, 76, 11; 18, 78, 10 (for MltExp); 25, 65, 21; 20, 74, 13; 25, 72, 19; 19, 78, 13; 20, 76, 11; 18, 73, 11 (for PMltExp); 26, 68, 18; 22, 75, 15; 28, 73, 22; 22, 79, 15; 23, 78, 13; 22, 79, 10 (for MltReg); 26, 68, 22; 22, 75, 15; 28, 73, 22; 22, 79, 15; 23, 78, 13; 22, 79, 10 (for PMltCab); 26, 68, 22; 22, 75, 15; 28, 73, 19; 22, 79, 15; 23, 78, 13; 22, 79, 10 (for Parties); 26, 68, 23; 22, 75 15; 28, 73, 22; 22, 79, 15; 23, 78, 13; 22, 79, 10 (for CenAss); 22, 64, 18; 20, 73, 13; 24, 71, 19; 18, 76, 12; 17, 71, 8; 16, 61, 9 (for Budget); 15, 47, 12; 15, 57, 9; 18, 55, 14; 13, 55, 19; 11, 49, 5; 8, 42, 4 (for Educ); 13, 45, 12; 12, 53, 7; 16, 51, 12; 11, 50, 9; 9, 44, 5; 7, 37, 3 (for Health); 25, 68, 21; 20, 72, 13; 26, 72, 21; 19, 79, 13; 19, 78, 10; 19, 77, 9 (for Doctors); and 26, 68, 22; 22, 75, 16; 28, 73, 22; 22, 79, 15; 23, 78, 13; 22, 79, 10 (for NLWV and LWV).
8. A fuller description of these military expenditure ANOVA results can be found in Chapter 4.
9. In Table 7.4, the number of cases in the NR and R categories is: 23, 12; 19, 16; 19, 19; 22, 22; 27, 31; 36, 41; 46, 36; 47, 38; 57, 35; 57, 37; 65, 32; 69, 28 (for MltExp); 19, 11; 16, 15; 16, 18; 22, 20; 27, 31; 36, 41; 46, 36; 47, 36; 56, 34; 57, 37; 65, 32; 69, 28 (for PMltExp); 27, 12; 21, 12; 22, 23; 24, 25; 27, 31; 36, 41; 46, 36; 49, 38; 59, 35; 60, 37; 69, 32; 73, 28 (for MltReg); 24, 10; 19, 17; 21, 18; 24, 20; 27, 31; 36, 41; 46, 36; 49, 38; 59, 35; 60, 37; 69, 32; 73, 28 (for PMltCab); 27, 12; 21, 20; 22, 23; 24, 25; 27, 31; 36, 41; 46, 36; 49, 38; 59, 35; 60, 37; 69, 32; 73, 28 (for Parties); 26, 12; 21, 19; 22, 23; 24, 25; 27, 31; 36, 41; 46, 36; 49, 38; 59, 35; 60, 37; 69, 32; 73, 28 (for CenAss); 20, 10; 16, 15; 15, 17; 19, 18; 24, 26;

34, 36; 43, 34; 47, 36; 52, 34; 57, 36; 64, 31; 68, 26 (for Budget); 18, 9; 15, 13; 15, 15; 18, 16; 19, 21; 17, 27; 27, 25; 31, 28; 35, 27; 41, 31; 47, 26; 47, 21 (for Educ); 15, 8; 13, 11; 13, 13; 16, 15; 18, 19; 17, 24; 26, 23; 30, 25; 34, 24; 38, 27; 45, 22; 44, 17 (for Health); 27, 12; 21, 21; 22, 23; 23, 25; 27, 31; 36, 41; 46, 36; 49, 38; 58, 35; 56, 36; 67, 31; 71, 27 (for Doctors) and 27, 12; 21, 21; 22, 23; 23, 25; 27, 31; 36, 40; 46, 36; 48, 38; 59, 35; 60, 37; 69, 32; 73, 28 (for NLWV and LWV).

10. Re-estimating the equations with outliers (1955, 1967, 1969, 1971, 1973 and 1975) does little to change the overall picture presented in Table 7.5. Its principal effect is to render another equation, the 1975 one, insignificant.

11. Again, re-estimating the years with an outlying case produces no change worthy of note.

12. In Table 7.7, the number of cases in each of the NR and R categories is: 68, 26; 71, 26; 64, 33; 62, 35; 58, 38 (for MltExp); 68, 26; 71, 26; 64, 33; 61, 35; 53, 38 (for PMltExp); 71, 26; 75, 26; 67, 34; 66, 35; 63, 38 (for MltReg, PMltCab, Parties, CenAss); 68, 25; 70, 25; 61, 33; 55, 33; 44, 33 (for Budget); 52, 20; 53, 20; 43, 25; 37, 23; 28, 22 (for Educ); 47, 18; 48, 19; 41, 20; 34, 19; 25, 19 (for Health); 67, 25; 73, 25; 65, 33; 63, 34; 59, 37 (for Doctors); 71, 26; 75, 26; 67, 34; 66, 35; 63, 38 (for NLWV and LWV).

13. The conceptual basis of the arms racing variable is that a Third World country is considered to be engaging in this practice if it and one or more of its neighbours spend more on arms than would be expected given their respective GDPs.

    The variable itself is calculated by means of annual regressions of each country's gross military expenditure on its GDP, both being measured in constant figures. The regressions themselves are run separately for each of four regions, the Middle East (including Egypt), Africa (including N. Africa), Asia and Central and South America. The runs are carried out by region both to control for the very substantial regional differences that exist in military expenditure scores and to take account of the logic of arms racing's presupposing some degree of territorial proximity between the participants in the process. Having completed the regressions, we then identify those countries with positive residual scores (i.e. whose expenditure on arms is greater than would be expected given their GDP) and then, taking this group, we further identify those in it with one or more neighbours also having a positive residual score. Countries satisfying both these criteria are then classified as engaging in arms racing and given the score '1' and those not satisfying them given the score '0'.

14. Health expenditure also figures with some frequency in the per capita aid and military assistance regressions. It is difficult to know how to interpret this variable, however. In the first place, unlike budget size, it is never an especially prominent estimator. Moreover, it seems a little extravagant to interpret it as evidence of a humanitarian dimension to US official transfers since it is rarely accompanied by other humanitarian variables like educational expenditure and population per doctor. For these reasons, we hesitate to attach substantive importance to it.

15. There is some relatively weak evidence that the United States also rewards political stability through its military assistance programme. This overlap only serves to emphasise that the various transfer programmes differ not so much in the foreign policy objectives that they pursue as in the relative emphasis that each places on common objectives.

16. A noteworthy feature of the arms sales regressions is the total absence from them of the left-wing insurgency variable. This idiosyncrasy reflects the relative commercial, as opposed to security, orientation of the arms sales programme and also highlights that the individual programmes differ in their goal emphasis.

8 Conclusion

This conclusion is organised to match the distribution and impact research objectives of our larger study so that the bulk of the chapter comprises two sections. The first, and more succinct, essentially summarises the key arguments developed in the body of the book by integrating them into a single general thesis explaining the distribution of US official transfers. The second section is more ambitious and more controversial since it presents a summary thesis that is based partly on the combined distribution and impact findings and partly on an appraisal of the transfers that goes beyond our empirical analysis. Finally, in a third and relatively brief section, this 'impact' thesis serves as the foundation stone for a speculative evaluation of the future of US official transfers.

The distributional thesis

The objective of the distributional analysis as a whole is to provide a general explanation of the patterns of US official transfer allocations and it has employed two heuristic devices to this end. The first of them is a demand–supply utility conceptualisation according to which the availability of transfers is explained by means of the first-order utilities of commitment and leverage potential that they confer on the supplier. That is, these utilities can be deployed to promote or protect the supplier's substantive foreign policy goals, i.e. its second-order utilities. This utility conceptualisation, however, does not specify precisely what these goals are so that it has been necessary for us to profile four clusters of substantive US foreign policy goals. (In this respect, the conceptualisation provides only the foundation of an empirical theory rather than the theory itself.) The second heuristic device employed in the distributional· analysis is the provision of theoretical rationales that explain why these goals, or second-order utilities, can be expected to be pursued by the United States through its official transfers. Our empirical analysis then concerns itself with testing for relationships between the variables operationalising the individual clusters and the volume of US official transfers. If found, these relationships are interpreted in terms of both the utility conceptualisation and appropriate theoretical rationale and thereby yield a corroborated empirical theory of the distribution of US official transfers.

In practice, the empirical analysis has demonstrated that the power politics and competition with communism clusters of foreign policy interests influence the distribution of official transfers far more decisively than the economic and political structure and performance clusters. Moreover, the substantive relationships

that do characterise these last two clusters have been shown to be more satisfactorily interpreted by integrating them into an explanation that is founded
on the United States' overwhelming foreign policy preoccupation with containing communism, and especially in the more powerful Third World states.
Thus, this explanation is rendered all the more convincing by its ability to
absorb rival explanations of US transfer allocations.

Our distributional thesis then, combines the foreign policy goals of power
politics and competition with communism under the general rubric of containment and can be summarised as follows:

> Guided by a rivalry and antagonism that is rooted in both power political
> and ideological conflict, the United States deploys its official transfers
> to promote the containment of communism. Over the post-war period,
> this objective has remained more or less constant in its overriding influence
> on transfer allocations, but the demands of containment have changed
> largely as a function of changing patterns of Soviet activity in the Third
> World. That is, within the parameters of a stable commitment to the
> containment of communism, US official transfers have shown an evolu-
> tionary pattern that attests to their substantial flexibility and adapt-
> ability and to an impressively co-ordinated division of labour between
> the economic aid, military assistance and arms sales transfer programmes
> in their individual pursuit of this goal.

To put some flesh on the bones of this thesis, its point of departure is the
collapse of the Euro-centric international system in the wake of World War II.
This collapse created a power vacuum that could be filled only by the establishment of some new international order, a task that fell to or, more accurately,
was imposed upon, the United States. Paradoxically, therefore, the situation
arose whereby a state that had been a relatively insignificant international
actor only a few years earlier was suddenly obliged to become the principal
architect in the design of a new international order.

The *sine qua non* from the US perspective was the establishment of some
form of liberal order since it believed this arrangement would avoid the devastat-
ing tariff and currency wars of the 1930s and at the same time enable its own
booming economy to expand overseas. Its basic problem, however, was that
the USSR had no place in such an order if for no other reason than that it
generally rejected the social, economic and political principles on which it was
premissed. To make matters worse from the US perspective, nor could the
USSR be dismissed easily since it had emerged from the war as the only state
that could possibly rival the USA in the filling of the prevailing international
power vacuum.

This 'problem' notwithstanding, however, the United States engineered a
new international order that was quasi-liberal in the sense that it anticipated
the free flow of trade and investment, but was to be managed by a dominant

United States rather than some 'hidden hand'. As it turned out, the United States and Western Europe were united in a liberal community that was monitored and overseen by the dollar-based Bretton Woods international monetary system and US-dominated international institutions like NATO, GATT, the IMF and the World Bank. But systematically excluded from this community was the state that the United States perceived to be the biggest threat to its own hegemony namely, the USSR. Its plan was to neutralise the threat by 'containing' the USSR within its existing territorial boundaries, while the rest of the world went about its business in the larger part of the globe. In effect, an international system of apartheid was institutionalised whereby the 'dark' part of the world was confined to its territorial quarters so that the 'light' part of it could flourish in a new liberal international community.

Since the USSR shared borders with a number of Third World countries, the US policy of containment could not be limited to Western Europe, even though this was the region of the world where the threat of Soviet expansionism was perceived to be greatest. Viewing containment as simple physical confinement, the United States set about achieving this goal by negotiating a number of mutual defence treaties and, more importantly, by establishing a programme of official transfers whose first-order utilities promised the effective promotion of the second-order utility of containing the USSR. Thus, the USA turned its attention to the Third World in the late 1940s not because of any intrinsic interest in it, but because parts of it were critical to its political strategy of isolating and excluding the USSR from the emergent liberal international economic order that was to be supervised and policed by a dominant United States.

The incorporation of the Third World into the containment enterprise represented a colossal expansion of the United States' international commitments. At first, however, it did not appear too daunting an undertaking since it could concentrate its attention on those relatively few independent countries sharing a border with the USSR. But even at this time there was a recognition that other Third World countries could not be ignored, not least because experience had already shown that communism could threaten to establish itself as the result of spontaneous indigenous developments as well as of Soviet expansionism. Thus, an early division of labour was created whereby US economic aid to the Third World rapidly moved to effectively blanket coverage, while military assistance was highly concentrated in forward defence countries.

The United States, then, very quickly expanded its commitment to contain the USSR and undertook to forestall the advance of communism on a global scale. While anticipated by some of President Truman's critics at the time, the implications of this expanded commitment only became fully apparent some ten years later when the USSR had implemented its own strategy for circumventing US containment. This strategy essentially entailed two co-ordinated responses to what the USSR perceived as US aggression. The first of them, and of which Afghanistan is the most recent example, was simply to pressure weak links in the encircling chain of countries in order to break down the containment barrier. The second, and complementary, response was to 'leap-frog' this same barrier. It was the success of this second response especially that allowed the USSR to expand its involvement in the Third World, thereby clearly signalling the failure of the US policy of direct physical confinement.

While not vitiating the United States' commitment to its established policy of containment, this failure did highlight the policy's inadequacy as it stood. It came to be supplemented, therefore, by two important and co-ordinated adjustments to existing transfer programmes.

The first of these adjustments entailed attaching greater weight to recipients' power capabilities in transfer allocation decisions and it amounted to nothing more than the extension of the power political, or realist, calculus that had already been applied to the USSR. This communist state was perceived as a threat not only because it did not fit into the United States' plans for a liberal international order, but also because it was deemed capable of subverting this order. Inevitably, therefore, the relations between the United States and the USSR came to take on a zero-sum character. Successful Soviet expansionism, in turn, meant that the United States found itself in a position where it had no choice but to project this zero-sum logic to the Third World. In consequence, the locus of Soviet influence came to be a matter of critical concern for the United States and the logic of the realist calculus ensured that, other things being equal, the more important a Third World country in terms of its general power capabilities, the more damaging for the United States would be its loss to the USSR. In this context, Chapter 4 delineates the United States' response to the spread of Soviet activity in the Third World; it neatly and systematically channels larger volumes of its official transfers to the states with greater power capabilities. In addition, it develops an impressive division of labour between its individual transfer programmes to match the varying capability profiles of different Third World states, with economic aid and military assistance picking up politico-security capabilities and arms sales economic ones.

In sum then, the increasing power capability emphasis in US official transfers is the direct product of its adaptation to the threat posed by the unwanted expansion of Soviet activity and influence in the Third World.

The second, and co-ordinate, element in the US response was to diversify its containment strategies. Initially, its overriding strategy was to isolate the USSR by rewarding and reinforcing ties with itself; this we term the reinforcement strategy. Successful 'leap-frogging' by the USSR, however, rendered this strategy inadequate and inappropriate in isolation so two others, aversion and mutual veto, were added to it to maintain the general containment enterprise. Aversion entails punishing extant communist ties by withholding transfers, whereas mutual veto is intended simply to stalemate them. Although elements of all three strategies continue to be deployed to this day, aversion is the least popular since it implies recognition that a country is lost to the USSR, and mutual veto has little by little become the most common of the three. The eclipse of reinforcement by mutual veto did not signal the end of containment; rather it indicated that containment had changed its goals and, consequently, its form. Reinforcement had in fact been designed to exclude the USSR from involvement in the Third World, but it necessarily became supplemented by a strategy that less ambitiously defined containment as countervailment. The explanation of this change on the part of the United States is straightforward; the more pervasive Soviet involvement became, the more the United States was obliged to resort to merely stalemating spreading Soviet influence. Chapter 5 documents both the evolution of the different mixes of US containment strategies and the subtlety and co-ordination of the division of labour that characterises the different transfers in their particular combinations of these strategies.

By way of summary then, it is changes in the relative international activity levels of the United States and the USSR that explain the distributional logic of US official transfers. The evidence points to a strong continuity in the basic US foreign policy goal, or second-order utility, of containing the spread of communism, and official transfers have been important, if not the principal, mechanism for pursuing this goal in the specific context of the Third World. The United States' more specific distributional criteria have had to change, however, to take account of expanding Soviet involvement in these same countries. The initial strategy of keeping the USSR within its extant territorial boundaries so as to exclude it from the Third World gradually gave way to a strategy dominated by the philosophy of countervailment. This change of approach, in turn, obliged the United States to attach increasing importance to the power capabilities of Third World states so as not to allow the development of an unfavourable balance of power that could eventually threaten the international order that it had been primarily responsible for creating. Against the background of an overwhelming preoccupation with containing communism, it is this adaptability, together with a subtle and sophisticated division of labour between the individual transfer programmes that necessitates the overall conclusion that US official transfers have followed a distributional logic that is little short of spectacular in its cogency and coherence.

The impact thesis

In concentrating its attention on the supply utilities of official transfers, the distributional thesis has all but ignored the question of their first-order and second-order disutilities. This omission will now be remedied by an impact thesis that is primarily concerned with the net utility ratio of transfers. Stated more simply, this thesis represents an attempt to assess and explain the net utilities (i.e. the balance of utilities over disutilities) accruing to the

United States from its official transfers programmes. Two reasons, however, necessitate that this thesis step outside the confines of the quantitative analysis that has hitherto been the hallmark of this book. Firstly, official transfers do not exist in a vacuum, but are an integral part of US foreign policy and cannot be fully understood without reference to this general context. Secondly, the research design problems discussed in Chapter 1 have obliged us to conduct the impact analysis as a largely *ad hoc* and descriptive exercise so that it seems both appropriate and desirable that we now proceed to to the explanation of the reasons why the United States has achieved the net utility ratio that it has. Thus, the impact thesis is more than just a summary of findings; it in fact goes beyond our findings to encompass a judgemental and evaluative dimension that is inevitable in an enterprise of this kind.

The general background to this thesis is the observation that the individual impact analyses show the United States to have achieved few of its second-order utilities through any of its economic aid, military assistance or arms sales programmes. It can only be concluded, therefore, that its net utility ratio is on the whole negative in value. This state of affairs will now be explained by means of an impact thesis that comprises seven cumulative propositions, each of which will be presented and justified in turn.

Proposition 1: In the absence of a passive Soviet response to the enterprise, the United States' attempt to set up a quasi-liberal international order has stimulated an action-reaction dynamic that has brought in its wake the institutionalisation of a zero-sum conflict between the United States and the USSR.

Given the totality of the collapse of the Euro-centric international system in the aftermath of World War II, there was no question that some new order was required and that the United States would play a dominant role in shaping it. Nor is it conceivable that the United States would have entertained any design that it perceived to be incompatible with its own interests so that the minimum prerequisite for any new order would be its inclusion of a strong liberal component.

This prerequisite automatically meant that the USSR became a major international problem since it not only failed to share the United States' commitment to liberalism, but also it was perceived by the United States as having the capability, if not to impose its own design, at least to confound the United States. The United States, therefore, was left with no option but to respond to the 'problem' of the USSR. Critically, however, its response could have taken any one of several alternative forms, which meant that the nature of the Soviet problem would become a function of the particular response adopted.

One response option was simply to remove the USSR by means of military conquest supplemented by the political ploy of installing a new and friendly regime or, more likely, balkanising the USSR into a number of less powerful and intimidating states. Assuming its success, this option would have effectively incorporated what is now the USSR into a liberal order and thereby removed it as a problem.

At the other extreme, the United States could have opted for accommodation with its Soviet rival. While this option is unlikely to have been easily realised, it was not altogether unfeasible. The two countries had already co-operated to some degree in the conduct of World War II and in the redefinition of the territorial boundaries of several European states after the defeat of Germany. More importantly perhaps, had the United States ensured the USSR's inclusion in the IMF, the World Bank and the Marshall Plan or had it, following the Baruch Plan, surrendered its atomic weapons and reinforced the UN as a collective security system, then, albeit with difficulty, the USSR could once again have been incorporated into the new liberal order and its status as a problem undercut.

The United States in fact opted for an intermediate strategy that was designed to exclude the USSR from this new, US-dominated order by way of containment. The immediate effect of choosing this option was to institutionalise the USSR as an enduring problem for the United States since it deliberately juxtaposed the two states against each other in a system of international apartheid in which the 'dark' part of the world was to be led by the USSR and the 'light' part by the United States. In the longer term, this juxtaposition also laid the basis for a zero-sum conflict that characterises the relations between the two states to this day. To state the matter simply, a loss for one of them means a commensurate gain for the other.

If it comes to apportioning blame, the United States must bear primary responsibility for this situation. Its action of dividing the world into 'light' and 'dark' parts, apart from being hardly flattering to the USSR, was not achieved by negotiated settlement, but was imposed by US fiat. It was a division, furthermore, that did not entail a partnership of equals, being characterised instead by a gross asymmetry in favour of the United States. The United States then set about protecting its dominance by organising Western Europe through NATO and the Marshall Plan and surrounding the remainder of the USSR with countries that were tied to the United States through various bilateral and multilateral defence treaties. In mirror image terms, the functional equivalent of the US policy of containment through exclusion would be for the USSR to arm and politically organise neighbouring countries to the United States. Given the current US concern, even paranoia, over what it sees as communist penetration of Cuba and a number of Central American states, its failure to appreciate that the USSR could only interpret containment as an aggressive and threatening action can only be explained by severe myopia or gross hypocrisy on its part.

However, containment within a quasi-liberal order might well have provided a successful solution to the problem of the USSR had one critical condition been satisfied, viz. that the USSR passively accept its territorial confinement. But such did not prove to be the case. Rather, the USSR set about redressing the advantage and superiority enjoyed by the United States and, in so doing, set in motion an action–reaction cycle that manifests itself most clearly in the area of weapons procurement. Here each superpower acts to counter the ever more sophisticated and deadly weaponry of the other and thereby contributes to a qualitative arms race. In other words, the superiority initially enjoyed by the United States has served not as a means of one-way deterrence, but as a stimulus to the USSR to achieve parity with the result that US strategic doctrine has, albeit reluctantly, been obliged to abandon the goal of superiority and embrace that of sufficiency. In the process, some form of mutual deterrence has currently been achieved, but it has been arrived at by accident rather than design and is in constant danger of being undermined since, in the absence of a negotiated balance, parity can be maintained only by matching escalation on the part of each superpower.

In sum then, while the roots of US–Soviet antagonism lie in ideological differences and power political rivalry, it was the US decision to safeguard its quasi-liberal international order by containing the USSR that was primarily responsible for defining the two superpowers as the principal antagonists in a zero-sum conflict that has taken on a life of its own. The asymmetry of their initial relative positions only served to encourage the USSR to strive for parity and, in the process, to trigger an action–reaction cycle that has entrapped the two superpowers in a vicious circle of institutionalised conflict that is entirely of their own making and of which the dominant outcome is mutual paralysis.

Proposition 2: While the United States and the USSR remain locked in an institutionalised conflict that has, if anything, intensified with the passage of time, this conflict has become progressively less relevant to the concerns of the United States' Western allies.

One of the two pillars sustaining US–Soviet anatagonism is ideological incompatibility. This factor has not, in contrast, had the same deterministic influence on Western European–Soviet relations because, unlike the United States, the countries of Western Europe have a well-established socialist tradition that emerged in large measure as a corrective to some of the structural inequities and imbalances of classical liberalism and has flourished with successive extensions of the suffrage. Socialism did not supplant liberalism, however; it fused with it so that the modal political party in these countries now embraces elements of both ideological traditions. Thus, there is variation both within and across European governments as their party composition periodically changes, but this variation represents not so much an oscillation between liberalism and socialism as oscillations within a liberal-socialist fusion.

Perhaps because it lacks any socialist tradition, the United States has never been able to accept socialism as a legitimate ideology. The result is that US ideological attacks on the USSR often denigrate goals or institutions that are widely accepted in Western Europe. For its part, the USSR, partly because of its lack of a liberal tradition, has developed a particularly authoritarian strain of socialism so that it is as implacable in its hostility to liberalism as is the United States to socialism. The overall result is that US–Soviet ideological exchanges often smack of great parochialism to a more pragmatic Western Europe.

But while a substantially less pronounced hostility to socialism helps to explain Western Europe's generally lower level of antipathy to the USSR, this factor has been relatively constant over the post-war period and so cannot account for the general reduction in European–Soviet tension over this same period. To understand this development, we in fact need to look to the second pillar of US–Soviet antagonism, namely, power politics.

Western Europe needed no encouragement to join the US crusade against the USSR after World War II. The Brussels Pact, for example, was signed initially only by European governments. Nor can this fear of the USSR be explained by ideological antipathy since the distribution of political ideologies between Western Europe and the USSR was hardly affected by the war. What the war did change, however, was the European perception of Soviet power capabilities. Especially with the demise and division of Germany, the USSR became clearly the dominant power on the European continent and the prospect of its stepping into the prevailing power vacuum was anathema to the countries of Western Europe. But their apprehension of the USSR has grown weaker with the passage of time as, having brought themselves to accept the permanence and inevitability of the USSR's presence, they have come round to the view that accommodation rather than confrontation is the key to a more secure future. This move away from the traditional Cold War mentality is perhaps best illustrated by the FRG policy of *Ostpolitik*, which was initiated in the late 1960s.

Of course, the extent of this reduction in tension should not be overstated, especially in the area of military and security affairs. Nor is it irreversible. None the less, it has occurred and its most striking manifestations are to be found with regard to economic interaction where its mutual benefits are most in evidence. Technology, manufactured goods and capital investment flow from Western Europe into the relatively underdeveloped Soviet economy in return for raw materials. The natural gas pipeline from the USSR is probably the best-known current example of this type of exchange. Nor is the European interest in such interaction confined solely to commercial considerations. Its own experience indicates that economic partnership can help to attenuate political differences. The existence of the European Community, for example, now makes it more or less inconceivable that France, the FRG and the United Kingdom will revert to their centuries-old tradition of waging war against each other as the means of settling national differences. Stated differently, while it

is obviously the case that economic interaction is no guarantee of peace, interdependence does seem to help it along. From a broader perspective, however,
economic interaction with the USSR appears to be undermining the US-led
Western alliance. On the one hand, it erodes the power politics-based antipathy
of Western Europe towards the USSR and, on the other, it strains Western
Europe's relations with a United States that remains largely unchanged in its
traditional anti-Soviet stance and is increasingly disillusioned and disaffected
in its efforts to organise its European allies against the USSR.

In sum then, our second proposition derives from the argument that the
twin pillars of US antipathy to the USSR rest on increasingly shaky foundations
in Western Europe. The simple fact of the matter is that the United States'
allies have never fully shared its revulsion against the ideology of socialism.
In addition, as their relations with the USSR have become less tense, so has
their fear of its power and military might become less acute and their impatience
with the United States' persistently confrontational approach more pronounced.
Generally speaking, therefore, the institutionalised superpower stalemate is
becoming ever less pertinent to the immediate, primarily economic, concerns
of the United States' traditional allies. That there is a certain hypocrisy in the
Europeans' expectation of ultimate protection against the Soviet military
threat by the US strategic umbrella makes the growing strains in the Western
alliance no less real.

> Proposition 3: The East–West (US–USSR) ideological debate has never
> had a great relevance for Third World countries whose most pressing
> political problem is not the choice between liberalism and socialism, but
> the creation of any kind of legitimate government. Moreover, despite the
> United States' wishes, whatever the precise form of government aspired
> to, it is, generally speaking, likely to entail a substantial socialist com-
> ponent. None the less, the debate between liberalism and socialism is not
> of immediate concern to a Third World that, in terms of macro-ideological
> debates, is increasingly preoccupied with North–South issues rather than
> East–West ones.

Viewing socialism as an externally induced scourge, the United States appears
initially to have assumed that as long as the USSR was physically contained, the
Third World would rush to embrace its quasi-liberal international order. As in
the case of Europe, a severe case of ideological myopia led it to discount the
possibility that socialism could be regarded as a legitimate nationalistic ideology
and developmental model. It ignored, and continues to ignore, that the great
majority of Third World countries labour under domestic and international
structural distortions and inequalities that at best distort and at worst invalidate
the workings of pluralistic competition in a 'free' economic or political market.
Precisely because it expressly functions to overcome problems of this kind,
however, socialism has proved to be a widespread developmental model in the

context of the Third World. US official transfers, therefore, have had to cope with the burden of being irrevocably tied to a foreign policy that is characterised in part by a blanket opposition to a political ideology that is often found preferable to liberalism.

This error on the part of the United States has only been compounded by the form that its opposition to socialism takes. Chapters 6 and 7 indicate that it is not an opposition that is grounded in the promotion of a liberal alternative. Rather, it is an opposition whose roots are once again to be found in a negative hostility to the USSR and the values for which it stands. The result is that in reacting insensitively to the sources of socialist sentiment in many Third World countries, the United States has often placed itself on the side of dominant ruling cliques whose principal preoccupation is the maintenance of their own privileged position in highly unequal and stagnant societies. US foreign policy, therefore, often appears as a source of support for force and repression rather than as the propagator of a powerful, persuasive and dynamic counter-ideology.

But even granting this problem, the liberal–socialist dichotomy remains a debate that is not very pertinent to Third World governments whose most pressing concern is not to choose rationally between these two alternatives, but to establish any kind of legitimate and effective form of government. Most of these countries are plagued by economic and political instability stemming from both domestic tribal, ethnic, linguistic and religious divisions and the workings of an international system over which they have little control.

Moreover, even when there are lulls in the struggle for domestic legitimacy, many Third World countries find that the activities of their immediate neighbours constitute their most problematic external concern. Thus, the last thirty years has seen an apparently endless series of wars and skirmishes between Third World states, often over boundary disputes that can be centuries old. That such regional tension does not always erupt into open violence does not gainsay the ubiquity of old-fashioned power political struggles. Just as East–West tension hinges, in part at least, on power rivalry, so too does much of the tension in the Third World. Vietnam's current occupation of Kampuchea (Cambodia) and Laos, for example, is more a function of power politics than of ideological differences. As, indeed, is ASEAN's opposition to, and fear of, Vietnam. The same characteristation applies to the struggles between India and Pakistan, Iran and Iraq, Chile and Argentina, and so on. When all is said and done, the hierarchy of nation-states does not end with the superpowers, but percolates down through all states with the main difference being one of territorial scope. In other words, Third World power struggles are distinctive only for their being much more localised.

In short, the principal concern of the majority of Third World governments is not their active participation in the global struggle between liberalism and socialism, but their holding on to office by whatever means in face of often severe domestic and regional instability. Furthermore, when their concerns are in fact broadened to encompass global issues, it is increasingly to the division between North and South and not East and West that perceptions of self-interest lead them to pay greatest attention.

The first sign of this new focus of concern emerged with the establishment of the Non-Aligned Movement in the mid-1950s. This organisation represented a clear statement of a widespread lack of interest in being closely identified with either superpower and not only is it a movement that has grown with the passage of time, but also, and more importantly, it has changed its goals. From an initial preoccupation with security issues, it had moved by the late 1960s to a predominant concern with global economic matters in the context of the relationship between the more and less developed countries. The first manifestation of this change of emphasis was the demand for a 'New International Economic Order' that would put an end to the North's domination of the world economy and bestow *de facto*, as well as *de jure*, independence on the South. What is more, Soviet protestations notwithstanding, the USSR was categorised with the West as the source of the South's economic troubles. Thus, when Third World countries do turn their attention to global matters, it is to North-South and not East–West issues that they tend to address themselves.

Proposition 4: As the USSR has responded in kind to the US official transfer programmes, the transfers of both superpowers have become transformed from instruments into objects of competition. Thus, US transfers have contributed to the exacerbation of the institutionalised East–West conflict and its attendant countervailing stagnation.

The US strategy of containment through exclusion was viable only to the extent that the USSR passively accepted its externally imposed confinement. Instead, however, it sought to 'leap-frog' the containment barrier by means of the very influence mechanisms, most notably official transfers, that the United States had deployed against it. Ironically, therefore, the exclusion strategy faltered because the USSR adopted the United States as a role model in its efforts to subvert containment. The United States then responded by courting the more powerful Third World countries and, once again, the USSR responded in kind. In other words, a transfer by either of them to whatever Third World country itself became the justification for the other to try to counter with its own transfers and it is this syndrome that underlies and explains the complex web of mutual veto outcomes identified in Chapter 5.

This process of mutual socialisation has had several important consequences. Firstly, as long as each antagonist is relatively successful in the sense of inhibiting reinforcement and aversion, then its dominant outcome is balanced stagnation. Secondly, to the extent that mutual veto does become the prevailing outcome in the 'transfers war', then the possibility of either superpower effecting behavioural change on the part of recipients reduces to zero precisely because each's transfers have lost their leverage potential. Finally, and perhaps most importantly, with the USSR imitating the United States, the latter's transfers have effectively ceased to be tools by means of which it can pursue its competitive superiority: Soviet imitation means that both its own and the United States' transfers have been transformed into objects, as opposed to instruments, of competition. A broad parallel can be drawn here with the superpowers' pattern of weapons development. Weapons themselves are most commonly viewed as responses to competition and conflict, but they can easily become sources of competition in their own right. That is, since, in the absence of a negotiated balance, weapons can create insecurity through the fear that the other side may achieve superiority, each superpower can rationalise the need to build better weapons by pointing to the other's military arsenal. Thus, the only alternative to a negotiated balance becomes constant escalation, which itself further feeds the cycle of fear and mistrust that instigated the weapons race in the first place.

Much the same situation is found with regard to official transfers. Transfers by one side are taken by the other to indicate hostility that has to be countered by matching transfers. In the absence of a negotiated balance, this distrust stimulates escalation as neither side dares to let the other achieve a position of superiority. Thus, in this prisoner's dilemma scenario, official transfers have in fact served to reinforce the institutionalisation of the zero-sum conflict between East and West so that, despite their no-gain and no-loss outcome, their true cost is that they have become transformed into self-justifying sources of competition with ever-diminishing leverage potential.

Proposition 5: The progressive diversification of Western sources of aid and arms transfers has further eroded the first-order utilities of US official transfers and, in the process, has diminished the viability of the second-order utility of containing communism.

The main result of the diversification of transfer sources, which is fully documented in Chapter 3, has been to change a monopolistic market into an oligopolistic one. Were this change to continue, there would eventually evolve a perfect market from which all supplier first-order utilities of commitment and leverage would be absent. While such a market is unlikely ever to emerge, any movement towards oligopoly must, other things being equal, reduce any extant supplier's first-order utilities simply because the scope of recipient choice has been broadened. The sole exception to such a reduction would take place where the dominant supplier can organise and orchestrate a cartel arrangement.

In the specific case of the United States, there is no evidence of the existence of such a cartel arrangement. It might well have expected the World Bank (and other multilateral agencies) to act as its surrogate when its own economic aid programme was cut back, but the correlational evidence indicates that its influence over Bank allocations has declined as its proportionate contribution to that institution's funds has diminished. Similarly, the other major bilateral suppliers are notable more for the busy pursuit of their own interests than for their participation in any burden-sharing arrangement orchestrated by the United States. Indeed they, and France in particular, have followed a neo-mercantilist strategy whereby their economic aid acts as a quid pro quo for recipients agreeing to give preference to the transfer supplier's exports and investments. Another manifestation of this neo-mercantilism is to make export credits part of aid and trade packages.

The absence of orchestration is even more apparent in an arms sales market that is characterised by fiercely competitive bidding. Again, the European arms suppliers have boosted their sales volume by incorporating purchase agreements into aid packages or by showing themselves to be less restrictive in their sales policies as a way of pre-empting the United States. Their 'theft' of Latin America, for example, was achieved essentially by ignoring the US-imposed restrictions on the volume and type of arms that could be sold in the region.

The move to oligopoly in both transfer markets had dealt the United States a number of blows. In the first place, by undermining the leverage potential of the United States' own transfers, it has impaired the latter's ability to pursue effectively its second-order utility of containing communism. Secondly, and relatedly, in addition to a lack of interest in burden-sharing, the other OECD suppliers have shown little independent concern to contain the spread of communist influence, preferring instead to cultivate their own neo-mercantilist interests through their transfers. Needless to say, this tendency only increases the strains on the Western alliance already discussed with reference to Proposition 2. Finally, and most importantly, the diversification of suppliers has provided Third World countries with a means of counter-leverage. If, for whatever reason, such a country is courted by more than one supplier, it can barter among the rivals and perhaps thereby bring about a situation of counter-dependence, i.e. a situation in which the supplier must look to maintain the goodwill of the recipient.

Proposition 6: Following the breakdown of its physical confinement strategy, an unreasonable burden, compounded by misallocation problems, was placed on US official transfers.

Although the United States' attempt to confine the USSR was almost bound to falter once the latter chose not to accept its captivity, the exclusion strategy none the less incorporated a viable role for US official transfers, namely, providing support for countries bordering the USSR. This support was in essence a repetition of the very successful Marshall Plan strategy and, while it had no in-built guarantee of a similar success, US official transfers could reasonably have been expected to effect some transformation in this relatively small number of countries. But once the USSR broke through the containment barrier and these transfers became obliged to contain it on a global scale, an unreasonable burden fell to them.

Firstly, the United States became obliged to deal with a massively larger number of potential recipients and it could not muster the political will to maintain the volume of the transfers that it had channelled to Western Europe in the years of the Marshall Plan. Secondly, Western Europe fully endorsed US foreign policy objectives at that time and its need for assistance was strictly short term, whereas neither of these features characterises the Third World. Despite the ravages of World War II, there are few similarities between the European economies of that time and those of the Third World countries in later years. The majority of these countries confronted then, and still do, a relatively staggering array of economic, social and political structural problem for which official transfers were hardly a sufficient panacea, especially when they were forthcoming in nothing like sufficient quantity to propel recipients into self-sustained growth.

This already unrealistic expectation of what official transfers could achieve has been compounded by allocation problems arising from the United States' ideological and power political preoccupations. In opposing socialism, whatever form it took, these transfers have often been seen to support repressive, anti-socialist regimes rather than to promote liberal ones. Indeed, they have often upheld clique regimes that are themselves among the biggest obstacles to structural change in the direction of liberalism. In other words, the United States has shown a propensity to associate with the forces of reaction rather than those of progress. One advantage of its attraction to recipient power political capabilities is that it has prevented it from indulging this propensity more often than it might otherwise have done. It is the case, however, that certain disadvantages go along with this advantage. For instance, the power political concerns of Third World countries are not always the same as the United States' so that the latter can find itself drawn into regional disputes in which it has little direct interest or influence and in which it becomes obliged to align itself with one antagonist rather than another. The repudiated country then turns to the USSR for assistance and the escalation of conflict begins. A second disadvantage of the power politics focus is that it enhances the potential for counter-dependence. The dominance of the mutual veto strategy means that virtually all Third World countries, and especially the more powerful ones, are of more or less equal interest to both suppliers. When taken together with the fact that the majority of them have no pressing ideological preference for either superpower, this means that they can relatively easily play one off against the other.

Proposition 7: US official transfers then, have proved to be an inappropriate means of pursuing an ill-conceived objective. As paradoxical as it may sound, however, this objective has for the most part been achieved, but it is an achievement that is inadvertent and largely independent of official transfers.

The crux of this proposition's argument is the uncontentious observation that the patent failure of the United States' exclusion strategy has brought in its wake countervailment and not a communist takeover of the Third World. In this narrow sense, the United States may be argued to have met with some success in its general containment endeavour. It is a success, however, that owes relatively little to its official transfer programmes, but is mainly a function of six inadvertent factors that by and large have nothing to do with these transfers.

Firstly, official transfers have not been the only, or even the most sizeable, vehicle of US interaction with the Third World. While its economic aid and military assistance in particular have floundered, its trade and investment have proceeded apace to create a pronounced disjuncture between official and private transactions. Indeed, had the United States co-ordinated its public and private transfer flows, it is eminently likely that it would have found itself far better able to effect transformations in the Third World. Moreover, given the United States' longstanding superiority over the USSR with regard to private, as opposed to public, flows, it seems reasonable to conclude that it is its private transfers that have contributed the more substantially to incorporating the Third World into the Western international economy.

Secondly, although there is ample evidence of real, and perhaps growing, conflicts of interest between the United States and its Western allies, it remains the case that, despite these conflicts, the allies' transfers serve the United States' interests in the sense that they help to fill a political void that might otherwise be occupied by the USSR. In the same vein, its allies have also been a major source of trade and investment for the Third World, which again has militated against Soviet expansionism. Thus, while the United States' allies might not always have subscribed to its specific foreign policy goals, they have always promoted its larger interests by dint of their restricting the USSR's room for manoeuvre in the Third World. This same argument holds equally for multilateral agencies like the World Bank.

Thirdly, official transfers and US hysteria notwithstanding, it is altogether inconceivable that the USSR could in any meaningful sense subvert or take over the whole Third World. Quite apart from the latter's staggering size, complexity and diversity, experience has repeatedly shown that it comprises independent and independently-minded countries that intend to remain that way. Indeed, all the signs are that Third World leaders have become more, rather than less, convinced of the need to establish their *de facto*, as well as *de jure*, independence and that *de facto* independence means minimally the absence of external manipulation. What is more, it is paradoxically the case that the regimes that are most open to superpower manipulation, namely corrupt clique regimes that lack national legitimacy, are precisely those that are least useful to any superpower 'grand design'. If the United States really wishes to steal a march on the USSR, it should strengthen its efforts to develop co-operative and mutually beneficial relations with Third World regimes that, whatever their political persuasion, are possessed of national legitimacy.

Fourthly, even holding constant the Third World's relative lack of malleability, it is again inconceivable that the USSR could possess the resources necessary for it to impose itself on the Third World. The simple fact of the matter is that, apart from military capabilities, the USSR pales into insignificance beside the West in terms of trading, investment and technological resources. Short of withdrawing completly into its shell, a Third World seeking 'telescoped' development simply cannot afford to cut itself off from the world economy and, if only by reason of their differential resources, the West constitutes a far more attractive pole in this economy than the East.

The fifth factor contributing to the US containment of communism differs from the first four in that it relates not to direct intervention or manipulation, but to the USSR acting as a role model for development. On close inspection, the argument that it does, or even could, play this role proves to be untenable. In the first place, there are a variety of strains of socialism. The United States ignores this variety because it seems incapable of even recognising the existence of the phenomenon, while the USSR ignores it because of its empirically mistaken conviction that it has a monopoly on socialist wisdom. In this regard, any doubts as to the USSR's ability to act as a role model for all Third World countries must surely be dismissed by the circumstances of the Sino-Soviet split where precisely this issue was in debate. In addition, the Third World as a whole has signalled its rejection of any notion of a benign Soviet model of development with its inclusion of the USSR with the West in a single group, the North, that it deems to be exploitative of the Third World.

The final, and perhaps most ironic, source of US success is that the USSR has substantially assisted the United States in its containment endeavour by encountering many of the same difficulties and making many of the same mistakes in its dealings with Third World countries. This similarity derives from the fact that the USSR has been socialised into adopting much the same approach to these countries as the United States and, as a result, is now equally caught up in the institutionalised zero-sum conflict. Thus, like the United States, it acquires strange bedfellows, experiences counter-leverage and is caught up, often unwittingly, in regional disputes. Or again, many of the development problems of the Third World, for example, regime circulation and instability, make it just as difficult for the USSR to hang on to its allies. So too does decreasing Third World malleability. But the most paradoxical assistance of all results from US errors encouraging countries to turn in part to the USSR, and vice versa. While illustrating perfectly the uncontrolled action–reaction dynamic of their conflict, this 'toing and froing' emphasises the extent to which the superpowers have to be grateful for each other. That is, given the not infrequent errors each makes, the extraordinary situation arises whereby each acts as the other's best recruiting agent.

Having elaborated these arguments, we are now in a position to state the impact thesis, which is a summary aggregation of the seven propositions:

Official transfers have been a driving force in the overriding US foreign policy objective of containing the spread of communism, a policy that itself derives from the United States' efforts to establish a quasi-liberal international order in the post-war world. But flaws in the policy's design and execution, which have become more acute as US hegemony has declined, have locked the United States into an institutionalised zero-sum conflict with the USSR whose dominant outcome is mutual negation and stalemate (Proposition 1). Although in many respects beneficial for the rest of the world, if only because superpower paralysis reduces the potential for superpower manipulation, this institutionalised conflict over global supremacy has become to some extent self-defeating since the ideological antipathy and power political rivalry sustaining it are of less pressing concern to the very countries that it seeks to mobilise (Propositions 2 and 3). Against this background, the superpowers' transfer programmes have been transformed from instruments to objects of competition and, as such, have come to perpetuate and justify the institutionalised stalemate that characterises their relations generally (Proposition 4). Faced with a burden that they might not have been able to carry in the first place, US official transfers, through a combination of misplaced application and eroding first-order utilities, have not proved to be an efficacious foreign policy instrument. Indeed, flowing to regimes that to all intents and purposes select themselves and over which it has precious little control, the United States' official transfers would appear on balance to have aggravated, rather than resolved, its foreign policy problems (Propositions 5 and 6). Ironically, however, the overriding objective of containing communism has for the most part been achieved, but it is an achievement that is inadvertent and largely independent of US official transfers. (Proposition 7).

Taking the picture overall, therefore, while the distributional thesis indicates that a spectacularly consistent and coherent logic governs US transfer allocations, the impact thesis points to this logic having decidedly unspectacular results.

The future of official transfers

Governments, like any body of decision-makers in an institutionalised setting, operate within a set of enduring constraints. While the decisions that they take are far from the uncontrolled, deterministic products of these constraints, it is none the less the case that decision-making usually takes place within relatively unchanging parameters that substantially reduce the latitude available to those taking the decisions.

The importance of these parameters for our assessment of the future of official transfers is that they facilitate prediction. That is, to the extent that critical decisional parameters do not change substantially, there can be little policy change. The importance of these parameters, therefore, is that they are critical to any consideration of policy change. Since all policy decisions entail parameters, there is little use suggesting policy changes that entail unrealistic or impractical parameter changes.

The major parameters structuring US foreign policy since World War II have been its commitment to a quasi-liberal international order and its power political rivalry with the USSR. These are the two considerations that have structured the distribution of US official transfers in a remarkably consistent manner and that also underlie and explain a number of the problems that have come to characterise its transfer programme. Of course, as our analysis shows, the influence of these parameters has not been altogether fixed, but the change in them that has taken place has been around the margin.

There is no reason to believe that their general form is likely to change in the near future. They are, however, likely to be joined by a third parameter, namely US competition with other Western transfer suppliers. It has already been argued that these other suppliers have taken advantage of the superpowers' fruitless and costly conflict to establish and develop their own self-interested and blatantly neo-mercantilist Third World transfer programmes. Quite apart from undermining the formerly hegemonic United States' commitment and leverage potential, these programmes have now come to impinge directly on the Third World economic interests of a United States in relative decline. It seems reasonable to anticipate, therefore, that the United States will sooner or later find itself obliged to compete with the other Western suppliers on their own terms. More specifically, this adaptation is likely to take the form of a continuing increase in the dollar value of arms sales relative to economic aid, a closer association between arms sales and specifically US trading and investment interests and a more pronounced tendency to use economic aid to promote arms and trade packages. A great potential irony, then, is that the United States may be forced to adapt its transfer programmes to the containment of a Europe and Japan that it initially helped to rebuild as part of its grand scheme to contain Soviet expansionism.

Nor should such adaptation on the part of the United States be thought of as out of the question, especially since several economic and political benefits would accrue to it immediately were it to move in a neo-mercantilist direction. In the first place, official and private US interests would probably become better synchronised and thereby increase the effectiveness of official transfers without having to increase their volume. In addition, much of the domestic opposition to economic aid in particular could be overcome since arms sales entail domestic economic gains rather than costs. Finally, the United States could continue its containment endeavour, but pursue it less through direct

government-to-government confrontation and more through economic competition, an area in which it enjoys a massive advantage over the USSR.

These immediate rewards notwithstanding, for the United States to strengthen
the neo-mercantilist dimension of its official transfers would have a number
of largely unwanted and deleterious consequences. For a start, it would com-
pound the problems of an international economic system that is already subject
to numerous illiberal distortions. In addition, it would quickly become self-
defeating since neo-mercantilist strategies work well only as long as all the partners
in the system do not use them. Once all resort to them, none achieves any
gains. If the United States were to resort to neo-mercantilism, therefore, it
would help to undermine the system that it was primarily responsible for designing in the years immediately following World War II, although the heavier
losers in the short term would be the other Western transfer suppliers that
had initiated this illiberal strategy in the first place.

But the heaviest costs of a US adoption of neo-mercantilism would be borne
by Third World countries. In the first place, the consequent increase in their
arms purchases would be more likely to exacerbate their security problems
than to alleviate them. In domestic terms, the use of arms imports to suppress
opposition tends to postpone and aggravate internal security problems rather
than remedy them. This same conclusion holds from a regional perspective
as well. That is, the growth of arms imports to individual countries is likely
not to remove regional security problems, but to enhance and institutionalise
them by virtue of stimulating arms racing. Secondly, an increase in arms imports
would also mean that more valuable capital is diverted from development
projects. While it can be argued that spending to maintain a standing army
helps to alleviate domestic social problems, like unemployment, or that domestic
weapons expenditure stimulates production, arms imports have no similarly
beneficial, domestic side-effects; they simply drain international liquidity
reserves and create, or exacerbate extant, balance of payments problems. Thirdly,
were the United States to become blatantly neo-mercantilist, its transfers would
necessarily generate more Third World dependence than they have hitherto
done. In large measure, the Third World has escaped this fate up to this point
precisely because the United States' preoccupation with containing communism
has meant that it has not manipulated its transfers to promote its own short-
term economic interests.

Thus, were the United States to de-emphasise the mutual veto bias of its
transfer allocations and become strongly neo-mercantilist, the Third World
would seem best advised to organise itself, most likely through UNCTAD, and
take the initiative to terminate all bilateral economic aid and arms sales in
order to escape the dependence that they would most likely bring in their
wake. After all, official transfers exist only because of an interplay between
demand and supply so that if, say, UNCTAD could organise the cessation of
demand for them, their supply would automatically dry up. In place of bilateral

aid, UNCTAD would ideally arrange for multilateral funds to be allocated to the most needy for purely developmental purposes and, as such, transform itself into what would effectively be a Third World-managed IDA. As for arms, the better recourse here would be for it not to replace bilateral with multilateral suppliers, but for it to remove the need for arms transfers of any kind by organising regional collective security systems in the Third World. As with aid, it would be UNCTAD itself that would police these arrangements.

In the face of US neo-mercantilism, therefore, the Third World would have to take the initiative in its own defence. At least as it seems to us, no countries of the North would do so since their policy towards the Third World is already heavily constrained by their competition with each other, so that unilateral action on the part of one of them to alter the political status quo there would hardly prove acceptable to the others. Nor is it likely that any country in the North would wish to undertake such an action in the first place, whereas an initiative could emerge from a South where a rapidly crystallising decision-making parameter is already the desire to control its own destiny. The NIEO order demands are ample evidence of this desire. The North would aslo be unlikely to offer a great deal of resistance to such an initiative since no single country among them would suffer a disproportionate loss of manipulative advantage by it precisely because it would be an initiative involving a blanket assertion of independence. After all, the evidence suggests that transfer suppliers are concerned more about each other than about a Third World that is essentially a pawn in their larger mutual competition. Thus, were this pawn to be removed as an object of competition, there is no reason to believe that the major parameters constraining their foreign policy decisions would be fundamentally disturbed.

If, on the other hand, there is no change in US transfer policy, this scenario is unlikely to transpire since its emergence is predicated upon neo-mercantilism coming to dominate its transfer allocation decisions. If its policy does change, however, then the most optimistic assessment of our scenario is that it approaches the limits of the possible and feasible. It is only the fact that it does not violate the extant decision-making parameters of transfer suppliers that stops it from transgressing these limits. Faced with increasing dependence, the Third World can realise its desire to control its own destiny only through collective action, with UNCTAD as probably the best available vehicle for it. Such action would have two advantages. On the one hand, it would effectively do away with the direct involvement of the countries of the North in the internal affairs of their Third World neighbours and, on the other, it would offer the South the opportunity to turn intra-Northern competition to its own advantage by having the more developed countries collaborate in the achievement of goals set not by them, but by UNCTAD. In short, a US shift to neo-mercantilism could well provide an opening for the establishment of accommodative and co-operative relations that would work to the mutual benefit of both North and South.

Appendix A: Variables used and their sources

This appendix does not include a dicussion of the official transfers since these are dealt with at length in Chapter 2. Nor does it detail how particular variables are computed; this matter is dealt with in the appropriate chapters. Variables that are computed are so indicated below and their original data sources are placed in parentheses. The variables are presented in the chapter order in which they appear.

Power politics

Gross domestic product	UNYNAS, UNSY
Per capita gross domestic product	Computed (UNYNAS, UNSY)
Population size	UNSY
Absolute military expenditure	SIPRI
Relative military expenditure	Computed (SIPRI, UNYNAS)
Gross exports	UNYITS
Gross imports	UNYITS
International liquidity	IMFIFS
Percentage international liquidity	Computed (IMFIFS, UNYITS)
Total number of embassies overseas	Computed (EY, SY)
Total number of embassies accredited	Computed (EY, SY)

Competition with communism

Diplomatic representation in the USSR	EY, SY
Diplomatic representation from the USSR	EY, SY
Number of embassies accredited to the communist bloc (CB)	Computed (EY, SY)
Number of embassies accredited from the CB	Computed (EY, SY)
Bloc preference	Computed (EY, SY)
Percentage neighbours' embassies accredited by the CB	Computed (EY, SY)
Percentage neighbours' embassies accredited by the West	Computed (EY, SY)
Economic aid from the CB	UNSY
Gross trade with the USSR	UNYITS
Gross trade with the CB	Computed (UNYITS)
Percentage trade with the USSR	Computed (UNYITS)
Percentage trade with the CB	Computed (UNYITS)
Neighbours' gross trade with the CB	Computed (UNYITS)
Neighbours' percentage trade with the CB	Computed (UNYITS)
Neighbours' gross trade with the USA	Computed (UNYITS)
Neighbours' percentage trade with the USA	Computed (UNYITS)

Forward defence area	—
Gross arms sales from the USSR	SIPRI-ws
Gross arms sales from the CB	SIPRI-ws
Percentage arms sales from the USSR	Computed (SIPRI-ws)
Percentage arms sales from the CB	Computed (SIPRI-ws)
Neighbours' gross arms sales from the USSR	Computed (SIPRI-ws)
Neighbours' percentage arms sales from the CB	Computed (SIPRI-ws)
Neighbours' gross arms sales from the USA	Computed (SIPRI-ws)
Neighbours' percentage arms sales from the USA	Computed (SIPRI-ws)
Presence of a communist party	EY, PHAW, KCA
Presence of left-wing violence	KCA, PHAW, EY

Economic structure and performance

Gross domestic product	UNSY, UNYNAS
Per capita gross domestic product	Computed (UNSY, UNYNAS)
Per capita gross domestic prdocut (in constant prices)	Computed (UNSY, UNYNAS)
Gross domestic fixed capital formation	UNSY, UNYNAS
Industrial production	UNSY, UNYNAS
Agricultural production	UNSY, UNYNAS
Gross exports	UNYITS
Gross imports	UNYITS
Percentage exports	Computed (UNYITS)
Percentage imports	Computed (UNYITS)
Gross agricultural exports	UNYITS
Percentage gross agricultural exports	Computed (UNYITS)
Gross mining exports	UNYITS
Percentage mining exports	Computed (UNYITS)
Gross manufacturing exports	UNYITS
Percentage manufacturing exports	Computed (UNYITS)
Gross manufacturing imports	UNYITS
Percentage manufacturing imports	Computed (UNYITS)
Trade deficit	Computed (UNYITS)
Export diversification by commodity	Computed (UNYITS)
Export diversification by destination	Computed (UNYITS)
Import diversification by source	Computed (UNYITS)
International liquidity	IMFIFS
Percentage international liquidity	Computed (IMFIFS)
Net factor income from abroad	UNYNAS
Percentage net factor income	Computed (UNYNAS)
Investment income	IMFBPY
Percentage investment income	Computed (IMFBPY)
Foreign direct investment	IMFBPY
Percentage foreign investment	Computed (IMFBPY)
Commercial banks' foreign assets	IMFIFS
Percentage commercial banks' foreign assets	Computed (IMFIFS)

Commercial banks' foreign liabilities	IMFIFS
Percentage commercial banks' foreign liabilities	Computed (IMFIFS)
Export-Import Bank loans	USOLG

Political structure and performance

Presence of central assembly	EY, PHAW, KCA
Number of political parties	EY, PHAW, KCA
Presence of military regime	EY, PHAW, KCA
Percentage military personnel in cabinet	EY, PHAW, KCA
Budget as percentage of GDP	UNSY, UNYNAS
Educational expenditure as percentage of GDP	UNSY, UNYNAS
Health expenditure as percentage of GDP	UNSY, UNYNAS
Population per doctor (in 1000s)	UNSY
Presence of left-wing violence	KCA, PHAW, EY
Presence of non-left-wing violence	KCA, PHAW, EY
Absolute military expenditure	SIPRI
Relative military expenditure	Computed (SIPRI, UNYNAS)
Presence of arms racing	Computed (SIPRI, UNYNAS)

Appendix B: Classification of recipients in the distributional analysis by zero, small, medium and large categories

Any classification inevitably entails a number of alternatives and consequently a series of often difficult decisions among these alternatives. As such there will always be an element of arbitrariness though this can be reduced by justification in terms of the objectives being pursued through the classification. In our case we wanted a classification procedure that would be relatively easy to understand and compute, that would be comparable across different years with different population sizes, and that would produce a reasonable dispersion across the categories (excepting the zero category over which we have no control).

There are basically two strategies available for categorising recipients. One would be what might be termed a distribution-bound strategy that would classify by breaks or discontinuities in an actual distribution. We have not followed this strategy as discontinuities may be difficult to identify unambiguously but more importantly because we may have found varying numbers of discontinuities, and therefore categories, across different years which would have confounded comparative analysis.

The second strategy entails imposing some a priori rule on the actual distribution and it is this that we have followed. Within this general strategy there are still a multitude of different methods that could be followed. Perhaps the most obvious is one based on the standard deviation, though we rejected this as our distributions tend to be positively skewed and therefore we would have found cases loading disproportionately in the lower categories.

The method we employ entails the same logic for both gross and per capita allocations, though the calculations are different. For the gross classification we begin by calculating an expected percentage mean allocation for any year. This is given by dividing 100 by the number of potential recipients. In 1950, for example, with thirty-six potential recipients, the mean percentage allocation is 2.77. For each recipient we then calculate its receipt of the appropriate US transfer as a percentage of the total US allocation for that year. The zero category of course is defined by no receipt; the small category as zero to half the mean value (in the case of 1950 zero to 1.39); the medium category as half to one-and-a-half of the mean value (1.39 to 4.17); and the large category as anything greater than one-and-a-half of the mean value.

In the per capita classification, we initially compute the mean per capita allocation for any one year (i.e. the total transfer divided by the total population in all potential recipients). The classification then uses the sames rules as for the gross case. Unlike the gross classification, however, the category boundaries have to be calculated separately for each transfer.

The number of cases by alternate year for each transfer are as shown in Table A.1. The years mark the time point at which the classification is calculated, though the actual numbers apply to the preceding year as our analysis is lagged by one year.

For reference the total number of cases for each year are: 36 (1950), 36

(1951), 40 (1952), 40 (1953), 43 (1954, 1955), 46 (1956), 47 (1957), 49 (1958), 52 (1959), 58 (1960), 73 (1961), 77 (1962), 80 (1963), 82 (1964), 85 (1965), 87 (1966), 90 (1967), 94 (1968), 95 (1969), 97 (1970), 98 (1971), 101 (1972), 102 (1973, 1974), 101 (1975–79).

Table A.1.

	Zero	Small	Medium	Large	(Total)	Zero	Small	Medium	Large
	Gross economic aid					Per capita economic aid			
1951	16	13	2	5	(36)	15	9	6	5*
1953	7	20	5	8	(40)	7	13	8	11*
1955	6	21	7	9	(43)	6	11	7	18*
1957	6	22	10	8	(46)	6	9	12	18*
1959	3	23	15	8	(49)	3	11	14	21
1961	4	24	16	14	(58)	4	14	14	26
1963	6	41	15	15	(77)	6	28	11	32
1965	7	44	22	9	(82)	7	33	15	27
1967	10	51	13	13	(87)	10	35	22	20
1969	26	43	14	11	(94)	26	21	25	22
1971	22	46	15	14	(97)	22	22	26	27
1973	28	44	14	15	(101)	28	22	21	30
1975	22	50	17	12	(101)	22	21	26	32
1977	23	51	16	11	(101)	23	24	25	29
1979	22	48	21	10	(101)	22	22	24	23
	Gross military assistance					Per capita military assistance			
1953	28	5	0	7	(40)	27	2	4	6*
1955	21	9	8	5	(43)	21	2	11	8*
1957	22	13	4	7	(46)	22	7	4	12*
1959	24	14	4	7	(49)	24	9	5	11
1961	27	15	4	12	(58)	27	17	7	7
1963	36	22	7	12	(77)	36	7	23	11
1965	46	20	5	11	(82)	46	15	11	10
1967	49	23	7	8	(87)	49	15	13	10
1969	59	25	2	8	(94)	59	23	5	7
1971	60	27	2	8	(97)	60	27	1	9
1973	69	23	3	6	(101)	69	21	5	6
1975	73	17	2	9	(101)	73	8	12	8
	Gross arms sales					Per capita arms sales			
1971	71	13	4	9	(97)	71	8	11	7
1973	75	15	3	8	(101)	75	11	5	10
1975	67	22	3	9	(101)	67	17	5	12
1977	66	19	7	9	(101)	66	18	7	10
1979	63	21	8	9	(101)	63	20	5	13

* For these years the total N is one less than the gross classification due to one missing population score.

Appendix C: The classification of recipients in the impact analysis by zero, small, medium and large categories

The basic requirements for the impact classification are identical to those of the distributional classification. The main additional requirement is the need to incorporate a measure of stability over time. In other words, since we are searching for associations between transfer receipt and some performance variable, we do not want a classification scheme that would be disturbed by say one high transfer value.

We can produce such a scheme by relying initially on the classifications outlined in Appendix B. The distribution categories of zero, small, medium and large are scored respectively from one to four. For any one recipient its scores are aggregated over the appropriate four-year interval. The aggregated impact categories are then defined as: zero (4, 5); small (6, 7, 8, 9); medium (10, 11, 12, 13); large (14, 15, 16); Thus, for example, a recipient which in any one four-year period had been a large recipient on two occasions and a medium one on the other two would be scored as large (i.e. it would have scores of $4 + 4 + 3 + 3 = 14$).

The number of cases in each category for the various transfers for each of our impact periods are presented below. It will be recalled that these are lagged by one year on the performance variables. Thus the actual recipient categories for say 1950–3 have their performance measured over 1950–4. While countries are assigned to any one category by comparison with all other countries included in our population in that year, the actual number of countries assessed in any one impact period is set by the number of countries present in the first year of the impact period. (The only exceptions to this rule are the periods 1972–5 and 1974–7 which have one less case than in 1972 and 1974 due to the exclusion from 1975 of South Vietnam.)

Table A.2.

	Zero	Small	Medium	Large	(Total)	Zero	Small	Medium	Large
	Gross economic aid					Per capita economic aid			
1950–53	5	21	7	3	(36)	5	19	8	3*
1952–55	6	23	2	9	(40)	6	13	9	11*
1954–57	4	21	10	8	(43)	4	10	12	16*
1956–59	4	21	14	7	(46)	3	11	12	19*
1958–61	2	24	15	8	(49)	1	12	12	24
1960–63	1	26	21	10	(58)	1	13	21	23
1962–65	3	41	22	11	(77)	3	26	19	29
1964–67	5	48	20	9	(82)	4	32	21	25
1966–69	11	49	16	11	(87)	10	34	21	22
1968–71	21	43	17	13	(94)	14	35	18	27
1970–73	20	48	17	12	(97)	16	28	27	26
1972–75	25	44	19	12	(100)	25	22	23	30
1974–77	17	51	24	9	(101)	14	30	31	26
	Gross military assistance					Per capita military assistance			
1952–55	25	8	1	6	(40)	22	9	2	6*
1954–57	20	10	6	7	(43)	19	8	6	9*
1956–59	21	11	7	7	(46)	20	7	8	10*
1958–61	21	16	4	8	(49)	20	13	6	10
1960–63	21	20	5	12	(58)	18	17	12	11
1962–65	37	20	9	11	(77)	35	12	18	12
1964–67	45	19	9	9	(82)	43	14	15	10
1966–69	51	23	4	9	(87)	51	14	13	9
1968–71	56	28	3	7	(94)	56	26	5	7
1970–73	59	27	3	8	(97)	59	28	1	9
1972–75	69	20	4	7	(100)	68	18	7	7
	Gross arms sales					Per capita arms sales			
1970–73	69	13	7	8	(97)	68	13	7	9
1972–75	72	15	6	7	(100)	70	16	5	9
1974–77	66	22	5	8	(100)	65	20	9	7

* One case is missing in each of these impact periods due to a missing population score.

Appendix D: Project population

The population constituting the focus of attention of this study is the Third World, which we take to be all countries outside the OECD and the 'communist bloc'. In the designation of the OECD we include: Australia, Austria, Belgium Canada, Denmark, Finland, France, Federal Republic of Germany, Iceland, Ireland, Italy, Japan, the Netherlands, New Zealand, Norway, Portugal, Sweden, Switzerland, the United Kingdom and the United States of America. In the 'communist bloc' we include: Albania, Bulgaria, the People's Republic of China, Cuba (after 1958), Czechoslovakia, the German Democratic Republic, Hungary, the People's Democratic Republic of Korea, Mongolia, Poland, Romania, the USSR, Vietnam (prior to 1975 this country title refers solely to North Vietnam and after this date includes also South Vietnam) and Yugoslavia.

We present below the list of countries making up the Third World population of this project. There must always be some dispute as to precisely which countries constitute the Third World as there is no agreed operational definition of it. To improve variance we have taken a fairly comprehensive list, hence the inclusion of countries such as Israel, Greece or Spain. We include only independent countries as official transfers are largely irrelevant to non-independent countries. Below we indicate the year of independence except in the case of independence achieved prior to 1950. We also indicate the year of inclusion into our analysis. For those countries independent by 1950, the inclusion date is 1950 except in those instances, such as Afghanistan, where the lack of date has required a later inclusion date. For those countries becoming independent after 1950 we have included them, subject to data availability, from the year of independence if independence was achieved prior to 31 July and from the following year if after this date. We do not include any countries achieving independence after 1973 as there would be too short a time period for analysis. Several countries (Equatorial Guinea, Maldives, Nauru and the United Arab Emirates) have been excluded entirely due to lack of data.

Table A.3

Country	Year of Independence	Year of Inclusion
Afghanistan	–	1960
Algeria	1962	1962
Argentina	–	1950
Bahamas	1973	1973
Bahrain	1971	1972
Bangladesh	1971	1972
Barbados	1966	1967
Bolivia	–	1950
Botswana	1966	1967
Brazil	–	1950
Burma	–	1950
Burundi	1962	1962

Country	Year of Independence	Year of Inclusion
Cambodia (Democratic Kampuchea)	1954	1954
Cameroon	1960	1960
Central African Republic	1960	1961
Ceylon (Sri Lanka)	–	1950
Chad	1960	1961
Chile	–	1950
Colombia		1950
Congo	1960	1961
Costa Rica		1950
Cyprus	1960	1961
Dahomey (Benin)	1960	1961
Dominican Republic	–	1950
Ecuador	–	1950
Egypt	–	1950
El Salvador	–	1950
Ethiopia	–	1950
Fiji	1970	1971
Gabon	1960	1961
Gambia	1965	1965
Ghana	1957	1957
Greece	–	1950
Guatemala		1950
Guinea	1958	1959
Guyana	1966	1966
Haiti	–	1950
Honduras	–	1950
India	–	1950
Indonesia	–	1950
Iran	–	1950
Iraq	–	1950
Israel	–	1950
Ivory Coast	1960	1961
Jamaica	1962	1963
Jordan	–	1952
Kenya	1963	1964
Kuwait	1961	1961
Laos	1954	1954
Lebanon	–	1950
Lesotho	1966	1967
Liberia	–	1958
Libya	1951	1952
Madagascar (Malagasy)	1958	1959
Malawi	1964	1964
Malaya (Malaysia)	1957	1958
Mali	1960	1961
Malta	1964	1965
Mauritania	1960	1961
Mauritius	1968	1968
Mexico	–	1950
Morocco	1956	1956
Nepal	–	1960
Nicaragua	–	1950
Niger	1960	1961
Nigeria	1960	1961

Country	Year of Independence	Year of Inclusion
Oman (Muscat & Oman)	–	1970
Pakistan	–	1950
Panama	–	1950
Paraguay	–	1950
Peru	–	1950
Philippines	–	1950
Qatar	1971	1972
Rwanda	1962	1962
Saudi Arabia	–	1959
Senegal	1960	1961
Sierra Leone	1961	1961
Singapore	1965	1966
Somalia	1960	1960
South Korea	–	1952
South Vietnam*	1954	1954
Spain	–	1950
Sudan	1956	1956
Swaziland	1968	1969
Syria	–	1952
Taiwan	–	1950
Tanzania	1961	1962
Thailand	–	1950
Togo	1960	1960
Tonga	1970	1970
Trinidad and Tobago	1962	1963
Tunisia	1956	1956
Turkey	–	1950
Uganda	1962	1963
Upper Volta	1960	1961
Uruguay	–	1950
Venezuela	–	1950
Western Samoa	1962	1968
Yemen (Arab Republic)	–	1968
Yemen (People's Democratic Republic or S. Yemen)	1967	1968
Zaire	1960	1960
Zambia	1964	1965

* South Vietnam ceased to exist in 1975 and is excluded from our population of Third World countries from that year onwards.

Index